Seaforth WORLD NAVAL REVIEW 2024

HMS Glasgow – built with pride for the Royal Navy
ANGLEGARTH
MILFORD

Seaforth

WORLD NAVAL REVIEW

2024

Editor
CONRAD WATERS

Naval Institute Press
Annapolis, Maryland

Frontispiece: The lead Type 26 frigate *Glasgow* transits the Clyde on a submersible barge on 30 November 2022 prior to being floated out in the sheltered waters of Loch Mallan. It is likely to be 2028 before she enters operational service with the British Royal Navy. *(Crown Copyright 2023)*

First published in Great Britain in 2023 by
Seaforth Publishing
An imprint of Pen & Sword Books Ltd
47 Church Street, Barnsley
S Yorkshire S70 2AS

www.seaforthpublishing.com
Email info@seaforthpublishing.com

Published and distributed in the United States of America and Canada by the Naval Institute Press,
291 Wood Road, Annapolis, Maryland 21402-5043
www.nip.org

Library of Congress Cataloging Number: 2023944937

ISBN 978 1 68247 484 6

Typeset and designed by Stephen Dent
Printed and bound in India by Replika Press Pvt. Ltd.

FSC www.fsc.org MIX Paper from responsible sources FSC® C016779

CONTENTS

Section 1: Overview

Section 2: World Fleet Reviews

Section 3: Significant Ships

Section 4: Technological Reviews

Note on Tables: Tables are provided to give a broad indication of fleet sizes and other key information but should be regarded only as a general guide. For example, many published sources differ significantly on the principal particulars of ships, whilst even governmental information can be subject to contradiction. In general terms, the data contained in these tables is based on official information updated as of June 2023, supplemented by reference to a wide range of secondary and corporate sources, such as shipbuilder websites.

1.0 OVERVIEW INTRODUCTION

Author: Conrad Waters

'When you see contention amongst your enemies, go and sit at ease with your friends; but when you see them of one mind, string your bow, and place stones upon the ramparts' wrote the renowned thirteenth-century Persian poet Saadi Shirazi.[1] These words seem an appropriate opening for this fifteenth edition of *Seaforth World Naval Review* given the growing alignment of China and Russia – the leading revisionist powers – against the 'liberal world order' based on values such as democracy, the rule of law and free trade that was established in the aftermath of the Second World War. The last twelve months have seen elements of the Russian and Chinese fleets conduct a series of joint exercises as part of a pattern of strengthened military collaboration that has occurred despite – or possibly as a result of – Russia's February 2022 invasion of Ukraine. In the words of China's premier Xi Jinping, 'There is a clear historical logic and strong internal driving force for the growth of China-Russia relations … I look forward to working with President Putin to jointly adopt a new vision, a new blueprint and new measures for the growth of China-Russia comprehensive strategic partnership of coordination in the years to come.'[2] President Xi Jinping's remarks were published the day after the conclusion of trilateral naval serials in the Gulf of Oman that also included the participation of Iran, thereby adding a further unwelcome element into an accelerating strategic realignment.

China's Russian-built Project 956E *Sovremenny* class destroyer *Hangzhou* seen from the deck of an indigenous Type 052D 'Luyang III' class vessel in June 2023. Sino-Russian naval collaboration has now expanded beyond the supply of equipment as part of a growing alignment between the two nations, the world's leading revisionist powers. *(China Military Online)*

The response to this burgeoning alliance by those countries leading the current liberal world order has also been picking up pace. Positively, NATO and other Western nations have proved capable of providing a sustained stream of coordinated support for Ukraine's military in the aftermath of the Russian invasion in spite of early concerns to the contrary. There have also been signs that the previously tentative reversal of the long post-Cold War decline in Western defence spending is starting to accelerate. Notably, France has followed Germany's earlier *Zeitenwende* or 'turning point' in announcing a significant uplift in its military budget. Expenditure under the forthcoming 2024–2030 Military Programming Law will increase to €413bn (c. US$450bn), over a third more than the €295bn (c. US$295bn) found in its current iteration. Much of this will support naval programmes, including the renewal of the country's flotilla of strategic submarines and the construction of at least one new aircraft carrier to replace the existing *Charles de Gaulle.*

On the other side of the globe, Japan's new National Security Strategy announced in December 2022 strikes a similar, expansionary note. Notably, it includes a target of bringing expenditure on 'defence and other outlays' to two percent of gross domestic product (GDP) by 2027. This headline figure is notionally double the unspoken but 'de facto' cap of one percent that held good for Japanese defence spending until the turn of the current decade.[3] However, an interesting feature of both the French

The naming ceremony for *Jingei* (SS-515), the third of Japan's *Tagei* class submarines, took place at Mitsubishi Heavy Industries' Kobe Shipyard & Machinery Works on 12 October 2022. Japan has already steadily expanded its submarine flotilla in recent years and is now to set to embark on a further phase of naval investment as it significantly increases its defence budget. *(JMSDF)*

and Japanese plans is how little in the way of expansion they will actually provide; for example, in both cases naval force structures will be little changed from those previously envisaged. This, perhaps, suggests the extent of the effort needed to remedy the years of post-Cold War neglect in areas such as holdings of munitions and logistical resilience. Moreover, there is also a need for investment in expensive new technologies such as those related to air and missile defence, cyber warfare and autonomous systems that will inevitably soak up much of the new money.

DEFENCE PLANS AND BUDGETS

The latest, 2022 iteration of the annual summary of global defence spending produced by the Stockholm International Peace Research Institute (SIPRI) reflects the quickening pace of global rearmament. Further detail is provided in Table 1.0.1. World military expenditure rose by 3.7 percent in real terms (i.e. after adjustment for inflation) to reach US$2,240bn in 2022; the highest level ever recorded by SIPRI. Inevitably, the data was heavily influenced by events in Ukraine. These drove a 9.2 percent increase in Russian defence spending, pushing it to third in the global table. Also driven by Ukraine's vastly expanded defence budget, there was a 15 percent uplift in European expenditure overall. The United States and China continue to head the table, with American spending of nearly US$877bn still far surpassing the US$292bn spent by its Asian rival. However, underlying trends paint a different picture. Whilst the United States' military budget has grown only marginally, China's spending was up 4.2 percent over 2021 and 63 percent over the decade in real terms. China's defence expenditure has now increased for 28 consecutive years; the longest uninterrupted period of spending growth made by any country in the SIPRI Military Expenditure Database.

As regularly mentioned in previous editions of *Seaforth World Naval Review*, the disparity between trends in American and Chinese military spending is indicative of a broader economic shift driven by the

Table 1.0.1: COUNTRIES WITH HIGH NATIONAL DEFENCE EXPENDITURES: 2022

RANK 2022	(2021)	COUNTRY	TOTAL US$BN 2022[1]	SHARE OF GDP 2022	WORLD SHARE 2022	TOTAL US$BN 2021[1]	REAL CHANGE 2021–2022[2]	REAL CHANGE 2013–2022[2]
1	(1)	United States	876.9	3.5%	39.1%	806.2	0.7%	2.7%
2	(2)	China	[292.0]	[1.6%]	[13.0%]	[285.9]	[4.2%]	[63%]
3	(5)	Russia	[86.4]	[4.1%]	[3.9%]	65.9	[9.2%]	[15%]
4	(3)	India	81.4	2.4%	3.6%	76.3	6.0%	47%
5	(8)	Saudi Arabia	[75.0]	[7.4%]	[3.3%]	[63.2]	[16%]	[-2.7%]
6	(4)	United Kingdom	68.5	2.2%	3.1%	67.5	3.7%	9.7%
7	(7)	Germany	55.8	1.4%	2.5%	56.5	2.3%	33%
8	(6)	France	53.6	1.9%	2.4%	56.6	0.6%	15%
9	(10)	South Korea	46.4	2.7%	2.1%	50.9	-2.5%	37%
10	(9)	Japan	46.0	1.1%	2.1%	51.0	5.9%	18%
-	(-)	**World Total**	**2240**	**2.2%**	**100%**	**2104**	**3.7%**	**19%**

Information from the Stockholm International Peace Research Institute (SIPRI) – https://www.sipri.org/databases/milex
The SIPRI Military Expenditure Database contains data on countries over the period 1949–2022

Notes:

1. US$ totals for 2022 and 2021 are based on then current (i.e. non-inflation adjusted) prices and exchange rates for the years in question. Exchange rate movements, in particular, can therefore result in significant movements in the US$ figures and explain apparent discrepancies in the table. SIPRI also adjust previous-year calculations when more accurate data becomes available, potentially impacting prior year rankings.
2. The 'real' change figure is based on constant (2021-based) US$ figures. Figures over 10 percent have been rounded to the nearest percentage.
3. Figures in brackets are SIPRI estimates.

outperformance of the Asian economies in recent decades. Given this trend is unlikely to be reversed, it will be increasingly difficult for the United States to maintain the military – and, therefore, the unchallenged naval – supremacy that it has come to expect since the end of the Cold War. Further recent evidence of this strategic shift is provided by the political agreement reached to suspend the ceiling on US government debt reached in early June 2023. An important element of the deal is a cap on FY2024 defence spending to the US$886bn proposed by the Biden administration; an uplift that is less than the current rate of inflation. This will make it far more difficult, for example, for Congress to bolster the naval shipbuilding programme with funds for additional warships; a commonplace practice of recent years. It will be difficult to square this particular circle without a further strengthening of alliances to spread the military burden with partners sharing the same world view. The 2021 AUKUS alliance, including its sharing of sensitive submarine technology, is one tangible demonstration of this shift. American military collaboration with India is also steadily increasing, albeit constrained by the nationalist Modi administration's reluctance to loosen its long-standing Russian ties.[4] The Indian Navy became one of the very few countries to design and build an indigenous aircraft carrier when it commissioned *Vikrant* on 2 September 2022, demonstrating something of its potential value as a future ally.

FLEET STRENGTHS AND REVIEWS

Vikrant's commissioning is reflected in the summary of major fleet strengths in Table 1.0.2. As always, these can only provide a short-term snapshot of longer term trends, although there are a few noteworthy points. These include:

- The continued growth in the number of the People's Liberation Army Navy's (PLAN's) fleet of 'blue water' surface combatants. This has now surpassed that of the US Navy, partly aided by the latter's decommissioning of elderly *Ticonderoga* (CG-47) class cruisers.
- Conversely, the significant reduction in the number of smaller PLAN combatants. This reflects the transfer of relatively new Type 056 corvettes – which lack towed-array sonar – to coast guard service rather than any real diminution in maritime potential.
- The incremental growth in submarine numbers across Asia, with both Japan and the Republic of Korea steadily expanding their underwater flotillas in recent years. Whilst Japan has now achieved its targeted force structure, numbers of South Korean boats are likely to continue to grow.
- A slow decline in the number of specialist mine countermeasures vessels operated by many established navies. This is being counterbalanced by the introduction of autonomous, modular systems that can be deployed from outside the minefield.

TABLE 1.0.2: MAJOR FLEET STRENGTHS 2022-2023[1]

REGION	THE AMERICAS				EUROPE & RUSSIA										ASIA								IND. OCEAN	
COUNTRY	USA		BRAZIL		UK		FRANCE		ITALY		SPAIN		RUSSIA		CHINA		JAPAN		KOREA(S)		AUSTRALIA		INDIA	
	2022	2023	2022	2023	2022	2023	2022	2023	2022	2023	2022	2023	2022	2023	2022	2023	2022	2023	2022	2023	2022	2023	2022	2023
Carriers & Amphibious																								
CV/CVN	11	11	–	–	2	2	1	1	1	1	–	–	1	1	2	2	–	–	–	–	–	–	1	2
CVS/CVH	–	–	–	–	–	–	–	–	1	1	–	–	–	–	–	–	4	4	–	–	–	–	–	–
LHA/LHD/LPH	9	9	1	1	–	–	3	3	–	–	1	1	–	–	2	3	–	–	2	2	2	2	–	–
LPD/LSD	23	22	1	1	5	5	–	–	3	3	2	2	–	–	8	8	3	3	–	–	1	1	1	1
Submarines																								
SSBN	14	14	–	–	4	4	4	4	–	–	–	–	12	11	7	7	–	–	–	–	–	–	1	1
SSN/SSGN	54	53	–	–	5	6	6	5	–	–	–	–	25	25	9	9	–	–	–	–	–	–	–	–
SSK	–	–	5	5	–	–	–	–	8	8	2	2	20	20	50	50	22	23	19	20	6	6	16	16
Surface Combatants																								
BB/BC	–	–	–	–	–	–	–	–	–	–	–	–	2	2	–	–	–	–	–	–	–	–	–	–
CG/DDG/FFG	94	92	6	6	18	17	14	15	16	17	11	11	35	35	90	100	38	40	24	27	11	11	22	23
DD/FGS/FS	24	27	2	2	–	–	12	12	–	–	–	–	45	45	75	55	6	6	7	5	–	–	11	11
FAC[2]	–	–	–	–	–	–	–	–	–	–	–	–	30	25	75	75	6	6	18	18	–	–	7	7
Other (Selected)																								
MCMV	8	8	3	3	11	9	13	12	10	10	6	6	40	40	25	25	20	19	10	10	4	4	–	–
AO/AOR/AFS	31	31	1	1	7	7	2	3	4	4	2	2	20	20	12	12	5	5	3	3	2	2	4	4

Notes

1 Numbers are based on official sources, where available, supplemented by news reports, published intelligence data and other 'open sources' as appropriate. Given significant variations in available data, numbers should be regarded as indicative, particularly with respect to Russia, China and minor warship categories (which are sometimes rounded). There is also a degree of subjectivity with respect to warship classifications given varying national classifications and this can also lead to inconsistency.

2 FAC numbers relate to ships fitted with or for surface-to-surface missiles.

The Royal Navy aircraft carrier *Queen Elizabeth* pictured heading down Loch Long in February 2023. Although construction of the two *Queen Elizabeth* class carriers was eventually completed, their supporting air groups are far from their originally intended strength. Many other contemporary British naval projects were also cancelled or scaled back, often due to political dithering. *(Michael Leek)*

This year's fleet reviews focus on three specific navies. The last year has marked the 200th anniversary of the founding of the *Marinha do Brasil*; a fleet which has subsequently experienced many ups and downs. Felipe Salles and Alexandre Galante provide a history of the navy, explore the fleet's current structure and assess its future priorities. Protection of the 'Blue Amazon' – the country's resource-rich and massive Exclusive Economic Zone (EEZ) – is central to the navy's strategic vision. However, there has only been sufficient money to fund the fleet's most pressing equipment requirements in light of financial instability as well as, arguably, lack of any clear external threat.

Our other two reviews both relate to European fleets. Guy Toremans assesses the current status of Greece's Hellenic Navy. The fleet has also suffered as a result of previous economic problems but is now embarking on a significant programme of renewal. Meanwhile, Richard Beedall provides his biennial assessment of the Royal Navy, examining how the fleet has evolved since his first review of the British fleet some fifteen editions ago. Many of the ambitious projects envisaged at the time have either been cancelled or delivered only in part. Whilst much of this has been down to underfunding and ongoing international and technological change, continuing political vacillation seems to have been another significant factor in ensuring a less than optimal result. Nevertheless, the Royal Navy's willingness to embrace both new technologies and mission requirements, for example in the areas of mine countermeasures and seabed operations, are indicative of an organisation that remains in the forefront of current thinking.

SIGNIFICANT SHIPS

The importance of consistency and persistence to the satisfactory achievement of naval modernisation is demonstrated by two of the significant warship classes analysed this year. India's Project 15A *Kolkata* and Project 15B *Visakhapatnam* destroyers – described by Mrityunjoy Mazumdar – trace their

The Indian Navy's indigenously designed and constructed aircraft carrier *Vikrant* – commissioned on 2 September 2022 – sails alongside the lead Project 15A destroyer *Kolkata* in July 2022. Although Indian shipyards are still taking a long time to complete complex warships, they are delivering increasingly sophisticated vessels that few navies can match. *(Indian Navy)*

The Spanish S-80 class submarine *Isaac Peral* pictured at the time of her preliminary sea trials. After considerable delays caused by design problems, her delivery to the Spanish Navy is now imminent. *(Navantia)*

origins to before the turn of the Millennium. However, their construction was significantly delayed due to hesitancy over selecting their primary combat systems. Nevertheless, their progressive delivery from 2014 onwards has been accompanied by the modernisation of indigenous shipbuilding techniques and the introduction of sophisticated capabilities – including Cooperative Engagement Capability – which few navies can emulate. Spain's four S-80 *Isaac Peral* class submarines have an equally long gestation period, with contracts for their construction first signed in 2004. Initially planned for delivery from 2011 onwards, they were subject to significant delay due to the need for extensive redesign after they were found to be materially overweight. However, the Spanish government and shipbuilder Navantia have persevered with the project. Accordingly, the lead boat is now in the course of final trials to meet a revised delivery date before the end of 2023. In addition to providing the *Armada Española* with an important capability, they place Spain amongst the handful of countries worldwide that can successfully design and build a modern submarine.

The third significant ship chapter focuses on a different type of vessel in the form of *Auguste Bénébig*, the first of six new French overseas patrol vessels. Specifically designed to police the vast waters that surround France's overseas territories, they are representative of growing numbers of specialist ships that have been built in response to the creation of extensive EEZs under the United Nations Convention on the Law of the Sea (UNCLOS) regime. Bruno Huriet's article explains the origins and design of the new vessels. Although lightly armed, they incorporate advanced communications and surveillance equipment. An interesting design feature is a flight deck and hangar optimised for drone rather than helicopter operation in an indication as to how unmanned systems are making their presence felt across the maritime sphere.

TECHNOLOGICAL DEVELOPMENTS

A further demonstration of the increasing importance of unmanned systems is contained in David Hobbs' annual review of world naval aviation. His chapter includes a detailed assessment of Boeing's MQ-25A Stingray unmanned combat air vehicle, which will initially be optimised for air-to-air refuelling. A prototype of the autonomous aircraft became the first unmanned aerial vehicle to transfer fuel to another aircraft in flight in June 2021 and entry into operational service is planned for 2026. At this stage, it will become the first autonomous aircraft to be integrated into a carrier's air wing. Here, the MQ-25A will have an important role in extending the range of the US Navy's relatively 'short-legged' F/A-18E/F Super Hornet and F-35C Lightning II strike fighters, thereby potentially facilitating carrier operations outside of China's growing anti-access/area-denial (A2/AD) bubble. In due course, it is also possible that the type will be developed to perform other missions, such as long-range intelligence surveillance and reconnaissance.

Another area where technological progress is making itself felt is in the field of naval propulsion. Norman Friedman's chapter examines recent developments in the field, focusing on the shift towards electric ships. As well as providing important advantages in the area of stealth and design, increasing amounts of generating capacity are required by directed energy weapons such as lasers and, potentially, rail guns. The flexible architecture inherent in utilising electric power – there only needs to be a limited physical connection between the electrical generator and a ship's propellers – could also act as a bridge to future sources of propulsion, such as scaled-up fuel cells. Our technological reviews conclude with Richard Scott's analysis of Norway's Naval Strike Missile (NSM). Developed as an affordable precision stand-off weapon for use against both warships and land-based targets, it has been increasingly adopted by NATO and allied navies in replacement for the veteran Harpoon. Relying largely on stealth and manoeuvrability to penetrate enemy defences, it makes an interesting contrast to the philosophy behind the high-speed hypersonic missile technologies explored in last year's edition.

SUMMARY

The last year has been dominated by the continued fallout from Russia's 2022 invasion of Ukraine. Although the impact has inevitably been most keenly felt in Europe, President Vladimir Putin's act of aggression has had ramifications that have been felt across the globe. In the words of Japan's revised National Security Strategy, 'In the course of almost a century, humanity has invested itself in defining a fundamental international principle of the general prohibition of the use of force. Yet, a permanent member of the United Nations Security Council … has overtly trampled on this very principle … Russia's aggression against Ukraine has easily breached the very foundation of the rules that shape the international order. The possibility cannot be precluded that a similar serious situation may arise in the future in the Indo-Pacific region, especially in East Asia.'[5]

Whilst the outcome of the war in Ukraine remains uncertain, it is clear that governments – and navies – worldwide are scrambling to adapt to the new geopolitical reality of major state-on-state conflict for the first time in a generation. The availability of adequate funding will have a significant influence on the extent to which the Western navies successfully adapt to the new environment. However, it is equally apparent that the adoption of new and emerging technologies will also play a significant part.

A prototype MQ-25 Stingray unmanned combat air vehicle seen aboard the US Navy aircraft carrier *George H. W. Bush* (CVN-77) in November 2021. The navy hopes to deploy the type operationally as part of carrier air wings from 2026. *(US Navy)*

ACKNOWLEDGEMENTS

Seaforth World Naval Review has now reached the milestone of its fifteenth edition; an achievement that is primarily due to the ongoing support of its readers. The author is grateful for this continued loyalty. Other elements critical to the annual's success have been the backing of the small production team. Publisher Rob Gardiner, designer Stephen Dent and proof reader Stephen Chumbley have all been involved in the project from the start. Also important have been the high-quality contributions of a wide range of authors – some also dating from the first edition – and the consistently excellent drawings produced by John Jordan, often from limited material. In addition to the help provided by navies and industry, the photographic contributions of Lorenz Amiet, Andy Amor, Derek Fox, Eugene Gillet, Vincent Groizeleau, Michael Leek, Marc Piché, Bernard Prézelin, Arjun Sarup and Devrim Yaylali have proved invaluable in maintaining a broadly-based photographic record of current naval activity. The assistance of my wife, Susan, in proof reading the initial drafts of the text has been another enduring contribution to the book's success.

The author continues to welcome engagement with *Seaforth World Naval Review's* wide readership. Please send any comments or criticisms marked for my attention at info@seaforthpublishing.com.

Conrad Waters, Editor

30 June 2023

Notes

1. Saadi Shirazi was an influential and widely-travelled Persian writer and poet who lived around the time of the Mongol invasion of Persia. He is recognised as a noted wordsmith and his writings had a lasting impact on Middle Eastern and European scholars alike.

2. See Xi Jinping, 'Forging Ahead to Open a New Chapter of China-Russia Friendship, Cooperation and Common Development' in a press release issued by the Ministry of Foreign Affairs of the People's Republic of China on 20 March 2023. The statement was published as the Chinese leader arrived in Moscow for a meeting with his Russian counterpart.

3. There is, however, some question as to what extent the headline figures will flow through to actual spending on the military. The two percent target covers all security-related spending under what Japan refers to as a 'Comprehensive Defence Architecture', including public security and civil defence measures. The Stockholm International Peace Research Institute calculates that real spending on defence will equate to around 1.5 percent in 2027, admittedly still a substantial increase. See Xiao Liang and Nan Tian, 'The proposed hike in Japan's military expenditure' posted to the sipri.org website on 2 February 2023.

4. See for example, John Reed and Demetri Sevastopulo, 'How India is slowly moving into the American orbit' published in the *Financial Times* on 23 June 2023.

5. See *National Security Strategy of Japan* (Tokyo: Government of Japan, December 2022).

2.1 REGIONAL REVIEW

NORTH AND SOUTH AMERICA

Author:
Conrad Waters

On 9 March 2023, the Biden administration submitted its FY2024 Defense Budget Request to Congress. It requested headline Department of Defense (DOD) spending of US$842bn; an increase of US$26bn over FY2023 levels and US$100bn more than the US$742bn enacted in FY2022. The total increases to US$886bn when non-DOD defence-related spending is taken into account. Proudly proclaimed by American Secretary of Defense Lloyd J. Austin III as, ' … the most strategy-driven request we've ever produced …', it focused squarely on the People's Republic of China as the United States' 'pacing challenge'. Declaring that the budget, '… seeks to meet this critical challenge today, tomorrow, and into the future by providing the resources today to continue to implement our National Defense Strategy …', Secretary Austin confidently declared that, '… this budget will sharpen our edge by making critical investments across all timeframes, theaters, and domains'.[1]

Beyond the political hyperbole, the reality is different. When taking inflation into account, core American defence spending is little higher in real terms than when the Biden administration entered office. Moreover, the current quantum of the defence budget has been largely driven by Congressional action, which has consistently increased Presidential proposals to more robust figures during the budget approval process. The US Navy's shipbuilding account has been a big beneficiary of this political manoeuvring. Its funding has been typically 'marked up' with approvals for additional warships.

The political compromise relating to the total amount the US government can borrow – referred to in the Introduction – will upset this process. The agreement caps total defence spending at the US$886bn proposed by President Biden, effectively preventing the Congressional budget increases that have been a feature of recent years. Whilst it would, for example, still be possible for Congress to promote additional shipbuilding contracts, something else would have to give. This would hazard a return to the 'hollowing out' of capabilities that was experienced during the previous financial restrictions of the sequestration era, when higher-profile acquisitions of new equipment were sometimes prioritised over routine repairs and maintenance.[2]

The squeeze on spending comes at a difficult time for the US Navy. Since 2019, it has been working on a successor to the current force-level goal of 355 ships; a figure set as long ago as 2015. This was before plans for a distributed fleet architecture – including emphasis on a larger number of smaller warships, as well as increased reliance on unmanned vessels – driven, inter alia, by the Distributed Maritime Operations (DMO) concept became established. Unfortunately, completion of this work has been repeatedly delayed through the changing years of the Trump and Biden administrations, leaving ongoing warship procurement decisions to be made in something of a vacuum. The latest, FY2024 long-range shipbuilding plan that was released in March 2023 stated that the navy was close to concluding a revised Battle Force Ship Assessment and Requirement Report (BFSAR), which was due to be ready by June 2023. Hopefully the completion of this analysis will lend clarity to what has become an ever-shifting and confusing picture.[3]

Irrespective of the outcome of the BFSAR, the fundamental problem is that the US Navy does not have the funding to achieve what has been described as a once-in-a-generation change in fleet architecture. The navy budget has been growing slightly as a share of total spending under the Biden administration, amounting to a proposed US$255.8bn or 30.4 percent of the overall 'cake' in FY2024. Around US$32bn of this is devoted to warship procurement; a not-insignificant sum. However, nearly a fifth is being allocated to the extremely costly *Columbia* (SSBN-826) strategic submarines, a proportion that will only grow over the decade ahead. The expense of this programme is a major influence behind the navy's leadership implementing what is essentially a policy of 'robbing Peter to pay Paul'. Under this, existing warships are being decommissioned before the end of their expected lives to free up additional resources for shipbuilding and other priorities. Whilst many ships are being retired only a little ahead of schedule, the withdrawal of Littoral Combat Ships after only a few years' service is a particularly egregious example of a strategy that has encountered significant Congressional resistance. The end result is that – although a distributed architecture depends on fielding more ships – US Navy force numbers are currently predicted to go backwards over the next few years.

The US Navy Littoral Combat Ship *Kansas City* (LCS-22) leads the destroyer *Hopper* (DDG-70) during tactical training in the Pacific in March 2023. Ongoing delay in concluding a future fleet structure plan – including the optimum mix of large, small and unmanned combatants – is hindering decisions on American warship procurement. *(US Navy)*

Table 2.1.1: FLEET STRENGTHS IN THE AMERICAS – LARGER NAVIES (MID 2023)

COUNTRY	ARGENTINA	BRAZIL	CANADA	CHILE	COLOMBIA	ECUADOR	PERU	USA
Aircraft Carrier (CVN/CV)	–	–	–	–	–	–	–	11
Strategic Missile Submarine (SSBN)	–	–	–	–	–	–	–	14
Attack Submarine (SSN/SSGN)	–	–	–	–	–	–	–	53
Patrol Submarine (SSK)	–[1]	5	4	4	4	2	6	–
Fleet Escort (CG/DDG/FFG)	4	6	12	8	4	2	6	92[2]
Patrol Escort/Corvette (FFG/FSG/FS)	9	2	–	–	2	6	2	27
Missile Armed Attack Craft (PGG/PTG)	2	–	–	3	–	3	5	–
Mine Countermeasures Vessel (MCMV)	–	3	12	–	–	–	–	8
Major Amphibious Units (LHD/LPD/LPH/LSD)	–	2	–	1	–	–	1	31

Note:

1. Argentina's two remaining submarines are non-operational and unlikely to be returned to service. A number of other vessels are of uncertain operational status.
2. Includes one *Zumwalt* class destroyer that is not fully operational.

MAJOR NORTH AMERICAN NAVIES – CANADA

The current strength of the Royal Canadian Navy is set out in Table 2.1.2. As has been the case for several years now, there have been no changes in the fleet's inventory of major warships. A number of significant programmes remain ongoing under the Canadian National Shipbuilding Strategy (NSS) and these are starting to deliver minor vessels against a backdrop of cost overruns and delays. However, it will be a while yet before material progress in recapitalising the fleet's major units is achieved.

The most important and expensive element of the current NSS is the project to build fifteen new Canadian Surface Combatants (CSCs); a derivative of the British Type 26 Global Combat Ship. The design was selected as the preferred option towards the end of 2018, with the subsequent years spent evolving this to meet the Royal Canadian Navy's specific requirements. On current planning, an order for an initial batch of three vessels will be placed with Irving's Halifax Shipyards within the next twelve months so as to allow construction to commence during 2024. This would allow initial deliveries to follow during the early 2030s. Contracts for some long-lead items have already been placed. Current procurement costs are estimated to be between C$56–60bn (c. US$42–45bn), an already eye-watering cost that past experience suggests is likely to be exceeded. It would also be an achievement if projected timelines are maintained.

The evidence for this assertion is based on progress with the two contracts for Royal Canadian Navy vessels that have already been placed under the NSS framework. The furthest advanced for these is for the *Harry DeWolf* class Arctic and Offshore Patrol Ships (AOPSs), which are also being built at Halifax. In January 2023 it emerged that the cost of the six ships being constructed for the navy – a further two are being built for the coast guard – had increased from by another C$680m (c. US$510m) to C$5bn (c. US$3.75bn).[4] This compares with an estimated project cost of C$3.5bn (US$2.6bn) when construction commenced in 2015. Experience with the lead ship has also not been altogether positive, with initial teething troubles including a major generator failure and contamination of the ship's potable water. More positively, second of class *Margaret Brooke* was commissioned on 28 October 2022 and sister-ship *Max Bernays* – the third vessel – delivered on 2 September that same year. Other programme highlights during the past year included the launch of the fourth AOPS, *William Hall*, on 27 November 2022 and a first steel-cutting ceremony for the sixth vessel, *Robert Hampton Gray*, on 15 August. In July 2022, Irving Shipbuilding strengthened its management team with the appointment of Dirk Lesko, previously longstanding President of General Dynamics Bath Iron Works, as its new President. The presence of a leader with extensive experience of the US Navy's major destroyer programmes will doubtless provide considerable assurance as CSC production commences.[5]

Meanwhile, on Canada's west coast, it has been confirmed that construction of the two *Protecteur* class joint support ships being built to Germany's Type 702 *Berlin* class combat support ship design at Seaspan's Vancouver Shipyard has been further delayed. New project timelines announced in mid-

The Royal Canadian Navy's supply ship *Asterix* (centre) is seen replenishing the Canadian frigate *Montréal* (left) and US Navy destroyer *Truxtun* (DDG-103) (right) during a deployment in the Red Sea in May 2023. Leased to provide an interim solution to a gap in Canadian naval replenishment capability pending completion of the new joint support ships, *Asterix*'s service with the navy has been extended as delivery of the new vessels has been progressively shifted to the right. *(US Navy)*

Table 2.1.2: CANADIAN NAVY: PRINCIPAL UNITS AS AT MID 2023

TYPE	CLASS	NUMBER	TONNAGE	DIMENSIONS	PROPULSION	CREW	DATE
Principal Surface Escorts							
Frigate – FFG	**HALIFAX**	12	4,800 tonnes	134m x 16m x 5m	CODOG, 29 knots	225	1992
Submarines							
Submarine – SSK	**VICTORIA** (UPHOLDER)	4	2,500 tonnes	70m x 8m x 6m	Diesel-electric, 20+ knots	50	1990

2022 now envisage delivery of the lead ship in 2025, two years later than previously envisaged. Her sister, *Preserver*, will follow in 2027, also two years behind the former schedule. Sustained supply chain delays due to the pandemic and further challenges related to a first-of-class delivery have been held responsible. The leasing contract for the interim supply vessel *Asterix* has been extended by a further two years at a cost of C$187m (US$140m) to cover the delay. This takes the total expense of these interim arrangements to C$878m (US$660m), not much more than the total cost of the British Royal Fleet Auxiliary's four 'Tide' class tankers.

In addition to current NSS naval programmes, two additional major warship procurement projects are starting to appear on the radar screen. One is the Canadian Patrol Submarine Project (CPSP), first stood up in 2021 to explore options for the existing *Victoria* (former British *Upholder*) class's replacement. In June 2023 Britain's Babcock – which supports the existing boats – entered a technical collaboration agreement with South Korea's Hyundai Heavy Industries (HHI) to cooperate on a CPSP bid. Press reports suggest that the Royal Canadian Navy would like to acquire twelve submarines; a substantial uplift on its current four-strong flotilla. The other requirement is a replacement for the existing elderly *Kingston* class coastal defence vessels, which is now seen as an additional requirement to the AOPSs. Commodore Jason Armstrong, the Royal Canadian Navy's Director-General Naval Force Development has been reported as stating that the envisaged replacement is a relatively small vessel in the 1,000–2,000-tonne range that will, however, be internationally deployable. Key characteristics will include a minimal crew and some self-defence capability, as well as an emphasis on leveraging autonomous systems.[6] A major question, particularly with respect to submarine numbers, is whether funding will be forthcoming to support the navy's aspirations. A Defence Policy Update to the 2017 *Strong, Secure, Engaged* strategy document that is expected in the second half of 2023 might provide the answer.

MAJOR NORTH AMERICAN NAVIES – UNITED STATES

The US Navy retained 298 warships in its front-line 'battle force' as of mid-2023, a figure that was unchanged year-on-year. In very broad terms, deliveries of *Arleigh Burke* (DDG-51) class destroyers and Littoral Combat Ships more than compensated for withdrawals of *Ticonderoga* (CG-47) class cruisers, whilst there were small declines in the number of submarines and amphibious ships. Last year's FY2023 Presidential Budget Request envisaged battle force numbers falling to 285 by September 2023. However, Congressional refusal to sanction premature retirement of a number of vessels – including a cruiser, four dock landing ships and five Littoral Combat Ships – mean that the decline has not been as precipitous as first envisaged. Nevertheless, it seems that the pain has only been deferred because the navy – as has often happened in the past – is seeking to overcome Congressional resistance by seeking to revisit its proposals in FY2024 and subsequent years. As such, current estimates of a battle force of 290 ships at the end of the decade are little changed from previous calculations.

Where the fleet goes from there will depend on the conclusions to the revised BFSAR referred to in the Introduction, as well as the extent of the political will to fund its conclusions. A previous, classified iteration of the BFSAR study (BFSAR 2022) delivered to Congress in July 2022 and summarised in Table 2.1.3 suggested that a total battle force of as many as 373 manned warships, together with 150 large surface and sub-surface unmanned vessels, were required in a notional 2045 US Navy.[7] Whilst navy leadership believe that the total of 373 vessels contained in BFSAR 2022 will set a floor on the required future fleet structure, they expect the detail to change in the revised assessment that will soon be completed.

Given this continued uncertainty, the US Navy's official FY2024 long-range shipbuilding plan and associated force structure assessments essentially exclude the current BFSAR deliberations from its calculations. Instead, its focus is largely on the short term impact of the latest, five year FY2024–28 Future Years Defense Program (FYDP) on the estimates contained in the previous plan, which had contained three different scenarios for the fleet's future trajectory. Given that planned disposals and construction have changed little from previous plans year-on-year, the overall effect on calculations that, in any case, will soon be overtaken by events is only marginal.[8]

The FY2024–28 FYDP shipbuilding programme is set out in Table 2.1.4. It envisages the procurement of fifty-five warships at a total cost of

Table 2.1.3: US NAVY FLEET STRUCTURE EVOLUTION

PLANNED FLEET STRUCTURE 'BATTLE FORCE' SHIPS	FSA 2016[1] (PRE-DMO)	BFSAR 2022[2] (POST-DMO)	CURRENT[3] (MID-2023)
Strategic Submarines (SSBNs)	12	12	14
Attack Submarines (SSGNs/SSNs)	66	66	53
Aircraft Carriers (CVNs)	12	12	11
Large Surface Combatants (CGs/DDGs)	104	96	91
Small Surface Combatants (FFGs/FFs/MCMVs)	52	56	35
Large Amphibious Vessels (LHAs/LHDs/LPDs/LSDs)	38	31	31
Small Amphibious Vessels (Medium Landing Ship)	Nil	18	Nil
Auxiliary Vessels	71	82	63
Sub Total	**355**	**373**	**298**
Large Unmanned Surface & Sub-Surface Vessels	Not Stated	c. 150	Nil
Total	**355+**	**c. 523**	**298**

Notes:

1. Numbers based on the Force Structure Assessment (FSA) released in 2016.
2. Numbers based on the classified Battle Force Ship Assessment and Requirement (BFSAR) submitted to Congress in mid-2022 and summarised in the *Chief of Naval Operations Navigation Plan 2022.* The US Navy would hope to achieve this force design by 2045. A revised BFSAR is now being developed.
3. Based on information contained in the Naval Vessels Register as of June 2023.

US$146.4bn over FY2024–28 compared with the previous year's initial plan to spend US$132.8bn on fifty-one vessels during FY2023–27. The programme remains consistent with previous years' plans in envisaging the continued production of *Virginia* (SSN-774) class attack submarine and *Arleigh Burke* class destroyer production throughout the life of the FYDP at an annual 'drumbeat' of two units p.a. The other major commitment is, inevitably, construction of the *Columbia* class strategic submarines. These will be ordered at a steady rate of one unit p.a. from FY2026. Taken together, these three programmes will cost a total of

The second *Ford* class carrier *John F. Kennedy* (CVN-79) pictured fitting out at Huntington Ingalls Industries' Newport News yard. A revised building strategy will bring forward work which was previously scheduled post-delivery, hopefully helping to smooth her entry into operational service. *(Huntington Ingalls Industries)*

Table 2.1.4: USN FY2023 FIVE-YEAR SHIPBUILDING PLAN (FY2024–FY2028)

SHIP TYPE	FY2023 Request	FY2023 Funded	FY2024 Request[1]	FY2025 Plan[1]	FY2026 Plan[1]	FY2027 Plan[1]	FY2028 Plan[1]	FY2024-28 Total FYDP[1]
Aircraft Carrier (CVN-78)	0	0	0 ($1,916)	0 ($3,083)	0 ($3,081)	0 ($3,854)	1 ($3,845)	**1 ($15,780)**
Strategic Submarine (SSBN-826)	0	0	1 ($5,834)	0 ($7,276)	1 ($8,468)	1 ($8,788)	1 ($8,729)	**4 ($39,095)**
Attack Submarine (SSN-774)	2	2	2 ($10,346)	2 ($9,964)	2 ($8,670)	2 ($8,090)	2 ($7,553)	**10 ($44,621)**
Destroyer (DDG-51)	2	3	2 ($4,483)	2 ($4,410)	2 ($4,172)	2 ($4,220)	2 ($4,609)	**10 ($21,984)**
Frigate (FFG-62)	1	1	2 ($2,174)	1 ($1,037)	2 ($1,933)	1 ($1,041)	2 ($2,058)	**8 ($8,243)**
Amphibious Assault Ship (LHA-6)[2]	1	1	0 ($1,830)	0 ($79)	0 ($367)	1 ($3,479)	0 ($0)	**1 ($5,755)**
Amphibious Ship (LPD-17 F II)	1[2]	1[2]	0 ($0)	0 ($0)	0 ($0)	0 ($0)	0 ($0)	**0 ($0)**
Medium Landing Ship (LSM(X))	0	0	0 ($0)	1 ($188)	1 ($150)	2 ($297m)	2 ($296m)	**6 ($931m)**
Expeditionary Fast Transport (T-EPF-1)	0	2[3]	0 ($0)	0 ($0)	0 ($0)	0 ($0)	0 ($0)	**0 ($0)**
Replenishment Oiler (T-AO-205)	1	1	1 ($815m)	0 ($0)	2 ($1,632m)	1 ($861m)	2 ($1,752m)	**6 ($5,061m)**
Light Replenishment Oiler (T-AOL(X))	0	0	0 ($0)	0 ($0)	1 ($150m)	1 ($156m)	1 ($159m)	**3 ($465m)**
Submarine Tender (AS(X))	0	0	1 ($1,733m)	0 ($0)	1 ($1,101m)	0 ($0)	0 ($0)	**2 ($2,834m)**
Fleet Tug (T-ATS-6)	1	1	0 ($0)	0 ($0)	0 ($0)	0 ($0)	0 ($0)	**0 ($0)**
Surveillance Ship (T-AGOS-25)	0	0	0 ($0)	1 ($434)	1($417)	1 ($421)	1 ($427m)	**4 ($1,699)**
Total	**9**	**12**	**9 ($29,131)**	**7 ($26,470)**	**13 ($30,141)**	**12 ($31,207)**	**14 ($29,428)**	**55 ($146,378)**
Projected Battle Force			**293**	**286**	**285**	**285**	**291**	

Notes:

1. Figure in brackets relates to the dollar cost of the period's acquisitions in millions. Funding for some major units, such as aircraft carriers, is spread over the programme's life. This explains why funding is sometimes allocated in years when no procurement of a particular class is proposed.
2. There is a dispute between the US Navy and Congress as to when this ship, LHA-9, was actually authorised. Consistent with past Congressional action, Congress believes that it was actually approved in the FY2021 programme year.
3. Expeditionary Medical Ship variant.

a little more than US$105bn over the life of the FYDP; approaching three-quarters of total expenditure on warship procurement over the period.

In view of the importance of distributed operating concepts, it is noteworthy how little of warship procurement is taken up with the new generation of ships that will be required to put the new vision into practice. For example, orders for the new *Constellation* (FFG-62) class frigates are projected to continue at a rate of three units every two years, with the total FYDP bill of US$8.2bn for eight ships being little more than a third of the US$21.9bn spent on ten destroyers despite the supposed plan to shift to a larger number of smaller ships. Similarly, acquisitions of next-generation landing ships and small oilers that are supposedly vital to the effective implementation of DMO are allocated less than US$1.5bn of funding over the period. Planned spending on the development of large unmanned vessels also remains at a relatively low level despite their supposed future significance.

Table 2.1.5 provides a summary of the fleet's major combatants as of mid-2023, with analysis of the principal warship types following below.

Aircraft Carriers: The last year has seen *Gerald R. Ford* (CVN-78) finally enter the US Navy's operational deployment cycle, over five years after she was first commissioned. Whilst some of this gap was down to resolving inevitable first-of-class teething troubles, the US Navy also hope to narrow this interval with the next *Ford*, *John F. Kennedy* (CVN-79), by bringing forward work that was previously due to be implemented post-delivery into the build process. The revised scheme therefore envisages the ship's delivery slipping by around a year to 31 July 2025 but her entry into operational service remaining in line with previous plans. *Enterprise* (CVN-80), the third ship, is due to complete in March 2028 and be followed by *Doris Miller* (CVN-81) in February 2032. Despite the progress made with getting the class to sea, concerns remain with respect to the reliability of many of the new technologies they introduce. Notably, the ships electro-magnetic aircraft launch system (EMALS) and advanced arrestor gear (AAG) have remained significantly less reliable than required.[9]

Surface Combatants: The last year has seen the start of the withdrawals of the vertical launch system (VLS)-equipped *Ticonderoga* (CG-47) class cruisers, essentially marking the end of Congressional efforts to keep these ships in the fleet over the medium term.[10] *Vella Gulf* (CG-72) was the first to be retired

Table 2.1.5: UNITED STATES NAVY: PRINCIPAL UNITS AS AT MID 2023

TYPE	CLASS	NUMBER	TONNAGE	DIMENSIONS	PROPULSION	CREW	DATE
Aircraft Carriers							
Aircraft Carrier – CVN	**FORD** (CVN-78)	1	100,000 tonnes+	333m x 41/78m x 12m	Nuclear, 30+ knots	4,600	2017
Aircraft Carrier – CVN	**NIMITZ** (CVN-68)	10	100,000 tonnes+	333m x 41/78m x 12m	Nuclear, 30+ knots	5,200	1975
Principal Surface Escorts							
Cruiser – CG	**TICONDEROGA** (CG-47)	17	9,900 tonnes	173m x 17m x 7m	COGAG, 30+ knots	365	1983
Destroyer – DDG	**ZUMWALT** (DDG-1000)	2[1]	15,800 tonnes	186m x 25m x 8m	IEP, 30+ knots	175	2016
Destroyer – DDG	**ARLEIGH BURKE** (DDG-51) – Flight III	1	9,700 tonnes	155m x 20m x 7m	COGAG, 30 knots	360	2023
Destroyer – DDG	**ARLEIGH BURKE** (DDG-51) – Flight II-A	44	9,400 tonnes	155m x 20m x 7m	COGAG, 30 knots	330	2000
Destroyer – DDG	**ARLEIGH BURKE** (DDG-51) – Flights I/II	28	8,900 tonnes	154m x 20m x 7m	COGAG, 30+ knots	305	1991
Littoral Combat Ship – FS	**FREEDOM** (LCS-1)	12	3,500 tonnes	115m x 17m x 4m	CODAG, 45+ knots	<50[2]	2008
Littoral Combat Ship – FS	**INDEPENDENCE** (LCS-2)	15	3,000 tonnes	127m x 32m x 5m	CODAG, 45+ knots	<50[2]	2010
Submarines							
Submarine – SSBN	**OHIO** (SSBN-726)	14	18,800 tonnes	171m x 13m x 12m	Nuclear, 20+ knots	155	1981
Submarine – SSGN	**OHIO** (SSGN-726)	4	18,800 tonnes	171m x 13m x 12m	Nuclear, 20+ knots	160	1981
Submarine – SSN	**VIRGINIA** (SSN-774)	21	8,000 tonnes	115m x 10m x 9m	Nuclear, 25+ knots	135	2004
Submarine – SSN	**SEAWOLF** (SSN-21)	3[3]	9,000 tonnes	108m x 12m x 11m	Nuclear, 25+ knots	140	1997
Submarine – SSN	**LOS ANGELES** (SSN-688)	25	7,000 tonnes	110m x 10m x 9m	Nuclear, 25+ knots	145	1976
Major Amphibious Units							
Amph. Assault Ship – LHD	**AMERICA** (LHA-6)	2	45,000 tonnes	257m x 32/42m x 9m	COGAG, 22+ knots	1,050	2014
Amph Assault Ship – LHD	**WASP** (LHD-1)	7[4]	41,000 tonnes	253m x 32/42m x 9m	Steam, 20+ knots	1,100	1989
Landing Platform Dock – LPD	**SAN ANTONIO** (LPD-17)	12	25,000 tonnes	209m x 32m x 7m	Diesel, 22+ knots	360	2005
Landing Ship Dock – LSD	**WHIDBEY ISLAND** (LSD-41)	10[5]	16,000 tonnes	186m x 26m x 6m	Diesel, 20 knots	420	1985

Notes:

1 Includes one ship commissioned but not included in the 'battle force' pending completion of combat systems installation.

2 Plus mission-related crew.

3 Third of class, SSN-23 is longer and heavier.

4 LHD-8 has many differences.

5 Includes four LSD-49 HARPERS FERRY variants.

The writing is on the wall for the US Navy's dwindling number of *Ticonderoga* (CG-47) class cruisers as plans to remove them from service to free up resources for new shipbuilding start to overcome Congressional resistance. *Lake Erie* (CG-70), seen here in February 2023, is to be retired before the end of 2025. *(Lorenz Amiet)*

The immediate future of the US Navy's force of larger surface combatants is in the hands of the new *Arleigh Burke* class Flight III iterations equipped with the improved, modular AN/SPY-6(V)1 Air and Missile Defense Radar (AMDR). This can be distinguished by its larger dimensions compared with the previous AN/SPY-1. This photograph shows the first Flight III Burke, *Jack H. Lucas* (DDG-125) running trials from Huntington Ingalls Industries' Pascagoula yard in April 2023. *(Huntington Ingalls Industries)*

when she was decommissioned at a ceremony at Norfolk naval base on 4 August 2022. Four more members of the class – *Monterey* (CG-61), *Hué City* (CG-66), *Anzio* (CG-69) and *Port Royal* (CG-73) – followed in short order the following month. Although two additional ships were temporarily saved by Congressional order, they – and two more cruisers – will be retired by the end of September 2023. Barring a further political rear-guard action, it remains the plan to dispose of all the rest by 2027. Although most of these ships are being retired close to – and sometimes in excess of – their planned service lives, loss of their relatively large missile capacity will be severely felt at a time when this is commanding more of a premium in navy thinking.

In another significant end of an era, production of *Arleigh Burke* Flight IIA variant destroyers is also drawing to a close. Huntington Ingalls Industries' (HII's) Ingalls Shipbuilding yard at Pascagoula delivered *Lenah Sutcliffe Higbee* (DDG-123), its final Flight IIA, on 30 November 2022. General Dynamics Bath Iron Works (BIW) – which shares construction of the class – subsequently handed over *Carl M. Levin* (DDG-120) in January 2023 but still has three further Flight IIAs to deliver after previous production problems. Once these are completed, there will be a total of twenty-eight Flight I/II and forty-seven Flight IIA *Burke*s in the class.

Deliveries of the follow-on *Arleigh Burke* Flight III variant have now commenced following the acceptance of *Jack H. Lucas* (DDG-125) from Ingalls on 27 June 2023. Displacing around 200 tonnes more than her immediate predecessors, she is equipped with the improved, modular AN/SPY-6(V)1 Air and Missile Defense Radar (AMDR) and incorporates increased generating power to match the demands of the new array. After Congress voted to add a third Flight III *Burke* to the FY2023 procurement programme, a total of seventeen Flight IIIs have been authorised to date. When combined with the ten destroyers contained in the 2024–28 FYDP, this suggests total production will encompass over 100 ships of all variants. After a recent decision to increase the life of the lead ship by a further five years, withdrawal of the older members of the class will now commence with *Barry* (DDG-52) and *John Paul Jones* (DDG-53) during FY2027, when each will have been in service for 35 years.

Although two of the *Zumwalt* (DDG-1000) destroyers have been commissioned and actually deployed on exercises, only the lead ship officially forms part of the battle force as the navy develops options for the future of the truncated, three-ship class. Work will soon start on replacing their existing 152mm guns – which lack their intended guided ammunition – with launch tubes for the hypersonic Conventional Prompt Strike missile. The aim is to test this weapon at sea from *Zumwalt* by the end of 2025. The other two ships will follow in due course. Work is also underway to implement a *Zumwalt* Enterprise Upgrade Solution (ZEUS) that will see radar and other systems revised to provide greater commonality with the rest of the fleet. In the meantime, delivery of the third and final ship – *Lyndon B. Johnson* (DDG-1002) – continues to be delayed. It will now be late 2024 before her acceptance.

Design work is now underway on the next-generation DDG(X), about which details are slowly starting to emerge. The baseline design has a displacement of 13,500 tonnes and – in an evolutionary approach – will utilise the same AN/SPY-6 radar and combat management system incorporated in the *Arleigh Burke* Flight III variant. Its VLS missile load-out remains at the ninety-six cells found in the Flight IIA and Flight III *Burkes* but an optional additional mid-body hull section – called the Destroyer Payload Module – will provide the possibility of increasing magazine capacity if required. Given orders won't be placed during the current decade, it is likely to be the second half of the 2030s before the DDG(X) makes its presence felt in the US Navy's force structure.

Turning to smaller surface combatants, the last year has seen deliveries of the odd-numbered *Freedom* (LCS-1) variant Littoral Combat Ships *Cooperstown* (LCS-23) and *Marinette* (LCS-25) by Marinette Marine and their even-numbered *Independence* (LCS-2) variant counterparts *Santa Barbara* (LCS-32) and *Augusta* (LCS-34) by Austal USA. These arrivals were counterbalanced by the decommissioning of *Coronado* (LCS-4) at San Diego in September 2022, leaving twelve LCS-1 types and fifteen LCS-2 variants in the current inventory. Austal USA laid the keel of *Pierre* (LCS-38), their final Littoral Combat Ship, on 16 June 2023. As the US Navy's ultimate requirement is now only for fifteen *Independence* class variants, they propose decommissioning the oldest two members of the *Independence* class – *Jackson* (LCS-6) and *Montgomery* (LCS-8) – during FY2024 to balance the future arrival of LCS-38 and her sister *Kingsville* (LCS-36). With only six *Freedom* variants now required, the cull of existing ships will be more severe. Whilst three additional ships will be delivered by FY2027, a further nine vessels (*Freedom* has already been decommissioned) will have been deleted over that period if the US Navy gets its way. It is hoped that many of these vessels will be transferred to foreign navies to recoup some of the money essentially wasted on their construction.

The *Freedom* (LCS-1) variant Littoral Combat Ship *Cooperstown* (LCS-23) – pictured here in November 2022 – is one of the latest members of the class to be delivered, helping to stabilise fleet numbers over the last year. However, planned premature retirements of earlier members of the class will be a key factor in driving a reduction in the size of the US Navy in the period ahead. *(Marc Piché)*

Physical construction of the first of the Littoral Combat Ship's successors, the *Constellation* (FFG-62) class frigates, began at Marinette Marine on 31 August 2022. Her delivery was initially planned for 2026 but this may prove optimistic. Four members of the class have now been ordered following exercise of a contract option in May 2023, with the ship subsequently being named *Lafayette* (FFG-65) in honour of the French hero of the American Revolutionary War.

In addition to reducing their inventory of Littoral Combat Ships, the US Navy also continues to withdraw smaller combatants that do not form part of the headline 'battle force'. Notably, the last year has seen the withdrawal of the last five *Cyclone* (PC-1) class patrol ships, which have been transferred for further service with the Egyptian and Philippine navies. When combined with the deletion of smaller Mk VI patrol boats in 2021–2, a material part of the navy's littoral warfare assets have been divested without significant debate.

Amphibious and Support Shipping: The US Navy's force of large amphibious vessels dropped by one to thirty-one over the last year with the decommissioning of the lead *Whidbey Island* (LDS-41) class dock landing ship in July 2022. This is the minimum level currently set in law by Congress.[11] However, the navy's leadership continue to press for further retirements of 'legacy' vessels whilst putting a hold on plans for replacements. It was previously envisaged that these would be provided by ongoing construction of *San Antonio* (LPD-17) Flight II amphibious transport docks. However, orders for these have effectively been paused with effect from LPD-32, the third Flight II, which was contracted on 31 March 2023. The suspension has been implemented whilst the navy completes evaluation of the number of amphibious warships it needs as part of the revised BFSAR. However, the hiatus has caused fraction with US Marine Corps (USMC) Commandant General David Berger, who is strongly in favour of continued procurement. Current indications suggest that acquisition of more of the type will be added to the FY2025–29 FYDP once force structure deliberations have concluded.

Meanwhile, design work continues on the medium landing ship (LSM) – previously known as the light amphibious warship (LAW) – that is destined to support the USMC's Expeditionary Advanced Base Operations (EABO) concept; part of the wider shift to DMO.[12] The contract for the first will be placed in FY2025, with orders for a total of six planned within the lifespan of the current FYDP. The use of cheaper ships to 'pad out' the larger warships dedicated to supporting USMC operations is not new. The *Spearhead* (T-EPF-1) class expeditionary fast transports and *Lewis B. Puller* (ESB-3) class expeditionary mobile bases are previous examples of this approach. The last year has seen the delivery of *Apalachicola* (T-EPF-13), the last of the Flight I *Spearhead* class variants. Three additional Flight II versions – incorporating improved medical facilities – have also been ordered and a *Bethesda* (T-EMS-1) class expeditionary medical ship iteration approved. An adjustment to the FY2023 budget saw two further ships of this type added to one that had already been authorised. 2023 has also seen delivery of *John L. Canley* (ESB-6), the fourth expeditionary support base.

Construction of replenishment shipping continues to be dominated by *John Lewis* (T-AO-205) fleet replenishment oilers. The lead ship was delivered on 27 July 2022 and eight further vessels are at various states of construction or on order. Work on designing the supplementary light replenishment oiler (TAOL) is also underway but it will be a couple of years yet before an order for the first of the type – considered essential to supporting the demands of a dispersed fleet – is placed. Also at the design stage is a new class of AS(X) submarine tender that are destined to replace the two *Emory S. Land* (AS-39) class vessels that support US Navy boats operating out of Guam. L3 Harris, General Dynamics NASSCO and HII are all working on preliminary designs for the new ships under contracts awarded in April 2022. The latest FYDP proposes accelerating the start of actual procurement by around a year, with a contract for the first of two units now expected by mid-2024.

Also drawing closer to production is the new TAGOS-25 class of ocean surveillance ships. The navy eventually plans to acquire seven of these ships, which are larger and faster than ships that currently perform the role. The lead ship was authorised in the FY2022 budget. Subsequently, in June 2023, Austal USA was awarded a contract for the detailed design of the ships that also includes options for their subsequent construction.

General Dynamics NASSCO yard in San Diego, California delivered the first *John Lewis* (T-AO-205) fleet replenishment oiler in July 2022 and has received orders for eight further vessels in a planned twenty-strong class. This photograph shows the third member of the class, *Earl Warren* (T-AO-207), in the course of construction. *(General Dynamics NASSCO)*

Submarines: In February 2023, the strategic submarine *Louisiana* (SSBN-743) completed a 41-month engineered refuelling overhaul (ERO) at the Puget Sound Naval Shipyard. Delayed by the Covid pandemic, the mid-life refuelling was the longest undertaken on any of the eighteen-strong *Ohio* (SSBN-726) class. It was also the last concluded on an *Ohio* class boat. From FY2027, the *Ohio*s – starting with two of the reconstructed SSGN cruise missile variants – will begin to be withdrawn from service. Work is well advanced on the first of the following *Columbia* (SSBN-826) class, which is scheduled to be delivered in 2027. Achieving this timetable may prove to be a stretch given that the programme is reportedly running as much as 10 percent behind internal completion schedules whilst the American nuclear submarine sector struggles to accommodate a significant growth in demand.[13]

Production pressures are also impacting deliveries of the *Virginia* (SSN-774) class nuclear-powered attack submarines. The US Navy has sought to increase class deliveries from a rate of one to two per annum as 'legacy' Cold War-era boats start to decommission in increasing numbers, raising procurement to two submarines each year from FY2011 onwards in line with this aim. However, when combined with the subsequent transition to a larger *Virginia* class variant – incorporating additional missile capacity in the form of a Virginia Payload Module – this has proved too much for industrial capacity. As such, the actual current delivery rate is around 1.2 boats per year, with no new members of the class joining the fleet since March 2022. With *Chicago* (SSN-721) of the previous *Los Angeles* (SSN-688) transferred to reserve in preparation for disposal in January 2023, submarine numbers have dropped by one boat over the past 12 months. Given a bulge of submarine retirements in the years ahead, the situation is likely to deteriorate further in the medium term. An added strain will be the promised transfer of at least three *Virginia* class submarines to Australia in the early 2030s as part of the AUKUS agreement. Two of these are likely to be drawn from the US Navy's existing inventory.

Unmanned Vessels: The US Navy remains committed to operating considerable numbers of unmanned vessels as part of a distributed fleet. It has developed plans for deploying large unmanned surface vehicle (LUSV), medium unmanned surface vehicle (MUSV) and extra-large unmanned undersea vehicle (XLUUV) type vessels as part of these plans. The recent emphasis has been on exploring the likely capability of such units through extensive trials of various prototypes. However, transition to series production is likely in the years ahead.

As of mid-2023, evaluation of the LUSV – which seems primarily intended to operate as an unmanned platform for anti-ship and land attack missiles – appears to be furthest advanced following completion of a Distributed / Offensive Surface Fires Analysis of Alternatives during the past year. The aim is to complete detail design and construction preparations during 2023–4 prior to commencing series production in 2025. Recent statements suggest the LUSV will continue to house a small crew, at least at the start. There has been more hesitancy relating to the MUSV following the success of smaller USVs in deploying the distributed sensors that are their key function. However, recent navy pronouncements suggest that trials during the RIMPAC 2022 exercises have demonstrated its continued utility. A MUSV prototype was ordered from L3 Harris in July 2020 but there are no current plans to exercise additional production options contained in the contract. Meanwhile, assessment of the five 'operationally relevant' Orca XLUUVs ordered from Boeing in 2019 has been delayed due to problems at the contractor. Deliveries of these prototype systems, initially intended for trialling autonomous minelaying operations, will now extend to mid-2024. This, in turn, has pushed back series production by at least two years to FY2026.

The US Navy's *Ohio* (SSBN-726) class strategic submarine *Louisiana* (SSBN-743) transits Puget Sound in February 2023 following a 41-month-long engineered refuelling overhaul at Puget Sound Naval Shipyard. She is the last *Ohio* class submarine to be refuelled, with work on the replacement *Columbia* (SSBN-826) class now underway. *(US Navy)*

Operational Highlights: The snapshot of US operations provided in the press briefing that accompanied the FY2024 Department of the Navy Presidential Budget request indicated that a total of 105 out of 296 ships were deployed as of 13 March 2023, around 35 percent of the total. Although this was lower than the exceptionally high 43 percent figure recorded the previous year – which possibly reflected the impact of Russia's invasion of the Ukraine on force deployment – it remains a high figure. The distribution of forces was largely unchanged from March 2022, with the sixty-seven (sixty-nine) vessels in the Asia-Pacific region and ninety-five (ninety-four) on the Pacific Coast continuing to emphasise the priority given to these theatres.

A major problem in maintaining this high operational tempo has been a growing backlog of repairs and maintenance on existing ships. The hard-pressed submarine force has proved particularly susceptible to this problem. As of FY2023, eighteen (37 percent) of the navy's forty-nine nuclear-powered attack submarines were either in or awaiting maintenance, an increase from twelve (23 percent) of fifty-three boats a decade ago. The deterioration has been primarily due to neglect of the four government-operated shipyards which perform most of the overhauls of these boats, although supply chain issues impacting the availability of spare parts has also been a problem. In 2018, the navy began a 20-year investment plan, the Shipyard Infrastructure Optimization Program (SIOP), to modernise these facilities. However, it is taking time to gain traction. Spending on SIOP is planned to increase by almost a third (from US$1.86bn to US$2.73bn) in FY2024, with almost half allocated to a replacement dry dock at Pearl Harbor. In addition to making greater use of the privately-owned submarine builders, which have experienced problems of their own, some consideration is being given to adding a fifth public shipyard to put the refit schedule on a more sustainable footing.

Evolving the Distributed Maritime Operations concept – alongside supporting approaches such as EABO, Stand-In Forces and Littoral Operations in a Contested Environment – continue to exert a significant influence on exercises and training as the navy seeks to counter China's ever-strengthening anti-access/area denial (A2/AD) bubble in the Western Pacific. A particularly important programme of experimentation during the first half of 2023 involved the use of the *Carl Vinson* (CVN-70) carrier strike group to test technology associated with the highly secretive Project Overmatch. Forming part of the Department of Defense's wider Joint All-Domain Command and Control (JADC2) initiative, this aims to expand on previous network-centric warfare efforts to provide better connectivity between the navy's warships, aircraft, weapons and sensors. The intention is to use the results of the trials with *Vinson* and her escorts to inform efforts to roll out Overmatch across the navy. Unsurprisingly, the initial focus will be on the Pacific. Interestingly, it has been revealed that there has been collaboration with key allies such as Australia, France and the United Kingdom in developing the project's evolving technology.[14]

US Coast Guard: The US Coast Guard's procurement continues to be driven by a program of record drawn up as long ago as 2004 that essentially required replacing ninety old cutters of various shapes and sizes with three new classes. These comprised eight large 'Legend' or *Bertholf* (WMSL-750) class national security cutters; twenty-five slightly smaller 'Heritage' or *Argus* (WMSM-915) offshore patrol cutters; and sixty-four (now sixty-five) small 'Sentinel' or *Bernard C. Webber* (WPC-1101) fast response cutters.

The *Los Angeles* (SSN-688) class nuclear-powered attack submarine *Topeka* (SSN-754) is seen in the course of undocking from Pearl Harbor Naval Shipyard in July 2021 towards the end of a planned overhaul. Previous neglect of the navy's state-owned shipyards is having a significant impact on submarine availability, although large sums are now being expended on modernisation. *(US Navy)*

Nearly 20 years on, the programme's implementation can be viewed as being broadly successful. Indeed, Congressional largesse has seen the purchase of vessels additional to the original requirement. For example, the coming months will see the delivery of the tenth 'Legend' class cutter *Calhoun* (WMSL-759), which completed builder's sea trials on 30 June 2023. An eleventh vessel has also been ordered but it seems that a possible twelfth ship may not be progressed. At the other end of the size spectrum, fifty-two fast response cutters are now in service and thirteen more either under build or authorised. Six are allocated to the Coast Guard's Patrol Forces Southwest Asia in Bahrain. The Coast Guard is seeking to expand its overseas activities and has an unfunded priority to acquire four additional 'Sentinel' class vessels to expand presence and engagement activities in the Indo-Pacific region. To an extent, the US Coast Guard is replacing the capacity lost to the US Navy as its own patrol vessels are retired.

Realisation of the offshore patrol cutter element has proved problematic. Eastern Shipbuilding Group of Florida – the original contactor for the programme – has faced significant challenges delivering the lead ship, most recently due to defects found with her shaft lines. Originally scheduled for delivery in August 2021, it now seems that it will not be until 2024 that the Coast Guard takes delivery. In mid-2023, Austal USA was brought in as a replacement builder for the fifth ship in the class and is likely to be awarded options for ten more vessels in due course.

Another programme encountering delays is that for three polar security cutters; essentially heavy icebreakers. The former Halter Marine received a contract for the first of these in April 2019 and exercised an option for a second vessel at the end of 2021. It was initially planned that the lead ship – *Polar Sentinel* (WMSP-21) – would be delivered in 2024. However, this was later pushed back to 2025; a schedule that now looks hopelessly optimistic. As of mid-2023, the detailed design of the new class had still to be finalised and *Polar Sentinel* is unlikely to be completed before 2027 at the earliest. In November 2022 Bollinger Shipyards, an unsuccessful bidder for the original deal, acquired Halter Marine from previous owner, Singapore's ST Engineering at a cost of just US$15m. Halter Marine's Pascagoula yards had reportedly racked up losses of more than US$250m in the previous five years.[15]

OTHER NORTH AND CENTRAL AMERICAN NAVIES

With **Mexico's** previously successful programme of naval construction effectively suspended by the current Obrador administration, there is little in the way of news flow from Central America's largest navy. There has been some speculation that Mexico may be interested in acquiring some of the US Navy's prematurely retired Littoral Combat Ships as replacements for its older frigates and patrol vessels, although firm details have yet to emerge.

Elsewhere in Central America and the Caribbean, local navies and coastguards continue to benefit from a flow of '85 Defiant' near costal patrol vessels (NCPVs). These are being built by America's Metal Shark to a Damen Stan Patrol 2606 design under the auspices of a US Southern Command Foreign Military Sales Program. The latest countries to receive the new vessels are **Costa Rica** and **Guatemala**, which both took delivery of a single vessel each in the first half of 2023.[16] **The Dominican Republic, Honduras, El Salvador** and **Panama** have also previously received NCVPs under a programme that is eventually envisaged encompassing thirteen of the class. Metal Shark is also gaining Latin American orders beyond the NCPV programme, being reportedly close to launching a larger, 35m '115 Defiant' patrol vessel ordered by Guyana for its defence force's coast guard component.

MAJOR SOUTH AMERICAN NAVIES – BRAZIL

A full review of the Brazilian Navy, including recent developments, is included in Chapter 2.1A.

OTHER SOUTH AMERICAN NAVIES

The most significant South American naval developments in the last year have occurred in **Colombia**, which has taken a series of strides in putting its Naval Development Plan 2042 into effect. In September 2022, the country's Ministry of National Defence announced the selection of Damen's SIGMA 10514 as the preferred design for its flagship *Plataforma Estratégica de Superficie* (PES) programme. This envisages the acquisition of five new frigates to replace the existing four FS-1500 *Almirante Padilla* class vessels. The new ships will be

The US Coast Guard national security cutter *Calhoun* (WMSL-759) will be the tenth member of her class when delivered in the second half of 2023. This photograph shows her on builder's sea trials in June 2023. All-in-all, recapitalisation of the Coast Guard's fleet of cutters is progressing well. *(Huntington Ingalls Industries)*

The Mexican Navy's sole SIGMA 10514 light frigate *Benito Juárez* pictured whilst participating in the RIMPAC exercises in July 2022. Effective suspension of the navy's construction programme means that she is the only one of a planned class of eight ships to be completed to date. However, a variant of the Damen SIGMA 10514 design has been selected for the Colombian Navy's five-strong frigate programme. *(US Navy)*

constructed under licence by state-owned shipbuilder COTECMAR, which has received a firm contract for the first of the new ships. COTECMAR has also been entrusted with building the first of another significant new warship class as a result of an order for the initial *Patrullero Océanico Colombiano* (POC), previously referred to as the OPV-93. Larger than the country's previous three licence-built Fassmer OPV-80 type vessels, it is reportedly a fully indigenously-produced design and will be fitted 'for but not with' surface-to-surface missiles. A first steel cutting ceremony for the new ship was held on 31 March 2023. The Naval Development Plan ultimately envisages the acquisition of four POCs.

Peru also has ambitious naval recapitalisation plans that will eventually encompass twenty-three vessels under a project to strengthen the country's naval sector that was launched in 2022. Key components of the plan are six multi-role frigates, three offshore and four coastal patrol vessels as well as – eventually – four new submarines. Whilst all will be built by local shipbuilding group SIMA, extensive use of licensed designs is likely. Sufficient funding has already been advanced to make a start on the lead offshore patrol vessel and two further *Río Pativilca* class patrol boats, the seventh and eighth units of what will ultimately be a ten-ship class.

Somewhat more surprising has been the allocation of nearly US$100m to commence the programme for new frigates, which has probably been driven by the increasing age of the navy's existing surface combatants. A ceremony in September 2022 saw the withdrawal of the *Carvajal* (*Lupo*) class frigates *Villavicencio* and *San Martin* – the latter re-roled as a patrol vessel in 2013 – as well as the lead PRP-72 type fast attack craft *Velarde.* Current plans envisage upgrades to at least some of the six remaining frigates until their replacements can be commissioned. The fate of another of the fleet's dwindling force of surface combatants is also unclear following a serious engine-room fire aboard the corvette *Guise* – the former South Korean *Suncheon* – on 17 July 2022 during the RIMPAC 2022 exercises. Although the fire was extinguished after around five hours, two of her crew members were seriously injured in the blaze. More positively, 9 December 2022 saw the launch at Callao of *Paita*, the second of two *Pisco* class amphibious transport docks built under licence to the *Makassar* design.

In neighbouring **Ecuador**, local shipbuilder ASTINAVE has reported that construction of the Fassmer MPV70 Mk III multi-role vessel ordered in 2020 is now around 40 percent complete. Delivery is scheduled by the end of 2024, a timetable that looks optimistic. The Guayaquil shipyard is also working on a second phase of a modernisation plan for the *Esmeralda* class corvettes that form the core of the surface fleet. This will see *Esmeraldas*, *El Oro* and *Galápagos* refitted to the same standard as the work that was concluded on the other three members of the class in 2018.[17]

Moving southwards, the most significant naval development in **Chile** over the past year has been the launch of the icebreaker *Almirante Viel* – previously referred to as 'Antártica 1' – from ASMAR's Talcahuano shipyard on 22 December 2022. Built to a VARD 9-203 design, the 10,500-tonne ship will be the most complex completed in Chile when she is delivered in August 2024. She forms part of a Continuous National Shipbuilding Plan that has the completion of four amphibious transport ships, also based on a VARD concept, as its next target. Firm orders for two of these have been placed to date. Construction will then progress to a new frigate class, likely based on a foreign design, as part of long-term plans to replace the navy's flotilla of eight major surface combatants. The navy's older pair of submarines – both Type 209/1400 boats dating from the early 1980s – will also need replacement within the next decade but overseas construction is likely.

There have been few recent tangible developments in **Argentina,** which continues to explore options to re-constitute its defunct submarine fleet.

The Peruvian corvette *Guise* – formerly the South Korean *Po Hang* class corvette *Suncheon* – suffered a major engine-room fire whilst participating in the RIMPAC exercises on 17 July 2022. This photograph of the ship was taken four days previously. *(US Navy)*

Proposals from France's Naval Group and Germany's tkMS apparently for new-build submarines are being considered alongside transfers of second-hand Brazilian Type 209 boats. However, there has been little real process against a backdrop of questions as to how the expensive programme will be financed. Proposed local construction of a new amphibious transport – most likely based on Damen's LST-100 design – seems to be further advanced and fabrication might start before the end of 2023. More broadly, the Argentine Navy continues to struggle to deploy ships to police its extensive economic zone despite the boost to capabilities provided by deliveries of the new *Bouchard* class.

The saga of adjacent **Uruguay's** efforts to acquire new offshore patrol vessels continues to progress. The Spanish shipyard Astilleros Gondán is now seemingly the favourite to win a reported c. US$120m contract for two 80m vessels after a previously preferred bid from China was turned down on political grounds. The armament and surveillance capabilities of the new ships have been significantly downgraded as Uruguay struggles to fund their purchase, which was previously estimated to cost around US$200m.

The political and economic situation in **Venezuela** means that there have been no major developments of note beyond strenuous efforts to keep existing warships operational in the face of significant logistical challenges.

Notes

1. The Defense Secretary's remarks were contained in a press release, 'Department of Defense Releases the President's Fiscal Year 2024 Defense Budget' posted to the defense.gov site on 13 March 2023. Full details of the FY2024 defense budget request can be found at: comptroller.defense.gov/Budget-Materials/#press. The equivalent Department of the Navy budget materials are at: secnav.navy.mil/fmc/fmb/Pages/Fiscal-Year-2024.aspx

2. The sequestration process, put in place by the 2011 Budget Control Act, was intended to reduce the large US government financial deficit by placing strict caps on both military and non-military spending. In practice, Congress found the extent of the restrictions unpalatable and found ways to avoid some of their effects, particularly by channelling spending through budget headings not impacted by the controls. There has been speculation Congress will attempt similar measures again.

3. The FY2024 shipbuilding plan, the *Report to Congress on the Annual Long-Range Plan for Construction of Naval Vessels for Fiscal Year 2024* (Washington DC: Office of the Chief of Naval Operations, 2023) can be found at: govexec.com/media/navy_2024_shipbuilding_plan.pdf. It is essentially a holding document pending completion of the revised BFSAR. A previous, classified iteration of this assessment was produced in 2022 and is summarised later in this chapter.

4. See the ever-informative David Pugliese, 'Cost of new Arctic patrol ships jumps by $780 million' posted to the *Ottawa Citizen* website – ottawacitizen.com – on 5 January 2023. In addition to the CS$680m price increase for the Royal Canadian Navy's AOPSs, the cost of the two ordered for the coast guard has increased by C$100m. Reduced labour availability, the impact of Covid and higher transportation and spares costs were all blamed for the uplift.

5. As mentioned in last year's *Seaforth World Naval Review*, the widely-respected Lesko had unexpectedly resigned from BIW in April 2022 in an abrupt parting of ways that had produced considerable comment in the local press at the time.

6. See Norman Jolin, 'Highlights from the ShipTech Forum 2023' posted to the Canadian *Vanguard* trade media site – vanguardcanada.com – on 23 May 2023.

7. The BFSAR 2022 numbers in the classified report to Congress were summarised in the *Chief of Naval Operations Navigation Plan 2022* (Washington DC: Office of the Chief of Naval Operations, 2022).

8. In addition to the FY2023 shipbuilding plan, Ronald O'Rourke's *Navy Force Structure and Shipbuilding Plans: Background and Issues for Congress RL32665* (Washington DC: Congressional Research Service, 2023) provides invaluable information on the history and current status of the US Navy's force structure plan. Mr O'Rourke, the Congressional Research Service's (CRS's) longstanding Specialist in Naval Affairs, produces large numbers of periodically updated reports on a wide range of topics pertinent to US Navy policy and procurement, many of which have been referred to in the preparation of this chapter. They can be accessed by searching the Congressional Research Service's website at crsreports.congress.gov or via the Federation of American Scientists' site at sgp.fas.org/crs

9. For further detail on the *Ford* class programme, see Ronald O' Rourke's *Navy Ford (CVN-78) Class Aircraft Carrier Program: Background and Issues for Congress RS20643*.

10. The first five *Ticonderoga* class cruisers – which were equipped with traditional missile launchers – were decommissioned prematurely between 2004 and 2005.

11. The FY2023 National Defense Authorization Act of 23 December 2022 contained a provision making it clear that this requirement related to 'larger' amphibious ships, including ten LHA/LHD type amphibious assault ships and 21 LPD or LSD type amphibious docks.

12. The highly significant Distributed Maritime Operations concept, which has been discussed in several previous editions of *Seaforth World Naval Review*, essentially seeks to use the US Navy's technological leadership, particularly in the area of command and control, to defeat China's expanding A2/AD capacity in a 'high-end' war in the Pacific. For further information on the concept's evolution and its key components see also the author's, 'Preparing for the Next Pacific War: The US Navy and Distributed Maritime Operations' in John Jordan (ed) *Warship 2023* (Oxford: Osprey Publishing, 2023), pp.173–87.

13. Further information on the pressures facing *Columbia* and *Virginia* class submarine construction are provided by John Grady's 'Navy Will Have Challenges Meeting Submarine Delivery Schedules, Admiral Tells Senate' posted to the *USNI News* site – news.usni.org – on 20 April 2023.

14. See Jon Harper, 'Gilday: 7th Fleet to receive Project Overmatch capabilities' posted to the *Defense Scoop* website – defensescoop.com – on 7 June 2023.

15. Ronald O' Rourke's CRS reports *Coast Guard Cutter Procurement: Background and Issues for Congress* R42567 and *Coast Guard Polar Security Cutter (Polar Icebreaker) Program: Background and Issues for Congress* RL34391 provide considerable additional detail on current Coast Guard procurement.

16. *Seaforth World Naval Review 2023* incorrectly reported the delivery of a NCVP to Guatemala in July 2021. It was Honduras and El Salvador that received NCVPs in that month, accepting *Río Aguán* and *PM-15* respectively.

17. See Carlos Vanegas, 'Puesta a punto de la Corbeta CM 13 "Los Ríos" de la Armada Ecuatoriana y modernización de la CM 15 "Galápagos" en ASTINAVE' posted to the defensa.com site on 6 July 2023. Along with official navy websites, the Spanish-language defensa.com and its rival infodefensa.com remain invaluable sources of additional information on naval developments in Latin America.

2.1A FLEET REVIEW

THE BRAZILIAN NAVY

Entering its Third Century

Authors:
Felipe Salles & Alexandre Galante

The year 2022 marked the 200th anniversary of Brazil's independence from the Kingdom of Portugal and, also, the formation of the country's *Marinha do Brasil.* The events were celebrated by a naval parade and fleet review off Rio de Janeiro during the period between 7 and 9 September that year in which over twenty ships from Brazil and friendly navies took part. This chapter looks at the development and future prospects for South America's leading fleet as the Brazilian Navy enters its third century of naval service.

HISTORICAL BACKGROUND

The Brazilian Navy was established in 1822 at the time of Brazil's declaration of independence from Portugal. It was initially formed largely by Portuguese sailors and British Royal Navy veterans using ships seized from the former colonial power. The initial focus was on ensuring Brazil's territorial integrity in the war for independence and, subsequently, in a series of conflicts against what is now

The Brazilian Navy held a fleet parade and review off Rio de Janeiro in September 2022 to mark the 200th anniversary of Brazil's independence and the creation of the *Marinha do Brasil.* This picture shows, from left to right, the 'Round Table' class logistic landing ship *Almirante Sabóia* (the former British *Sir Belvidere*), the *Amazonas* class offshore patrol vessel *Apa* and the *Niterói* class frigate *Liberal. (Brazilian Navy)*

Argentina and other former Spanish colonial possessions. Later, the fleet played a decisive role in the War of the Triple Alliance (1864–70), which was fought alongside Argentina and Uruguay against Paraguay. The navy developed rapidly during this period, with the deployment of advanced riverine monitors playing a particularly important part in the Paraguayan War. By the late 1880s, ongoing investment meant that the Brazilian Navy was amongst the leading navies in the world.

The 1889 army-led coup that resulted in the Brazilian monarchy being replaced by a republic heralded a decade or more of naval neglect, a situation exacerbated by the Naval Revolt of 1893–4. An improving economy and concerns over lack of naval parity with Argentina and Chile in the early 1900s saw the naval establishment convince Brazil's politicians of the urgent need to remedy this situation. This led to approval of an ambitious expansion programme in late 1904 that had three battleships and three armoured cruisers at its core. Changing priorities and subsequent budgetary constraints saw many changes to this programme. However, delivery of the dreadnought-type battleships *Minas Gerais* and *São Paulo* in 1910 placed Brazil back amongst the leading naval powers, sparking a 'dreadnought race' with its South American rivals that was only ended by the First World War.[1]

Brazil aimed to maintain a neutral stance in the First World War but eventually declared war against Germany on 26 October 1917 as a result of U-boat attacks on the country's merchant shipping. Brazil was thus the sole South American country to take part in the conflict. The fleet subsequently assembled a modest squadron of cruisers and destroyers – the War Operations Naval Division (DNOG) – to join the Allied forces patrolling the sea routes off North West Africa between Gibraltar and Dakar.

Following a period of limited naval investment in the inter-war period, Brazil found itself again drawn into global conflict in the aftermath of the Japanese attack on Pearl Harbor and the strong showing of support for the United States gathered from Latin America during the Rio Conference of 1942. The basing of United States forces in the country, particularly around the strategically important city of Natal in north-eastern Brazil, and a severing of diplomatic ties with the Axis powers was accompanied by a spate of U-boat attacks on Brazilian merchant shipping.[2] In August 1942, following the sinking of five Brazilian freighters – resulting in the

By the late 1880s, investment in modern warships such as the ironclad battleship *Riachuelo* – named after a famous Brazilian naval victory in the War of the Triple Alliance against Paraguay – made the Brazilian Navy amongst the most powerful in the world. This photograph was taken in the early twentieth century towards the end of the ship's career. *(Library of Congress LC-DIG-det-4a15955)*

After a period of neglect, newfound economic prosperity saw Brazil acquire two *Minas Gerais* class dreadnought battleships early in the twentieth century, triggering a South American 'dreadnought race'. This photograph of a much-modernised *Minas Gerais* was taken from a US Navy warship several decades later during the Second World War. The conflict brought the Brazilian Navy closer to its American counterpart and had a significant impact on the country's post-war naval development. *(US Navy Heritage & History Command NH 59893)*

The *Niterói* class frigate *Defensora* photographed during the Brazilian Navy's Operation 'Aderex' in May 2023. She is one of six Vosper Thornycroft Mk 10 frigates ordered in September 1970 under a programme that had a significant impact on the Brazilian Navy's force structure throughout the following decades. As of mid-2023, five of these vessels remained in the Brazilian fleet. *(Brazilian Navy)*

loss of 607 lives – by the German submarine *U-507*, Brazil entered the war. Subsequently, Brazilian President Getúlio Vargas placed the Brazilian Navy under the authority of US Navy Vice-Admiral Jonas H. Ingram, Commander of America's South Atlantic Force. The Brazilian fleet played an important part, particularly in protecting convoys from South America to the Caribbean during the remainder of the conflict. Ultimately Brazilian sailors escorted 574 Allied convoys comprising 3,164 ships.

An important aspect of the Brazilian Navy's involvement in the Second World War was the receipt of several warships of American origin. This flow of ships was maintained in the post-war era as the US Navy and British Royal Navy – holding a massive surplus of vessels whose upkeep was unaffordable in the new environment – sought to transfer them to allies around the world. Notable acquisitions included two former US Navy *Brooklyn* (CL-40) class cruisers in 1951 and the aircraft carrier *Minas Gerais* (formerly HMS *Vengeance*) five years later. These transfers continued throughout the first part of the Cold War, including seven former *Fletcher* (DD-445) class destroyers from 1959 and seven *Sumner* (DD-692) and *Gearing* (DD-710) class ships from 1972 onwards. A downside of this tide of cheap warships was the drowning out of hopes of sustaining significant indigenous production at the Rio de Janeiro Naval Arsenal, which had completed two destroyer classes during and immediately after the war.[3]

ORIGINS OF THE CURRENT FLEET

A list of current major Brazilian Navy vessels is set out in Table 2.1A.1. A major part of the fleet traces its origins to programmes commenced in the 1970s and early 1980s, the most significant of which are summarised below. Many of the vessels constructed under these programmes are now in the course of retirement, adding urgency to the process of replacement and renewal that is now underway.

The *Niterói* Frigate Programme: In 1968, Brazil determined to replace many of its obsolescent major surface vessels through an international tender process. Subsequently, in September 1970, it was announced that the British Vosper Thornycroft Mk 10 design – loosely based on the Royal Navy's Type 21 *Amazon* class frigate – had been selected to meet the requirement. A total of six of the new *Niterói* class were included in the agreement; four built in the United Kingdom and two at the Naval Arsenal at Rio de Janeiro. Encompassing features such as combined diesel or gas (CODOG) propulsion using MTU diesels and Rolls-Royce Olympus gas turbines, Exocet, Ikara and Seacat missiles, and an embarked Westland Lynx helicopter, the frigates marked a step change in the Brazilian Navy's capabilities.

The ships were originally built in two variants.

Table 2.1A.1: BRAZILIAN NAVY: PRINCIPAL UNITS AS AT MID 2024

TYPE	CLASS	NUMBER	TONNAGE	DIMENSIONS	PROPULSION	CREW	DATE
Submarines (5)							
Submarine – SSK	**RIACHUELO** (Scorpène)	1	1,900 tonnes	71m x 6m x 6m	Diesel-electric, 20+ knots	35	2022
Submarine – SSK	**TIKUNA** (Type 209 – modified)	1	1,600 tonnes	62m x 6m x 6m	Diesel-electric, 22 knots	40	2005
Submarine – SSK	**TUPI** (Type 209)	3	1,500 tonnes	61m x 6m x 6m	Diesel-electric, 22+ knots	30	1989
Principal Surface Escorts (8)							
Frigate – FFG	**GREENHALGH** (Type 22-Batch 1)	1	4,700 tonnes	131m x 15m x 4m	COGOG, 30 knots	270	1979
Frigate – FFG	**NITERÓI**	5[1]	3,700 tonnes	129m x 14m x 4m	CODOG, 30 knots	220	1976
Corvette – FSG	**BARROSO**	1	2,400 tonnes	103m x 11m x 4m	CODOG, 30 knots	145	2008
Corvette – FSG	**INHAÚMA**	1	2,100 tonnes	96m x 11m x 4m	CODOG, 27 knots	120	1989
Principal Amphibious Units (4)							
Helicopter Carrier – LPH	**ATLÂNTICO** (OCEAN)	1	22,500 tonnes	203m x 35m x 7m	Diesel, 18 knots	490	1998
Landing Ship Dock – LSD	**BAHIA** (FOUDRE)	1	12,000 tonnes	168m x 24m x 5m	Diesel, 20 knots	160	1998
Tank Landing Ship – LST	**MATTOSO MAIA** (NEWPORT)	1	9,000 tonnes	159m x 21m x 5m	Diesel, 20 knots	265	1969
Logistic Landing Ship – LSL	**ALMIRANTE SABOIA** ('Round Table')	1	6,800 tonnes	134m x 18m x 4m	Diesel, 17 knots	65	1964
Patrol Vessels (23)							
Offshore Patrol Vessel – OPV	**AMAZONAS** ('River Batch 2')	3	2,000 tonnes	90m x 14m x 4m	Diesel, 25 knots	50	2012
Offshore Patrol Vessel – OPV	**MACAÉ** ('Vigilante 400')	3	500 tonnes	56m x 8m x 3m	Diesel, 21 knots	35	2009
Offshore Patrol Vessel – OPV	**BRACUÍ** ('River MCMV')	4[2]	900 tonnes	47m x 11m x 3m	Diesel, 14 knots	30	1984
Offshore Patrol Vessel – OPV	**CABOCOLO** (IMPERIAL MARINHEIRO)	1	1,000 tonnes	56m x 10m x 4m	Diesel, 16 knots	65	1955
Patrol Vessel – PV	**GRAJAÚ**	12	225 tonnes	47m x 8m x 2m	Diesel, 27 knots	30	1993
Mine Countermeasures (3)							
Minesweeper – MCMV	**ARATU**	3	300 tonnes	47m x 7m x 2m	Diesel, 24 knots	30	1971

Notes:
1. A modified variant serves as the training ship *Brasil*
2. Three other members of the class serve in the Brazilian Navy in other roles.
3. In addition to the ships listed, the navy operates a number of oceanographic and hydrographic vessels, including two ice-strengthened Polar ships. There is also a single replenishment oiler, *Almirante Gastão Motta*, and the usual logistical support, tugs and harbour craft. The district forces are supported by a sizeable riverine flotilla that include a river monitor, around ten other patrol vessels, specialised hospital ships and other logistics assets.

Four were focused on anti-submarine warfare (A/S in Brazil) and were equipped with the Australian anti-submarine Ikara missile aft. The other two were delivered in general purpose (E/G in Brazil) configuration. This saw a second 4.5in gun replace the Ikara system aft, as well as the installation of Exocet missiles. Later, in 1981, a seventh ship – the unarmed training ship *Brasil* – was ordered using the *Niterói* hull.

These two variants would be eventually unified into a single version under the midlife MODFRAG (frigate modernisation) programme implemented during the late 1990s and early 2000s. This programme was managed by the Rio de Janeiro Naval Arsenal. One of its most significant elements was the replacement of the original Ferranti CAAIS command and control system by the Brazilian-designed Siconta Mk2 system. Amongst other changes was the replacement of British radar equipment by systems from Italy's Selex (now Leonardo) and the deletion of, respectively, the Ikara missiles and second 4.5in gun. Surface-to-air missile capability was upgraded with the installation of the Italian Aspide system to replace Seacat. Five of the *Niterói* class remain in service, forming the core of Brazil's surface fleet.[4]

The *Inhaúma* Class Corvettes: The arrival of the

Construction of the *Niterói* class was followed by a programme for smaller and cheaper corvettes that was never fully completed in its original form. *Barroso*, pictured here under maintenance at the Rio de Janeiro Naval Arsenal in August 2022, was intended to be the lead ship of an improved, follow-on class to these *Inhaúma* class vessels but eventually became the sole ship of her type after an extremely protracted construction period. *(Brazilian Navy)*

Acquisition of German-designed Type 209/1400 submarines formed the third major plank of Brazilian naval modernisation implemented in the later part of the twentieth century. *Tikuna*, completed by the Rio de Janeiro Naval Arsenal in 2005, was built to a modified Type 209/1400 design and was the last boat in this series. *(Brazilian Navy)*

Niterói class marked the start of a period of rapid technological development for the Brazilian Navy. The newly-acquired ships were clearly a successful design and the navy sought to build on this through the acquisition of still modern, but cheaper ships to replace obsolete destroyers and corvettes in the fleet. However, the Brazilian Navy decided that the new corvettes should have much of the armament and sensor fit of the *Niterói* class, leading to them being more expensive than first envisaged. As a result, although a numerous class was initially planned, orders were only ultimately placed for four (two in 1982 and two in 1986). All were built in Brazil, two at the Rio de Janeiro Naval Arsenal and two at Estaleiro Verolme. Only one now remains in service.

A follow-on corvette design, the *Barroso* class, was intended to correct seakeeping problems that were identified after the *Inhaúma* class entered service. Ordered in 1994, this single ship was not commissioned until 2009 and became a rare example of a vessel that effectively underwent a mid-life upgrade whilst still being built. When finally delivered, she incorporated much of the technology that had been used in the *Niterói* MODFRAG modernisation. Economic considerations prevented further planned members of the class being ordered.

***Tupi* Class Submarines:** The third major element in the historic programmes that continue to influence current Brazilian fleet structure is its acquisition of German Type 209/1400 class submarines. This was driven by a need to replace American-built 'Guppy' and British *Oberon* class submarines with more modern units. Ultimately, in 1984, the Brazilian Navy decided to adopt what had become the 'de facto' regional standard in the form of the IKL/HDW Type 209 design. The first of the class was built in Kiel, Germany, and the other three at Rio de Janeiro through technology transfer. Three of these remain in service. A fifth improved, Type 1400 mod unit – *Tikuna* – was constructed later, becoming operational in 2006.

THE 'PAEMB' DREAM FLEET

The programme of Brazilian fleet modernisation that commenced with the *Niterói* frigate acquisition was ultimately curtailed by persistent national economic problems that continued throughout the 1980s and into the 1990s. However, economic reforms implemented during the latter part of the decade coincided with the benefits of increased demand for Brazil's commodity-rich resources. In the first decade of the new Millennium, Brazil was one of the fastest growing major economies in the world, becoming a major constituent of the BRICS (Brazil-Russia-India-China-South Africa) economic grouping. During this period, exploitation of the country's oil reserves also resulted in Brazil achieving self-sufficiency in energy requirements. The vast majority of Brazil's oil and gas production is located offshore, driving a need to protect this critical asset.

Against this backdrop, the Brazilian Navy drew up an extremely bold strategic plan that envisaged equipping itself with a world-class fleet – both quantitatively and qualitatively – by the 2030s. The so-called *Plano de Articulação e Equipamento da Marinha* (PAEMB) – the Navy Articulation and Equipment Plan – aimed at a fleet structure comprising two 50,000-tonne aircraft carriers, four multi-role amphibious assault ships, six nuclear-powered and fifteen diesel-electric submarines, and thirty major surface combatants as well as patrol vessels and auxiliaries. It is questionable whether the political and financial support needed to achieve this programme was ever likely to be attainable but, in any event, a steady deterioration in the economic outlook rendered the ambition unreachable. In essence, this resulted in the PAEMB in its original form being shelved.

In spite of this setback, a number of specific naval modernisation programmes have either survived or emerged from the PAEMB's collapse that will have a significant impact on fleet structure in the years ahead.

The *Amazonas* class offshore patrol vessel *Araguari* pictured in front of an offshore energy installation in what appears to be a 'doctored' PR image. The economic wealth created by the exploitation of Brazil's offshore energy resources and the need to protect these assets were key factors behind the ultimately abortive PAEMB expansion plan. *(Brazilian Navy)*

PROSUB SUBMARINES

The huge *Programa de Desenvolvimento de Submarinos* (PROSUB) project forms part of a strategic partnership agreed between Brazil and France by then-presidents Luiz Inácio Lula da Silva and Nicolas Sarkozy in December 2008. As a result of this agreement, previous plans to maintain construction of German Type 209 submarines were replaced by the selection of France's Naval Group as Brazil's new technological partner in this field. Under a series of contracts reportedly valued at c. €7bn (c. US$7.5bn) signed in 2009, a new shipyard and naval base complex for the construction and sustainment of an initial four S-BR 'Scorpène' type conventionally-powered and one SN-BR submarines was established at Itaguaí, less than 100km west of Rio de Janeiro. The latter, to be named *Álvaro Alberto*, will be the first Brazilian nuclear-powered attack submarine when she is eventually delivered.[5]

As the PAEMB projected a total of twenty-one submarines, PROSUB was initially envisaged as just the start of a major construction programme. However, no additional boats have been ordered to date. *Riachuelo* (S40), the first S-BR submarine, entered service on 1 September 2022. The second, *Humaitá* (S41), started pre-acceptance trials in August 2022 and is expected to be delivered in the second half of 2023. *Tonelero* (S42) is set to be floated out in December 2023 whilst *Angostura* (S43) has had its hull segments transferred to the massive ship construction hall for its final assembly prior to delivery to the Fleet by the end of 2025.

The construction of the much-delayed *Álvaro Alberto* (SN-10) nuclear-powered submarine has yet to formally begin, with only a limited test segment currently being worked on. The submarine's designation has been changed from SN-BR to *submarino convencionalmente armado com propulsão nuclear* (SCPN): conventionally-armed submarine with nuclear propulsion. This is because the navy wants to emphasise that the submarine will not carry nuclear weapons. She is likely to be delivered in the course of the 2030s.

The delay to *Álvaro Alberto* has created a production gap between the last S-BR and the first SCPN submarine. To address this, the navy is studying the use the Itaguaí Naval Complex to build surface ships in addition to submarines.

Hull sections of the submarine *Angostura*, the final member of the four *Riachuelo* ('Scorpène') class submarines ordered under the massive PROSUB programme, seen entering the tunnel that links the northern and southern sections of the vast construction, maintenance and base facility at Itaguaí in May 2023. PROSUB is currently the Brazilian Navy's most important construction programme. *(Brazilian Navy)*

TAMANDARÉ CLASS FRIGATES

The ambitious PAEMB plan aimed to replace existing frigates and corvettes with a new 'high-low' surface fleet. The 'high' end component would consist of c. 6,000-tonne frigates. An initial tranche of five were to be acquired under the ultimately abortive PROSUPER programme (the surface counterpart of PROSUB) and would have been built to an overseas design. The 'low' component would be an affordable, complementary 2,700-tonne corvette. The corvette would support local design and manufacture of sensors and weapons. It was to be built to a CV03 design developed by the Brazilian branch of Fincantieri's Vard. However, foreign countries approached to provide technical support to the construction programme favoured a development of one of their own designs and – faced with a pressing need to replace warships that had already retired – the navy was prepared to be flexible. In March 2019, it was announced that the Águas Azuis consortium – comprising thyssenkrupp Marine Systems (tkMS) in partnership with Brazil's Embraer Defence & Security and Atech – were the preferred bidders for four new *Tamandaré* class vessels. A formal construction contract followed on 3 March 2020 at a cost of BRL 9.1bn (c. US$1.7bn).

The new ships are to be constructed to the tkMS A-100BR design. With a displacement of c. 3,500 tonnes, the ships are considerably larger than the c. 2,500-tonne CV03 and will be classified as frigates. By offering a larger hull, tkMS have been able to claim that the class will be better suited to replacing the navy's Type 22 and *Niterói* class frigates, as well as the corvettes. The ships will be built at the Oceana shipyard in Itajaí, Brazil, now purchased by tkMS and renamed thyssenkrupp Estaleiro Brasil Sul. A keel laying ceremony for the first vessel was held on 24 March 2023.

A notable feature of the *Tamandaré* contract is the government's decision to provide Emgepron – the naval projects management organisation – with the funding required from the Brazilian Treasury in advance of the project's commencement. In theory, this means that Emgepron already has all the money it needs to pay for construction, a move that should lower contractor risk by bypassing subsequent restrictions that might emerge with respect to government funding. The approach has also subsequently been followed for the NApAnt Antarctic Support Ship (see further below).

The *Tamandaré* class will incorporate an Atech-developed combat management system based on Atlas Elektronik's ANCS. Atech will also design the platform management system with assistance from America's L3 Harris. tkMS' influence on equipment sourcing is also evidenced by the specification of the Hensoldt TRS-4D multifunction radar over the BAE Systems Artisan already used aboard the helicopter carrier *Atlântico*, as well as that of the Atlas Elektronik ASO 713 sonar. Other key sensors will include Raytheon search and navigation radars. Electronic warfare will be focused on the Brazilian-developed MB/Omnisys Defensor Mk 3 ESM suite, with Terma's C-Guard chaff and flare dispensers providing physical countermeasures. Weapons will include a Leonardo 76mm/62 main gun, a Rheinmetall Sea Snake 30mm weapons station and MBDA CAMM missiles. Indigenous MANSUP surface-to-surface missiles are also likely to be fitted.

This computer-generated image shows the current configuration of the *Tamandaré* frigate class. Four of these ships will be completed in Brazil to tkMS's MEKO A100BR design, replacing existing frigates and corvettes. The keel of the lead ship was laid on 24 March 2023. *(tkMS)*

ANTARCTIC SUPPORT SHIP

Brazil's ongoing Antarctic program, PROANTAR, conducts scientific research in the remote continent. The Comandante Ferraz Station, located on King George Island, serves as Brazil's permanent research base in the Antarctic, whilst logistical support is provided by the Brazilian Navy. Two ice-strengthened oceanographic research ships are used in this task. One of these, *Ary Rongel*, has reached the end of her operational life, resulting in the need for a replacement. This resulted in the *Navio de Apoio Antártico* (NApAnt) programme.

The Antarctic support vessels *Almirante Maximiano* (H41) and *Ary Rongel* (H44) pictured in company on 4 February 2022. A new Antarctic support ship was ordered in June 2022 to replace *Ary Rongel,* which is now close to the end of her service life. *(Brazilian Navy)*

The selected design, named *Almirante Saldanha*,

Delays to new construction programmes have forced the Brazilian Navy to continue a long tradition of acquiring second-hand vessels from other navies to fill gaps in the fleet. Perhaps the most prominent recent example was the purchase of *Atlântico*, the former British Royal Navy helicopter carrier *Ocean*, which was recommissioned into the Brazilian Navy in June 2018. This photograph was taken during Exercise 'Poseidon 2021' in September that year. *(Brazilian Navy)*

is a development of the Australian research ship RV *Investigator*. Polar 1 Construção Naval, a special-purpose-entity formed by Brazil's Estaleiro Jurong Aracruz (EJA) and Sembcorp Marine of Singapore, was awarded a construction contract reportedly valued at US$150m to build the new ship in June 2022. The diesel-electric powered vessel will displace 6,800 tonnes and have a length of 103.2m, width of 18.5m and draft of 6.3m. She is scheduled to enter service in 2025, enabling extended stays at sea for up to 70 days.

OTHER RECENT ACQUISITIONS

Given the delays encountered in realising new construction, the Brazilian Navy has had to resort to the acquisition of second-hand vessels to maintain a balanced fleet. Perhaps the most significant of these is the former British amphibious helicopter carrier *Ocean*, which was acquired in 2018 as a replacement for the aircraft carrier *São Paulo* (the former French *Foch*). She was commissioned into the navy as *Atlântico* on 29 June 2018 at Devonport in the United Kingdom before sailing for her new home-port of Rio de Janeiro. The vessel has subsequently been designated as a *navio-aeródromo multipropósito* (NAM) or multi-purpose aircraft carrier, with the idea of operating fixed-wing UAVs from its flight deck. She is currently the largest vessel in Brazil's fleet.[6]

Another major acquisition of the last decade is the amphibious transport dock *Bahia*, the former French *Foudre* class *Siroco*. She was acquired in 2015 after Portuguese attempts to buy her fell through. The navy also benefitted from another failed agreement when it acquired three British-built 'River' class offshore patrol vessels when Trinidad and Tobago's coast guard cancelled a contract for their construction. They were commissioned as the *Amazonas* class between 2012 and 2013.

More recently, the navy has started to take delivery of a second pair of smaller NPa500 *Macaé* class (French CMN Vigilante 400) patrol vessels that were first laid down by the EISA shipyard over a decade ago but suspended after their shipbuilder suffered financial collapse. Their completion has been assigned to the Rio de Janeiro Arsenal, where *Maracanã* entered the operational fleet in December 2022 following delivery the previous September. Her sister, *Mangaratiba*, should be handed over in due course. Policing Brazil's extensive waters mandates a large fleet of constabulary assets and the need for additional vessels is urgent. This may be achieved through the PRONAPA programme. This will be focused on building the NPa 500BR design, an improved version of the NPa 500.

BRAZILIAN NAVY ORGANISATION

The navy is currently led by the Commander of the Brazilian Navy, Admiral Marcos Sampaio Olsen, who assumed office in January 2023. He is advised by an Admiralty Board and carries out his role with the support of a Naval Staff, the *Estado-Maior da Armada* (EMA). The bulk of the 'operational' Brazilian Navy – its personnel and equipment – falls under the responsibility of the Naval Operations Command, the *Comando de Operações Navais* (CON). CON's key subordinate commands are:

- **The Commander-in-Chief of the Fleet:** This encompasses the fleet's 'blue water' surface warships, submarines and its naval aviation component, as well as supporting base infrastructure. It is headquartered at Rio de Janeiro, the country's principal naval base.[7]
- **The Nine Naval District Commands:** These are spread out across the country, including along the coastline and Amazon. The navy's patrol vessels are allocated to many of these commands and all include marine formations. Four also have their own helicopter squadrons operating various utility rotorcraft. As there is no separate coast guard in Brazil, the navy needs to fulfil this function in addition to its other tasks.
- **The Fleet Marine Corps Command:** The seagoing component of the naval infantry.[8]
- **The Maritime Operations Command:** Responsible for ensuring the real-time safety of maritime traffic in the South Atlantic on the basis of AIS and other tracking and monitoring data collected by satellite, radar systems and other means. The navy eventually intends to enhance this data collection and analysis system with the creation of a brand-new 'Blue Amazon Management System', better known locally by its Portuguese language acronym, SisGAAz.
- **The Naval Warfare Doctrinal Development Centre**

Sitting alongside CON and reporting to the navy's commander are a number of other major commands and directorates. These comprise the General Command of the Marine Corps, the General Directorate of Personnel, the General

The *Niterói* class frigate *Liberal* photographed during trials of the indigenous MANSUP surface-to-surface missile in April 2023. Like the rest of the navy's major surface combatants, *Liberal* falls under the control of the Commander-in-Chief of the Fleet as part of the wider *Comando de Operações Navais* (CON).

Responsible for a wide range of constabulary missions in the absence of a separate Brazilian coast guard, the Brazilian Navy operates a large number of coastal and riverine patrol vessels, which are deployed across many of the nine geographical district commands. Here the river patrol vessel *Rondônia* is seen operating in the Amazon in May 2023. *(Brazilian Navy)*

The Brazilian Navy's promotion of the 'Blue Amazon' concept has served to highlight the need to protect the valuable resources found within its EEZ. In this photo, the *Niterói* class frigate *Constituição* is pictured on a visit to the remote Brazilian island of Trindade in 2023. *(Brazilian Navy)*

Directorate of Navy Materiel (responsible for acquisition and maintenance programmes), the General Directorate for Nuclear and Technological Development, the General Directorate for Navigation, and the Naval General Secretariat. Also reporting directly to Admiral Olsen are a number of other functions, including the Navy Intelligence Organisation, the Navy Public Relations Organisation and the Inter-ministerial Commission for the Resources of the Sea.

Recently the Brazilian Navy has developed much closer inter-agency relationships with key Brazilian government agencies that have relevance to its own mission. These include ANTAQ (dealing with aquatic transport), IBAMA (environmental protection) and ICM (natural conservation and biodiversity), as well as the Brazilian Internal Revenue Service and the Federal Police.

CURRENT AND FUTURE MISSION PRIORITIES

The Brazilian Navy has worked successfully to convey the concept of the 'Blue Amazon' to the general populace. This concept has been used to illustrate the importance and economic value of the country's 4.5 million km^2 Exclusive Economic Zone (EEZ) to the average Brazilian, piggy-backing on the well understood value of the actual 'green' Amazon on land.

It is fair to say that protection of the Blue Amazon lies at the heart of the navy's current strategic vision. This reflects the importance to the Brazilian economy of the so-called 'Blue Economy', namely shipping, fishing, offshore energy extraction and mining, and other existing and developing sea-related activities. By publicly emphasising Brazilian rights over these riches, the navy expects to pre-empt any attempted foreign encroachment over them. Moreover, it also hopes to use their importance to obtain political leverage to persuade the Brazilian government to provide the funds necessary for the navy needed to control and protect the EEZ.

Beyond the Blue Amazon, there is the *Entorno Estratégico Brasileiro*, which can be loosely translated as the Brazilian strategic neighbourhood. This comprises the geographic area where Brazil may need to take action to preserve its territorial sovereignty and the broader interests of the Brazilian state. The neighbourhood spans the complete South American continent and the South Atlantic Ocean but also extends as far as the African continent, from Cape Verde in the north to Mozambique in the east. A 2016 revision to Brazil's strategic policy documents also added the Caribbean and Antarctic to these areas of interest.

The scope of the Brazilian Navy's strategic vision is therefore vast but the funding needed to further this vision has, as of yet, failed to materialise. Sufficient money has been made available to support the highest-priority requirements, viz. the PROSUB submarine programme, the associated naval nuclear programme, and the construction of the new *Tamandaré* class frigates. However, with – for example – much of the surface fleet approaching 40 years of age, the quartet of new ships currently envisaged is not sufficient to counter the imminent spectre of block obsolescence. Unless the political will can be found to increase its resources, the Brazilian Navy will be left with a capacity far below its responsibilities.

The Brazilian Navy's lead *Riachuelo* class submarine pictured shortly after her commissioning. Whilst sufficient funding has been found to support priority programmes such as PROSUB, the Brazilian Navy will not be able to meet its full responsibilities without more resources. *(Brazilian Navy)*

Notes

1. A third battleship, *Rio de Janeiro*, was sold to Turkey in 1913 in the aftermath of an economic downturn and the 1910 mutiny aboard *Minas Gerais*. She eventually became the British *Agincourt*.

2. Natal became a crucial strategic location, known locally as the 'Springboard to Victory'. It allowed the US to transport aircraft from American factories to Europe via a safe route, bypassing hazardous northern air routes in winter.

3. Another development over this period was the evolution of Brazil's marines – the *Corpo de Fuzileiros Navais* (CFN) – into a modern amphibious force. The CFN was increasingly equipped with standard US Marine Corps' equipment and was modelled after its American counterpart. Two US Navy tank landing ships were acquired in the 1970s to support CFN operations. Later, in 1989, the dock landing ships *Ceará*, the former *Hermitage* (LSD-34), and *Rio de Janeiro*, previously *Alamo* (LSD-33) were purchased to form the basis of a truly modern amphibious force.

4. Three of the *Niterói* class are being further modernised to retain them in service. The remainder are being replaced by the new *Tamandaré* class.

5. The PROSUPER project was assessed in detail by Richard Scott in 'PROSUB: Building Brazil's Future Submarine Capability', *Seaforth World Naval Review 2020* (Barnsley: Seaforth Publishing, 2019), pp.184–91. The selection of Itaguaí as the construction site and base was likely prompted by nuclear security considerations.

6. As previously noted Brazil acquired its first aircraft carrier, *Minas Gerais*, in 1956. Although expensively refitted with an angled deck, a dispute with the air force meant that her air group was limited to anti-submarine aircraft and helicopters until Skyhawk aircraft were acquired at the end of the 1990s. *Minas Gerais* was replaced by the larger and more modern *São Paulo* at the turn of the millennium. Unfortunately, the new ship faced numerous costly breakdowns during its service, limiting her operational effectiveness and eventually resulting in her withdrawal in 2017. Subsequently sold to Turkish shipbreakers, her entry into Turkish waters was prohibited due to a dispute over the amount of contaminants aboard when she had already crossed the Atlantic. Returning to Brazil, she was scuttled by the navy in the South Atlantic on 3 February 2023.

7. Brazilian naval aviation is focused on the Naval Air Force Command (ComForAerNav), which reports to the Commander-in-Chief of the Fleet. It is based at São Pedro da Aldeia east of Rio de Janeiro and comprises one fixed wing and five helicopter squadrons together with training and support elements. The fixed-wing squadron operates around six A-4KU Skyhawks – a legacy of the fleet's previous fast-jet carrier operations – whilst front-line helicopters include Sikorsky S-70B Seahawk, AgustaWestland Lynx, and Eurocopter EC725 and AS350 types. A new remotely-piloted aircraft squadron was stood up to operate Scan Eagle drones in July 2022.

8. The Fleet Marine Corps Command is focused on an Amphibious Division, which is based at Ilha do Governador in Rio de Janeiro. It provides the navy with the capacity to undertake limited amphibious and land-based operations. It comprises three Marine Infantry Battalions – named the Riachuelo, Humaitá and Paissandu Battalions – as well as command and control, armoured, artillery and anti-aircraft formations. The Fleet Marine Corps Command also encompasses other units, including a Reinforcement Troop that includes marine and engineering elements. There is also a Special Forces formation.

9. The Brazilian Navy's Portuguese language website – marinha.mil.br – provides much supplemental information on the navy's strategy, structure and composition.

2.2 REGIONAL REVIEW

Author:
Conrad Waters

ASIA AND THE PACIFIC

On 16 December 2022, the Japanese Government released three interrelated documents setting out its response to the growing security challenges afflicting the Asia-Pacific region. The *National Security Strategy of Japan*, the first since 2013 and only its second ever, aims to establish the main threats to Japan's national interests and determine how these can be dealt with. The associated *National Defense Strategy* (previously known as the *National Defense Program Guidelines*) provides an overview of the defence policy and capabilities that are required to support Japan's overarching security objectives. Finally, the *Defense Build-up Program* (the former *Medium Term Defense Program*) gives greater granularity on the procurement and force structures needed to support the defence strategy over a five- to ten-year horizon.[1]

Taken together, this trinity of documents reflect both continuity and change in Japan's security policy.[2] As in 2013, the activities of China and North Korea remain the focal points of Japanese concern. However, the language used in the documents reflects a view that the scale and urgency of the challenges that these two countries pose has substantially increased over the last decade. A notable change is the view of Russia. Previously a potential partner in the quest for stability across the Pacific, it is now viewed as 'a strong security concern'. It is clear that Russia's invasion of Ukraine has had a dramatic impact on Japan's strategic thinking, largely because its actions might encourage a similar act by China somewhat closer to home.

There is a similar evolution in defence posture. The principle of *senshu boei* (strictly defensive national defence) remains at the heart of defence planning. However, this concept has been expanded to incorporate the acquisition of a counterstrike capability; the ability to attack the enemy missile bases that are considered to form a growing threat to the Japanese homeland. Whilst a pre-emptive strike against enemy territory is explicitly excluded, the change marks a further blurring of the post-Second World War prohibition on offensive weapons that has already been eroded, for example, by the decision to acquire F-35B strike fighters to operate from Japan's 'helicopter carrying destroyers'. Rather than rely exclusively on the United States to provide a retaliatory strike capacity, Japan is now increasingly taking responsibility for all aspects of its defence. Nevertheless, the American alliance remains a cornerstone of overall security policy. Similarly, missile defence continues to form an essential component of defensive preparations. Relevant technology will continue to be upgraded with a view to defeating the latest ballistic and hypersonic missile threats.

From a practical perspective, these changes to defence thinking will prioritise qualitative rather than quantitative improvements in the Japan Self Defense Force, including its Japan Maritime Self Defense Force (JMSDF) component. Indeed, the number of JMSDF combatants in key areas such as submarines, destroyers and patrol vessels are unchanged from the objectives set out in 2018. Projected numbers of manned combat aircraft will actually decline slightly. However, the focus on counterstrike capacity is reflected in an intention to acquire as many as 400 Tomahawk cruise missiles for deployment aboard the existing Aegis-equipped destroyers. These will plug the immediate gap pending the development of indigenous strike missiles, as well as the installation of vertical launch systems in submarines. Another major development that has been confirmed is the acquisition of two Aegis System Equipped Vessels (ASEVs), replacing previous plans for land-based, 'Aegis Ashore' ballistic missile defence (BMD) sites. Essentially large, multi-role cruisers, these ships will counter North Korea's ballistic missiles and release the existing Aegis destroyers for their primary air defence role in high priority areas such as the East China Sea.

Japan's new strategic documents were followed by the publication of Australia's *Defence Strategic Review* in April 2023.[3] Whilst arguably less explicit in calling out China as Australia's main area of security concern, its emphasis on developing a more focused force structure targeted at the country's most significant military risks leaves little question as to threat perceptions. The review confirms investment in the new AUKUS nuclear-powered submarines as a key objective, thereby facilitating Australia's ability to operate at distance throughout South East Asia in pursuit of a deterrence strategy. The acquisition of long-range precision strike missiles and integrated missile defence capabilities are other priorities in a similar vein. A major outstanding question is what will have to be sacrificed to fund these expensive programmes. Surface warship procurement may be one area that is vulnerable to the necessary trade-offs.

The Japanese replenishment oiler *Omi* refuels the Australian frigate *Arunta* in November 2022 during the course of the annual Malabar exercises. The last year has seen both Japan and Australia publish new security strategies in view of a deteriorating security picture in the Asia-Pacific region. *(Royal Australian Navy)*

Table 2.2.1: FLEET STRENGTHS IN ASIA AND THE PACIFIC – LARGER NAVIES (MID 2023)

COUNTRY	AUSTRALIA	CHINA[1]	INDONESIA	JAPAN	S KOREA	SINGAPORE	TAIWAN	THAILAND
Aircraft Carrier (CV)	–	2	–	–	–	–	–	–
Support/Helicopter Carrier (CVS/CVH)	–	–	–	4	–	–	–	1
Strategic Missile Submarine (SSBN)	–	7	–	–	–	–	–	–
Attack Submarine (SSN)	–	9	–	–	–	–	–	–
Patrol Submarine (SSK/SS)	6	50	4	23	20	4	4[4]	–
Fleet Escort (DDG/FFG)	11	100	7	40	27	6	26	8
Patrol Escort/Corvette (FFG/FSG/FS)	–	55	24	6	5	14	4	10
Missile Armed Attack Craft (PGG/PTG)	–	75	24[2]	6	18	–	c. 30	–
Mine Countermeasures Vessel (MCMV)	4	25	11	19	10	4	c. 6	5
Major Amphibious Units (LHD/LPD/LSD)	3	11	8[3]	3	2	4	2	2

Notes:

1: Chinese numbers approximate. **2:** Some additional Indonesian patrol gunboats are able to ship missiles. **3:** Includes three vessels configured as hospital ships. **4:** Taiwan's submarines are reported to have limited operational availability.

MAJOR REGIONAL POWERS – AUSTRALIA

The defence strategic review referenced in the introduction has provided a broad outline of the Royal Australian Navy's (RAN's) future direction. However, many details were left unanswered. There is most clarity with respect to the submarine force as a result of decisions announced in a joint statement by Australian Premier Anthony Albanese, his British counterpart Rishi Sunak and US President Joe Biden at a joint press conference in San Diego on 13 March 2023. The statement builds upon the AUKUS security partnership first revealed in September 2021 to set out a long-term pathway to the RAN's acquisition of a nuclear-powered attack submarine capability. This will commence later in 2023 when Australian military and civilian personnel start to be embedded alongside their American and British counterparts. This will be followed by increased US Navy and Royal Navy visits to Australian ports, including the establishment of a rotational presence by these boats in Western Australia by 2027. Subsequently, from the early 2030s, the RAN will acquire between three and five American *Virginia* (SSN-774) class submarines. In the final stage from the early 2040s onwards, Australia will take delivery of a class of new AUKUS nuclear-powered attack submarines that will be developed for the RAN and RN under a joint programme that will also benefit from the input of US technology. The RAN boats will be assembled at the Osborne Naval Shipyard in Adelaide, South Australia, utilising nuclear reactors produced by Rolls-Royce in Derby in the United Kingdom.[4]

The acquisition of nuclear-powered submarines makes considerable sense for the RAN given their superior characteristics in the areas of speed, range and stealth, facilitating their deployment in both offensive and defensive roles across the vast waters of the Pacific region. The main potential downside, given that the threat of a capability gap arising from the retirement of the existing *Collins* class patrol submarines appears to have been mitigated by the planned acquisition of *Virginia* class boats, is the potential huge expense involved. Estimates of total costs of the AUKUS programme – including running and maintenance costs of the acquired submarines – range from AUS$268bn to US$368bn (c. US$180bn to US$245bn) over the next 30 years. Of the total, estimated spend over the next decade will be at least AU$50bn (c. US$33bn). This is more than double the previous, cancelled programme for French-designed *Attack* class patrol submarines. Whilst the Australian defence budget is steadily expanding, being expected to reach 2.3 percent of GDP by 2022/23, the defence strategic review acknowledges that trade-offs will be required to pay for the AUKUS submarines and other priority capabilities.

A preliminary graphic of the planned AUKUS nuclear-powered attack submarine that is destined to serve in both the Royal Australian Navy and the Royal Navy. *(Crown Copyright 2023)*

Against this backdrop, the RAN's surface re-equipment programme looks exposed to reductions. The 'high end' of this programme currently comprises nine *Hunter* class frigates, an evolved variant of the British Type 26 Global Combat Ship, being acquired under Project SEA 5000 Phase 1. These will be supplemented by a second tier of at least twelve *Arafura* class offshore patrol vessels (OPVs), which are based on the NVL OPV-80 design, under Project SEA 1180 Phase 1. Both programmes have been subject to significant criticism against a background of problems of varying severity.

Fabrication of the first block to be used in actual *Hunter* class assembly began at BAE Systems' facilities at Osborne in May 2023 as part of pre-production preparations. However, the build schedule to complete the lead ship is running behind initial estimates by around 16 months due to difficulties in squeezing all the RAN's required capabilities into the Type 26 hull. Pressures on programme costs are also considerable. Internal Australian Department of Defence estimates suggest that the overall total will be significantly higher than the AU$44.3bn (c. US$30bn) approved in 2018. In May 2023, an Australian National Audit Office report criticised management of the procurement process to date, stating that it had been only 'partly effective'. Problems identified included gaps in records relating to the selection of designs shortlisted for the original competition and a lack of a value-for-money assessment when the Type 26 was chosen as the preferred option from this shortlist. As of mid-2023, a decision to proceed with the construction of an initial batch of three *Hunter* class frigates is waiting completion of the pre-production phase. Current plans envisage two further batches following in due course.[5]

Construction of the *Arafura* class OPVs is much further advanced. The lead pair are being completed at Osborne under arrangements made to maintain local shipbuilding skills prior to the ramp-up of *Hunter* class production. However, the bulk will be built in Henderson, Western Australia by a joint venture between NVL and Australia's Cimvec. The lead vessel was launched in December 2021 but has yet to be delivered against a backdrop of rumours that her seaworthiness has failed to meet civilian standards.[6] All-in-all, six of the class were under assembly across the two facilities by the end of 2022. A common criticism of both the *Hunter* and *Arafura* classes is that they lack the offensive firepower that is required by Australia's evolving strategy. This criticism was, to an extent, reflected in the defence strategic review, which called for 'an enhanced lethality combat fleet'. Whilst this will still comprise higher end, Tier 1, and lower end, Tier 2, vessels, the review states that the surface fleet's structure should be 'consistent with a strategy of a larger number of smaller surface vessels' in an echo of the current US Navy distributed lethality concept. An independent analysis of the planned surface fleet is currently being conducted with a view to devising its optimum size, structure and composition in relation to the new fleet of nuclear-powered submarines. There has been speculation that this could result in reductions in *Hunter* and *Arafura* class orders, possibly in conjunction with the purchase of cheaper alternatives.

For the time being, deliveries of new ships are being dominated by the 'Evolved Cape' class patrol boats that are being built at Austal's Henderson yard. Five of these had been accepted as of mid-2023 following the arrival of *Cape Woolami* on 22 June 2023. *Cape Peron*, *Cape Naturaliste* and *Cape Capricorn* have also been delivered over the past 12 months. They join the lead ship, *Cape Otway*, and two of the original 'Cape' class – *Cape Fourcroy* and *Cape Inscription* – operated by the RAN under a lease arrangement. Six other 'Capes' are operated by the Australian Border Force. The new ships are effectively compensating for progressive withdrawals of the previous *Armidale* class. Five of these have been decommissioned since June 2022: *Ararat* (2 July 2022); *Glenelg* (6 October 2022); *Wollongong* (8 December 2022); *Armidale* (30 March 2023); and *Launceston* (1 June 2023). This left just six of the original fourteen-strong flotilla in service as of mid-2023.

The second 'Evolved Cape Class' patrol boat *Cape Peron* leads the French frigate *La Fayette* into Cairns, Queensland in April 2023. These vessels are slowly taking over from the *Armidale* class as the older ships are decommissioned. *(Royal Australian Navy)*

A summary of the RAN's major warships, unchanged since last year, is contained in Table 2.2.2.

MAJOR REGIONAL POWERS – CHINA

The expansion of China's military capabilities – particularly those of the People's Liberation Army Navy (PLAN) – had been the defining feature of the Asian geopolitical landscape over the past decade or more. Already numerically stronger overall than its US Navy counterpart, the PLAN passed another milestone in the last year, with the number of its major surface combatants now also surpassing that of its American rival for the first time. Whilst it continues to lag behind the US Navy in important technological areas such as underwater warfare, the gap is seemingly closing all the time. The main concern is that China might use its increasing power

Table 2.2.2: ROYAL AUSTRALIAN NAVY: PRINCIPAL UNITS AS AT MID 2023

TYPE	CLASS	NUMBER	TONNAGE	DIMENSIONS	PROPULSION	CREW	DATE
Principal Surface Escorts							
Frigate – FFG	**HOBART** (F-100)	3	6,300 tonnes	147m x 19m x 5m	CODOG, 28 knots	200	2017
Frigate – FFG	**ANZAC**	8	3,600 tonnes	118m x 15m x 4m	CODOG, 28 knots	175	1996
Submarines							
Submarine – SSK	**COLLINS**	6	3,400 tonnes	78m x 8m x 7m	Diesel-electric, 20 knots	45	1996
Major Amphibious Units							
Amph Assault Ship – LHD	**CANBERRA** (JUAN CARLOS I)	2	27,100 tonnes	231m x 32m x 7m	IEP, 21 knots	290	2014
Landing Ship Dock – LSD	**CHOULES** (LARGS BAY)	1	16,200 tonnes	176m x 26m x 6m	Diesel-electric, 18 knots	160	2006

to adopt a military solution to the long-held objective of reunification with Taiwan.

Opinion on this subject remains divided. In addition to its substantial economic consequences, any invasion of Taiwan would be fraught with hazard and subject to a high risk of failure. The initial outcome of Vladimir Putin's assault on Ukraine may well influence China's President Xi Jinping against any similar action with respect to Taiwan. In January 2023, the Washington DC-based Center for Strategic and International Studies (CSIS) released the findings of a series of wargames it had run to determine the likely outcome of any invasion. In most scenarios, combined American, Japanese and Taiwanese forces defeated a Chinese amphibious operation, albeit with the loss of tens of ships, hundreds of aircraft and thousands of servicemen.[7] Nevertheless, tensions across the Taiwan Strait remain high. In August 2022, China responded to then House or Representatives speaker Nancy Pelosi's visit to the island with a series of exercises that included the firing of multiple ballistic missiles around and over Taiwan, some falling into Japan's EEZ. Subsequently, on 3 June 2023, the Chinese Type 052D 'Luyang III' class destroyer *Suzhou* came close to colliding with her US Navy counterpart *Chung-Hoon* (DDG-93) whist the American ship – in company with the Canadian frigate *Montreal* – was conducting a freedom of navigation operation along the Taiwan Strait.

Table 2.2.3 summarises PLAN strength as of mid-2023, with comments on various warship types below.

Aircraft Carriers and Amphibious Vessels: Work continues fitting out China's first catapult assisted

Table 2.2.3: PEOPLE'S LIBERATION ARMY NAVY: PRINCIPAL UNITS AS AT MID 2023

TYPE	CLASS	NUMBER	TONNAGE	DIMENSIONS	PROPULSION	CREW	DATE
Aircraft Carriers							
Aircraft Carrier – CV	Type 001A (Modified Kuznetsov)	1	65,000 tonnes	315m x 35/75m x 10m	Steam, 32 knots	Unknown	2019
Aircraft Carrier – CV	Type 001 **LIAONING** (Kuznetsov)	1	60,000 tonnes	306m x 35/73m x 10m	Steam, 32 knots	Unknown	2012
Principal Surface Escorts							
Destroyer – DDG	Type 055 **NANCHANG** ('Renhai')	8	c. 12,000 tonnes	180m x 20m x 7m	COGAG, 30 knots	c.300	2019
Destroyer – DDG	Type 052D **KUNMING** ('Luyang III')	25	7,500 tonnes	156m x 17m x 6m	CODOG, 28 knots	280	2014
Destroyer – DDG	Type 051C **SHENYANG** ('Luzhou')	2	7,100 tonnes	155m x 17m x 6m	Steam, 29 knots	250	2006
Destroyer – DDG	Type 052C **LANZHOU** ('Luyang II')	6	7,000 tonnes	154m x 17m x 6m	CODOG, 28 knots	280	2005
Destroyer – DDG	Type 052B **GUANGZHOU** ('Luyang I')	2	6,500 tonnes	154m x 17m x 6m	CODOG, 29 knots	280	2004
Destroyer – DDG	Project 956E/EM **HANGZHOU** (Sovremenny)	4	8,000 tonnes	156m x 17m x 6m	Steam, 32 knots	300	1999
Destroyer – DDG	Type 051B **SHENZHEN** ('Luhai')	1	6,000 tonnes	154m x 16m x 6m	Steam, 31 knots	250	1998
Destroyer – DDG	Type 052 **HARBIN** ('Luhu')	2	4,800 tonnes	143m x 15m x 5m	CODOG, 31 knots	260	1994
Frigate – FFG	Type 054A **XUZHOU** ('Jiangkai II')	40	4,100 tonnes	132m x 15m x 5m	CODAD, 28 knots	190	2008
Frigate – FFG	Type 054 **MA'ANSHAN** ('Jiangkai I')	2	4,000 tonnes	132m x 15m x 5m	CODAD, 28 knots	190	2005
Frigate – FFG	Type 053 H3 **LIANYUNGANG** ('Jiangwei II')	8	2,500 tonnes	112m x 12m x 5m	CODAD, 27 knots	170	1992
Frigate – FSG	Type 056/056A **BENGBU** ('Jiangdao')	50[1]	1,500 tonnes	89m x 12m x 4m	CODAD, 28 knots	60	2013
Plus c. 5 remaining obsolescent frigates of the Type 053 H1/H1G **TAIZHOU/BEIHAI** ('Jianghu II & V') classes that remain active in second-line roles.							
Submarines							
Submarine – SSBN	Type 094/094A ('Jin')	c. 6	9,000 tonnes	133m x 11m x 8m	Nuclear, 20+ knots	Unknown	2008
Submarine – SSBN	Type 092 ('Xia')	1[2]	6,500 tonnes	120m x 10m x 8m	Nuclear, 22 knots	140	1987
Submarine – SSN	Type 093/093A ('Shang')	c. 6	6,000 tonnes	107m x 11m x 8m	Nuclear, 30 knots	100	2006
Submarine – SSN	Type 091 ('Han')	3[2]	5,500 tonnes	106m x 10m x 7m	Nuclear, 25 knots	75	1974
Submarine – SSK	Type 039A/039B (Type 041 'Yuan')	c. 20+	2,500 tonnes	75m x 8m x 5m	AIP, 20+ knots	Unknown	2006
Submarine – SSK	Type 039/039G ('Song')	13	2,300 tonnes	75m x 8m x 5m	Diesel-electric, 22 knots	60	1999
Submarine – SSK	Project 636 ('Kilo')	10[3]	3,000 tonnes	73m x 10m x 7m	Diesel-electric, 20 knots	55	1997
Plus c. 10 obsolescent patrol submarines of the Type 035 ('Ming' Class), some in reserve. A Type 032 'Qing' trials submarine has also been commissioned for strategic missile trials.							
Major Amphibious Units							
Amph. Assault Ship – LHD	Type 075 HAINAN ('Yushen')	3	40,000 tonnes	237m x 36m x 8m	CODAD, 20+ knots	Unknown	2021
Landing Platform Dock – LPD	Type 071 KULUN SHAN ('Yuzhao')	8	25,000 tonnes	210m x 27m x 7m	CODAD, 20 knots	Unknown	2007

Notes:

1. The 22-strong Type 056 variant has been transferred to the Coast Guard after refit.

2. The operational status of these vessels is questionable.

3. It has been reported that the two older Project 877 EKM 'Kilos' have been decommissioned.

take-off but arrested recovery (CATOBAR) aircraft carrier, *Fujian*, at the Jiangnan Shipbuilding yard on Changxing Island off Shanghai. Chinese press reports suggest that mooring trials commenced in the first half of 2023 but recent satellite imagery suggest work is still underway on her electromagnetic catapults and arrestor gear. There has been speculation that the ship, the first Type 003 carrier, will commence sea trials before the end of 2023. If so, this would be a remarkable achievement given she was launched as recently as 17 June 2022.

Meanwhile, the PLAN's amphibious forces have been bolstered by continued deliveries of Type 075 'Yushen' class amphibious assault ships from Hudong–Zhonghua Shipbuilding, with *Anhui* joining her sisters *Hainan* and *Guangxi* around the end of 2022. On 30 June 2023, *Guangxi* was photographed passing through the Osmui Strait into the Pacific Ocean, suggesting that she has now achieved operational status. It is possible that there may be a pause in further deliveries as Hudong–Zhonghua's activities are transferred from its current shipyard in central Shanghai to a new facility being completed on Changxing Island.

Surface Combatants: The last year has seen the PLAN's force of major surface combatants continue to grow as a result of ongoing construction of Type 055 and Type 052D destroyers, as well as of Type 054A frigates. The top end of these vessels remains the Type 055 'Renhai' class. The first batch of eight of these large and imposing c. 12,000-tonne ships has been completed with the deliveries of *Zunyi* and *Xianyang* from the Dalian Shipbuilding Industry Company (DSIC). An initial two vessels of a second batch are under construction by DSIC and Shanghai's Jiangnan Shipbuilding, which share construction of the class. The two yards also continue to work on the smaller but more numerous Type 052D destroyers. Twenty-five of these c. 7,500-tonne ships have now been delivered and at least ten of what will form a fourth batch are currently at various stages of assembly. As of mid-2023, it is too early to know whether either of the new batches of Type 055 and Type 052D vessels will incorporate significant improvements over their predecessors.

Deliveries of the 'intermediate', 4,100-tonne Type 054A 'Jiangkai II' frigate design by Hudong–Zhonghua and Guangzhou's Huangpu Wenchong Shipbuilding are now approaching forty

The Chinese Type 052D 'Luyang III' class destroyer *Suzhou* cuts across the bows of the US Navy destroyer *Chung-Hoon* (DDG-93) on 3 June 2023 as the American ship conducts a freedom of navigation transit of the Taiwan Strait. China's PLAN is in the forefront of the country's efforts to exert its authority in the region as tensions remain high. *(US Navy)*

The PLAN Type 055 'Renhai' class destroyers, eight of which have been commissioned to date, are the most powerful in their surface fleet. These photographs show *Xianyang* and *Zunyi*, both of which have been commissioned in the last 12 months, operating in company during exercises held in May 2023. *(China Military Online)*

units as the latest batch of ten are steadily completed. It was once thought that this group might number twenty vessels. However, a number of reports in early 2023 suggest that the first of the long-awaited Type 054B iteration – sometimes also referred to as the Type 057 – is now under construction by Hudong–Zhonghua. If speculation is confirmed, the new ships are likely to be around 147m in length and displace c. 6,000 tonnes, therefore falling between the Type 054A and Type 052D destroyers in size. The two prototype Type 054 'Jiangkai I' and eight remaining Type 053H3 'Jiangwei II' frigates have reportedly been upgraded with HQ-10 point defence surface-to-air missiles in replacement for their obsolescent HQ-7 systems, suggesting they will remain in the operational fleet for a while yet. The few earlier frigates of the 'Jianghu' series that remain in service have all now seemingly been transferred to second-line roles.

In an exception to recent trends, the number of the PLAN's smaller, littoral warfare corvettes has declined in number over the past year with the transfer of all twenty-two of the Type 056 class to China Coast Guard from late 2021 through to mid-2022. The handover has seen these ships' former missile armament removed in favour of the addition of more constabulary-focused equipment, such as water cannon, acoustic hailing devices and instructional LED displays. The original Type 056 design arguably has increasingly limited relevance to China's front-line naval operations given that the national anti-access/area-denial (A2/AD) bubble has steadily extended beyond the littoral. However, their potential to contribute to 'grey zone' policing remains. Conversely, the fifty ships of the improved, Type 056A variant have greater military value by virtue of the anti-submarine capacity provided by their towed-array sonar and, accordingly, they remain in PLAN service.

Submarines: The ongoing development of the PLAN's secretive submarine service continues to remain difficult to assess. Most open sources believe that there are currently around six Type 094/094A 'Jin' strategic submarines and six Type 093/093A 'Xia' nuclear-powered attack submarines in service, possibly supplemented by obsolete Type 92 and Type 91 series boats from the Cold War era. The development of next-generation Type 096 and Type 095 designs has been anticipated for some time but it seems that an interim Type 093B variant – first reported in May 2022 – may precede these new boats. There has been considerable speculation that current expansion of the Bohai shipyard at Huludao is being driven with the new programmes in mind. The next generation-submarines will likely close the gap on Western submarine designs in terms of stealth, an area in which the PLAN's current boats significantly lags its rivals, when they eventually arrive. In the interim, US intelligence assessments suggest that the existing Type 094 series submarines are being retrofitted with the new, longer-range JL-3 submarine-launched ballistic missile, significantly increasing China's ability to strike targets in the continental United States.[8]

The PLAN's force of patrol submarines notionally comprises forty-eight boats – plus additional training units – to maintain two, eight-strong divisions in each of the three fleets. These are increasingly comprised of the indigenously-designed, air-independent propulsion (AIP)-equipped series of Type 039A/041 'Yuan' class submarines, which have been progressively improved. The latest, Type 039C variant incorporates an unusual stealth fin (US Navy: sail) that has a close resemblance to that destined for Sweden's A26 *Blekinge* class. The pace of Chinese patrol submarine production has slackened off in recent years. This is likely due to a combination of export orders, the Covid pandemic and the relocation of the Wuchang Shipyard in Wuhan where many of the 'Yuan' class have been built. Nevertheless, current US Department of Defense estimates suggest that twenty-five 'Yuan' series submarines will be in service by 2025.[9]

A major feature underlying the PLAN's expansion has been significant investment in the country's shipbuilding sector, by now far the largest in the world. In addition to modernisation of existing facilities, a notable feature of infrastructure development has been the relocation of entire shipyards to more spacious, greenfield sites. Nowhere has this been more evident than in Shanghai, where the main naval shipyards have been progressively transferred from the heart of the city to Changxing Island as part of a two decade-long plan to establish a colossal shipbuilding enterprise. The first phase of the project saw Jiangnan Shipbuilding relocate to a new 5.6km^2 facility built on Changxing between 2005 and 2008; a shipyard which was subsequently

A photograph of an unidentified 'Yuan' class submarine attached to China's Northern Fleet in March 2023. The increasingly numerous 'Yuan' class, which have now been built in a number of iterations, have come to dominate the patrol submarine divisions found in each of China's three fleets. *(China Military Online)*

expanded by a further 2km² between 2016 and 2020 as part of efforts to support the carrier *Fujian*'s construction. More recently, starting in 2021, work has been underway on an adjacent yard for Hudong–Zhonghua Shipbuilding. Being completed in two phases, this will add 4.3km² to the shipbuilding facilities on the island. All-in-all, the massive shipbuilding centre will reportedly stretch nearly 7.7km along the Shanghai River, encompassing a total area nearly twice that of midtown Manhattan.[10]

MAJOR REGIONAL POWERS – JAPAN

The strategic and defence reviews discussed in the introduction set a force structure encompassing twenty-two submarines, four 'helicopter carrying destroyers', two Aegis System Equipped Vessels (ASEVs), fifty other destroyers/frigates, twelve patrol vessels and c. 170 combat aircraft to be achieved within the next decade. This represents an increase of two ASEVs and a reduction of around twenty manned combat aircraft compared with the previous force structure announced in December 2018. The main changes from the actual force structure as of mid-2023 set out in Table 2.2.4 will be an increase in number of destroyers and frigates from the existing forty-six vessels and the addition of the new patrol vessels to the order of battle.

The submarine force reached its targeted strength of twenty-two boats – first set in the National Defense Program Guidelines of 2010 – with the delivery of the lead *Taigei* (SS-513) class boat in March 2022.[11] The arrival of her sister *Hakugei* (SS-514) on 20 March 2023 temporarily takes submarine numbers to twenty-three (plus two additional boats used for training). However, one unit will be used exclusively for trials and evaluation, maintaining the operational force at the targeted level. The FY2023 defence budget includes 80.2bn Japanese yen (c. US$570m) for a seventh member of the *Taigei* class. However, it seems that subsequent construction will shift to a new design given the desire to induct vertically-launched missiles in future submarines.

The destroyer and frigate force has grown by two vessels year-on-year as a result of the commissioning of the third and fourth *Mogami* (FFM-1) class multi-mission frigates *Noshiro* (FFM-3) and *Mikuma* (FFM-4) without counter-balancing withdrawals. The class will continue to be delivered by Mitsubishi Heavy Industries (MHI) at a rate of two per annum for the next four years, with FFM-11 and FFM-12 being approved at a total cost of 116.7bn yen (c. US$810m) in the FY2023 budget. Subsequent production will transition to a new design that will benefit from lessons learned from the existing class. The frigates utilise a modular design that encompasses the use of autonomous systems for mine countermeasures duties, thereby allowing the traditional MCM force to continue to

Table 2.2.4: JAPAN MARITIME SELF-DEFENCE FORCE: PRINCIPAL UNITS AS AT MID 2023

TYPE	CLASS	NUMBER[1]	TONNAGE	DIMENSIONS	PROPULSION	CREW	DATE
Support and Helicopter Carriers							
Support Carrier – CVL[2]	**IZUMO** (DDH-183)	2	27,000 tonnes	248m x 38m x 7m	COGAG, 30 knots	470	2015
Helicopter Carrier – CVH	**HYUGA** (DDH-181)	2	19,000 tonnes	197m x 33m x 7m	COGAG, 30 knots	340	2009
Principal Surface Escorts							
Destroyer – DDG	**MAYA** (DDG-179)	2	10,500 tonnes	170m x 21m x 6m	COGLAG, 30 knots	300	2020
Destroyer – DDG	**ATAGO** (DDG-177)	2	10,000 tonnes	165m x 21m x 6m	COGAG, 30 knots	300	2007
Destroyer – DDG	**KONGOU** (DDG-173)	4	9,500 tonnes	161m x 21m x 6m	COGAG, 30 knots	300	1993
Destroyer – DDG	**HATAKAZE** (DDG-171)	0 (2)	6,300 tonnes	150m x 16m x 5m	COGAG, 30 knots	260	1986
Destroyer – DDG	**ASAHI** (DD-119)	2	6,800 tonnes	151m x 18m x 5m	COGLAG, 30 knots	230	2017
Destroyer – DD	**AKIZUKI** (DD-115)	4	6,800 tonnes	151m x 18m x 5m	COGAG, 30 Knots	200	2012
Destroyer – DDG	**TAKANAMI** (DD-110)	5	6,300 tonnes	151m x 17m x 5m	COGAG, 30 knots	175	2003
Destroyer – DDG	**MURASAME** (DD-101)	9	6,200 tonnes	151m x 17m x 5m	COGAG, 30 knots	165	1996
Destroyer – DDG	**ASAGIRI** (DD-151)	8	4,900 tonnes	137m x 15m x 5m	COGAG, 30 knots	220	1988
Frigate – FFG	**MOGAMI** (FFM-1)	4	5,300 tonnes	133m x 16m x 5m	CODAG, 30+ knots	90	2022
Frigate – FFG	**ABUKUMA** (DE-229)	6	2,500 tonnes	109m x 13m x 4m	CODOG, 27 knots	120	1989
Submarines							
Submarine – SSK[3]	**TAGEI** (SS-513)	2	4,300 tonnes	84m x 9m x 8m	Diesel-electric, 20+ knots	70	2022
Submarine – SSK	**SORYU** (SS-501)	12	4,200 tonnes	84m x 9m x 8m	AIP, 20+ knots[4]	65	2009
Submarine – SSK	**OYASHIO** (SS-590)	9 (2)	4,000 tonnes	82m x 9m x 8m	Diesel-electric, 20+ knots	70	1998
Major Amphibious Units							
Landing Platform Dock – LPD	**OSUMI** (LST-4001)	3	14,000 tonnes	178m x 26m x 6m	Diesel, 22 knots	135	1998

Notes:
1. Figures in brackets refer to trials or training ships.
2. In the course of conversion to operate F-35B STOVL strike fighters.
3. Some sources suggest that one of these submarines will be operated as a dedicated trials submarine, thereby keeping the operational flotilla at twenty-two boats.
4. The last two units of the class have their AIP plant replaced by lithium-ion batteries; an arrangement also adopted in the follow-on *Tagaei* class

Although construction of a seventh *Taigei* (SS-513) class submarine was authorised in Japan's latest defence budget, there are now plans to transition to a new design equipped with vertical launch cells. This photograph shows *Taigei* herself in November 2022. *(Arjun Sarup)*

Surface warship construction for the Japan Maritime Self Defence Force (JMSDF) is currently dominated by the *Mogami* (FFM-1) class frigates, which are being ordered at the rate of two each year. However, current plans envisage future orders being focused on a modified variant of the type. This photograph depicts *Kumano* (FFM-2). *(Arjun Sarup)*

shrink. The budget included funding for new unmanned surface and underwater drones that will be acquired for this purpose.

Other new classes of vessel that will enter service over the coming years include both the two ASEVs and the new patrol vessels. The FY2023 budget allocated 220.8bn yen (c. US$1.5bn) for the procurement of long-lead items for the ASEVs. Financing for actual construction is expected to follow in 2024 to allow them to enter service during 2027–8. The ships will be equipped with Standard Missile SM-3 and SM-6 variants to intercept ballistic and hypersonic missiles in various phases of their flight, as well as self-defence and strike weaponry. The offshore patrol vessels will be much simpler constabulary and surveillance vessels equipped with a light main gun but incorporating containerised equipment and facilities for helicopter and drone operation. An initial order for four ships at a cost of 35.7bn yen (c. USUS250m) was approved in the 2023 budget. Japan Marine United will build the first four ships but MHI will also be involved in later production.

MAJOR REGIONAL POWERS – SOUTH KOREA

The continued development of North Korean capabilities in the fields of missiles and nuclear weapons have effectively put paid to the Republic of Korea Navy's ambitions to acquire its first true aircraft carrier; at least for the time being.[12] Instead, the new administration of President Yoon Suk Yeol has prioritised reinforcement of the so-called 'Three-Axis' system that is designed to deter and punish any North Korean nuclear strike. The system combines (1) a 'Kill Chain' of detection, targeting and strike capabilities to pre-empt an imminent attack; (2) a 'Korean Air and Missile Defence' (KAMD) to intercept any missiles that are launched; and (3) a 'Korean Massive Punishment and Retaliation' (KMPR) to launch a massive conventional response. The annual 2023–7 Mid-Term Defense Plan announced at the end of 2022 confirmed that an expanded defence budget would be focused on securing 'overwhelming' deterrence capabilities through ongoing investment in weapons and technologies relevant to these three elements.[13] In July

2022, the president also announced that a new strategic command would be initiated by 2024 to coordinate the various tri-service components of the 'Three-Axis' system's architecture into a more cohesive whole.

Whilst negative for aircraft carrier acquisition, renewed focus on the 'Three-Axis' system is positive news for the development of the navy's submarine flotilla, which continues to expand. Current construction is focused on the KSS-III *Dosan Ahn Chang-ho* class. These boats are equipped with K-VLS vertical-launch cells for conventionally-armed Hyunmoo 4-4 ballistic missiles, which form a key component of the KMPR capability. *Ahn-moo*, the second of an initial batch of three of the class, was delivered by Daewoo Shipbuilding & Marine Engineering (DSME) in April 2023 and will be followed by a sister, the Hyundai Heavy Industries (HHI) built *Shin Chae-ho*, within the next 12 months. DSME had previously held a formal keel-laying ceremony for *Lee Bong-chang*, the first of an enlarged second batch, on 30 March 2023.[14] She will be equipped with more K-VLS cells – ten as opposed to six – to increase her second-strike capacity. The shipbuilding company are also working on a second member of this batch, with HHI likely to receive the order for the third in due course. Current planning then anticipates orders for a third trio, taking total production to nine vessels. When combined with the existing KSS-I Type 209 (*Chang Bogo*) and KSS-II Type 214 (*Son Won-il*) classes, their completion would give South Korea a substantial flotilla of twenty-seven submarines, although it seems questionable whether some of the older boats will last that long.

Another important naval contribution to the 'Three-Axis' system will be the ballistic missile defence capability provided by the three KDX-III Batch II Aegis-equipped destroyers that are currently been built by HHI. Displacing well over 10,000 tonnes at full load, these ships are larger, upgraded variants of the trio of existing KDX-III Batch I *Sejong the Great* destroyers and will reportedly be equipped with both Standard SM-3 and SM-6 missiles to perform an integrated air and missile defence role. The first ship of the second batch, *Jeongjo the Great*, was formally named at HHI's Ulsan yard on 28 July 2022 and should be delivered by the end of 2024. HHI was also contracted to build the third and final ship in December 2022.

The Republic of Korea Navy's lead KDX-III Batch I destroyer, *Sejong the Great*, pictured whilst operating with US Navy units in June 2022. A larger and more technologically advanced KDX-III Batch II *Jeongjo the Great* variant will start to enter service during the next year. *(US Navy)*

The KDX-III destroyers will ultimately be followed into production by a new class of KDDX vessels for which HHI are already working on the basic design. Somewhat smaller than the KDX-III with a full load displacement of around 9,000 tonnes, the new destroyers will be notable for incorporating a greater level of indigenous equipment, including an integrated mast and combat management system developed by Hanwha Systems. Current plans involve procurement of a total of six ships from 2024 onwards, with deliveries running into the middle of the next decade. There are also more esoteric plans for acquisition of three 'Arsenal ships', for which DSME was contracted to produce the basic design in April 2023. Known locally as 'joint firepower ships', they would be equipped with ballistic and cruise missiles to reinforce the 'Kill Chain' element of the 'Three-Axis' deterrent.

As reflected in Table 2.2.5 summarising current fleet strength, current surface procurement remains focused on completing the replacement of the legacy frigate and corvette force that form an important part of the navy's littoral warfare capabilities. Little more than a handful of the once-numerous *Ulsan* and *Po Hang* class ships remain in service as deliveries of FFX Batch II *Daegu* class frigates draw to a close. Three *Daegu* class frigates – *Daejeon*, *Po Hang* and *Cheonan* – have been delivered in the last year.[15] *Chuncheon*, the eighth and final member of the batch, is expected to follow before the end of 2023. Work is already well underway on the follow-on FFX Batch III *Chungnam* class, with HII conducting a ceremonial 'launch' of the lead ship on 10 April 2023.[16] The new ship continues the progressive increase in size and capability seen in previous transitions between batches, displacing over 600 tonnes more than the *Daegu* class at full load. It incorporates new technology – including an integrated mast – that will be eventually used in the KDXX destroyers. Orders for a further three of a planned total of six frigates in this batch have now been placed. All were

Table 2.2.5: REPUBLIC OF KOREA NAVY: PRINCIPAL UNITS AS AT MID 2023

TYPE	CLASS	NUMBER	TONNAGE	DIMENSIONS	PROPULSION	CREW	DATE
Principal Surface Escorts							
Destroyer – DDG	KDX-III **SEJONG THE GREAT**	3	10,000 tonnes	166m x 21m x 6m	COGAG, 30 knots	300	2008
Destroyer – DDG	KDX-II **CHUNGMUGONG YI SUN-SHIN**	6	5,500 tonnes	150m x 17m x 5m	CODOG, 30 knots	200	2003
Destroyer – DDG	KDX-I **GWANGGAETO THE GREAT**	3	3,900 tonnes	135m x 14m x 4m	CODOG, 30 knots	170	1998
Frigate – FFG	FFX-2 **DAEGU**	7	3,600 tonnes	122m x 14m x 4m	CODLOG	140	2017
Frigate – FFG	FFX **INCHEON**	6	3,000 tonnes	114m x 14m x 4m	CODOG, 30 knots	140	2013
Frigate – FFG	**ULSAN**	2	2,300 tonnes	102m x 12m x 4m	CODOG, 35 knots	150	1981
Corvette – FSG	**POHANG**	5	1,200 tonnes	88m x 10m x 3m	CODOG, 32 knots	95	1984
Submarines							
Submarine – SSK	KSS-3 **DOSAN AHN CHANG-HO**	2	3,800 tonnes	84m x 8m x 8m	AIP, 20+ knots	50	2021
Submarine – SSK	KSS-2 **SON WON-IL** (Type 214)	9	1,800 tonnes	65m x 6m x 6m	AIP, 20+ knots	30	2007
Submarine – SSK	KSS-1 **CHANG BOGO** (Type 209)	9	1,300 tonnes	56m x 6m x 6m	Diesel-electric, 22 knots	35	1993
Major Amphibious Units							
Amph Assault Ship – LHD	LPX **DOKDO**	2[1]	18,900 tonnes	200m x 32m x 7m	Diesel, 22 knots	425	2007

Notes:
1. *Marado*, the second ship of the class, is built to a slightly different design.

The lead FFX Batch III frigate, *Chungnam*, was ceremonially launched at Hyundai Heavy Industries' Ulsan shipyard on 10 April 2023. Prominent in this photograph is the integrated mast that forms a key feature of the design. *(Korean Ministry of National Defence)*

allocated to SamKang M&T, one of South Korea's mid-sized yards, in a move that drew criticism from the more established warship builders burdened with heavier developmental overheads.

OTHER REGIONAL FLEETS

Brunei: The Royal Brunei Navy has been reinforced by the gift of two former Republic of Singapore Navy warships; the *Fearless* class patrol vessels *Brave* and *Gallant.* The two ships will take the names *As-Siddiq* and *Al-Faruq* in Brunei's service, with the former being handed over at Changi Naval Base on 15 March 2023. The pair will operate alongside the two quartets of more modern NVL *Darussalam* class offshore patrol vessels and *Ijtihad* class inshore patrol boats that form the core of the current fleet.

Indonesia: Indonesia's programme of fleet modernisation has had mixed success over the past year. Questions about the ability of a constrained defence budget to fund a raft of new acquisitions that were raised in last year's *Seaforth World Naval Review* appear to have been validated by subsequent events. In particular, it appears that the large contract agreed with Italy's Fincantieri in June 2021 to acquire six new-build FREMM and two second-hand *Maestrale* class frigates has failed to make any progress because the necessary financing has yet to be put in place. There is speculation in the local press that the contract may be re-negotiated to encompass a smaller number of ships. The delay follows problems realising a previous 2019 agreement with South Korea's DSME to acquire a second batch of three Type 209 *Nagapasa* class submarines to join the trio that have already entered service. Instead, Indonesia is seemingly keen to pursue the prospect of acquiring a pair of more advanced 'Scorpène' type boats, which would be license-built by PT PAL at Surabaya with technical assistance from France's Naval Group. In the light of continued delays to procurement of new major warships, priority is being given to expediting the refit and upgrading of a wide range of existing assets, including some of the relatively recent *Bung Tomo* and *Diponegoro* classes.

One programme that has made progress over the last year has been the construction of two 'Arrowhead 140' corvettes by PT PAL under licence from Britain's Babcock International. A first steel-cutting ceremony for the lead ship was held at Surabaya on 9 December 2022, with delivery scheduled by the end of 2026. Known locally as the *Merah Putih* class after the red and white colours of the Indonesian flag, the new vessels will be equipped with vertical launchers for surface-to-air missiles and utilise a Turkish Havelsan Advent combat management system. This system has also been specified for a new modular 90m offshore patrol vessel design that commenced construction in the second half of 2021 and some of the 60m KCR 60M missile-armed fast attack craft.

Progress with local construction of the large fleet of second-line patrol vessels and logistical support ships that supplements the navy's relatively small force of major warships has continued to make better progress. Topping the list has been the hybrid presidential yacht *Bung Karno*, a lightly-armed 650-tonne patrol ship-like vessel equipped with a helicopter pad and a suite of bulletproof accommodation, that was delivered at the start of June 2023. The previous month saw the inauguration of *Kapak* and *Panah*, respectively the fifth and sixth members of the KCR 60M *Sampari* class. In similar fashion to Indonesia's previous 40m fast attack craft, the larger 60m type is also being constructed in a patrol vessel variant. This has a lower speed but can also be armed with surface-to-surface missiles in times of emergency. Two of these PC-60 vessels – named *Dorang* and *Bawai* – were accepted in the second half of 2022 and at least four more are under construction. Orders also continue for smaller, PC-40 *Pari* class vessels, of which nearly twenty will soon be in service.

The Indonesian Navy corvette *Bung Tomo* seen training with the US Navy destroyer *Momsen* (DDG-92) in April 2022. Delays in ordering new major warships mean that the three members of the *Bung Tomo* class remain an important part of the navy's relatively small force of major surface combatants. *(US Navy)*

Logistical and amphibious forces have been bolstered by the arrival of *dr. Radjiman Wedyodiningrat*, the second of two specialised hospital ships derived from the *Makassar* class of amphibious transport docks. This design continues to gain export success, with the United Arab Emirates being the latest to place an order from PT PAL in July 2022. Another significant arrival has been *Teluk Calang*, the ninth of twelve planned *Teluk Bintuni* class tank landing ships. Although local construction is being increasingly preferred for second-line vessels, some specialist naval shipping continues to be procured from overseas. Notable recent examples have been the two *Pulau Fani* mine countermeasures vessels based on the German Navy's Type 332 *Frankenthal* class, which were ordered from Abeking & Rasmussen in 2019. The ships were delivered in Germany at the end of May 2023 and are due to arrive in home waters before the end of the year.

Malaysia: The Royal Malaysian Navy's longstanding plan to reconfigure its fleet around five classes of warship totalling fifty-five major combatants – known as the '15 to 5 Transformation Plan' – has struggled to make headway against a backdrop of funding constraints and procurement problems. The most significant difficulty has related to the construction of six *Maharaja Lela* class 'Gowind' type frigates by Boustead Heavy Industries. Problems that emerged during the outfitting stage of the lead vessels saw the programme grind to a halt in 2019 against a backdrop of allegations of financial irregularities. The Malaysian government determined to proceed with the project – often referred to locally as the little combat ship programme – in 2021 but it was not until May 2023 that contracts that will see it recommence were finally concluded. The new plan will see the shipyard taken under government ownership and the scope of the project reduced to five ships to try to reduce the extent of the additional funding required to ensure its completion. It is hoped that physical construction of the lead ship will be concluded by the end of 2024 so as to allow delivery by 2026 after an extensive programme of first-of-class trials.

With restructuring of the little combat ship programme now seemingly complete, attention is turning to the acquisition of a second batch of littoral mission ships. These are supposed to be cheaper and less-sophisticated vessels than the littoral combat ships, with as many as eighteen being

The Royal Malaysian Navy's *Kasturi* class corvette *Lekir* pictured replenishing from the Royal Australian Navy oiler *Supply* during the course of the RIMPAC 2022 exercises. *Lekir* – commissioned in 1984 – is due to be replaced as part of Malaysia's '15 to 5 Transformation Plan' but its implementation has been slow. *(US Navy)*

envisaged under the '15 to 5' plan. An initial batch of four, 700 tonne *Keris* class variants were delivered from China between 2020 and 2022. However, the navy seemingly wants something more potent for the second batch, for which financial approval for three units was recently received. Local press reports suggest that Turkey's 'Ada' class design is a front-runner for the contract award. Whilst these large, c. 2,400-tonne ships would clearly bring a much higher level of capacity, it also seems that the principle of standardisation that was one of the key arguments for the transformation plan is being steadily unwound.

New Zealand: The future direction of the Royal New Zealand Navy will be given greater clarity during the second half of 2023 with publication of the New Zealand government's current Defence Policy Review. Its work will be driven by the preparatory *Defence Assessment 2021* published in December that year and which recognised the criticality of being able to deliver presence, awareness and response across the maritime domain.[17] Whilst this would appear to be positive for naval investment, the recent picture has not been altogether promising. The postponement of procurement of a planned Southern Ocean Patrol Vessel due to financial and other resource constraints in early 2022 has been followed by a manpower crisis that has seen the navy's two existing *Otago* class offshore patrol vessels, as well as the inshore patrol vessel *Hawea*, laid up for lack of crew. As is the case for other navies, a shortage of technical specialists is a particular problem in view of better pay in civilian jobs ashore. Whilst the navy is taking steps to address workforce attrition, the position doesn't augur well for any expansion in mission requirements the Defence Policy Review might identify.

North Korea: Assessment of Korean People's Navy (KPN) developments is inevitably influenced by the wider context of North Korea's nuclear and missile programmes. Although the last North Korean nuclear weapons test was in 2017, the country has continued to develop and test a range of ballistic, hypersonic and cruise missiles aimed at undermining the South's 'Three Axis' deterrence strategy. A BBC News report in March 2023 assessed that the Democratic People's Republic carried out a total of nearly ninety missile launches during 2022, more than three times the previous record. The same month saw the 'Sinpo' class submarine *8.24 Yongung* launch two cruise missiles in a further expansion of the range of strike weapons that North Korea can deploy.

Whilst the North's numerous conventional naval forces attract little attention, reports emerged in early June 2023 that the country plans to induct two new frigates. The ships have been registered with the International Maritime Organization (IMO) and are due for delivery in 2026. Speculatively reports suggest they will be helicopter-equipped vessels optimised for anti-submarine warfare similar to the two 'Nampo' class light frigates commissioned around a decade ago.[18] Somewhat more typical of the KPN's asymmetric approach to naval warfare are the 'Haeil' and 'Haeil-1' underwater 'suicide drones' announced by North Korean state television in March 2023. It is claimed that these can be equipped with nuclear warheads; a capability that would further complicate the South's deterrence planning.

The Philippines: Last year's *Seaforth World Naval Review* reported on the slew of naval acquisitions that coincided with the end of the previous Duterte administration and the final year of the 2018–22 'Horizon 2' phase of the Revised Armed Forces of the Philippines Modernization Program (RAFPMP). The contracts that were placed amounted to a veritable fleet, including two frigate-sized corvettes, six offshore patrol vessels, two additional *Makassar* type amphibious transport docks and batteries of coastal defence BrahMos missiles. Understandably, there is now a pause in new procurement as the previous contracts start to be implemented.

The highlight of the last year has been the start of deliveries of 'Shaldag' Mk V fast patrol boats from Israel Shipyards under a contract previously signed in February 2021. Known as the *Acero* class, the vessels displace less than 100 tonnes but incorporate a powerful armament that includes Spike-NLOS surface-to-surface missiles and a remotely-operated weapon station for a 25mm cannon, all controlled by a Rafael combat management system.[19] Four of the class have been built in Israel – being commissioned in pairs upon arrival in the Philippines in November 2022 and May 2023 – but a further five will be assembled under licence at the Cavite naval shipyard. The Philippine Navy hopes to obtain funding for a further fifteen members of the class in the 2023–7 'Horizon 3' phase of the RAFPMP. In the meantime, the navy's patrol forces will be further bolstered by the transfer of two additional former US Navy *Cyclone* (PC-1) class costal patrol vessels to join the lead unit, *General Mariano Alvarez*, acquired in 2004. The former *Monsoon* (PC-3) and *Chinook* (PC-9) were decommissioned from US Navy service at a ceremony in Bahrain on 28 March 2023.

The centrepiece of 'Horizon 3' is likely to be the acquisition of inaugural Philippine Navy submarine capability. French, South Korean and Spanish shipbuilders are all jockeying for what will be a lucrative contract. However, government statements suggest conclusion of the deal is not an immediate priority given the volume of new equipment already under order.

Nestor Acero is the lead ship of at least nine 'Shaldag V' or *Acero* class patrol gunboats ordered from Israel Shipyards for the Philippine Navy. She was commissioned on 28 November 2022. The class is capable of speeds in excess of 40 knots and armament can include the medium-range Spike-NLOS surface-to-air missile system. *(Rafael)*

Singapore: The Republic of Singapore Navy is now close to implementing the replacement of its existing Swedish-built submarines with the four tkMS Type 218SG *Invincible* class boats ordered in two batches in 2013 and 2017. On 13 December 2022, a high profile ceremony attended by German Chancellor Olaf Scholz and Singapore's Prime Minister Lee Hsien Loong saw the naming of *Impeccable* and *Illustrious*, respectively the second and third members of the class, by the premier's wife, Ms Ho Ching. Subsequently, on 18 May 2023, *Impeccable* was loaded onto the transport ship *Rolldock Storm* prior to departing for the long voyage east on 1 June. She is expected to be followed by *Illustrious* before the end of the year. As of mid-2023, the lead boat – *Invincible* – remained completing trials in German waters whilst the fourth unit, *Inimitable*, is in the course of construction at Kiel. An answer to a question posed in Singapore's parliament in January 2023 indicated that the project has cost in the region of US$2.4bn to achieve.[20]

There has also been progress with the programme for the future Multi-Role Combat Vessels (MRCVs), which will replace the six existing *Victory* class corvettes from 2028 onwards. In a series of contracts announced in March 2023, it was revealed that Saab will work with Singapore's Defence Science and Technology Agency (DSTA) to develop the basic design of the new vessels, with Singapore's ST Engineering undertaking detailed design and construction work. Press reports suggest that Saab will collaborate with Denmark's Odense Maritime

The Republic of Singapore Navy's Type 218SG submarines *Illustrious* (pictured) and *Impeccable* were named at a high-profile ceremony at the tkMS shipyard in Kiel on 13 December 2022. *(tkMS)*

Technology – responsible, inter alia, for originating the *Iver Huitfeldt* and 'Arrowhead 140' series of ships – in developing the new vessels. Significantly larger than the ships that they will replace, the new MRCVs will be optimised for deployment of autonomous vessels and make substantial use of the latest developments in the area of artificial intelligence.

The Republic of China Navy's prototype catamaran corvette *Tuo Chiang* pictured on exercises with the first of the series-built vessels, *Ta Chiang*, in December 2021. The series-built corvettes are slightly larger than the prototype and incorporate a number of differences, including provision for surface-to-air missiles. At least twelve of the ships are planned. *(Republic of China Navy)*

Taiwan: The long-delayed modernisation of Taiwan's Republic of China Navy has made headway on several fronts over the past year. One of the furthest-advanced programmes is for series production of the *Tuo Chiang* class catamaran-hulled missile corvettes. A joint ceremony held on 28 June 2023 at the Lungteh Shipbuilding facility at Suao saw the delivery of the second series-built ship *Fu Chiang* – third member of the class overall – and the naming of her sister, the fourth series-built ship *Wu Chiang*. A total of twelve *Tuo Chiang* class corvettes have been ordered to date. All are expected to be in service before the end of 2026. Local press reports suggest that orders for further members of the class – which are intended to work with the navy's thirty *Kuang Hua* fast attack craft in disrupting any Chinese amphibious invasion across the Taiwan Strait – are planned

With significant numbers of smaller vessels either delivered or under construction, attention is turning to modernising the navy's force of twenty-six major surface combatants; four former US Navy *Kidd* (DDG-993) class destroyers and twenty-two frigates of various classes. In May 2023, a contract was placed with the Jong Shyn Shipbuilding Group for an initial pair of what might ultimately be a class of twelve light frigates. With a length of c. 100m and a displacement in the region of 2,500 tonnes, the ships will reportedly be built in both anti-air and anti-submarine warfare variants. Some of the new ships will probably be earmarked to replace the navy's remaining six former US Navy *Knox* (FF-1052) class patrol frigates, all of which have now completed around 50 years' service.

A major new arrival in the past year has been the amphibious transport dock *Yushan*, which was delivered at a ceremony held in the presence of Taiwanese President Tsai Ing-wen on 30 September 2022. Construction of the navy's prototype next generation submarine also continues, with local press reports suggesting its launch will take place before the end of 2023.

The Royal Thai Navy's corvette *Sukhothai* capsized and sank in a storm in the Gulf of Thailand on 18 December 2022. The c. 1,000-tonne warship, which was completed in the United States by the former Tacoma Boatbuilding Company in 1987, was one of two members of the *Ratanakosin* class. *(Royal Thai Navy)*

Thailand: It has not been the best of years for the Royal Thai Navy. On 18 December 2022, the *Ratanakosin* class corvette *Sukhothai* suffered significant flooding after encountering severe weather whilst transiting the Gulf of Thailand. A resulting power failure eventually saw the warship capsize and sink. Twenty-nine members of her 105-strong crew were lost in the incident, one of the highest peacetime losses to afflict a warship's crew in recent years.

Meanwhile, there has been continued delay to the navy's flagship submarine programme. China's ongoing inability to procure an export licence for the German MTU396 diesel engines contracted for the submarines has seen construction of the lead S26T type boat – the only one of a planned three-strong class based on the PLAN's 'Yuan' series firmly ordered to date – effectively stalled. China is making strenuous efforts to persuade Thailand to agree the substitution of its indigenous CHD620 and recent press commentary suggests that a compromise may be agreed. In better news, the navy has taken delivery of its Hudong-Zhonghua-built Type 071E amphibious transport dock, which will become the largest warship in its fleet. The 25,000-tonne *Chang* was delivered in April 2023, arriving at the Sattahip naval base in Thailand on the 25th of the month.

The delay to the submarine programme may

result in previously-delayed surface warship programmes being prioritised. There is renewed interest in acquiring a second modern frigate to join the existing DSME-built *Bhumibol Adulyadej*, which was commissioned at the start of 2019. Bangkok Dockyard are also reportedly pushing various derivatives of its licence-built Krabi (BAE Systems Batch 2 'River') class design, including extension of the existing 90m hull to as much as 111m to accommodate various additional weapons options.

Vietnam: Largely reliant on Russian weaponry, the Vietnam People's Navy (VPN) has shown signs of attempting to diversify its supplier base over the last year. Vietnam is reportedly in advanced discussions to acquire BrahMos surface-to-surface missiles, which – although the product of an Indo-Russian joint venture – would mark a further stage of an evolving relationship with the Indian defence sector. The rumoured deal, which would be the second in the region after the Philippines' previous acquisition of BrahMos, may be associated with the planned gift of the Indian Navy *Khukri* class corvette, *Kirpan*, to the VPN. India has previously supplied patrol vessels to Vietnam's Boarder Guard. Vietnam also hopes to obtain further decommissioned *Po Hang* class corvettes from South Korea, whilst its coast guard could benefit from the transfer of a third former American *Hamilton* (WHEC-715) class high endurance cutter in coming months.[21]

Notes

1. The *National Security Strategy of Japan*, *National Defense Strategy* and *Defense Build-up Program* – all Tokyo: Government of Japan, 2022 – can be readily accessed by searching the web.

2. Commentators differ as to the extent the new strategic documents mark a fundamental change in Japan's defence strategy. Kana Inagaki's 'Japan scraps pacifist post-war defence strategy to counter China threat' for the *Financial Times* website – ft.com – on 16 December 2022 represents one stance. The article 'More of the Same or Different? Japan's New Security and Defense Policy' by Guibourg Delamotte and Hideo Suzuki posted to *The Diplomat* website – thediplomat.com – on 17 February 2023 provides a more nuanced view.

3. See *National Defence: Defence Strategic Review 2023* (Canberra: Commonwealth of Australia, 2023). It can be accessed at: defence.gov.au/about/reviews-inquiries/defence-strategic-review. An excellent summary of its principle conclusions can be found in an article 'Australia's 2023 Defence Strategic Review' posted to the *International Institute for Strategic Studies* (IISS) website; iiss.org

4. Many details of the RAN's future journey towards nuclear-powered submarine are provided in a document entitled *The AUKUS Nuclear-Powered Submarine Pathway: A Partnership for the Future* published jointly by the three partner governments. It can be found, inter alia, at: defence.gov.au/about/taskforces/aukus

5. See *Department of Defence's Procurement of Hunter Class Frigates* (Canberra: Australian National Audit Office, 2023). The report, Auditor-General Report No. 21 of 2022–3, was published to the audit office's website – anao.gov.au – on 10 May 2023. It contains much detail on the decisions surrounding the selection of the Type 26 design and the programme's progress to date.

6. The problems were first reported in an article by Andrew Greene, 'Federal government concerned as problems emerge with $4 billion offshore patrol vessel project' posted to the *ABC News* site – abc.net.au/news – on 9 October 2022.

7. See Mark F. Cancian, Matthew Cancian and Eric Heginbotham, *The First Battle of the Next War: Wargaming a Chinese Invasion of Taiwan* (Washington: CSIS, 2023) available at the think tank's website – csis.org

8. This development was assessed by Luke Caggiano in 'China Deploys New Submarine-Launched Ballistic Missiles' posted to the Arms Control Association site – armscontrol.org – in May 2023.

9. The annual report *Military and Security Developments Involving the People's Republic of China* (Washington DC, US Department of Defense, 2022) includes regular updates of PLAN force development.

10. See Matthew P. Funaiole, Brian Hart, Joseph S. Bermudez Jr., Jennifer Jun, and Samantha Lu, 'Changxing Island: The Epicenter of China's Naval Modernization' posted to the CSIS's *ChinaPower* project site – chinapower.csis.org – on 18 May 2023.

11. The previous target for submarine numbers was sixteen; a figure derived from the need to maintain two submarines to cover each of the La Pérouse, Tsugaru, and Tsushima Straits during the Cold War era whilst factoring in the demands of replenishment, maintenance and training. The increase seemingly reflected the heightened threat from China and North Korea and a greater focus on intelligence-gathering missions. An interesting overview of the development of the JMSDF's submarine strategy is provided by Tanida Kuniichi, 'Lack of Personnel Threatens to Torpedo Japan's Reiwa-Era Submarine Strategy' posted to the nippon.com website – nippon.com/en – on 3 April 2023.

12. The Republic of Korea Navy still hopes to procure an even larger aircraft carrier in due course that will be capable of operating a navalised KF-21N variant of the KAI KF-21 Boramae strike fighter. This ambition is only likely to be achieved in the longer term. For further detail see, Jamie Chang, 'South Korea Eyeing Larger Aircraft Carrier For Its CVX Program' posted to the *Naval News* website – navalnews.com – on 12 March 2023. *Naval News* is an excellent source of news on South Korean naval developments, as well as on other navies around the world.

13. See 'S. Korea's military to focus on "overwhelming" capabilities against N. Korean nuke, missile threats' posted to the *Korea Times* website – koreatimes.co.kr – on 28 December 2022,

14. DSME was renamed Hanwha Ocean in May 2023 after its acquisition by South Korea's Hanwha Group, a large business conglomerate, was confirmed. A previously planned merger with HHI had been prevented on competition grounds.

15. Last year's fleet summary did not take account of the deliveries of the third and fourth *Daegu* class frigates – respectively *Seoul* and *Donghae* – during the second half of 2021.

16. Confusingly, the FFX Batch III was previously known as the (new) *Ulsan* class.

17. See *Defence Assessment 2021: A Rough Sea Can Still Be Navigated* (Wellington: New Zealand Ministry of Defence, 2021).

18. The new frigates were reported by Anton Sokolin, 'North Korea plans to build two new naval frigates by 2026, IMO data shows' posted to the *NK News* site – nknews.org – on 27 June 2023.

19. A number of sources suggest only four ships will be equipped with Spike-NLOS.

20. For further information, see Hans Uwe Mergener, 'Second Type 218SG Submarine Prepared for Transit to Singapore' posted to the *European Security & Defence* website – euro-sd.com – on 2 June 2023.

21. A detailed review of the VPN by Mrityunjoy Mazumdar was published in *Seaforth World Naval Review 2023*.

2.3 REGIONAL REVIEW

Author:
Conrad Waters

THE INDIAN OCEAN AND AFRICA

On 2 September 2022, Indian Prime Minister Narendra Modi commissioned *Vikrant*, the country's first indigenously-built aircraft carrier, at the Cochin Shipyard Ltd (CSL). Laid down in February 2009 and launched in August 2013, the new warship's delivery has been repeatedly delayed. Her cost – reportedly some INR 230bn (c. US$2.8bn) – has also turned out to be much greater than first envisaged. Nevertheless, the carrier's completion marks a major technical achievement for India's naval sector. In the words of the premier, 'INS *Vikrant* is not just a warship. It is a testament to the hard work, talent, influence and commitment of 21st century India.'[1] Importantly, her arrival also strengthens the Indian Navy's ability to project power across the vast Indian Ocean region, an area of ever-increasing interest to China's People's Liberation Army Navy (PLAN). Prime Minister Modi's remarks acknowledged the changing strategic situation. Accepting that security concerns in the Indian Ocean had often been ignored in the past, he confirmed that the area is now a major defence priority.

Vikrant's commissioning was accompanied by the unveiling of a new Indian Navy ensign that dispenses with the longstanding Cross of Saint George. The aim is to disassociate it from its British Royal Navy roots and the Indian colonial era. Perhaps revealing a degree of post-colonial insecurity, Premier Modi noted that the new ensign allowed the Indian Navy to dispense with '… the identity of slavery …' that had previously remained on its flag. Instead, he dedicated the new ensign to Chhatrapati Shivaji Maharaj, the seventeenth century founder of the Maratha Empire whose historical legacy is presumably better aligned with the prime minister's vision of Hindu nationalism.[2]

More significantly, the ship's commissioning allowed the assembled dignitaries to extoll the merits of the policy of a self-reliant India (*Atmanirbhar Bharat*) that is an important tenet of the Modi administration. As part of this drive, the Indian Navy has pledged to become self-sufficient by 2047, the 100th anniversary of Indian independence. This commitment seems to be a double-edged sword. Positively, it has served to promote the expansion of an indigenous maritime sector capable of delivering complex warships, *Vikrant* being a prime example. Investment to support self-sufficiency has also meant that the performance of Indian shipbuilders in meeting cost and timescale requirements has improved, albeit from the dismal to the merely disappointing. As such, there is some way to go before local yards can aspire to international best practice. Equally, India's home-grown naval technology still lags behind that produced by many rivals. Its most sophisticated systems – such as the MF-STAR radars and Barak 8 missiles found aboard *Vikrant* and the latest surface combatants – remain reliant on overseas technology. At present, it seems difficult for the navy to maintain its current progress if this input is dispensed with.

Although the acquisition of 'high end' capabilities such as *Vikrant* has dominated regional news flow, the ongoing fight against lower-level threats such as drug trafficking, illegal fishing and piracy continues to have a major day-to-day impact on operational naval activities across the broad Indian Ocean and African region. The Gulf of Guinea off Africa's west coast has become a focal point of piracy in the last few years, supplanting the previous hotspot off the Horn of Africa. However, 2022 brought a further welcome decline in reported incidents to a recent low of nineteen. This compares with thirty-five in 2021 and a peak of as many as eighty-four in 2020. The fall contributed to an overall reduction from 132 to 119 in incidents of piracy reported globally, the lowest recorded level for some decades. However, in a sign of the need for continued vigilance, there has been a surge in attacks at the other end of the region in the Singapore Straits. Here there were thirty-eight reported incidents in 2022 compared with just three five years previously.[3]

The overall progress in the fight against piracy can be attributed to a number of factors. Notably, the International Chamber of Commerce's International Maritime Bureau (IMB) has commended efforts made by coastal authorities along the Gulf of Guinea for their concerted efforts in tackling this regional scourge. These have encompassed greater collaboration on a regional and international level, including ongoing 'capacity-building' initiatives sponsored by, for example, the US Navy and Coast Guard. Equally, it seems that there has been greater willingness to invest in surveillance, communications and patrol capabilities as the financial importance of the 'blue economy' has been increasingly recognised.

African navies have been steadily improving their ability to perform constabulary activities in protection of their maritime interests over the past decade. This is due both to acquisition of purpose-built patrol assets and also to 'capacity-building' support from larger fleets. One consequence has been a welcome reduction in piracy across the region. This photograph shows the Namibian Navy's offshore patrol vessel *Elephant* at the Brazilian Navy's bicentennial review in September 2022. Constructed by China's Wuhan Shipyard and commissioned in September 2012, *Elephant*'s efficiency has benefited from an extensive training of Namibian Navy personnel carried out by Brazil. *(Brazilian Navy)*

Table 2.3.1: FLEET STRENGTHS IN THE INDIAN OCEAN, AFRICA AND THE MIDDLE EAST – LARGER NAVIES (MID 2023)

COUNTRY	ALGERIA	EGYPT	INDIA	IRAN	ISRAEL	PAKISTAN	SAUDI ARABIA	SOUTH AFRICA
Aircraft Carrier (CV)	–	–	2	–	–	–	–	–
Strategic Missile Submarine (SSBN)	-	-	1	–	–	–	–	–
Attack Submarine (SSN/SSGN)	–	–	–	–	–	–	–	–
Patrol Submarine (SSK/SS)	6	8	16	4	5	5	–	3
Fleet Escort (DDG/FFG)	2	14	23	–	–	9	10	4
Patrol Escort/Corvette (FFG/FSG/FS)	11	3	11	8	6	2	4	–
Missile Armed Attack Craft (PGG/PTG)	c. 12	c. 30	7	c. 25	8	10	9	1
Mine Countermeasures Vessel (MCMV)	3	c. 14	–	1	–	5	3	2
Major Amphibious (LPD)	1	2	1	–	–	–	–	–

Notes:

1 Algerian fast attack craft and Egyptian fast attack craft and mine-countermeasures numbers approximate.

2 Iranian fleet numbers exclude large numbers of indigenously-built midget and coastal submarines, as well as numerous additional missile-armed patrol boats operated both by the Iranian Navy and Revolutionary Guard.

3 The South African attack craft and mine countermeasures vessels serve in patrol vessel roles. Not all the latter are operational.

INDIA

India's defence budget for 2023/24 has been set at INR 5.94 trillion (c. US$72bn); a nominal 13 percent increase on last year's initial allocations.[4] Although an impressive figure, around a quarter of this continues to be swallowed up by pensions and non-military allocations, with less than a third of the total allocated to capital expenditure when salaries and other revenue costs are taken into account. A noteworthy feature of the latest figures is an increase in the navy's INR 851bn (c. US$10.5bn) share of the core Defence Services budget – largely the non-pensions element of defence spending – to 20 percent, an all-time high. This possibly reflects India's perception of an increasing threat to security in its maritime domain, as reflected in Prime Minister Modi's remarks at *Vikrant*'s commissioning. However, the navy's modernisation budget is only destined to expand at a pedestrian six percent, a figure that remains insufficient to fund planned procurement. As such, the recent picture of a fleet that is able to replace life-expired warships but which is struggling to achieve meaningful expansion seems set to continue for the time being. This is reflected in Table 2.3.2 summarising current fleet strength and in the analysis of major warship categories that follows.

Aircraft Carriers and Major Amphibious Ships: *Vikrant*'s commissioning has been followed by ongoing trials as the new carrier works up to operational status. The first landings of jet aircraft – by, initially, a naval prototype of the Indian Tejas light fighter and, then, a MiG 29K – were completed in February 2023. Subsequently, the return of the navy's other carrier, *Vikramaditya*, from an 18-month refit allowed multi-carrier operations to be conducted for the first time since the former *Viraat* (ex HMS *Hermes*) was withdrawn from active service in 2016. The two-carrier battle group performed a range of training exercises in the Arabian Sea involving upwards of thirty-five aircraft of various types in early June 2023. In normal service, however, it is believed that one of the carriers will be allocated to each of India's main Western and Eastern Commands, thereby allowing organic naval power to be deployed on both sides of the sub-continent.

The navy's request for information for four amphibious assault ship-like LPDs that was released in August 2021 has yet to reach a tangible conclusion. Current speculation is that it will be 2025 at the earliest before a request for proposals is issued and a contract signed. The French *Mistral* and Spanish *Juan Carlos I* designs were front runners in a previous, ultimately abortive tender process that commenced as long ago as 2011. In line with the *Atmanirbhar Bharat* philosophy, the chosen design will be constructed by an Indian shipyard, with deliveries likely to commence in the early 2030s.

Major Surface Combatants: The last 12 months have seen the commissioning of the second Project 15B *Visakhapatnam* class destroyer, *Mormugao*, whilst the third member of the class, *Imphal*, has commenced sea trials.[5] It seems likely that the remaining members of the elderly Project 61E *Rajput* class will be withdrawn as Project 15B deliveries are completed, leaving the destroyer force standing at ten units. Details are starting to emerge of a follow-on, Project 18 Next Generation Destroyer (NGD) that is currently at the preliminary design stage and which will likely start to enter service in the second half of the next decade. Speculation suggests that it will be a much larger vessel than the current destroyers, possibly due to

Table 2.3.2: INDIAN NAVY: PRINCIPAL UNITS AS AT MID 2023

TYPE	CLASS	NUMBER	TONNAGE	DIMENSIONS	PROPULSION	CREW	DATE
Aircraft Carriers							
Aircraft Carrier (CV)	**VIKRANT**	1	45,000 tonnes	263m x 62m x 9m	COGAG, 28 knots	1,650	2022
Aircraft Carrier (CV)	Project 1143.4 **VIKRAMADITYA** (KIEV)	1	45,000 tonnes	283m x 60m x 10m	Steam, 30 knots	1,600	1987
Principal Surface Escorts							
Destroyer – DDG	Project 15B **VISAKHAPATNAM**	2	7,400 tonnes	163m x 17m x 7m	COGAG, 30+ knots	300	2021
Destroyer – DDG	Project 15A **KOLKATA**	3	7,400 tonnes	163m x 17m x 7m	COGAG, 30+knots	330	2014
Destroyer – DDG	Project 15 **DELHI**	3	6,700 tonnes	163m x 17m x 7m	COGAG, 32 knots	350	1997
Destroyer – DDG	Project 61 ME **RAJPUT** ('Kashin')	3	5,000 tonnes	147m x 16m x 5m	COGAG, 35 knots	320	1980
Frigate – FFG	Project 17 **SHIVALIK**	3	6,200 tonnes	143m x 17m x 5m	CODOG, 30 knots	265	2010
Frigate – FFG	Project 11356 **TALWAR**	6	4,000 tonnes	125m x 15m x 5m	COGAG, 30 knots	180	2003
Frigate – FFG	Project 16A **BRAHMAPUTRA**	3	4,000 tonnes	127m x 15m x 5m	Steam, 30 knots	350	2000
Corvette – FSG	Project 28 **KAMORTA**	4	3,400 tonnes	109m x 13m x 4m	Diesel, 25 knots	195	2014
Corvette – FSG	Project 25A **KORA**	4	1,400 tonnes	91m x 11m x 5m	Diesel, 25 knots	125	1998
Corvette – FSG	Project 25 **KHUKRI**	3	1,400 tonnes	91m x 11m x 5m	Diesel, 25 knots	110	1989
Submarines							
Submarine – SSBN	**ARIHANT**	1	7,500+ tonnes	112m x 11m x 10m	Nuclear, 25+ knots	100	2016
Submarine – SSK	Project 75 **KALVARI** ('Scorpène')	5	1,800 tonnes	68m x 6m x 6m	Diesel-electric, 20 knots	45	2017
Submarine – SSK	Project 877 EKM **SINDHUGHOSH** ('Kilo')	7	3,000 tonnes	73m x 10m x 7m	Diesel-electric, 17 knots	55	1986
Submarine – SSK	**SHISHUMAR** (Type 209)	4	1,900 tonnes	64m x 7m x 6m	Diesel-electric, 22 knots	40	1986
Major Amphibious Units							
Landing Platform Dock – LPD	**JALASHWA** (AUSTIN)	1	17,000 tonnes	173m x 26/30m x 7m	Steam, 21 knots	405	1971

the influence of the PLAN's Type 055 'Renhai' class.

Indigenous frigate construction continues to be dominated by the Project 17A *Nilgiri* class. Four are being constructed by Mazagon Dock Shipbuilders Ltd (MDSL) of Mumbai and three by Garden Reach Shipbuilders & Engineers (GRSE) of Kolkata under contracts signed in 2015. Deliveries were expected to commence in 2022 and be completed in 2025. However, construction has been badly delayed and it will be the middle of the decade at the earliest before the class starts to enter operational service. *Dunagiri* – the fourth of the seven ships and GRSE's second unit – was launched on 15 July 2022. Her sister *Taragiri* – MDSL's third ship – followed on 11 September. Displacing around 6,700 tonnes at full load, the Project 17A frigates share much equipment with the Project 15A and Project 15B destroyers, including their MF-STAR radar and Barak 8 missiles. It seems likely that repeat orders for either further Project 17As or a slightly revised Project 17B variant will be placed within the next couple of years to maintain production of complex warships at India's main two naval shipyards.

The Indian Navy is also awaiting delivery of a third batch of Project 11356 *Talwar* class frigates. Two of these are being completed by Yantar in Kaliningrad using hulls originally destined for the Russian Navy and another pair under licence by Goa Shipyard Ltd (GSL) in India. Construction has been impacted by the Russo-Ukrainian war. Although it has been reported that delivery of the first vessel, the Russian-built *Tushil*, will be achieved by the end of 2023, this must be regarded with a considerable degree of scepticism.

Smaller Surface Combatants: The construction of major surface warships continues to be supplemented by a number of programmes for smaller combatants and second-line vessels. The last year has seen progress with the contracts for sixteen Anti-Submarine Warfare Shallow Water Craft (ASW-SWC), which are optimised for littoral operations. Eight of these vessels were ordered from each of GRSE and CSL in April 2019 at a unit cost approaching US$100m and are being built to their own distinct designs. GRSE has sub-contracted four of its ships to Larsen & Toubro's (L&T's) Kattupalli shipyard, which carried out the launch of *Arnala* – the first vessel to hit the water – on 20 December 2022. A second ship, named *Androth*, was launched at GRSE in March 2023, followed by L&T's

The Indian Navy's new indigenous aircraft carrier *Vikrant* (foreground) sails in company with the former Soviet Project 1143.4 carrier *Vikramaditya* (formerly *Admiral Gorshkov*) in June 2023. *Vikrant*'s arrival gives India the option of conducting multi-carrier operations for the first time since 2016. *(Indian Navy)*

Built by Larsen & Toubro at Kattupalli, Chennai under a sub-contract from Kolkata's GRSE, *Arnala* was the first of eight anti-submarine warfare shallow water craft ordered for the Indian Navy from GRSE in April 2019 to be launched after a ceremony held on 20 December 2022. Displacing c. 900 tonnes, she has a length of 77.6m and is capable of a maximum speed of 25 knots. Another eight vessels with a similar function but different design are being completed by Cochin Shipyard Ltd. *(Indian Navy)*

Anjadip on 13 June 2023. Progress at CSL has been less swift due to delays in the delivery of propulsion equipment. However, launch of the first pair of their vessels is expected before the end of 2023.

Despite CSL's problems with ASW-SWC production, it was announced in March 2023 that it had been awarded an INR 98bn (c. US$ 1.2bn) contract to build six Next Generation Missile Vessels. Optimised for anti-surface warfare, these ships will replace the remaining Project 1241.RE *Veer* class fast attack craft but will be larger vessels with a displacement in the region of 2,500 tonnes. Deliveries are anticipated to commence in March 2027. The Indian Navy also continues to develop its plans for eight NGC Next Generation Corvettes, which will ultimately replace the existing *Khukri* and *Kora* classes.

The order for the Next Generation Missile Vessels was announced alongside the award of contracts to GRSE and GSL to build a total of eleven Next Generation Offshore Patrol Vessels. These effectively replace the previous Project 21 *Shachi* class patrol vessel programme with the former Pipavav Shipyard, which was cancelled for non-performance with contractual obligations after two of the ships had been launched. The new contract will see GRSE complete four ships and GSL seven, each to their own design. The contracts were awarded under an increasingly common process in India by which contracts have been allocated to both the lowest (L1) and second lowest (L2) bidders for warship construction. Deliveries are expected to begin in late 2026 and conclude by the end of the decade. Although primarily intended for constabulary duties, the new ships will also be able to perform mine countermeasures operations through a modular payload of autonomous systems.

Submarines: Firm news on India's top-secret strategic submarine programme continues to be largely elusive. In an exception to this general rule, the Indian Ministry of Defence announced that the lead *Arihant* class boat had carried out a successful launch of a ballistic missile in the Bay of Bengal on 14 October 2022 as part of an ongoing process to validate crew and weapon system proficiency. The delivery of *Arighat*, the second, improved member of the class had yet to be confirmed as of mid-2023 but this is likely to be imminent.

Conventional submarine numbers have remained unchanged at sixteen boats, with the

The Indian Navy are now close to completing their six 'Scorpène' type *Kalvari* class submarines after *Vagsheer* – the final boat – commenced sea trials from MDSL at Mumbai on 18 May 2023. In spite of the progress achieved with this programme, delays to ordering the follow-on, Project 75I class mean that Indian Navy submarine numbers will remain under pressure for the foreseeable future. *(Indian Navy)*

retirement of the Project 877EKM *Sindhugosh* class *Sindhudhvaj* in July 2022 being balanced by the commissioning of the fifth 'Scorpène' type *Kalvari* class *Vagir* on 23 January 2023. The sixth and final boat, *Vagsheer*, commenced sea trials from MDSL on 18 May 2023 and is scheduled for delivery in 2024, bringing the programme to a close. Tenders for the next, Project 75I, programme close in August 2023, with Germany's tkMS (in partnership with MDSL) and Spain's Navantia (teamed with L&T) believed to be the only shipyards likely to submit proposals. Given that a number of both the remaining seven *Sindhugosh* and the four *Shishumar* (Type 209) class submarines are fast approaching their fortieth birthdays, it seems inevitable that the submarine flotilla will decline before the new class is delivered.

OTHER INDIAN OCEAN NAVIES

Bangladesh: On 23 March 2023, Bangladesh's Prime Minister Sheikh Hasina officially inaugurated the country's first submarine base, which was named in her honour. The new facility is located at Cox's Bazar, close to the border with Myanmar. It was completed under a contract with China that was signed in September 2019, with construction commencing in February 2021. It will be the home for the country's two Type 035G 'Ming' class submarines that were previously delivered second-hand after completing PLAN service, both being commissioned in 2017.

The Bangladesh Navy has benefitted from ongoing modernisation under the lengthy Hasina administration, acquiring frigates, corvettes, patrol vessels and maritime patrol aircraft in addition to its submarines as part of the 'Forces Goal 2030' military renewal programme first launched in 2009. However, the pace of acquisitions has slackened in recent years, possibly due to a desire to shift from overseas purchases of new and second-hand equipment to a greater focus on indigenous construction. Current naval shipbuilding remains dominated by the contract for a second batch of 52m *Padma* class patrol vessels that were contracted from the state-owned Khulna Shipyard in mid-2019. Three of these are now in the fitting-out stage after the launch of *Shaheed Farid* and *Shaheed Mohibullah* in mid-2022. The Khulna facility has also been contracted to supply a class of three 70m tank landing craft, which will be based on a Fincantieri Vard Marine 7 507 design. Longer-term plans to build a class of indigenous frigates at Chittagong Dry Dock Limited remained under discussion as of mid-2023.

Myanmar: The Myanmar Navy has completed a series of high-profile acquisitions that have included deliveries of its first, second-hand submarines from both India and China – not to mention the South Korean-built amphibious transport dock *Mottama* – in recent years. However, the traditional commissioning ceremonies for new vessels that typically accompany the annual navy day celebrations were more muted affairs in December 2022. The most significant new arrivals were two additional licence-built Israeli Super Dvora Mk 3 fast patrol boats, the fifth and sixth vessels of the type to enter Myanmar Navy service. Construction work continues on the fleet's new 135m frigate, the fourth of a series of progressively improved vessels built at the Myanmar Naval Dockyard south of Yangon (Rangoon). Satellite images have suggested that her launch has been imminent for some time now, although it is likely to be the second half of the decade before she is ready for operational service.

Pakistan: Modernisation of the Pakistan Navy's force of major surface combatants has continued to make progress over the past year. On 10 May 2023, a commissioning ceremony was held at the Hudong Zhonghua Shipbuilding facility at Shanghai for *Tippu Sultan* and *Shah Jahan*, the second pair of Type 054A/P *Tughril* class frigates that were ordered in 2018. Along with their two sisters and the older quartet of Type 22P *Zulfiqar* class vessels, they complete the 'high end' of Pakistan's surface fleet renewal around a homogenous flotilla of Chinese-built vessels. Their arrival paves the way for the disposal of *Tariq* (formerly HMS *Ambuscade*), the last of six Type 21 frigates that have formed the core of the surface fleet from the mid-1990s. *Almagir* – formerly the US Navy's *McInerney* (FFG-8) and the country's sole FFG-7 class frigate – also looks vulnerable to disposal in the interest of standardisation.

The second, middle-tier element of surface fleet renewal encompasses the acquisition of four Turkish-designed *Babur* class light frigates, which are essentially a variant of the 'Milgem' or 'Ada' class corvettes. Construction is being split between Istanbul Naval Shipyard (ISN) and Pakistan's Karachi Shipyard & Engineering Works (KSEW), with each yard assembling a pair of ships. ISN launched *Khaibar*, the second of its two units, on 25 November 2022 and is likely to deliver its first vessel, *Babur*, within the next 12 months. A stretched, *Jinnah* class variant is likely to succeed the class into production at KSWE in the medium term.

The third, 'low end' of the surface fleet is being provided by a series of Dutch Damen-designed patrol vessels, that are designated corvettes in Pakistan Navy service. Two OPV1900 *Yarmook* class variants were commissioned in 2020. They are now being followed by two larger OPV2600 types that will be larger and, probably, better armed. Like their predecessors, the two vessels are being built at Damen's yard in Galati, Romania, where a keel-laying ceremony for the first was held in October 2022. Pakistan also received two former Dutch 'Tripartite' minehunters in late 2022, bringing its inventory to five vessels.

In addition to large surface vessels, the Pakistan Navy are also expanding their littoral security forces through licensed construction of a new series of high-speed coastal gunboats at KSEW. Interestingly, given reliance on China for much new equipment, the navy has turned to American company Swiftships to assist the design and construction of the new 39m vessels, which will have a top speed of 33 knots and a main armament of a Turkish Aselsan stabilised 30mm mounting. Fabrication of the lead ship in the programme commenced at KSEW in October 2022 and was followed by a keel-laying ceremony on 27 January 2023. Completion is expected early in 2024 and up to twenty of the class may eventually be acquired.

There has also been news on renewal of Pakistan's submarine flotilla. Here, modernisation of the three Agosta 90B type submarines under the supervision of Turkey's STM has passed the halfway mark with the completion of work on *Khalid*, the second boat to pass through the programme. Work also continues on the eight *Hangor* class submarines that are derived from China's PLAN's Type 039A design and on which assembly is being shared between Chinese yards and KSEW. The latter held a ceremony in December 2022 to mark initial steel-cutting for the second of its four boats. Keel-laying for its first boat – to be named *Tasnim* – that had commenced construction a year previously also took place at the same event. The overall submarine programme is progressing more slowly than expected, possibly because of restrictions on the export of German MTU diesel engines that were to form the class's main propulsion. It seems that the

Pakistan Navy has agreed to accept Chinese-built CHD620 diesels as a replacement for the original power plant, clearing the project's way ahead.[6]

Sri Lanka: Sri Lanka's economic woes have not prevented it taking delivery of *Vijayabahu* – the former US Coast Guard high endurance cutter *Douglas Munro* (WHEC-724) – to increase its flotilla of large, ocean-going offshore patrol vessels to eight units. The cutter, the second member of the *Hamilton* (WHEC-715) class to be transferred to Sri Lanka, was handed over in October 2021 but needed to complete repair, maintenance and crew training before beginning the lengthy journey to her new home from Seattle, WA in September 2022. The ship was formally commissioned at a ceremony held at Colombo on 22 November that year. Although Sri Lanka has made considerable strides re-orientating its navy towards seagoing constabulary duties after the end of the country's lengthy civil war, further progress seems unlikely until the country's financial heath improves.

Slow delivery of the three 750-tonne Damen Stan Patrol 6211 inshore patrol vessels being built under Project Biro means that the South African Navy's patrol forces have been temporarily reduced to just two vessels following the withdrawal of the re-roled 'Warrior' fast attack craft *Isaac Dyobha* in 2022. This photograph shows the veteran warship during the course of exercises with the British Royal Navy in August 2015. *(Crown Copyright 2015)*

AFRICAN NAVIES

News from **South Africa** – the continent's most significant naval power south of the Sahara – has been dominated by the country's continued close ties to Russia despite the Ukraine war. In December 2022, the Russian cargo vessel *Lady R*, which is subject to Western sanctions, made a secretive stopover at South Africa's Simon's Town Naval Base. Subsequent speculation, most notably by the United States' ambassador to the country, suggested that the ship's visit was associated with the supply of South African munitions to aid Russia's war. The *Lady R* incident was later followed by extensive exercises between the South African Navy and Russian and Chinese warships off the country's eastern coast in February 2023 that reinforced both domestic and international criticism of the South African government's stance.

The South African Navy itself continues to suffer from poor availability of its major warships, with insufficient funding for regular refits leaving the majority of the fleet's frigates and submarines unable to deploy. ZAR 1.4bn (c. US$75m) has recently been made available to fund the refurbishment of one frigate and one submarine during 2023–4 but this is only around a third of the sum necessary to address the total refit backlog.[7] There is more bad news with respect to new vessels. Construction delays mean that *King Sekhukhune I* currently remains the only one of the three 750-tonne Damen Stan Patrol 6211 inshore patrol vessels being built under Project Biro to have entered service. The second unit should be delivered before the end of 2023 but the third will not commission until early 2026, around three years later than originally envisaged. It remains unclear at the current time whether an option for a fourth vessel will be exercised. Work has also been delayed on a new hydrographic survey vessel, which will be named SAS *Nelson Mandela*. The original date set for her completion was November 2022 but it now seems that it will be 2025 before she can be handed over.

Procurement in the rest of Sub-Saharan Africa continues to be dominated by the acquisition of patrol vessels of varying levels of sophistication intended for territorial and Exclusive Economic Zone (EEZ) constabulary missions. Typical of these vessels is the **Cote d'Ivoire's** new patrol vessel *Esperance*, the first of two Israel Shipyards OPV-45 vessels ordered in 2020. Delivered early in 2023, she is relatively lightly armed with a 30mm main gun but has a useful endurance of around 3,000 nautical miles at an economical speed. However, a relatively recent trend is the procurement of increasingly sophisticated vessels, of which **Senegal's** three French Piriou-built OPV 58S patrol vessels are a good example. Displacing c. 600 tonnes, they are armed with a 76mm main gun and surface-to-air and surface-to-surface guided missiles. The lead vessel, named *Walo*, was delivered on 2 June 2023. Her sisters *Niani* and *Cayor* were launched, respectively, in September 2022 and May 2023. Both will be in service by mid-2024.

Another regional navy steadily expanding its capabilities is **Angola.** Previously focused on relatively inexpensive patrol boats, the country has signed a €1bn (c. US$1.1bn) contract with Abu Dhabi Ship Building (ADSB) to acquire three advanced BR71 Mk II corvettes that are derived from the CMN *Baynunah* class design. The deal marks a major step forward for the United Arab Emirates-based shipyard, being its largest export contract to date. The award is in line with the increasing presence of new competitors into the African naval market, a development best illustrated by **Nigeria's** growing partnership with Turkish industry to support its own naval renewal. September 2022 saw keel-laying ceremonies held at Dearsan Shipyard in Istanbul for two 1,100-tonne OPV-76 patrol vessels under a contract announced in October the previous year. Subsequently, in June 2023, Dearsan announced that it had concluded further contracts with Nigeria encompassing refurbishment of the veteran MEKO 360 frigate *Aradu* and the supply of a 400-tonne *Tuzla* class patrol ships. However, Nigeria also continues to maintain links with existing suppliers, ordering additional patrol boats from France's Ocea – a long-term partner – over the past 12 months.

In North Africa, **Egypt** continues to set the pace of naval acquisitions, taking delivery of several sophisticated warships during the last year. The most significant arrivals have been the first two of a quartet of MEKO A-200 EN frigates ordered from Germany's tkMS in September 2018. The lead ship, named *Al Aziz*, was handed over at Kiel on 14 October 2022. The event was subsequently followed by delivery of the second member of the class, *Al Qahhar*, in May 2023, with a third German-built unit expected to follow before the end of 2023. The fourth vessel is being assembled in Egypt at Alexandria Shipyard, which has previously built French Naval Group-designed 'Gowind' type corvettes. *El Moez* – the second locally-built Egyptian 'Gowind' and third of the overall series – entered operational service in the past year. Delivery of a fourth and final vessel is believed to be imminent.

Completion of current acquisitions will leave Egypt with a flotilla of eleven modern major surface combatants – two Italian and one French FREMM frigates, four German MEKO A-200 EN frigates and four French 'Gowind' corvettes – that are as notable for their disparate sources of supply as the capabilities that they bring. Nine older ships – four former US Navy FFG-7 and *Knox* class frigates, two Spanish *Descubierta* class corvettes and a single South Korean *Po Hang* type corvette – comprise the balance of the force. The arrival of new ships should allow retirement of some of the fleet's older vessels, with two Chinese-built Type 053H frigates reportedly already decommissioned. However, the navy continues to acquire vessels from varied sources,

Senegal's three French Piriou-built OPV 58S patrol vessels are a good example of the increasing levels of sophistication and combat capability being introduced into some current African navies. This picture shows *Walo*, the first of the class, which was delivered early in June 2023. *(Bruno Huriet)*

The Egyptian Navy has undergone a significant qualitative and quantitative expansion in recent years but the diverse origins of the ships that it now operates gives rise to questions over its longer-term efficiency. This photograph shows the Italian-built FEMM Frigate *Al Galala* and the French-built amphibious assault ship *Gamel Abdel Nasser* exercising with the US Navy destroyer *Delbert D. Black* (DDG-119) in August 2022. *(US Navy)*

with its patrol forces recently being supplemented by three retired US Navy *Cyclone* (PC-1) class patrol boats that were handed over at Alexandria in March 2023. Whilst, therefore, Egypt has a large and seemingly impressive fleet that also includes eight submarines and two amphibious assault ships, its operational effectiveness must be questionable.

The same concerns hold good for **Algeria's** navy, which has also prioritised security of supply through the diversification of its equipment over homogeneity. Although the pace of warship deliveries has eased in recent years, the last 12 months have seen the arrival of a third *El Kasseh* (improved *Lerici*) class minehunter from Italy and an initial Type 056 corvette from China in a sign that this policy is likely to continue. The new corvette – named *El Moutassadi* – arrived in Algerian waters in early February 2023 and could be followed by as many as five additional vessels.

MIDDLE EASTERN NAVIES

The growing competence of naval shipyards in the Middle East was further demonstrated on 28 December 2022 when ADSB held a first steel-cutting ceremony for the lead ship in the **United Arab Emirates'** 'Falaj 3' offshore patrol vessel programme. The quartet of new vessels – corvettes in all but name – is being built with design support from ST Engineering and reportedly draws heavily on the Republic of Singapore Navy's former *Fearless* class. The new 60m, 650-tonne vessels will be able to achieve a maximum speed of 26 knots from four diesel engines and are optimised to reduce crewing requirements. Despite the growing role of local industry, the Emirates continue to work closely with France for their naval requirements and will shortly take delivery of two 'Gowind' type corvettes from Naval Group. The initial unit, named *Bani Yas*, commenced sea trials from Lorient in March 2023. The two ships, which are generally similar to the Egyptian 'Gowinds' previously mentioned, will be the largest vessels in the United Arab Emirates Navy when completed.

Qatar is now close to completing its own modernisation and expansion programme. Fincantieri has now completed deliveries of the four *Al Zubarah* class air-defence 'corvettes' and two *Musherib* class 'offshore patrol vessels' ordered under the construction programme first agreed in June 2016. The corvette *Semaisma* was the last of these vessels to be delivered when she was handed over at the company's Muggiano yard near La Spezia on 16 May 2023. Fincantieri has still to finish work on *Al Fulk*, the heavily-armed amphibious transport dock that will complete the seven-ship, €4bn (c. US$4.4bn) order. The vessel was launched at Palermo on 24 January 2023 and should be delivered during 2024.

A photograph of *Al Emarat*, the second of two 'Gowind' type corvettes being built by France's Naval Group for the United Arab Emirates Navy, fitting out at Lorient in January 2023. Although the navy continues to order warships overseas, the capabilities of its indigenous shipbuilding sector are also expanding. *(Bruno Huriet)*

Saudi Arabia is also making progress with fleet renewal under the Saudi Naval Expansion Programme II (SNEP II). Work is now underway at Fincantieri's Marinette Marine yard in Wisconsin on all four *Saud* class multi-mission surface combatants (MMSCs) that are based on the *Freedom* (LCS-1) class Littoral Combat Ship variant. Trials of the first are expected to begin before the end of 2023. In a surprise development, it has been announced that the ships will be armed with MBDA's CAMM (Royal Navy Sea Ceptor) surface-to-air missile as their primary air-defence weapon, adding another navy to the missile's growing list of customers. The Royal Saudi Navy has already taken delivery of three of the five Navantia-built 'Avante 2000' *Al-Jubail* corvettes that also form part of the programme following a ceremony at the company's San Fernando yard in the Bay of Cádiz on 4 December 2022 to hand over *Hail*. Commissioning of the final two ships will take place in Saudi Arabia, presumably reflecting the greater level of indigenous industrial involvement in completing these vessels. Navantia has already signed a memorandum of understanding to supply further multi-mission combatants to the Royal Saudi Navy.

A major driver for the considerable naval investment being made by states bordering the Persian Gulf has been ongoing tension with **Iran,** which has been exacerbated by Yemen's lengthy civil war. However, in March 2023 discussions brokered by China saw Saudi Arabia – arguably Iran's main regional rival – re-establish diplomatic relations with the Tehran regime in a rapprochement that has considerable potential to ratchet down regional anxieties. The Iranian Navy's commander, Rear Admiral Shahram Irani, subsequently claimed in June 2023 that Iran and several Gulf countries plan to form a naval alliance to bolster maritime security; an assertion given some credibility by an earlier United Arab

Emirates' announcement that it is to withdraw from the US Navy-led Combined Maritime Forces security partnership. Whilst it is not inconceivable that a closer naval relationship will develop between Iran and its neighbours, it would be surprising if this were to overturn existing regional partnerships with the West.[8] In the meantime, the regular Iranian Navy and the parallel Iranian Revolutionary Guard Corps (IRGC) Naval Forces have continued their low-level harassment of shipping transiting the critical waterway.

Given Iran's nuclear ambitions remain unabated, the country continues to be regarded by **Israel** as its primary strategic threat. The need to upgrade its own nuclear forces may explain the continued delay in delivery of the Israeli Navy's submarine *Drakon*, the final boat in a second and improved three-strong batch of *Dolphin* class boats that have been built by tkMS in Kiel. There has been considerable speculation that *Drakon*'s design has been modified to accommodate vertical-launch tubes that would be capable of housing nuclear-tipped cruise or, even, ballistic missiles. Israel's other *Dolphin* class submarines are already equipped with a number of larger-diameter torpedo tubes for cruise missile launch but, if confirmed, the addition of a vertical launch system would presumably increase the design's second strike potential. Meanwhile, design work continues on the new tkMS *Dakar* class that will replace the initial trio of *Dolphin* class boats early in the next decade.

In the more immediate term, Israel has also been bringing into service its quartet of new 'Sa'ar 6' corvettes that were constructed in Germany but which have been outfitted by Israel Shipyards in Haifa. The 1,900-tonne corvettes are equipped with the same ELM-2248 MF-STAR multi-function radar and Barak 8 missiles found aboard the Indian Navy's Project 15A/B series of destroyers. They also carry, inter alia, a naval C-Dome variant of the famous Iron Dome air defence system. The new systems have been extensively tested as outfitting has been completed and reports from Israel suggest the new ships are starting to enter operational service. Israel Shipyards also expect to be prime contractor for a new class of smaller 'Reshef' class fast attack craft to replace the eight existing 'Sa'ar 4.5' vessels, which will reportedly be outfitted from modules built in the United States. The lead ship should be delivered by 2027 but the anticipated build contract had yet to be awarded as of mid-2023.

The fifth Saudi Arabian *Al-Jubail* class corvette *Unayzah* pictured shortly after launch from Navantia's San Fernando yard in the Bay of Cádiz. Recent reports suggest that her final outfitting and commissioning will take place in Saudi Arabia as part of increased local input in the final members of the class. *(Navantia)*

Notes

1. The premier's remarks were contained in an India Ministry of Defence press release, 'Prime Minister Shri Narendra Modi commissions India's first indigenous aircraft carrier INS Vikrant in Kochi' published on the date of the ship's launch.

2. The new Indian ensign comprises two main constituents overlaid on a white background. The national flag remains in the upper left canton whilst a blue, gold-bordered octagon – supposedly inspired by Shivaji's shield – has been added to its fly side. The octagon contains the national emblem – the Lion Capital of Ashoka – resting atop an anchor and superimposed on a shield. The Indian Navy's motto – *Sam No Varunah* (May the Lord of the Seas be favourable to us) – is inscribed below the shield. This is the second time the Indian Navy has attempted to dispense with the Cross of Saint George, a similar change in 2001 proving to be short-lived.

3. These figures are derived from periodic reports produced by the International Chamber of Commerce's (ICC's) International Maritime Bureau (IMB) and available at: icc-ccs.org/

4. As is frequently the case, the 2022/23 budget was subject to a mid-year uplift, in this case largely due to revisions to pension benefits. A full analysis of the 2023/24 budget is provided by Laxman K Behera in 'High on Revenue, Low on Capital: India's Defence Budget 2023-24' posted to the *Observer Research Foundation*'s orfonline.org website on 11 February 2023.

5. Chapter 3.2 contains a detailed description of the Project 15A and Project 15B series of destroyers.

6. As noted in Chapter 2.2, a similar problem has impacted the Royal Thai Navy's Chinese submarines. For further detail on Pakistan's submarine programmes, see 'The "Silent Service" is still the Future of Pakistan's Navy' posted to the *Quwa* website – quwa.org – on 8 January 2023.

7. See Guy Martin, 'SA Navy frigate and submarine refits less than half funded' posted to the *defenceWeb* news portal, defenceweb.co.za, on 23 May 2023. The *defenceWeb* site remains an excellent source of news on African naval developments.

8. A good assessment of the Iranian Navy announcement is provided by an article titled 'Iranian talk of new naval alliance puts focus on regional buy-in' posted to the *Amwaj Media* site – amwaj.media – on 6 June 2023.

2.4 REGIONAL REVIEW

Author:
Conrad Waters

EUROPE AND RUSSIA

On 29 October 2022, the Ukrainian Armed Forces launched a coordinated drone assault on naval shipping and facilities in Sevastopol, the Russian Navy's principal base in the Black Sea. The attack followed a period of relative naval inactivity in the Russo-Ukrainian conflict. The earlier destruction of the cruiser *Moskva* and the recapture of Snake Island had already demonstrated the growing effectiveness of Ukraine's anti-access/area-denial (A2/AD) bubble, changing the nature of Russia's naval deployments and essentially confining their fleet to long-distance strike and blockade roles. Details of the Sevastopol operation remain clouded by the fog of war. However, it seems that relatively small numbers of uncrewed surface and aerial vehicles were involved in a series of 'suicide' strikes. These likely caused only minor damage to warships and infrastructure.

On one level, therefore, the October attack's consequences were of limited significance. Arguably, it caused little beyond nuisance to Russian naval operations that had already been severely restricted by previous setbacks. Sevastopol's defences have since been strengthened and subsequent assaults by maritime drones, now lacking the element of surprise, have seemingly been more easily dealt with. Moreover, the October assault hardly represented the first time that unmanned vehicles had been used against naval vessels in the course of a conflict.

Irrespective of these qualifications, a number of naval analysts view the operation as being of historic significance.[1] Echoing previous surprise attacks such as the Japanese assault on Port Arthur in 1904 at the start of the Russo-Japanese War and the British 1940 airborne strike against the Italian fleet at Taranto, it highlighted the continued relevance of asymmetric warfare against a more powerful naval opponent in the modern era. It will undoubtedly have had a psychological effect on personnel who previously felt secure within the defences of their principal base. More importantly still, the attack vividly pointed the way to how developing technology – in this case possibly including the commercial Starlink communications network – could actualise the implementation of effective swarm attacks by unmanned aerial and marine vehicles against naval targets. Many believe that such tactics could have a defining impact on future naval conflicts.

Irrespective of one's views of the significance of the Sevastopol attack, it is clear that wider developments in drone technology comprise some of the most important factors influencing current naval force structures and warship design. To give one example, the British Royal Navy is already on course to abolish its traditional force of mine countermeasures vessels around the end of the current decade. They will be replaced by a new Mine Hunting Capability (MHC) built around maritime autonomous systems. In June 2023, its new mine-hunting 'mothership', RFA *Stirling Castle*, conducted inaugural operations with the motor boats *Apollo*, *Hydra* and *Hazard* in the waters off Portland as part of a programme of trials aimed at demonstrating how the craft could be controlled or remotely-piloted from the ship. Some have questioned this rapid shift to unmanned mine clearance technology as being precipitous. However, the encouraging results of previous trials in speeding and simplifying clearance operations have only tended to accelerate the current switch. Many other European leaders in the field of naval mine countermeasures are also adopting similar technologies; the Belgo-Dutch rMCM programme being a case in point.

Another indication of the current direction of travel was revealed with the publication in March 2023 of *Das Zielbild für die Marine ab 2035*; the German Navy's vision for its future in the period for 2035 and beyond.[2] A noteworthy feature of the new plan is the inclusion of large numbers of unmanned 'future surface combat systems', large unmanned underwater vehicles, and both land- and sea-based unmanned aerial vehicles in the future fleet structure. These will supplement the fleet's growing numbers of more conventional warships, submarines and aircraft. The vision makes it evident that expanded use of unmanned systems, alongside greater reliance on artificial intelligence, is critical to the navy's future plans. The overall approach has similarities to the US Navy's embryonic manned-unmanned teaming philosophy, with drones being used as sensors and weapon-carriers across all domains whilst acting in conjunction with their 'manned twins'. In essence, the German Navy is balancing another current trend – that towards bigger and more extensive manned units – by investment in potentially cheaper unmanned systems that will provide the necessary mass.

The British Royal Fleet Auxiliary's new mine countermeasures 'mothership' *Stirling Castle* seen training with the motor boats *Apollo*, *Hydra* and *Hazard* in Portland Harbour in June 2023 as part of a wider switch to the use of unmanned and autonomous MCM systems. Initial trials were focused on the ability of the mothership to deploy and recover the boats but the programme also aims to demonstrate how the craft can be controlled or remotely-piloted from the ship. *(Crown Copyright 2023)*

TABLE 2.4.1: FLEET STRENGTHS IN WESTERN EUROPE – LARGER NAVIES (MID 2023)

COUNTRY	FRANCE	GERMANY	GREECE	ITALY	NETHERLANDS	SPAIN	TURKEY	UK
Aircraft Carrier (CVN/CV)	1	–	–	1	–	–	–	2
Support/Helicopter Carrier (CVS/CVH)	–	–	–	1	–	–	–	–
Strategic Missile Submarine (SSBN)	4	–	–	–	–	–	–	4
Attack Submarine (SSN)	5	–	–	–	–	–	–	6
Patrol Submarine (SSK)	–	6	10[2]	8	4	2	12	–
Fleet Escort (DDG/FFG)	15	11	13[2]	17	6	11	16	17
Patrol Escort/Corvette (FFG/FSG/FS)	12	5	–	–	–	–	9	–
Missile Armed Attack Craft (PGG/PTG)	–	–	16	–	–	–	18	–
Mine Countermeasures Vessel (MCMV)	12	8[1]	3	10	5	6	11	9
Major Amphibious (LHD/LPD/LPH/LSD)	3	–	–	3	2[3]	3	1	5

Notes:

1 Two further units used as support vessels and two as recruitment platforms.

2 Headline figures overstate the actual position, as some old units are of doubtful operational status.

3 Also one joint support ship with amphibious capabilities.

MAJOR REGIONAL POWERS – FRANCE

The future trajectory of France's *Marine Nationale* has been set by the new *Loi de Programmation Militaire* 2024-2030 (LPM 2024-30), which is currently close to being approved by the French National Assembly.[3] Setting both the guidelines and budget for defence policy for the next seven years, its headline figures appear ambitious. Overall funding for the period is set at €413bn (c. US$460bn), around 40 percent more than the €295bn (c. US$330bn) allocated for the previous LPM 2019-25. Annual expenditure will grow from €43.9bn (c. US$50bn) in 2022 to €68.9bn (c. US$75bn) in 2030, with the NATO target of spending more than two percent of GDP on defence achieved from 2025 onwards. Despite this largesse – and as mentioned in this book's Introduction – the overall size and shape of the French Armed Forces will be little different than previously planned. This reflects a number of factors. They include the need to invest in new capabilities in the areas of cyber and drone defence, as well as undersea warfare; the need to rebuild depleted stocks of munitions; and the large sums required to realise previously planned programmes. The impact of inflation must also be taken into account. All-in-all, therefore, the LPM 2024-30 preserves previous naval force structure and procurement plans but provides for little in the way of new initiatives.

Table 2.4.2 summaries the French Navy's major units as of mid-2023, with commentary on major warship categories following:

Aircraft Carriers: Design development work continues on the *Porte-Avions de Nouvelle Génération* (PANG) prior to the planned start of construction at Chantiers de l'Atlantique in Saint-Nazaire at the end of 2025 or the beginning of 2026. Around €5bn is allocated for the new carrier's assembly in the LPM 2024-30. However, that much again will be required before the as yet unnamed ship begins sea trials around the end of 2036 prior to replacing the existing *Charles de Gaulle* two years later. The question of acquiring a second aircraft carrier to ensure one is available at all times remains under consideration, with a decision likely to be taken before the next LPM.

Submarines: In early November 2022, the lead *Rubis* class nuclear-powered attack submarine arrived at Cherbourg for the final time. She was subsequently decommissioned on 2 December 2022, nearly 40 years after she had first entered service. In the short term her place in the fleet will be taken by the newly-refurbished *Perle. Perle* commenced sea trials from Toulon in May 2023 after completing a programme of work that was significantly delayed by a serious fire in her forward sections on 12 June 2020. Accordingly, she returns to sea incorporating the forward part of her decommissioned sister *Saphir*, which was joined to *Perle's* undamaged aft sections in a complex project undertaken at Naval Group's Cherbourg yard in the course of 2021.

Duguay-Trouin, the second of the six *Suffren* class boats that will eventually replace the remaining members of the *Rubis* class, commenced trials from Cherbourg in late March 2023. If the programme goes well, she should be delivered before the end of 2023. *Tourville*, the third member of the class, is scheduled to be launched in the same timeframe and all six boats should have been accepted by the end of the decade. Meanwhile, design work continues on the SNLE 3G strategic submarines that will start to replace the existing *Le Triomphant* class from the mid-2030s.

Major Surface Combatants: The French element of the FREMM multi-mission frigate programme was brought to an end on 16 November 2022 with delivery of *Lorraine*. The eighth member of the class in *Marine Nationale* service, she subsequently assisted the evacuation of French and other foreign nationals from Sudan in April 2023 whilst still preparing for acceptance into full operational service.[4]

Amiral Ronarc'h – the first of the five FDI type

TABLE 2.4.2: FRENCH NAVY: PRINCIPAL UNITS AS AT MID 2023

TYPE	CLASS	NUMBER	TONNAGE	DIMENSIONS	PROPULSION	CREW	DATE
Aircraft Carriers							
Aircraft Carrier – CVN	CHARLES DE GAULLE	1	42,000 tonnes	262m x 33/64m x 9m	Nuclear, 27 knots	1,950	2001
Principal Surface Escorts							
Frigate – FFG	AQUITAINE (FREMM)	8[1]	6,000 tonnes	142m x 20m x 5m	CODLOG, 27 knots	110	2012
Frigate – FFG	FORBIN ('Horizon')	2	7,100 tonnes	153m x 20m x 5m	CODOG, 29+ knots	195	2008
Frigate – FFG	LA FAYETTE	5	3,600 tonnes	125m x 15m x 5m	CODAD, 25 knots	150	1996
Frigate – FSG	FLORÉAL	6	3,000 tonnes	94m x 14m x 4m	CODAD, 20 knots	90	1992
Frigate – FS[2]	D'ESTIENNE D'ORVES (A-69)	6	1,300 tonnes	80m x 10m x 3m	Diesel, 24 knots	90	1976
Submarines							
Submarine – SSBN	LE TRIOMPHANT	4	14,400 tonnes	138m x 13m x 11m	Nuclear, 25 knots	110	1997
Submarine – SSN	SUFFREN	1	5,300 tonnes	100m x 9m x 7m	Nuclear, 25+knots	65	2020
Submarine – SSN	RUBIS	4	2,700 tonnes	74m x 8m x 6m	Nuclear, 25+ knots	70	1983
Major Amphibious Units							
Amph Assault Ship – LHD	MISTRAL	3	21,500 tonnes	199m x 32m x 6m	Diesel-electric, 19 knots	160	2006

Note:

1 Includes two slightly-modified *Alsace* variants.

2 Now officially reclassified as offshore patrol vessels.

frégates de défense et d'intervention that are following the FREMMs into service – was floated out at Lorient on 9 November after a formal 'launching ceremony' two days previously. Her first sea trials are scheduled to take place before the end of 2023 and she should be accepted during 2024. However, the need to accommodate the FDI variants being built for Greece's Hellenic Navy in the production schedule looks set to delay deliveries of subsequent French members of the class, with a total of only three vessels likely to have joined the *Marine Nationale* by 2030. This means that two of the three modernised *La Fayette* class light frigates dating from the late 1990s will have to remain in front-line service longer than was previously envisaged. *La Fayette* herself became the second ship to complete this limited upgrade in November 2022, with *Aconit* currently in dockyard hands to complete the programme. The other two members of the class will not be upgraded.

The LPM 2024-30 also anticipates starting the replacement of the *Floréal* class surveillance frigates by 2030 with the delivery of the first of France's European Patrol Corvettes (EPCs). This schedule might prove ambitious given the inevitable complexities of managing the European Union's first foray into warship procurement.

The French element of the FREMM multi-mission frigate programme was brought to an end on 16 November 2022 with delivery of *Lorraine*, the eighth and final FREMM to join the *Marine Nationale*. This photograph shows the frigate in the course of sea trials in June 2022. *(Pierre Ollier/REA via Naval Group)*

Minor Warships and Auxiliaries: *Jacques Chevallier*, the first of four force replenishment vessels – *bâtiments ravitailleurs de force* or BRFs – undertook her first voyage from Chantiers de l'Atlantique in late December 2022. She was preliminarily handed over to the French Navy on 3 March 2023 prior to continuing acceptance trials in the Mediterranean. Work is already underway on *Jacques Stosskopf*, the second member of the class. However, the LPM 2024-30 confirms that it will be after 2030 before *Gustave Zédé*, the fourth and final BRF, will be delivered. The arrival of *Jacques Chevallier* will be balanced by the imminent retirement of the 36-year-old command and replenishment ship *Marne*, leaving only *Somme* of the five original *Durance* class vessels in the French Navy's list.

The ongoing, if belated, renewal of France's patrol vessel force saw the arrival of *Auguste Bénébig*, the first of six new *patrouilleurs outre-mer* (POMs), a class described in detail in Chapter 3.1. Naval Group has been contracted to design the ten larger *patrouilleurs océaniques* (POs) that are intended to be based in Metropolitan France. It is envisaged that

Jacques Chevallier, the first of the French Navy's four BRF replenishment oilers, was delivered by Chantiers de l'Atlantique in March 2023 but is still undergoing a programme of trials. This photograph was taken off Saint-Nazaire in February 2023. *(Bruno Huriet)*

these will be ordered from a number of smaller French shipyards during 2023 to allow the delivery of the first by 2025 but this had not happened as of mid-year. In a delay to previous plans, the LPM 2024-30 now expects only seven being delivered by 2030, with the three *La Fayette* class frigates not required for front-line service being re-roled as patrol vessels until the new class is completed. The National Assembly are not altogether happy with this delay and are pressing for delivery of the POs to be accelerated.

The LPM 2024-30's roll-out of the navy's new mine warfare force will also proceed at a relatively leisurely pace. The eventual vision is for six BDGM *bâtiments de guerre des mines* 'motherships' supporting eight 'toolboxes' of MCM drones, as well as five NG BBPD *bâtiments base support plongeurs*. However, only around half the new vessels will have been delivered by 2030 in a further indication of the pressures faced in achieving the planned force structure. Meanwhile, the minehunter *Cassiopée* was retired from service on 1 July 2022 as the existing MCM force starts to be drawn down.

Francesco Morosini, commissioned on 21 October 2022, is the second of the Italian Navy's frigate-like multi-purpose offshore patrol vessels. She is spending much of 2023 on an extended Asia-Pacific deployment. 2023 has seen the *Marina Militare* undertake its largest-ever number of simultaneous missions outside the Mediterranean. *(Italian Navy)*

MAJOR REGIONAL POWERS – ITALY

In May 2023, Italy's *Marina Militare* issued a press release announcing that no fewer than eleven of the navy's warships were deployed beyond the Mediterranean; an achievement which it claimed was an all-time record. The geographical extent of the navy's deployments was certainly impressive. They extended from the US freeboard across the North Sea, Gulf of Guinea and Indian Ocean into the Asia-Pacific region, where the new PPA multi-purpose offshore 'patrol ship' *Francesco Morosini* was engaged in an extended diplomatic and marketing campaign. The announcement reflected the continuing growth in the capacity of the Italian Navy which – assisted by an ongoing programme of modernisation – has been slowly closing the gap with its British and French rivals, currently Europe's leading fleets.

Table 2.4.3 summarises the Italian Navy's principal components as of mid-2023. In comparison with the previous year, the only material change to fleet strength has been the arrival of the aforementioned *Francesco Morosini.* The second PPA-type patrol vessel, she was commissioned on 21 October 2022. However, this snapshot does not provide the full picture, as the following projects are set to deliver further increases in capability in the near to medium term:

- **Amphibious Assault Ship *Trieste*:** The c. 38,000-tonne *Trieste*, which will be Italy's largest warship when delivered, is currently completing extended pre-acceptance trials. Current reports suggest that she is likely to be commissioned before the end of 2023.
- **FREMM Multi-Mission Frigates:** Two additional FREMM frigates – which will be the Italian Navy's ninth and tenth members of the class – are currently under construction. They will replace *Spartaco Schergat* and *Emilio Bianchi*, which were both sold to Egypt in 2020 when almost ready for delivery. These new ships are expected to be completed in 2025.
- **PPA Multi-Mission Patrol Vessels:** *Francesco Morosini* will be followed by five additional members of the class between now and the end of 2026. Three of these have already been launched and started sea trials; the most recent being *Marcantonio Colonna* which was launched on 22 November 2022. Being completed in various 'light', 'light plus' and 'full' armament configurations, these ships are frigates in all but name.
- ***Vulcano* Class Logistic Support Ships:** *Atlante*, the second ship in a planned three-strong class that also forms the basis for France's BRFs, was subject to a formal keel-laying ceremony at Fincantieri's Castellammare di Stabia yard on 28 June 2023. Delivery is expected in 2025.
- **Type 212NFS Submarines:** Two of the evolved Type 212A Near Future Submarines are now under construction following commencement of work on the second boat at Muggiano near La Spezia on 7 June 2023. An order for a third boat has already been approved by the Italian Parliament and a fourth is planned as part of a programme that aims to replace the remaining elderly *Sauro* class submarines on a numerical like-for-like basis. Deliveries are anticipated to run from 2027 onwards. The submarine flotilla will also be supported by a new submarine rescue vessel under a contract signed with the T Mariotti shipyard in Genoa in mid-2021.

These current programmes will likely be supplemented over the coming years by a significant number of new projects that are currently in the development phase. Key elements of these plans

Table 2.4.3: ITALIAN NAVY: PRINCIPAL UNITS AS AT MID 2023

TYPE	CLASS	NUMBER	TONNAGE	DIMENSIONS	PROPULSION	CREW	DATE
Aircraft Carriers							
Aircraft Carrier – CV	**CAVOUR**	1	28,100 tonnes	244m x 30/39m x 9m	COGAG, 29 knots	800	2008
Aircraft Carrier – CVS	**GIUSEPPE GARIBALDI**[1]	1	13,900 tonnes	180m x 23/31m x 7m	COGAG, 30 knots	825	1985
Principal Surface Escorts							
Frigate – FFG	**CARLO BERGAMINI** (FREMM)[2]	8	6,700 tonnes	144m x 20m x 5m	CODLOG, 27 knots	145	2013
Frigate – FFG	**ANDREA DORIA** ('Horizon')	2	7,100 tonnes	153m x 20m x 5m	CODOG, 29+ knots	190	2007
Destroyer – DDG	**DE LA PENNE**	2	5,400 tonnes	148m x 16m x 5m	CODOG, 31 knots	375	1993
Frigate – FFG	**MAESTRALE**	3	3,100 tonnes	123m x 13m x 4m	CODOG, 30+ knots	225	1982
Frigate – FFG/FF[3]	**PAOLO THAON DI REVEL**	2	5,800 tonnes[3]	143m x 17m x 5m	CODAG, 32+ knots	90	2022
Submarines							
Submarine – SSK	**TODARO** (Type 212A)	4	1,800 tonnes	56m x 7m x 6m	AIP, 20+ knots	30	2006
Submarine – SSK	**PELOSI** (Improved SAURO)	4	1,700 tonnes	64m x 7m x 6m	Diesel-electric, 20 knots	50	1988
Major Amphibious Units							
Landing Platform Dock – LPD	**SAN GIORGIO**	3	8,000 tonnes	133m x 21m x 5m	Diesel, 20 knots	165	1987

Note:
1 Now operates largely as a LPH.
2 Class includes *Bergamini* (GP) and *Fasan* (ASW) variants.
3 Varies dependent on armament configuration.

include two large air defence destroyers to replace the 30-year-old *Durand de la Penne* class and twelve modular mine countermeasures vessels, as well as many as eight corvettes. The last-mentioned will be ordered under the framework of the European Union's EPC programme but may be supplemented by a series of less-sophisticated offshore patrol vessels of indigenous design. Of the remaining ships, it seems likely that it will be the destroyers that will be the first to enter the production phase. Another project that is moving closer to implementation is that for three LxD next-generation amphibious vessels, that will replace the existing *San Giorgio* class amphibious transport docks. Design studies for these ships are expected to conclude by the end of 2023, paving the way for transition to the construction phase.

Fincantieri commenced construction of its second Type 212NFS submarine in June 2023 and is shortly to receive an order for the third of an eventual planned total of four boats. They will join the Italian Navy's earlier quartet of Type 212A submarines; this picture shows *Pietro Venuti*, the third member of this earlier class. *(Fincantieri)*

MAJOR REGIONAL POWERS – RUSSIA

Russia's ongoing war in Ukraine means that any assessment of the Russian Navy is inevitably influenced by the trajectory of the wider conflict. As already referenced in this chapter's introduction, the successful establishment of increasingly potent Ukrainian A2/AD defences along the country's remaining coastline during the first half of 2022 has acted as a powerful deterrent to Russian naval activity, limiting its role in the conflict. The Black

Sea Fleet has continued to exercise important long-range strike functions through, notably, use of the 3M14 'Kalibr' (SS-N-30A 'Sagaris') missile. It has also been able to blockade Ukrainian trade across much of the Black Sea, whilst Russian naval infantry have played an important part in some of the land fighting. Overall, however, the navy has arguably become largely irrelevant to the campaign's outcome.

At the present time, it is impossible to state with certainty what this outcome might be. However, given the huge financial and materiel cost of the war to date, it is relevant to question how the navy will fare during its aftermath. The current Putin administration remains firmly wedded to the concept of naval power being fundamental to Russia's wider status in the world, a belief emphasised in an updated *Naval Doctrine of the Russian Federation* published on 31 July 2022 to coincide with that year's Navy Day. Many commentators have opined on the implications of a document – the first since 2015 – that places greater emphasis on Russia's deepening confrontation with the United States and NATO, as well as a more overt recognition of its willingness to use force to promote Russia's global interests. A common observation is that the scope of the document's ambitions far outweighs Russia's practical ability to implement them.[5]

Given this innate disconnect, it seems probable that the Russian Navy will focus what are likely to be increasingly constrained resources on objectives of paramount national interest. These include protection of the strategic submarine force, including the maritime 'bastions' in which it operates, and the maintenance of security in Russia's near seas. As the new Naval Doctrine makes clear, the Arctic, particularly, is seen as a vital area given the growing importance of the 'Northern Sea Route' to the country's maritime trade and the importance of the region's mineral resources. Investment in vessels – including submarines – that are able to operate in this environment looks set to be sustained. The corollary is that the revitalisation of traditional 'blue water' surface naval forces, largely neglected for much of the post-Soviet era, will again be relegated to a low priority.

For the time being, Table 2.4.4 provides an overview of Russia's major combatants, with commentary on the principal warship types following:

Submarines: The ongoing modernisation of Russia's flotilla of strategic submarines continued to hit important milestones over the last year. The acceptance of *Generalissimus Suvorov* – sixth member of the 'Borey' class and the third Project 955A variant – on 29 December 2022 was accompanied by the launch of *Emperor Alexander III*, the fourth Project 955A boat, on the same day. Three other members of the class are under construction and two more planned

TABLE 2.4.4: RUSSIAN NAVY: SELECTED PRINCIPAL UNITS AS AT MID 2023

TYPE	CLASS	NUMBER[1]	TONNAGE	DIMENSIONS	PROPULSION	CREW	DATE
Aircraft carriers							
Aircraft Carrier – CV	Project 1143.5 **KUZNETSOV**	1	60,000 tonnes	306m x 35/73m x 10m	Steam, 32 knots	2,600	1991
Principal Surface Escorts							
Battlecruiser – BCGN	Project 1144.2 **KIROV**	2	25,000 tonnes	252m x 29m x 9m	CONAS, 32 knots	740	1980
Cruiser – CG	Project 1164 **MOSKVA** ('Slava')	2	12,500 tonnes	186m x 21m x 8m	COGAG, 32 knots	530	1982
Destroyer – DDG	Project 956/956A **SOVREMENNY**	c. 2	8,000 tonnes	156m x 17m x 6m	Steam, 32 knots	300	1980
Destroyer – DDG	Project 1155.1 **CHABANENKO** ('Udaloy II')	1	9,000 tonnes	163m x 19m x 6m	COGAG, 29 knots	250	1999
Destroyer – DDG	Project 1155 **UDALOY**	c. 7	8.500 tonnes	163m x 19m x 6m	COGAG, 30 knots	300	1980
Frigate – FFG	Project 22350 **GORSHKOV**	2	5,500 tonnes	135m x 16m x 5m	CODAG, 30 knots	210	2018
Frigate – FFG	Project 11366M **GRIGOROVICH**	3	4,000 tonnes	125m x 15m x 4m	COGAG, 30 knots	200	2016
Frigate – FFG	Project 1154 **NEUSTRASHIMY**	2	4,400 tonnes	139m x 16m x 6m	COGAG, 30 knots	210	1993
Frigate – FFG	Project 1135 **BDITELNNY** ('Krivak I/II')	c. 2	3,700 tonnes	123m x 14m x 5m	COGAG, 32 knots	180	1970
Frigate – FFG	Project 20385 **GREMYASHCHIY**	1	2,500 tonnes	106m x 11m x 5m	CODAD, 27 knots	100	2020
Frigate – FFG	Project 20380 **STERGUSHCHIY**	8	2,200 tonnes	105m x 11m x 4m	CODAD, 27 knots	100	2008
Frigate – FFG	Project 11611 **TATARSTAN** ('Gepard')	2	2,000 tonnes	102m x 13m x 4m	CODOG, 27 knots	100	2002
Submarines							
Submarine – SSBN	Project 95/955A **YURY DOLGORUKY** ('Borey')	6	20,000+ tonnes	170m x 13m x 10m	Nuclear, 25+ knots	110	2010
Submarine – SSBN	Project 677BDRM **VERKHOTURYE** ('Delta IV')	5[2]	18,000 tonnes	167m x 12m x 9m	Nuclear, 24 knots	130	1985
Submarine – SSGN	Project 855/855M **SEVERODVINSK** ('Yasen')	3	13,500+ tonnes	120m x 14m x 9m	Nuclear, 30+ knots	90	2013
Submarine – SSGN	Project 949A ('Oscar II')	c. 7	17,500 tonnes	154m x 8m x 9m	Nuclear, 30+ knots	100	1986
Submarine – SSN	Project 971 ('Akula I/II')	c. 10	9,500 tonnes	110m x 14m x 10m	Nuclear, 30+ knots	60	1986
Submarine – SSK	Project 636.3 (Improved 'Kilo')	10	3,200 tonnes	73m x 10m x 7m	Diesel-electric, 20 knots	55	2014
Submarine – SSK	Project 877 ('Kilo')	c. 10	3,000 tonnes	73m x 10m x 7m	Diesel-electric, 20 knots	55	1981

Notes:

1. Table only includes main types and focuses on operational units and/or ships under active modernisation or refit.
2. One additional unit is being used in an experimental role. It is unclear whether *Ryazan*, the sole surviving 'Delta III' class submarine, continues to deploy ballistic missiles.

to give a revitalised strategic submarine force of at least twelve modern vessels in due course. The progress made with delivering the new submarines has allowed the withdrawal of last serving Project 941 'Akula' (NATO: 'Typhoon') class boat *Dmitriy Donskoy*, which had previously supported trials of the RSM-56 'Bulava' (SS-N-32) ballistic missile used in the 'Borey' class. The remaining Project 677 BDR/BDRM 'Delta' class boats also look set to dwindle rapidly as their replacements arrive.

The Project 855M 'Yasen M' class nuclear-powered attack submarine *Krasnoyarsk* – third of the modified series and the fourth Project 855 'Yasen' ('Severodvinsk') type boat overall – continues to undergo protracted sea trials prior to joining her sister *Novosibirsk* in the Pacific Fleet in late 2023. A further five 'Yasen Ms' remain under construction. Although builders Sevmash failed to achieve *Krasnoyarsk*'s delivery during the last year, they did ensure the handover of the secretive Project 09852 'research submarine' *Belgorod*. A much-modified variant of the Project 949A 'Antey' ('Oscar II') type, she was accepted on 8 July 2022. In addition to acting as a mothership for a mini-submarine, *Belgorod* can be armed with the 2M39 'Poseidon' autonomous nuclear-powered torpedo, capable of delivering a nuclear warhead at intercontinental range.

Deliveries of Project 636.3 (Improved 'Kilo') class submarines to the Pacific Fleet from the Admiralty Shipyards continue at a rate one each year. *Ufa* – fourth of this second, six-boat batch and the tenth Project 636.3 overall – was delivered in December 2022. The fifth, *Mozhaysk*, was subsequently launched on 27 April 2023. Additional Project 636.3s have been ordered for the Northern and Pacific Fleets but it seems that their construction has yet to commence. Work is underway on four of the newer Project 677 'Lada' class design, of which two are said to be under trials. However, a decision has been taken to decommission the prototype Project 677, *Sankt Peterburg*, which was accepted in 2010 but has never performed to the navy's satisfaction. It seems that lessons learned from these problems will be incorporated in the following members of the class.

The British Royal Navy Type 23 frigate *Portland* shadows the prototype Russian Project 855 'Yasen' class submarine *Severodvinsk* in July 2022. Russia's submarine arm is likely to remain a priority for investment after the current war in Ukraine comes to an end. *(Crown Copyright 2022)*

Aircraft Carriers and Amphibious Warships: The lengthy and troubled refit of the sole Russian Project 1143.5 aircraft carrier, *Admiral Kuznetsov*, is seemingly drawing to a conclusion. The docking phase of her refurbishment concluded early in 2023 and it is hoped that she will return to the fleet before the end of 2024, six years after the refit commenced. There is no further news on progress with either the two Project 23900 *Ivan Rogov* class amphibious assault ships being built at the Zaliv shipyard in Crimea or the second pair of modified Project 11711 *Ivan Gren* class large landing ships entrusted to Yantar at Kaliningrad. The construction of the former, particularly, must be vulnerable to logistical disruption arising from the war in Ukraine.

Surface Combatants: Progress with the construction of large surface warships for the Russian Navy continues to be painfully slow. Sea trials of *Admiral Golovko*, the third Project 22350 *Admiral Gorshkov* class frigate being built by Saint Petersburg's Severnaya Verf, commenced in November 2022 and she should be delivered in the course of 2023. Five additional members of the class are being built and two more ordered, a position unchanged since last year. Given the lead ship was laid down in February 2006, this is hardly an impressive performance.

The second tier series of Project 20380/20385/20386 corvettes is faring slightly better. Eight of the Project 20380 *Steregushchiy* class variant have now been delivered following the acceptance of *Merkuriy* (previously named *Retiviy*) from Severnaya Verf in May 2023. Another four of the type are under construction at Saint Petersburg and at the Amur Shipbuilding Plant in the Far East for delivery by the middle of the decade. The Severnaya Verf-built *Gremyashchiy* remains the sole, enlarged Project 20385 iteration to have been commissioned following the delay caused by the fire aboard her sister *Provornyy* in December 2021. However, the Amur yard seem to be making reasonable progress with the quartet of vessels they have been allocated, holding out the prospect of six vessels of this type being in service by the end of the decade. It is possible that further Project 20380 and Project 20385 corvettes will be ordered given reported dissatisfaction with the follow-on Project 20386 prototype *Derzkiy* (formerly *Merkuriy*), on which work commenced in 2016. It is believed that no series orders for this variant will be placed pending a redesign of the existing ship.

Construction of the smaller 'green water' corvette-like missile boats that increasingly form the bulk of the navy's modern surface fleet is achieving mixed results. Positively, ten of twelve planned Project 21631 'Buyan M' small missile ships have been completed by the Zelenodolsk yard. The final two are likely to be delivered in the next year. Negatively, production of the follow-on, more seaworthy Project 22800 'Karakurt' type continues to be beset by problems, with no deliveries over the past year. Only three of sixteen firmly contracted units have been completed to date; a delay which will be keenly felt as older Soviet-era light units increasingly reach the end of their service lives.

For some years, the Russian Navy's 'blue water' operations have been kept alive by refurbished Soviet-era ships. This is becoming increasingly difficult to sustain as many of these vessels enter their fifth decade of service. Nearly all the Project 956 *Sovremenny* class destroyers have now been retired, although many of their Project 1155 *Udaloy* class contemporaries remain in service. This is possibly because their gas turbine propulsion has been easier to maintain.[6] It is expected that 2024 will see the return of the Project 1144.2 nuclear-powered battle-cruiser *Admiral Nakhimov* after completion of her ten-year-long refit at Sevmash. However, the expense and difficulty involved in implementing her refurbishment may result in cancellation of plans to perform similar work on her sister *Pyotr Velikiy*, currently flagship of the Northern Fleet.

Minor Warships and Auxiliaries: The Russian Navy's construction programmes for major combatants continue to be supplemented by a wide range of other projects of varying cost and complexity, many of which were summarised in last year's edition. Amongst these, deliveries of Project 12700 'Alexandrite' mine countermeasures vessels appear to be progressing well, with two further units – the sixth and seventh vessels *Pyotr Ilyichev* and *Anatoly Shlemov* – being delivered from Saint Petersburg's Sredne-Nevsky Shipyard in late 2022. Five other members of the class, possibly of an improved design, are in production and more are planned.

Saint Petersburg's shipyards are also heavily involved in production of icebreakers. These include large, nuclear-powered vessels for the civilian but state-owned FSUE Atomflot, an enterprise that has increasing military relevance as the Arctic's strategic importance increases. On 22 November 2022, the city's Baltic Shipyard hosted a ceremony that saw the delivery of the third Project 22220 icebreaker, *Ural*, and the ceremonial launch of the fourth, *Yakutiya*. The yard has been contracted to build two additional members of this 33,000-tonne class – the sixth and seventh vessels – due to delays impacting the construction of the first, even larger Project 10510 'Leader' icebreaker at the rebuilt Zvezda shipbuilding complex in Russia's Far East. Saint Petersburg's Admiralty yard also has orders for icebreakers. It is close to completing *Ivan Papanin*, first of four Project 23550 multi-role diesel-powered vessels. These have a modular armament and are being built for both the navy and coast guard.

The Russian Navy continues to make slow progress with recapitalising the 'blue water' elements of its surface fleet, with only two of the Project 22350 *Admiral Gorshkov* class frigates commissioned to date. As a consequence, its 'blue water' operations continue to be dependent on aging Soviet-era ships, a strategy that is becoming increasingly difficult to maintain over time. This photograph of *Admiral Gorshkov* was taken from a Norwegian maritime patrol aircraft in January 2023; note the 'Z' – which has become the symbol for Russia's invasion of Ukraine – on the frigate's funnel. *(333 Squadron/Norwegian Armed Forces)*

MAJOR REGIONAL POWERS – SPAIN

Spain's *Armada Española* is seemingly starting to turn the corner after a decade or more of challenges. The highlight of the year has undoubtedly been the steady progression of the lead S-80 class submarine, *Isaac Peral*, through a trials programme that should see her delivery by Navantia's Cartagena yard before the end of 2023. This programme is described further in Chapter 3.3. Construction of the first of the five new F-110 *Bonifaz* class frigates is also underway following first steel-cutting in April 2022, with a formal keel-laying ceremony expected to take place at Ferrol before the end of 2023. As both of these projects are now seemingly on a firm footing, the navy is in a good position to make progress realising other long-delayed objectives.

A major priority seems to be acquisition of additional patrol vessels. The original *buque de acción marítima* (BAM) programme was intended to encompass ten patrol ships in addition to a number of specialised variants. Due to past financial constraints, only six *Meteoro* class offshore patrol vessels have been delivered to date. An additional single BAM-IS submarine rescue vessel, named *Poseidón*, will also shortly commence construction at

Table 2.4.5: SPANISH NAVY: PRINCIPAL UNITS AS AT MID 2023

TYPE	CLASS	NUMBER	TONNAGE	DIMENSIONS	PROPULSION	CREW	DATE
Principal Surface Escorts							
Frigate – FFG	**ÁLVARO DE BAZÁN** (F-100)	5	6,300 tonnes	147m x 19m x 5m	CODOG, 28 knots	200	2002
Frigate – FFG	**SANTA MARÍA** (FFG-7)	6	4,100 tonnes	138m x 14m x 5m	COGAG, 30 knots	225	1986
Submarines							
Submarine – SSK	**GALERNA** (S-70/AGOSTA)	2	1,800 tonnes	68m x 7m x 6m	Diesel-electric, 21 knots	60	1983
Major Amphibious Units							
Amph Assault Ship – LHD	**JUAN CARLOS I**	1	27,100 tonnes	231m x 32m x 7m	IEP, 21 knots	245	2010
Landing Platform Dock – LPD	**GALICIA**	2	13,000 tonnes	160m x 25m x 6m	Diesel, 20 knots	185	1998

Navantia's shipyards in the Bay of Cádiz. However, in June 2023 it emerged that €550m (c. US$615m) has been allocated to finance two additional members of the class, which will be equipped as specialised anti-submarine warfare (ASW) BAM variants. The ships will effectively replace the two remaining *Descubierta* class corvettes, which have been serving as patrol vessels for a number of years. Of these, *Infanta Elena* was decommissioned in March 2023, whilst *Infanta Cristina* will follow shortly. In the longer term, the prospect of additional BAMs may be overtaken by Spain's participation in the EPC programme. The navy reportedly has a requirement for six EPCs, presumably to replace the *Serviola* and *Chilreu* class patrol vessels. However, the prospect of construction of a proposed BAM hydrographic ship variant remains

Another pressing requirement is recapitalisation of the Spanish Naval Air Arm. In April 2023, the navy received approval to acquire eight MH-60R helicopters at an estimated cost of €820m. They will replace twelve existing SH-60B models, which are fast approaching the end of their service lives. The navy's fleet of twelve EAV-8B Matador II plus Harriers will also need replacing before the end of the decade but, with the F-35B Lightning II the only potential contender, this will be a more expensive proposition. The *Armada Española* will have to hope that its recent run of good fortune continues if it is to retain its organic fixed wing aviation component.

Table 2.4.5 summarises the current status of the Spanish fleet.

MAJOR REGIONAL POWERS – UNITED KINGDOM

A summary of current Royal Navy fleet strength is provided in Table 2.4.6. The main development in the last year has been the arrival of the new *Astute* class submarine *Anson.* She was commissioned in August 2022 prior to departing her builder's yard at Barrow on 19 February 2023 to begin sea trials. Lengthy refits of the nuclear-powered attack submarine *Triumph*, last operational member of the *Trafalgar* class, and the strategic submarine *Vanguard* have also been completed at Devonport Dockyard, easing pressure on the underwater flotilla. Conversely, the force of major surface combatants has continued to decline with the decommissioning of the Type 23 frigate *Montrose* on 17 April 2023 after completing a near four year-long forward deployment to Bahrain in the Persian Gulf. This takes the surface fleet down to seventeen destroyers and frigates; two fewer than the targeted number. This position may deteriorate further before new Type 26 and Type 31 frigates start to enter operational service in the second half of the decade.

Triumph, the last remaining British Royal Navy *Trafalgar* class submarine, pictured entering the Firth of Clyde from Loch Long in February 2023. She completed a refit at Devonport Dockyard at the end of 2022 and is destined to serve for a few years yet. The 'Hunt' class mine countermeasures vessel *Hurworth* is in the background. *(Michael Leek)*

Table 2.4.6: BRITISH ROYAL NAVY: PRINCIPAL UNITS AS AT MID 2023

TYPE	CLASS	NUMBER	TONNAGE	DIMENSIONS	PROPULSION	CREW	DATE
Aircraft Carriers							
Aircraft Carrier – CV	QUEEN ELIZABETH	2	65,000 tonnes	284m x 73m x 11m	IEP, 26 knots+	1,600	2017
Principal Surface Escorts							
Destroyer – DDG	DARING (Type 45)	6	7,500 tonnes	152m x 21m x 5m	IEP, 30 knots	190	2008
Frigate – FFG	NORFOLK (Type 23)	11	4,900 tonnes	133m x 16m x 5m	CODLAG, 30 knots	185	1990
Submarines							
Submarine – SSBN	VANGUARD	4	16,000 tonnes	150m x 13m x 12m	Nuclear, 25+ knots	135	1993
Submarine – SSN	ASTUTE	5	7,800 tonnes	93m x 11m x 10m	Nuclear, 30+ knots	100	2010
Submarine – SSN	TRAFALGAR	1	5,200 tonnes	85m x 10m x 10m	Nuclear, 30+ knots	130	1983
Major Amphibious Units							
Landing Platform Dock – LPD	ALBION	2[1]	18,500 tonnes	176m x 29m x 7m	IEP, 18 knots	325	2003
Landing Ship Dock – LSD (A)	LARGS BAY	3	16,200 tonnes	176m x 26m x 6m	Diesel-electric, 18 knots	60	2006

Notes:
1. One at extended readiness.

The pressure on fleet numbers is also impacting smaller vessels as the advent of new technology makes itself felt. The last 12 months have seen the decommissioning of the hydrographic survey ship *Enterprise* and the *Sandown* class mine countermeasures vessels *Grimsby* and *Shoreham*. In all cases their role has been supplanted by unmanned and autonomous systems, either in whole or in part. The arrival of the Royal Fleet Auxiliary (RFA) MCM 'mothership' *Stirling Castle* – referred to in this chapter's introduction – and the acquisition of the multi-role ocean surveillance ship RFA *Proteus* – which has yet to enter service – provide some compensation. The Gibraltar-based *Cutlass* class fast patrol boat *Dagger* was also officially commissioned on 14 July 2022.

The final German F122 frigate, *Lübeck*, was decommissioned on 15 December 2022, bringing an era to a close. This photograph shows the frigate departing Portsmouth Harbour in November 2019. *(Conrad Waters)*

The longer-term future looks somewhat more promising. Orders for the second batch of five Type 26 frigates placed on 15 November 2022 and three fleet solid support ships on 18 January 2023 put two of the Royal Navy's most important procurement programmes on more solid ground. The announcement of the AUKUS submarine programme holds out the possibility of an increase in submarine numbers in the longer term.

A more detailed review of the Royal Navy's current status is provided in Chapter 2.4B.

MID-SIZED REGIONAL FLEETS

Germany: On 15 December 2022, a decommissioning ceremony was held for the F122 frigate *Lübeck*, the final member of the eight *Bremen* class frigates to be withdrawn from service. Their replacements, in the form of the quartet of F125 *Baden-Württemberg* class stabilisation frigates, have already joined the fleet, leaving the navy's number of major surface combatants at eleven units for the time being. Equipment selections continue for the follow-on F126 class and an initial steel-cutting ceremony for the first unit is expected before the end of 2023.

Meanwhile, significant problems encountered in integrating the combat management systems in the second batch of five K130 *Braunschweig* class corvettes ordered in 2017 are resulting in delays to their acceptance. As such, it is unlikely to be before

2024 at the earliest before the initial batch of five K130s will start to be reinforced. *Köln*, the first of the new ships, had previously commenced sea trials in June 2022, whilst the second – *Emden* – was christened at NVL's Blohm & Voss shipyard in Hamburg on 4 May 2023.

Whilst the *Zeitenwende* (turning point) in German defence spending announced by Chancellor Olaf Scholz in early 2022 has yet to feed its way through to new orders, progress has been made with programmes that had been previously announced in June 2021. Notably, work commenced on the lead ship of a pair of new Type 707 fleet replenishment tankers – replacements for the existing Type 704 *Rhön* class – at Meyer Werft, Papenburg on 29 June 2023. Construction of the new Type 212CD class submarines being built under a joint project with Norway is also likely to commence before 2023's end. An order for three Type 424 signals intelligence vessels – like the Type 707s replacements for an existing class – approved at the same time, is believed to be imminent.

The fleet's longer-term structure has effectively been set by the 'Vision 2035+' referenced in the chapter's introduction. In addition to the focus on autonomous solutions, a noteworthy feature of the proposed structure is the consistent application of a 1:3 ratio; both for manned and unmanned platforms. In effect, for every one deployable unit, there is a total requirement of three to support such factors as training and maintenance.

Greece: A full review of the Hellenic Navy is contained in Chapter 2.4B.

The Netherlands and Belgium: The joint recapitalisation programme encompassing the major surface elements of the Royal Netherlands Navy and Belgian Naval Component has seemingly put past challenges behind it. Most significantly, on 29 June 2023, a contract was signed with Damen for four new 'ASWF' anti-submarine warfare frigates, encompassing a pair of ships for each of the two navies. Intended to replace the existing 'M' or *Karel Doorman* class frigates serving in both fleets on a like-for-like basis, the new ships will be fabricated at Damen's Galati shipyard in Romania before final outfitting in the Netherlands. Earlier funding constraints and ongoing design changes had previously delayed finalisation of the flagship programme, which is likely to cost c. €4bn (c. US$4.5bn) in total. The first frigate will be delivered to the Royal Netherlands Navy in 2029, with the other three vessels following at annual intervals.[7]

Damen was awarded a contract for two pairs of ASWF anti-submarine warfare frigates for the Belgian and Dutch navies on 29 June 2023, bringing a protracted design development phase to a close. The new frigates will displace c. 6,400 tonnes and are reported to have a cost of around €1bn each. *(Damen)*

The new frigates are being acquired as part of a wider programme of collaboration in naval procurement that also encompasses the Belgian-led rMCM project. This involves the acquisition of six mine countermeasures motherships and associated drones for each navy. The contract is being overseen by the Belgium Naval & Robotics consortium of Naval Group and Exail (formerly ECA Group). Construction of the early motherships in the programme is being entrusted to the Piriou and Kership (the Naval Group-Piriou joint venture) shipyards in Brittany but reports suggest some of the later hulls might be fabricated in Romania. A formal launch ceremony for the first vessel, *Oostende*, took place at Piriou's yard at Concarneau on 29 March 2023, the keel for *Tournai* – Belgium's second ship and third member of the class overall – being laid the same day. Current plans envisage *Oostende* being delivered to the Belgian Naval Component by the end of 2024 with *Vlissingen*, the first Dutch vessel – laid down by Kership in June 2022 – following in 2025.

In addition to cooperation with Belgium, the Netherlands continues to pursue its much-delayed project to replace the *Walrus* class submarines. In November 2022, requests for quotations were sent to the three shipbuilding groups – Naval Group, Saab Kockums and tkMS – shortlisted for the contract. Delays encountered with the programme mean that two of the four existing boats will be retired before their replacements enter service, likely commencing with *Walrus* herself in the second half of 2023. The remaining submarines, as well as the LCF frigates, will be fitted with Tomahawk cruise missiles under a decision confirmed in April in 2023.

Longer-term plans envisage construction of replacement air defence frigates for the LCF type, as well as of a new class of 'LPX' amphibious ships. The former programme was to have been carried forward with Germany as part of their F127 requirement but recent reports suggest that Germany may be cooling on the idea. Interestingly, the LPX programme envisages it encompassing the roles both of the Dutch amphibious vessels and the *Holland* class patrol vessels in an unusual merging of two seemingly different requirements. In June 2023, it emerged that the project might be combined with the UK's programme for multi-role support ships that are needed to replace the British Royal Navy's own amphibious shipping.

The Turkish Navy commissioned its new amphibious assault ship *Anadolu* at a high-profile ceremony on 10 April 2023. A variant of Navantia's *Juan Carlos I* design, she is adapted for drone operations in addition to the rotorcraft seen on her flight deck in this image taken a week after her commissioning. *(Devrim Yaylali)*

Turkey: It has been a busy year for Turkish naval programmes. Most significantly, 10 April 2023 saw the commissioning of the navy's new flagship, the amphibious assault ship *Anadolu*, at a ceremony held in the presence of President Recep Erdoğan at the Sedef Shipyard in Istanbul. The c. 27,500-tonne vessel is derived from the Spanish *Juan Carlos I* design but incorporates a number of differences. These include the substitution of an all-diesel generating plant for the Spanish ship's gas turbine and diesel arrangement, both configurations being used to provide power to podded propulsors via an integrated electric propulsion system. Other changes include the incorporation of an indigenous Haveslan 'Advent' combat management system, as well as revisions to the ship's outfit of weapons and sensors. Notably, *Anadolu* is also intended to embark an outfit of drones; initially the propeller-driven Baykar Bayraktar TB3 but likely ultimately the jet-powered K›z›lelma unmanned combat air vehicle.

The lead Turkish Navy *Istanbul* class frigate commenced sea trials from the Istanbul Naval Shipyard on 20 June 2023. This photograph shows her four days previously. Three additional members of the class were ordered in January 2023. *(Devrim Yaylali)*

Vessels from two other significant Turkish naval programmes have also made their maiden voyages over the last year. The end of 2022 saw the commencement of trials for *Piri Reis*, the first of six licence-built Type 214 AIP-equipped boats originally contracted with tkMS in 2009. Whilst her delivery has been continuously pushed back, there is considerable optimism she will enter operational service before the end of 2023. The five remaining boats remain under construction at Gölcük Naval Shipyard, where *Hizir Reis* – the second boat – was launched on 25 May 2023.[8]

Subsequently, on Tuesday 20 June 2023, the lead *Istanbul* class frigate departed Istanbul Naval Shipyard (INS) to commence her own programme of sea trials. A significantly enlarged variant of the original 'Milgem' or 'Ada' class displacing around 3,000 tonnes and armed with an indigenous vertical-launch system, she will be the first of a class of four vessels. In January 2023, the Turkish Defence Agency awarded a contract for the other three ships to a consortium comprising the publicly-owned defence technology company STM and TAIS, itself a partnership of the leading Turkish shipyards

Anadolu, Sedef and Sefine. Each of the three shipbuilders has been allocated the construction of one of the class. The three ships will be built concurrently, with all being due for delivery within 36 months of the order being placed.

Two other important projects are also making headway. Having completed assembly of *Istanbul*, INS is reportedly now close to launching *Akhisar*, the first of a new class of corvette-like 'Hisar' offshore patrol vessels that are also based on the 'Ada' class design. The general concept appears to be to configure the class's weapons outfit on a 'for but not with' basis that has some similarities with the approach adopted for many of the Italian PPA patrol vessels. A total of ten of the class is eventually envisaged and work on a second vessel – *Koçhisar* – commenced in December 2022. It seems likely that initial vessels will be used to replace the six 'Burak' (French A69 *D'Estienne d'Orves*) class corvettes. One of these, *Bodrum*, was reportedly retired in October 2022.

Further down the line is a new class of indigenous fast attack craft, for which STM is carrying out the initial design work. This contract is now reportedly seemingly drawing to a close, paving the way for construction of a prototype to commence. The Turkish Navy urgently needs to replace the existing NVL-designed *Doğan* and *Rüzgar* classes, which date from the late 1970s and 1980s. The first withdrawal of a *Doğan* class fast attack craft, the 1978-built *Marti*, was reported in 2022.[9]

OTHER REGIONAL FLEETS

Black Sea and Mediterranean: The war in **Ukraine** makes it difficult to establish the current status of the country's existing fleet, which suffered heavily in the early stages of Russia's invasion. It is, however, known that the final Project 58155 'Gyurza-M' class gunboat *Bucha* was completed in May 2023, joining the three surviving vessels of the eight-ship class in Ukrainian service. Deliveries have also commenced of French OCEA FPB 98 Mk 1 patrol boats ordered for the country's border guard, with an initial pair reportedly transiting the Bosphorus aboard a civilian transport ship in May 2023.[10] In the longer term, the fleet's post-war strength will be bolstered by a slew of new and second-hand vessels acquired or donated from various sources. Prominent amongst these are the former British *Sandown* class minehunters *Chernihiv* (ex-*Grimsby*) and *Cherkasy* (ex-*Shoreham*), which are currently working up in British waters. Two Turkish 'Ada' type corvettes are also under construction. The lead ship, *Hetman Ivan Mazepa*, was launched by Istanbul Naval Shipyard on 2 October 2022.

Neighbouring **Romania** has been attempting to conclude arrangements for the modernisation of its own surface forces since 2019. The programme – encompassing the refit of its two existing Type 22 frigates and the construction of four new 'Gowind' corvettes – was to be implemented by a partnership of France's Naval Group and Romania's Santierul Naval Constanta (SNC). However, the two partners have reportedly failed to finalise the terms of their mutual relationship. It seems that – with four years having now elapsed since announcement of the original deal – Romania's patience is running out and it may turn to Damen to meet its requirements if negotiations are not concluded soon. However, the country is also reportedly in discussions with the French company to acquire three 'Scorpène' type submarines under a separate deal as part of plans to reconstitute its defunct underwater flotilla. Other projects that are closer to implementation include a c. US$200m to acquire the Naval Strike Missile Coastal Defence System and the US$150m purchase and modernisation of two former Royal Navy *Sandown* class minehunters. The problem of 'rogue' mines endangering navigation in the Black Sea has become a real one since the start of the Ukraine war. In September 2022, one of Romania's existing minesweepers, *Lt. Dimitrie Nicolescu*, was damaged whilst attempting to deal with one of these floating hazards.

Bulgaria's naval modernisation currently remains focused on the licensed construction of two 'Multipurpose Modular Patrol Vessels' (MMPVs) based on NVL's OPV-90 design. The keel for the second of these was laid at the MTG Dolphin shipyard in Varna on 22 June 2023.

Elsewhere in the Mediterranean, the new offshore patrol vessel *P71* was officially delivered to the Armed Forces of **Malta** by Italy's Cantiere Navale Vittoria at a ceremony in Valetta on 22 March 2023. The vessel, built to the yard's OPV748 design, was ordered in January 2019 and arrived in Maltese waters towards the end of 2022. Displacing 2,250 tonnes at full load, *P71* uses a hybrid diesel/diesel-electric propulsion system that can achieve a

Hetman Ivan Mazepa, the first of two 'Ada' class corvettes being built in Turkey for the Ukrainian Navy, was launched from Istanbul Naval Shipyard on 2 October 2022. *(Presidency of Ukraine)*

The Armed Forces of Malta took official delivery of their new offshore patrol vessel *P71* on 22 March 2023. Their largest vessel, with a displacement of some 2,250 tonnes, she was built by Italy's Cantiere Navale Vittoria. *(Justin Gatt/AFM Public Affairs Office)*

From left to right, three Irish Naval Service *Samuel Beckett* class patrol vessels *James Joyce* (P62), *George Bernard Shaw* (P64) and *William Butler Yeats* (P63) pictured operating in company in September 2021. In spite of longer-term plans to boost crewing, an ongoing manpower crisis meant that these ships represented three-quarters of Ireland's naval strength as of mid-2023. *(Irish Defence Forces)*

maximum speed in excess of 21 knots. She is equipped with two rigid-hulled inflatable boats and can land and refuel a medium weight helicopter. A 25mm-armed remotely-controlled weapons station constitutes her main armament.

The Atlantic and Northern Europe: It has been a mixed year for **Portugal's** navy. Its *Tridente* (Type 214) class submarine *Arpão* hit the headlines for the right reasons when she commenced a lengthy mission to West Africa in April 2023. She became the first Portuguese submarine to cross the Equator in a deployment that will also see her using her air-independent propulsion to travel for nearly a month underwater without resurfacing. Less positive headlines were garnered when thirteen crew members from the patrol vessel *Mondego* refused an order to sail to track a Russian vessel transiting near Madeira in March 2023 on grounds of the ship's poor serviceability. The so-called '*Mondego* Mutineers' face charges of refusing to obey an order in a case that has highlighted a potential maintenance backlog arising from previous austerity. The future looks brighter, however, with the publication of long-awaited tenders for the acquisition of six additional *Viana do Castelo* class offshore patrol vessels, as well as the innovative multi-purpose drone-carrier described in last year's *Seaforth World Naval Review.*

In July 2022, **Ireland's** government announced that the defence budget would rise from €1.1bn (c. US$1.25bn) to €1.5bn (c. US$1.7bn) per annum in real terms over the period to 2028, with 2,000 additional personnel being added to the Irish Defence Forces' existing 9,500 establishment. The announcement followed the report of a Defence Commission that set out three graduated Levels of Ambition (LOAs) for the Defence Forces' potential. These ranged from the maintenance of existing capacity (LOA1) to development of a full spectrum of capabilities comparable with Ireland's European peers (LOA3).[11] Perhaps predictably, the politicians selected the intermediate LOA2 pathway, at least for the time being. This includes improvements to situational awareness and better cyber protection but falls short of offering a full defensive capability across all domains. For the Irish Naval Service, LOA2 offers the accelerated replacement of older vessels as part of a notionally unchanged nine-strong fleet and a move to double crewing to make the most of existing assets. Ironically, the navy's ongoing crewing crisis has actually forced a reduc-

The Norwegian Type 210 *Ula* class submarine *Utvær* pictured in February 2022. Norway's Chief of Defence has advised that the government increase procurement of the replacement Type 212CD design from four to six boats in the light of the deteriorating security environment, thereby maintaining submarine numbers at existing levels. *(Thomas Haraldsen/ Norwegian Armed Forces)*

tion in the operational fleet to just four *Samuel Beckett* (PV90) offshore patrol vessels. The two older *Róisín* class (PV80) ships are both being held in operational reserve but the older *Eithne*, *Ciara* and *Orla* have all been permanently decommissioned. The last two ships will be replaced by the former Royal New Zealand Navy *Rotoiti* and *Pukaki*. The Antipodean pair arrived at Cork on a heavy lift vessel in May 2023 but still need to complete adaptation for Irish service.

Turning to Scandinavia, **Norway's** Chief of Defence submitted his formal advice on the future development of the Norwegian Armed Forces to the country's government in May 2023 as part of preparation for a new long-term defence plan.[12] In similar fashion to the Irish exercise, the advice is provided in the context of three alternative scenarios involving reduced, unchanged and higher funding. The most positive outcome – and perhaps the most likely given the current strategic context – would prioritise an increase in the acquisition of Type 212CD submarines from four to six boats. The existing frigates would also be replaced by six new ships if funding allowed. Much of the remaining fleet would be traded for two classes of large and small 'standard vessel' incorporating modular weapons and sensors.

Long a driver of modular technology, **Denmark** has kicked off the long-term renewal of its surface fleet with the June 2023 signature of an agreement with Danske Patruljeskibe K/S – a consortium of Odense Maritime Technology, Terma and PensionDanmark – to design a new class of modular patrol ship for the Royal Danish Navy. The new vessels will replace the existing *Thetis* class patrol frigates, with this initial contract seen as a first step to revitalising the country's naval sector. However, the precise trajectory of future construction will depend on the course of negotiations for a new political Defence Agreement covering the decade between 2024 and 2033, which have only just commenced.

Elsewhere in Scandinavia, **Sweden** continues to work on implementing its 'Total Defence' 2021-2025 programme. The naval centrepiece of this effort is construction of two A26 *Blekinge* class submarines at the Saab Kockums shipyard in Karlskrona as part of an objective to increase the submarine flotilla to five boats. The modernised A19 *Gotland* class will form the remainder of this force until eventually replaced by a 'U-båt 2030' project that might see the number of submarines further increased. Meanwhile work will soon start on an upgrade of the existing *Visby* corvettes as part of a package of enhancements to the surface navy that will also involve construction of 'Visby Generation 2' corvettes. Recent speculation suggests that these might be much larger, frigate-like ships equipped for an area air-defence role. Other improvements include modernisation of the five *Koster* class mine-hunters under a contract and options worth up to SEK620m (c. US$60m) awarded to Saab in December 2022 pending their eventual replacement in the 2030s. The commissioning of the intelligence gathering ship *Artemis*, which was handed over to the Swedish Defence Materiel Administration in April 2023, is a more imminent prospect.

Saab has been awarded a contract to modernise the Swedish Navy's existing *Koster* class mine countermeasures vessels prior to their eventual replacement in the 2030s. *(Copyright Saab AB)*

On 31 March 2023, **Finland** released an update on the status of its flagship 'Squadron 2020' programme to acquire four *Pohjanmaa* class corvettes. Reporting that the corvettes' design was nearing completion, the announcement noted a slight increase in length (119m) and beam (16m) over previous estimates. Displacement will be a substantial 4,300 tonnes. The changes were made to improve stability and to add a margin for future growth. Fabrication will start by the end of 2023. Sea trials of the lead ship will follow in 2026 and programme completion in 2029. This amounts to a delay of around two years compared with previous plans.

The last year has seen **Poland** continue preparations for the start of construction of its *Miecznik* ('Swordfish') frigate programme. First steel-cutting for the first of a planned three vessels – being built to the Babcock International 'Arrowhead 140' design – is due to take place in the second half of 2023. The country also plans to relaunch its long-delayed 'Orka' submarine programme and has concluded a contract with Saab for two signals intelligence ships similar to the Swedish *Artemis*.

Notes

1. For example, see I H Sutton's 'Why Ukraine's Remarkable Attack On Sevastopol Will Go Down In History' posted to the *Naval News* site – navalnews.com – on 17 November 2022.

2. *Das Zielbild für die Marine ab 2035* (Rostock: Inspector of the Navy, 2023). It can be found by searching the German Armed Force's website, bundeswehr.de

3. The full French text of the LPM 2024-30, as presented to the French National Assembly, can be accessed at: www.assemblee-nationale.fr/dyn/16/textes/l16b1033_projet-loi.pdf. Pages 103–07 provide a helpful tabular summary of future equipment plans.

4. Two additional French variant FREMMs have been built for export, one for Morocco and one for Egypt.

5. The new Naval Doctrine is available in Russian at kremlin.ru. Amongst numerous commentaries, Nick Child's 'Russia's new maritime doctrine: adrift from reality?' posted to the *International Institute for Strategic Studies* website – iiss.org – on 2 September 2022 provides a good summary from a Western perspective. From the other side of the hill, see Prokhor Tebin, 'The New Naval Doctrine of Russia' posted to the *Valdai Discussion Club* website – valdaiclub.com – on 4 August 2022.

6. This may not remain the case if alternative sources of spares for these Ukrainian-made turbines cannot be obtained.

7. Jaime Karremann's *Marineschepen* website – marineschepen.nl – remains an invaluable source of additional information and analysis on Dutch and Belgian naval programmes.

8. See further Tayfun Ozberk, 'Turkish Navy Launches The 2nd Reis-Class (Type 214TN) AIP Submarine' posted to navalnews.com on 25 May 2023. *Hizir Reis* had been rolled out of her construction hall the previous May.

9. Devrim Yaylali's *Bosphorus Naval News* blog at: turkishnavy.net remains a leading English-language source for Turkish Navy developments. The author thanks Mr Yaylali for his advice with respect to this section.

10. See Cem Devrim Yaylali and Kate Tringham, 'OCEA despatches first FPB 98 MKIs on order for Ukraine' posted to the *Janes* site – janes.com – on 7 June 2023.

11. The commission's guidance is contained in the *Report of the Commission on the Defence Forces* (Dublin: Commission on the Defence Forces, 2022).

12. See *Security in uncertain times: The Military Advice of the Chief of Defence 2023* (Oslo: The Norwegian Armed Forces, 2023), which can be found by searching the web.

2.4A FLEET REVIEW

THE ROYAL NAVY

Adapting to a Fast-Changing World

Author:
Richard Beedall

A major milestone for the Royal Navy is expected to occur in December 2023 when the United Kingdom Carrier Strike Group is expected to be declared fully operational, some 25 years after the concept was announced as a cornerstone of the Strategic Defence Review of 1998.[1] Since then the United Kingdom has had eleven government administrations, with contemporary First Sea Lords frequently battling to preserve the programme against cancellation. Cuts were instead often accepted to other parts of the naval service.[2]

When the first Royal Navy Fleet Review appeared in the 2010 edition of this publication it stated that the Royal Navy (RN) was 'in the midst of a revolution'. It then described numerous ambitious projects and initiatives underway to modernise and increase its capabilities. Fourteen years later, many of these projects are cancelled, reduced or still incomplete. Underfunding and cost overruns are often the cause, but another problem is that government policies and priorities change faster than the RN can implement them. For example, a plan announced in May 2021 for a 'National Flagship' operated by the RN was defunct by November 2022.

The Type 45 destroyer *Defender* pictured with allied naval units during the BALTOPS22 exercise in June 2022. Whilst the Royal Navy has invested in some expensive equipment in recent years, rapid changes in both technology and the geopolitical environment threaten to leave its fleet looking dated and ineffective. *(Crown Copyright 2022)*

However, time waits for no one and the potential threats to the United Kingdom have both grown and evolved significantly since 2010. In particular, the adoption by China of a coercive 'Wolf Warrior' approach to foreign policy – backed by enlarged and modernised armed forces – has become impossible to ignore. Meanwhile advances in technologies such as autonomous platforms, artificial intelligence and hypersonic weapons threaten to leave the RN's small but expensive fleet looking dated, vulnerable and ineffective.

In a rare sign of public frustration by a senior serving naval officer, the Second Sea Lord, Vice Admiral Nick Hine, published an open letter to the naval service on 12 January 2022 stating that the RN had 'lost its ambition', and needed to transform 'to regain the operational advantage'.[3] He separately suggested that underwater dominance, commando forces and autonomous air were areas that the RN must focus on to achieve this advantage.

The words of the Admiral became prescient when a month later Russian invaded Ukraine. A hurried reassessment of priorities led to several naval projects being progressed urgently, whilst others were cancelled or put on hold.[4] The British Secretary of State for Defence, Ben Wallace, also challenged the RN to justify its proposed future force structure – which prioritises additional escort vessels. For example, he asked if more emphasis should be placed on submarines and unmanned vessels.

Table 2.4A.1 illustrates the changing composition of the RN between mid-2009 and mid-2023.

THE UNITED KINGDOM'S SECURITY STRATEGY AND DEFENCE SPENDING

In March 2021, the government published an integrated review (IR2021) of the United Kingdom's security, defence, development, and foreign policy entitled *Global Britain in a Competitive Age*. This was followed in 2022 by a *National Strategy for Maritime Security*. However, both were quickly overtaken by events. A refresh of IR2021 was thus issued in March 2023, with a significant addition being the mention of the 'UK's growing concerns about the actions and stated intent' of China. As of mid-2023, the Ministry of Defence (MOD) is about to publish a Defence Command Paper describing how it will implement the refresh.[5]

The UK's defence budget (£50.9bn – c. US$65bn – in 2023/24, around two percent of GDP) is the highest in Europe but has been little better than static in real terms in recent years.[6] After the 2022 Russian invasion of Ukraine, France and Germany announced significant increases in their defence spending and could well outspend the United Kingdom over time. It initially seemed that the British defence budget would also grow substantially. However, after two rapid changes of leadership of the governing Conservative Party led to Rishi Sunak becoming Prime Minister on 25 October 2022, he decided against any major boost to the defence budget. Instead, a more limited expansion of funding that would grow defence spending to 2.25 percent of GDP by 2025 was announced in March 2023. Thereafter, there is an aspiration to increase this figure to 2.5 percent, but only if fiscal and economic conditions allow.

The Royal Navy ceased to have its own budget in 1964 when the MOD was formed. Tracking naval expenditure is now impossible, as most is included in joint budgets. One exception is the annual Defence Equipment Plan.[7] The latest version reveals that, in the ten-year period 2022–32, £41.1bn (c. US$52.5bn) of capital expenditure has been allocated to the RN, of which £22.3bn (c. US$28.5bn) will be spent on ships. A further £59.7bn (c. US$76.5bn) is allocated to the Defence Nuclear Organisation, much of which will be spent on delivering the *Dreadnought* and *Astute* class submarines.

Table 2.4A.1: THE CHANGING FACE OF THE ROYAL NAVY 2009–2023

SHIP TYPE & CLASS	MID-2009		MID-2023	
	NUMBER[1]	TOTAL DISPLACEMENT	NUMBER[1]	TOTAL DISPLACEMENT
Aircraft Carriers	**2 (1)**	**66,000 tonnes**	**2**	**130,000 tonnes**
CV – QUEEN ELIZABETH	–	–	2	130,000 tonnes
CVS – INVINCIBLE	2 (1)	66,000 tonnes	–	–
Major Surface Combatants	**23 (1)**	**122,800 tonnes**	**17**	**98,900 tonnes**
DDG – Type 45 DARING	1	7,500 tonnes	6	45,000 tonnes
DDG – Type 42 BIII EDINBURGH	4	20,800 tonnes	–	–
DDG – Type 42 BII EXETER	1 (1)	9,600 tonnes	–	–
FFG – Type 23 NORFOLK	13	63,700 tonnes	11	53,900 tonnes
FFG – Type 22 BIII CORNWALL	4	21,200 tonnes	–	–
Submarines	**12**	**105,300 tonnes**	**10**	**108,200 tonnes**
SSBN – VANGUARD	4	64,000 tonnes	4	64,000 tonnes
SSN – ASTUTE	–	–	5	39,000 tonnes
SSN – TRAFALGAR	7	36,400 tonnes	1	5,200 tonnes
SSN – SWIFTSURE	1	4,900 tonnes	–	–
Amphibious Ships	**7**	**124,300 tonnes**	**4(1)**	**85,600 tonnes**
LPH – OCEAN	1	22,500 tonnes	–	–
LPD – ALBION	2	37,000 tonnes	1 (1)	37,000 tonnes
LSD – LARGS BAY (RFA)	4	64,800 tonnes	3	48, 600 tonnes
Mine Countermeasures Vessels	**16**	**10,800 tonnes**	**9**	**11,300 tonnes**
LSV – 'CASTLE' (RFA)	–	–	1	5,000 tonnes[2]
MCMV – SANDOWN	8	4,800 tonnes	3	1,800 tonnes
MCMV – 'HUNT'	8	6,000 tonnes	6	4,500 tonnes

Notes:

1. Number figures in brackets relate to ships laid up in extended readiness.

2. Estimate.

THE DREADNOUGHT PROGRAMME

The United Kingdom's most expensive ever defence project is the £41bn (c. US$52.5bn) *Dreadnought* class strategic submarine programme. These four submarines will replace the *Vanguard* class in the provision of the British continuous at-sea deterrent. They will be the largest submarines ever operated by the RN.

The programme entered Delivery Phase 3, valued at £10bn (c. US$12.5bn), in March 2022.[8] This phase will see the completion of the lead boat, *Dreadnought*, and the commencement of her sea trials in the late 2020s. Most major components of *Dreadnought*, including her twelve missile tubes, have now been manufactured, and hull sections are being moved to the Devonshire Dock Hall at the BAE Systems shipyard in Barrow-in-Furness for fitting out and integration into the completed submarine. She is due to replace *Vanguard* in the early 2030s. The latter has now finally returned to service after completion of her second Long Overhaul Period and Refuel or LOP(R). This began in December 2015 and was due to be completed by early 2020 but ultimately overran by three years.

Meanwhile, construction of the second *Dreadnought* class boat, *Valiant*, is well underway and a ceremony to mark the start of work on *Warspite* was held on 9 February 2023. The final boat – to be named *King George VI* – will follow. Work has also started on the design, development and implementation of the support arrangements needed to facilitate the class's entry into service.

ATTACK SUBMARINES AND AUKUS

The six *Swiftsure* and seven *Trafalgar* class 'hunter killer' attack submarines (SSNs) were at the core of the RN's submarine flotilla during the 1980s and 1990s. It will thus be a significant moment when the last of these, *Triumph*, decommissions in 2024 or

2025. The two classes' replacements are the seven *Astute* class submarines which have been entering service at a glacial rate; the first of class commissioned in 2010 and the fifth, *Anson*, in 2022. The sixth, *Agamemnon*, should follow in 2024 and a final boat, *Agincourt*, in 2026.

The *Astute* class were designed with a nominal 25-year service life, and it takes two decades to design and build new class of attack submarines. After several false starts, the SSN(R) project – 'R' for *Astute* Replacement – entered the concept phase in early 2020. The project gathered momentum in early September 2021 when the MOD awarded two £85m (c. US$110m) contracts to BAE Systems and Rolls-Royce for initial design work on the new submarines. Whilst no details of the preliminary design have been published, it almost certainly uses the same PWR3 nuclear reactor as *Dreadnought* and likely has the same, c. 12.8m, pressure hull diameter. The hull length is likely to be over 100m, i.e. somewhere between the *Astute* and *Dreadnought* designs. The increased volume would allow improved habitability (including accommodation for female crew), a greater load of weapons, and space for autonomous underwater vehicles. Designed service life is expected to be 35 years, reflecting experience and reducing the need for expensive refits. When the concept phase began, the first of class was expected to enter RN service in the early 2040s.

An early hint that the schedule might change occurred when the trilateral AUKUS security pact between Australia, the United Kingdom and the United States was unexpectedly announced on 15 September 2021. This committed the UK and USA to supplying Australia with nuclear-powered submarines to help it counter regional threats, undoubtedly meaning China. This controversially replaced a previous deal that Australia had concluded with France for the supply of conventionally-powered submarines. It took over a year to negotiate the details of the submarine agreement, which were announced on 14 March 2023.[9] In summary:

Covered in black sheeting, the first pressure hull unit for the strategic submarine *Dreadnought* was transported to the Devonshire Dock Hall in Barrow-in-Furness on 30 November 2022 for outfitting and integration into the complete submarine. The image gives a good impression of the extensive diameter of the boat's hull. *(BAE Systems)*

The *Astute* class nuclear-powered attack submarine *Anson* left Barrow-in-Furness on her maiden voyage in February 2023, several months after commissioning on 31 August 2022. The *Astute* class are being commissioned at a glacial pace but there are hopes that the production of a successor class under the SSN-AUKUS programme will eventually lead to an increase in submarine numbers. *(Crown Copyright 2023)*

- Australian naval personnel will attend nuclear submarine-related courses in the United Kingdom and United States of America from 2023 onwards.
- Up to four American submarines and one British *Astute* class submarine will be based at HMAS *Stirling* in Western Australia from 2027, with Australian personnel forming part of their crew.
- Australia will buy or lease three *Virginia* (SSN-774) class nuclear-powered attack submarines from the United States, with an option for another two. These will start to enter Royal Australian Navy (RAN) service by the early 2030s.
- Australia will subsequently build submarines based on the UK's SSN(R) design, upgrading the Osborne Naval Shipyard in Adelaide, South Australia to undertake their assembly. The new submarines will be known as SSN-AUKUS.
- The UK will complete the first of the submarines for delivery to the RN by the late 2030s, with Australia then following with the first boat for the RAN by the early 2040s.
- Rolls-Royce UK will build the nuclear reactors for all of the RN and RAN submarines.

The British side of the project will now be accelerated, with construction of the first new Royal Navy submarine beginning 'later this decade', probably meaning 2029. The British government committed an additional £3bn to support the Defence Nuclear Organisation in the March 2023 defence spending announcements and it is expected that much of this will be used to expedite design work and boost British submarine industrial infrastructure. Australia has committed to making a proportionate financial investment. Senior RN officers are hoping that the economies of scale resulting from AUKUS will allow the construction of ten new attack submarines, a force level not seen since 2006. The SSN(R) baseline design is now being evolved to meet Australian as well as British requirements.

Meanwhile, the RN is developing a vision, known as Project Atlantis, for the future underwater battlespace. By the 2040s, it is envisaged that this will encompass unmanned, autonomous and remotely-operated underwater vehicles; mothership submarines; and underwater sensors that will all operate in concert. In similar fashion to the RAN, US Navy and many other fleets, the RN is already working on the development of extra-large uncrewed underwater vehicles (XLUUVs) under a programme known as Project Cetus. Although highlighting endurance, range and communication challenges – in particular the difference between automated and fully-autonomous operations – trials of an experimental Manta UUV in 2020/21 were considered successful. This has resulted in the award of a £15.4m (c. US$20m) contract to MSubs Ltd in December 2022 to build the RN's first XLUUV for delivery in late 2024. The 17-tonne, 12m long submarine will be 2.2m in diameter and have a range of 1,000 miles.

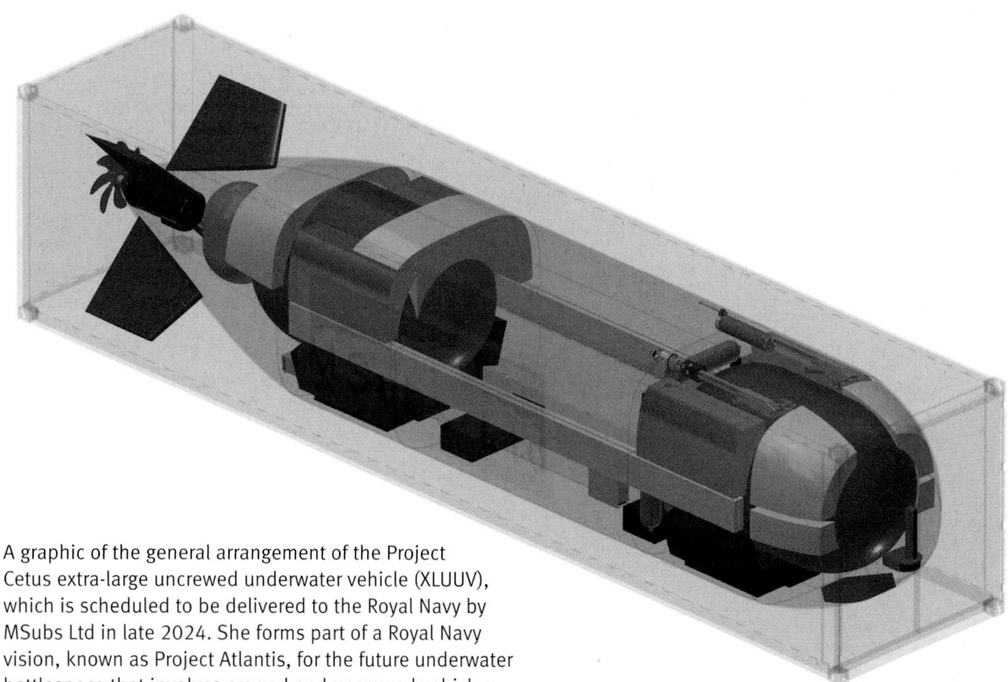

A graphic of the general arrangement of the Project Cetus extra-large uncrewed underwater vehicle (XLUUV), which is scheduled to be delivered to the Royal Navy by MSubs Ltd in late 2024. She forms part of a Royal Navy vision, known as Project Atlantis, for the future underwater battlespace that involves crewed and uncrewed vehicles working in unison. *(Crown Copyright 2022)*

CARRIER STRIKE AND THE FLEET AIR ARM

After years of anticipation, the inaugural operational deployment of *Queen Elizabeth* and Carrier Strike Group 2021 (CSG21) to the Far East was unfortunately badly affected by the COVID-19 pandemic, preventing high-profile events. Nevertheless, CSG21 demonstrated a power-projection capability that the United Kingdom and RN has not had since 2010, albeit assisted by the US Navy and US Marine Corps.

It was hoped that CSG21 would mark the start of substantial annual deployments. However, this was prevented when on 27 August 2022 *Prince of Wales* suffered a serious propeller-shaft failure at the start of her 'Westlant 22' deployment. *Queen Elizabeth* replaced her for part of the mission, but this restricted her own CSG22 deployment to just a few weeks. In October 2022 *Prince of Wales* was dry docked in Rosyth to begin repairs estimated to cost £25m. Once repaired she will again try to head to the United States' east coast in autumn 2023 for flying trials as part of a rearranged 'Westlant 23'.

August 2023 should see *Queen Elizabeth* deploy to the Mediterranean at the head of CSG23, before being replaced in 2024 by *Prince of Wales* as the UK's high-readiness strike carrier. She will then begin her first major refit since being completed in 2017. This will likely include improvements to her aviation arrangements to support the routine operation of fixed-wing unmanned air vehicles (UAVs). In 2025, *Prince of Wales* is expected to lead another major deployment 'East of Suez'.

On 15 December 2010 the Fleet Air Arm's (FAA's) last frontline fixed-wing Harrier squadron was decommissioned. Thirteen years later the formation of 809 Naval Air Squadron (NAS) with F-35B Lightning strike fighters seems imminent, although it will not be until 2025 that it is fully operational.

The FAA has completed a nearly two-decade-long update of its helicopter force, during which it halved in size. Its core strength is now twenty-eight Wildcat HMA2 maritime attack helicopters, twenty-five Merlin HC4/4A transport helicopters and thirty Merlin MH2 multi-role helicopters. The small number of the latter is a particular concern. They are in constant demand in their original role as a highly capable anti-submarine warfare platform, whilst five helicopters are now usually fitted with the Crowsnest Airborne Surveillance and Control (ASAC) system. Extraordinarily, they are also being used as a search and rescue (SAR) guard helicopter during fixed-wing operations from aircraft carriers, a role suited to a smaller and cheaper helicopter. Their out-of-service date has been extended from 2029 to 2040, by which time some airframes will be 50 years old.

Crowsnest has been a disappointment, suffering from performance issues that result from an attempt to save money by stretching 30+ year-old technology too far. The system should have entered initial operational service in March 2020, but is yet to achieve this three years later. Whilst Crowsnest was deployed as part of CSG21, it had significant limitations and reliability issues. The MOD has seemingly accepted that the system will never be fit for purpose against modern threats and it is likely to be replaced by the end of the decade.

Since 2020 the RN and FAA have been working on Project Vixen, an ambitious project to develop a substantial fixed-wing unmanned air vehicle, variants of which could be used in AEW, surveillance, air-to-air refuelling, electronic warfare and strike roles.[10] It was expected that the platform could be a derivative of the Spirit Mosquito UAV being developed by the RAF under Project LANCA (Lightweight Affordable Novel Combat Aircraft) but this was cancelled in June 2022. A more modest project took shape in July 2022 when the MOD awarded Leonardo a £60m (c. US$75m) contract to design and manufacture a prototype rotary-wing uncrewed air system (RWUAS) under a separate programme known as Project Proteus.

The RN increasingly uses contractor-owned helicopters such as the Dauphin 2 for fleet support duties, alleviating pressure on FAA assets. The RN is also seeking to reduce the use of helicopters by purchasing unmanned drones that can deliver or

An interesting aerial photo of *Queen Elizabeth* docked at Limassol in Cyprus on 30 June 2021, during the CSG21 deployment. Fifteen of the eighteen embarked F-35 Lightning II fighters are parked on her flight deck, and the aviation arrangement needed to operate these are clearly shown. These include two vertical landing areas with an expensive metallic covering that provides the deck with a thermal barrier against hot jet exhausts reaching 1500 °C. CSG21 was badly impacted by the Covid pandemic but demonstrated a revived Royal Navy power-projection capability. *(Crown Copyright 2021)*

A Merlin HC4 transport helicopter from 846 NAS exercising with a Portuguese Air Force counterpart in May 2023. The FAA has completed a nearly two-decade long update of its helicopter force but reduced numbers are stretching its ability to meet operational commitments. *(Crown Copyright 2023)*

cross-ship loads of at least 45kg (100lbs). The Malloy Aeronautics TRV-150s UAV with a maximum payload of 68kg (150lbs) was tested in 2021.

In the mid-2010s the RN successfully operated the Sea Eagle UAV for surveillance tasks from escorts operating in the Arabian Gulf, but this ceased due to a lack of money. A replacement has now been procured in the form of a S-100 Camcopter UAV manufactured by Schiebel. The single UAV, named Peregrine, will initially operate from the frigate *Lancaster* in 2024. Combined with her Wildcat helicopter, it will enable around-the-clock tasking and monitoring of targets such as smugglers and pirates.

On 30 March 2022, 736 NAS was disbanded. Equipped with BAE T1 Hawks, it was the RN's only fast jet squadron. As a partial replacement, the FAA has taken delivery of seven small remotely-piloted QinetiQ Banshee Jet80+ drones under Project Vixen. In March 2023, 700X NAS based at RNAS Culdrose formed a flight to operate these. The *Queen Elizabeth* class will operate Banshees as a step towards more capable unmanned systems.

DESTROYERS AND FRIGATES

The RN's escort force – destroyers and frigates – fell

A tired-looking *Montrose* shown making her final entry into Portsmouth naval base on 17 March 2023, before decommissioning. She is being escorted by the SERCO marine tugs *Indulgent* and *Bountiful*, which are providing a water cannon salute to the Type 23 frigate in honour of her long service. *(Andy Amor)*

to just seventeen warships when the 29-year-old frigate *Montrose* decommissioned on 17 April 2023. She had returned to UK waters in December 2022 after three and a half years forward deployed to the British naval support facility in Bahrain (HMS *Jufair*), averaging an extraordinary operational availability of over 300 days a year. This was enabled by using two rotating crews, named Port and Starboard. She has been replaced on station by her sister-ship, *Lancaster*.

The availability and operation of the six Type 45 destroyers has always been affected by their unreliable propulsion machinery, an issue highlighted by the breakdown of *Diamond* early in CSG21. A remedial Power Improvement Project (PIP) was approved in 2015 but implementation has been slow. *Dauntless* was the first to complete the work after two years in the shipyard, subsequently making her first post-refit operational deployment in mid-2023. *Daring* has also completed PIP and will soon return to service, whilst work on *Dragon* is currently underway.

The Type 45 class has also been criticised for being under-armed. However, several weapon upgrades have recently been approved: the urgent fitting of eight Naval Strike Missiles manufactured by Kongsberg in Norway, the replacement of the Aster 15 short-range air defence missile with Sea Ceptor (twenty-four CAAMS missiles being installed in a previously unused silo) and upgrading the Sea Viper area air defence system to provide a limited anti-ballistic missile capability (up to forty-eight of the latest Aster 30 Block 1 NT missiles will be carried). In the longer term, the MOD is studying a Type 83 destroyer to replace the Type 45; it is likely to succeed production of Type 26 frigates at BAE Systems shipyards on the Clyde.

The backbone of the RN escort force is formed by the eleven remaining elderly and hard-worked Type 23 frigates. However, their replacements are now in hand. The 'high end' of the frigate force will comprise a total of eight Type 26 'City' class anti-submarine warfare frigates ordered from BAE Systems. The initial three were ordered in July 2017 and the remaining five under a £4.2bn

The frigate *Westminster* monitors the Russian Project 1155 destroyer *Vice Admiral Kulakov* and tanker *Vyazma* during refuelling operations off the west coast of the United Kingdom in September 2022. The remaining eleven elderly and hard-worked Type 23 frigates are proving increasingly difficult to maintain in service and there have recently been rumours about *Westminster*'s own future. *(Crown Copyright 2022)*

The new Type 26 frigate *Glasgow* is towed to her fitting-out berth on 3 December 2022 following a lengthy float-out procedure using a submersible barge over the previous days. On current schedules, it will not be until 2028 that she enters operational service. *(Crown Copyright 2022)*

(c. US$5.4bn) contract announced in November 2022. The lead ship, *Glasgow*, was launched later that month on 25 November and is currently fitting out. Her sea trials should begin by 2026 prior to a currently planned in-service date of late 2028. This represents a year's delay compared with initial plans due to the Covid pandemic and problems related to manufacturing her gearbox. Work is also now underway on sister-ships *Cardiff*, *Belfast* and *Birmingham* following first steel-cutting on the last-mentioned ship on 4 April 2023.

The low end of the frigate force will comprise five Type 31 'Inspiration' class general-purpose frigates ordered in 2019 from Babcock International at headline cost averaging £250m (c. US$ 300m) each. However, the final cost including inflation and government-furnished equipment could exceed £400m (c. US$510m). The lead ship, *Venturer*, was formally laid down on 26 April 2022 and is being assembled at Rosyth. She is expected to be launched in December 2023 and enter service in 2027. If all five ships are delivered by 2030 as contracted, the RN escort force should then be back up to nineteen warships. It was confirmed in May 2023 that, like the Type 26 design, it is now planned to fit the Type 31 frigates with the Mk 41 vertical launch system, greatly increasing the range of missiles that they can potentially carry.

Studies on a new Type 32 class frigate – likely to be a variant of the Type 31 – are underway. In January 2023 it was officially stated that approximately c. £4m of funding has been allocated for this work, with a decision on ordering up to five ships expected by mid-decade. If the Type 32 project proceeds, then the early 2030s should see an increase in the number of RN escorts. This assumes that the final design equates to a traditional frigate, rather than morphing to a mothership for autonomous vessels and systems.

The veteran Royal Fleet Auxiliary *Argus* is being re-roled as an amphibious support ship to form the core of Littoral Response Group (South). This picture was taken in the Caribbean in August 2020. *(Crown Copyright 2020)*

The forward deployment of Royal Navy offshore patrol vessels across the globe has met with considerable success. Here the Batch 2 'River' class OPV *Spey* is seen exercising with the Royal Australian Navy patrol vessel *Wollongong* in August 2022. *(Australian Department of Defence)*

AMPHIBIOUS AND LITTORAL WARFARE

The last decade saw a decline in the importance of the Royal Marines and the United Kingdom's amphibious warfare capabilities. However, IR2021 set out a new strategic vision. It proposed to establish two permanent Littoral Response Groups. One – LRG (North) – would operate in the NATO region, covering the Atlantic, Baltic and Mediterranean. The second – LRG (South) – would operate in the Indo-Pacific region. In a crisis the two formations could combine to form a substantial Littoral Strike Group. One major challenge in meeting this vision has been finding enough specialist amphibious shipping for two LRGs. A plan previously announced in 2019 to build or convert two dedicated littoral strike ships (LSS) has not been implemented.

LRG (North) formed around March 2021 and includes the sole high-readiness *Albion* class amphibious transport dock (*Bulwark* from 2024), one of the three 'Bay' class auxiliary dock landing ships, 45 Commando Royal Marines and supporting elements. However, the creation of LRG (South) has been more problematic as no *Albion* class vessel is available and the 'Bays' are in high demand. It was eventually announced on 11 July 2022 that the 41-year-old veteran Royal Fleet Auxiliary (RFA) *Argus* would be converted to the LSS role at a cost of £50m (c. US$65m). She completed a refit in March 2023 that will allow her to remain in service until 2030. This did not include any obvious LSS-related upgrades other than the fitting of a Phalanx weapon system, although officially she is now an amphibious support ship. She is expected to be forward based at the port of Al Duqm in Oman, providing a naval platform for a force of up to 450 personnel from 40 Commando RM, the Army and the FAA. She will carry a small air group of Wildcat AH1 multirole and Merlin HC4 transport helicopters, plus Apache AH-64E attack helicopters when these are required.

It is planned that all current amphibious warfare ships, i.e., two *Albion*s, three 'Bays' and *Argus*, will be replaced by up to six new multi-role support ships (MRSS) in the first half of the 2030s. The possibility of their acquisition as a joint programme with the Royal Netherlands Navy is being explored. A decision on the replacement of the strategic sea lift capability provided by four commercially-operated 'Point' class vessels is expected soon, as their lease expires on 31 December 2024.

PATROL VESSELS

Due to a lack of escorts, the RN has resorted to the forward deployment of offshore patrol vessels (OPVs) to foreign stations. This has been a success.

The Royal Navy is transitioning from manned mine countermeasures vessels to an autonomous minehunting capability supported by logistics support vessels. These photographs show the support vessel RFA *Stirling Castle* and the autonomous minehunting vessel RNMB (Royal Navy Motor Boat) *Apollo* off Portsmouth in the spring of 2023. *(Derek Fox)*

The Batch 2 'River' class OPVs *Spey* and *Tamar* are deployed to the Indo-Pacific region, *Forth* to the South Atlantic, *Medway* to the Caribbean and *Trent* to Gibraltar for operations in the Mediterranean and West Africa.[11] To maximise availability, the ships are assigned a crew of three watches. Two are embarked with the other on leave and training, with the watches rotating every three months. These small, c. 2,000-tonne patrol vessels are punching far above their weight, as they are fulfilling tasks traditionally fulfilled by larger vessels, even cruisers. They are also visiting ports that have not seen the 'White Ensign' for decades. It is intended that two Type 31 frigates will replace the OPVs in the Indian Ocean and Pacific late this decade.

Two older original 'River' class OPVs – *Tyne* and *Mersey* – patrol UK waters on fishery protection type duties. A sister-ship, *Severn*, is primarily used for navigational training. It was briefly planned that these ships would be rebased at local ports related to their name, but a study found that this would be too expensive, and they thus still operate from Portsmouth. The Marine Scotland Directorate also operates two *Jura* class OPVs and a smaller inshore patrol vessel.

MINE COUNTERMEASURES

One part of the RN that will change radically over the next few years is the mine countermeasures force. It was announced in 2021 that all the manned mine countermeasures vessels (MCMVs) would be retired by 2031. At the time the RN was operating eight *Sandown* and six 'Hunt' class MCMVs. Instead, under the Mine Hunting Capability (MHC) programme, the RN will transition to an unmanned MCM future based around autonomous mine countermeasures systems and supporting logistic support vessels (LSVs). This process is already underway. Notably, just three *Sandown* class ships remained in service by June 2023 and these will decommission by 2025.

A foretaste of the future was provided in January 2023 when the offshore support vessel MV *Island Crown* – 97m long and displacing c. 5,000 tonnes – was purchased by the MOD to act as an interim LSV. Renamed RFA *Stirling Castle*, she has completed a three-month conversion at Devonport and will be based at Faslane as an offshore forward operating base for autonomous MCM systems. Her role will be 'to find and neutralise sea mines and other seabed threats in British waters'. Although

The three new fleet solid support (FSS) ships are primarily intended to replenish the Royal Navy's carrier strike groups. This graphic shows a FSS (left) and 'Tide' class fleet tanker (right) operating with a *Queen Elizabeth* class aircraft carrier. An order for the ships was confirmed in February 2023. *(Crown Copyright 2018. Modified by Team Resolute®)*

final decisions have yet to be taken, it is envisaged that three or four purpose-built LSVs will either join or replace *Stirling Castle* by 2030. These will be based in the UK and Bahrain, although available for operational tasks worldwide.[12]

The uncrewed systems include unmanned surface vessels, sonar and drones being developed by the joint Anglo-French Maritime Mine Countermeasures (MMCM) programme, a combined influence sweep (SWEEP) system and medium underwater autonomous vehicles (MAUVs). In February 2023, one of these demonstrator systems – the autonomous mine hunting vessel RNMB *Harrier* – was deployed to Bahrain as part of an ongoing programme of operational evaluation. With the auxiliary dock landing ship *Cardigan Bay* acting as her mothership, she is conducting trials to prove her capabilities in hot weather, having already proved her ability in UK waters.

ROYAL FLEET AUXILIARY (RFA) SERVICE

The RFA's decline in its traditional role of replenishing at sea (RAS) RN and NATO warships continued when the supply ships *Fort Rosalie* and *Fort Austin* were sold to Egypt in October 2021, leaving the aging and increasingly unreliable *Fort Victoria* as the only vessel able to resupply RN warships with significant quantities of solid stores. The downsizing continued when, in March 2022, the fast tanker *Wave Knight* joined her sister-ship in extended readiness, leaving just the four 'Tide' class vessels in the fleet tanker role.

However, there was good news in November 2022 when it was announced that Team Resolute, comprising BMT, Harland & Wolff and Navantia, had been selected as the preferred bidder for a £1.6bn (c. US$2bn) deal to build three fleet solid support (FSS) ships for the RFA. The contract was signed on 17 January 2023. The three vessels – 216m in length and displacing nearly 40,000 tonnes – will be built to a design by BMT and therefore share many features with the 'Tide' class tankers that the company also designed.

The FSS ships will be assembled at Harland & Wolff's shipyard in Belfast, which has not built a ship since the early 2000s. Navantia's shipyards in the Bay of Cadiz in Spain will therefore construct some of the more complex blocks and provide key skills and technology transfer. Harland & Wolff's shipyard in Appledore, Devon has also been subcontracted to build blocks and the company's other British facilities will also be involved in construction. Work is due to start in 2025. All three ships should be operational by 2032, replacing *Fort Victoria* and her already decommissioned partners.

As can be seen from other sections, the next few

Two images of the experimental vessel XV *Patrick Blackett* on trials after modification work by her builder Damen Shipyards – note the Dutch flag – a week before her delivery voyage and acceptance at Portsmouth on 29 July 2022. The vessel is named after former Royal Navy sailor and Nobel Prize winner Patrick Blackett. She will be used to test new technology, equipment and concepts. *(Damen)*

years will see the RFA moving into areas that were previously the preserve of the RN, such as the LSV role. A major question is whether it will be able to supply the crews to operate these vessels given ongoing recruitment difficulties.

DEFENCE OF SEABED INFRASTRUCTURE

IR2021 identified the vulnerability of the UK's underwater infrastructure – oil and gas pipelines, communication cables and electrical interconnectors – to hostile interference. It was thus proposed to convert or build a multi-role ocean surveillance (MROS) ship to help monitor and defend this critical undersea network. The programme gained urgency when, after its invasion of Ukraine, Russia became a prime suspect for attacks on the Nord Stream underwater gas pipelines on 26 September 2022.

The British Defence Secretary announced on 25 November 2022 that plans to build a 'National Flagship' had been cancelled, freeing funds to urgently progress MROS. The multi-purpose offshore vessel *Topaz Tangaroa* was subsequently purchased by the MOD, arriving at the Cammell Laird shipyard in Birkenhead on 19 January 2023 for conversion to the MROS role. She will enter service in mid/late 2023 as RFA *Proteus.* A second, more capable, MROS ship is in the concept phase and will be purpose-built. The target in-service date was 2029. However, this was extended after the retention of *Scott* (see note 12) which she will now replace, allowing time to refine the design. The MOD is also procuring a deep diving remotely-operated vehicle that will be deployable from the MROS ships.

NAVY-X

Since 2019 the RN has been studying advanced and innovative technologies, and conducting trials of small, unmanned vessels, under the umbrella title 'NavyX'.[13] As part of this work, the MOD purchased a newly-completed FCS4008 offshore supply ship from Damen Shipyards in the Netherlands in February 2022. After some modifications, the 42m long, 270-tonne ship arrived at Portsmouth naval base on 27 July 2022, being accepted into service as XV *Patrick Blackett* two days later. After further conversion work, she is now being used to trial a range of autonomous capabilities and other systems, including Persistent Operational Deployment Systems (PODS). The

Her Majesty Queen Elizabeth II and her husband Admiral of the Fleet Prince Philip on board the ice patrol ship *Endurance*, enjoying the Trafalgar International Fleet Review held on 28 June 2005. This proved to be the final fleet review of her reign as no further review were held to celebrate the Diamond or Platinum jubilees. Similarly, no review was held to mark the coronation of her son, King Charles III, on 6 May 2023, breaking a tradition that had run since 1902. *(Crown Copyright 2005)*

later are housed in twenty-foot equivalent unit (TEU) containers, two of which can be added or removed from the ship as needed.

FAREWELL QUEEN ELIZABETH II, LONG LIVE KING CHARLES III

Her Majesty Queen Elizabeth II passed away on 8 September 2022 after a reign of 70 years. No serving member of the RN, or of a Commonwealth navy where she was Head of State, had known any other monarch. She outlived her husband, Admiral of the Fleet Prince Philip, Duke of Edinburgh, who had served with distinction in the Second World War, by a year. She has been succeeded by her son King Charles III, who as a RN officer commanded the MCMV *Bronington* in 1976. The cypher on naval badges is now changing from EIIR to CIIIR. Disappointingly, a Fleet Review was not held to celebrate the coronation of the new King on 6 May 2023, breaking a tradition that dated back to 1902.

Notes

1. This will be despite the required thirty-six F-35B Lightning aircraft being unavailable, as was pointed out by a former First Sea Lord, Admiral West, in Parliament on 6 February 2023.

2. His Majesty's Naval Service consists of the Royal Navy (including the Fleet Air Arm), Royal Marines, Royal Fleet Auxiliary, Royal Naval Reserve, Royal Marines Reserve and the Naval Careers Service. This article uses the term 'Royal Navy' as a commonly accepted title for all of these, unless a branch is explicitly named.

3. Admiral Sir Nick Hine posted a copy of the letter on his Twitter account: @VAdmNickHine

4. A useful summary can be found in Louisa Brooke-Holland, *The Royal Navy's surface fleet* (London: House of Commons Library, 15 December 2022). This is accessible via commonslibrary.parliament.uk

5. See *National Strategy for Maritime Security CP 724* (London: Department for Transport, 2022) and *Integrated Review Refresh 2023: Responding to a more contested and volatile world* CP 811 (London: HM Government, 2023), both readily accessible by searching the web.

6. For an analysis, see Esme Kirk-Wade, *UK defence expenditure* (London: House of Commons Library, 23 April 2023).

7. *The Defence Equipment Plan 2022-32* (London: Ministry of Defence, November 2022). This annual report always contains information not previously officially published.

8. See further, *The United Kingdom's Future Nuclear Deterrent, 2022 Update to Parliament* (London: Ministry of Defence, 8 March 2023).

9. *The AUKUS Nuclear-Powered Submarine Pathway, a Partnership for the Future* (Canberra: Commonwealth of Australia, 2023). This is currently widely available online.

10. Chapter 4.1 provides a more comprehensive update on the Royal Navy's UAV programmes.

11. *Forth* has been in refit at Gibraltar since early 2023, with *Medway* covering her role as Falkland Islands' guardship.

12. It is also possible that one or two additional LSVs will be built for hydrographic service, rejuvenating a force which has been reduced to the ocean survey vessel *Scott*, the survey motor launch *Magpie* and the ice patrol ship *Protector*. *Scott* was due to decommission in 2022, but this was extended to, first, 2023 and, then, 2033 as no commercial replacement could be found that had equivalent seabed surveillance capabilities.

13. The work of 'NavyX', which operates as the RN's 'innovation engine' was detailed by Richard Scott as part of the article 'The Navy After Next in last year's *Seaforth World Naval Review 2023* (Barnsley: Seaforth Publishing, 2022), pp.182–91.

2.4B FLEET REVIEW

THE HELLENIC NAVY

A Flexible and Reliable Naval Force

Author:
Guy Toremans

Greece, a seafaring nation by tradition and tendency, is situated at the tip of the Balkan Peninsula, between the Ionian Sea to the west and the Aegean Sea to the east. The country has a total surface area of some 132,000km^2 and comprises two main parts. The mainland accounts for around 80 percent of the total mass whilst a myriad of thousands of islands and islets in the Aegean, Ionian and the Eastern Mediterranean seas makes up the balance. This geography gives Greece a lengthy coastline – from 13,000km to over 17,000km dependent on the source quoted – and an Exclusive Economic Zone (EEZ) in the region of 500,000 km^2. Moreover, Greece is located in a region where a range of maritime security issues remain prevalent. A crossing point for refugees, migrants and illicit drug traffickers alike, its seas are subject to the disruptive effects of disputes relating to jurisdictional rights over territorial waters and the EEZ, as well as associated issues relating to the security of energy supply routes and the potential vulnerability of undersea cables and pipelines. The discovery of significant offshore energy resources and the impact of unilateral interpretations of international law have only served to heighten regional geopolitical tensions.

It is obvious that, for a maritime nation located in such an unstable environment, the Hellenic Navy (HN) is a critical security provider, ensuring Greece's sovereignty and safeguarding the nation's interests. Moreover, this role extends to safeguarding maritime security across the wider Eastern Mediterranean. As such, the sea service needs to maintain a fleet that is capable of operating in multi-threat environments

The HN's *Hydra* (MEKO 200HN) class frigate *Salamis* pictured in the course of exercises off the Aegean island of Santorini in September 2017. The HN has responsibility for policing and protecting Greece's substantial maritime interests but has suffered from significant underinvestment until recently. *Salamis*, completed in 1998, is currently the fleet's most recent major surface combatant. *(Crown Copyright 2017)*

on, below and above the surface. However, the economic turmoil of a decade or so ago has had a significant impact on the HN, slowing modernisation programmes, mandating a reduction in operational commitments and forcing the service to re-evaluate its priorities. The need to replace many units that are nearing the end of their service lives, including major units that are between 30 and 40 years old, has become particularly pressing. It is only recently, with the Greek economy starting to recover, that the navy has slowly started to move ahead with its plans to update its fleet.

ROLES AND MISSIONS

The HN has to cover a broad spectrum of tasks and activities. Its national tasks are primarily oriented towards deterring external threats, defending the country's territorial integrity and protecting national interests. It also carries out joint operations with other government departments, notably the paramilitary Hellenic Coast Guard, in the containment of non-state actors that seek to exploit the vulnerabilities of the maritime environment. Principal activities include supervising territorial and EEZ waters, securing the safety of the country's sea lanes of communications (SLOCs) and ensuring coastal defence of the many islands. The HN also has to address challenges relating to illegal immigration, human trafficking the protection of maritime resources, as well as humanitarian tasks such as search and rescue (SAR), the evacuation of patients from remote islands and the transportation of personnel and equipment to similar areas.

On the international stage the navy fulfils its NATO commitments by assigning units and personnel to the NATO Standing Naval Forces SNMG2 and SNMCMG2. It also participates in joint international operations within, for example, NATO, European Union and United Nations contexts.

OVERALL ORGANISATION

As of mid-2023, the HN's inventory comprised c. 60 major combatants (submarines, frigates, fast attack craft, large patrol vessels and major amphibious units) and around 120 minor warships and auxiliaries. The navy operates from two main naval bases; one at Salamis opposite Piraeus on the mainland and the other at Souda Bay on the island of Crete.[1] There are also minor naval stations on some of the other islands. Due to its geographical

The lead MEKO 200HN frigate *Hydra* is seen here in company with the US Navy destroyer *Gonzalez* (DDG-66) and the Italian frigate *Antonio Marceglia* in the Ionian Sea in March 2022. In additional to meeting national obligations, the HN is also active supporting joint operations with allied navies. *(US Navy)*

Hellenic Navy fast attack craft at Amfiali Naval Station, part of the geographically-dispersed complex of facilities that supplement the HN's main naval base at Salamis, in 2014. Three of the now elderly 'La Combattante IIa' *Votsis* class can be seen in the foreground, with a mix of the larger 'La Combattante IIIa' and 'IIIb' types moored behind. The HN's Fast Attack Craft Command reports to Fleet Headquarters, which has responsibility for all the fleet's front-line combatants. *(Guy Toremans)*

position and deep-water harbour, Souda Bay is an important strategic facility for the US Navy and NATO, being capable of receiving ships as large as the *Nimitz* (CVN-68) class aircraft carriers. Souda naval base is also home to the NATO Maritime Interdiction Operational Training Centre (NMIOTC).

The HN is run by the Hellenic Naval General Staff (HNGS). As of the first half of 2023, this was headed by Chief of the HNGS, Vice Admiral Ioannis Drymousis, with the assistance of the Deputy Chief of the HNGS, Rear Admiral

Table 2.4B.1 HELLENIC NAVY FLEET COMPOSITION – MID 2023

PRINCIPAL UNITS

TYPE	CLASS	NO.	TONNAGE	DIMENSIONS	DATES[1]	MAIN ARMAMENT
Submarines (10)						
Submarine – SSK	Type 214 **PAPANIKOLIS**	4	1,800 tonnes	65m x 6m x 7m	2010–16	8 x TT. 16 torpedoes & guided missiles
Submarine – SSK	Type 209/1200 (Mod) **OKEANOS**	1	1,650 tonnes	62m x 6m x 6m	1979	8 x TT. 14 torpedoes & guided missiles
Submarine – SSK	Type 209/1200 **POSEIDON**	3	1,300 tonnes	56m x 6m x 5m	1979–80	8 x TT. 14 torpedoes
Submarine – SSK	Type 209/1100 **GLAVKOS**	2	1,250 tonnes	54m x 6m x 5m	1972	8 x TT. 14 torpedoes & guided missiles
The operational status of some of the older submarines must be considered doubtful.						
Major Surface Combatants (13)						
Frigate – FFG	MEKO 200HN **HYDRA**	4	3,400 tonnes	117m x 15m x 6m	1992–8	1 x 127mm gun, 16 x ESSM, 2 x quad Harpoon, 2 x triple TT, 1 x hel
Frigate – FFG	**ELLI** (KORTENAER)	9	3,750 tonnes	131m x 15m x 6m	1981–2003	1/2 x 76mm guns, 1 x oct Sea Sparrow SAM, 2 x quad Harpoon, 2 x twin TT, 1/2 x hel.
Fast Attack Craft (16)						
Fast Attack Craft – FAC	Super Vita **ROUSSEN**	7	675 tonnes	62m x 10m x 3m	2005–22	1 x 76mm gun, 2 x quad Exocet, 1 x Mk 49 RAM
Fast Attack Craft – FAC	'La Combattante IIIb' **KAVALOUDIS**	5	425 tonnes	56m x 8m x 3m	1980–1	2 x 76mm guns, 2 x twin Harpoon, 2 x TT
Fast Attack Craft – FAC	'La Combattante IIIa' **LASKOS**	4	425 tonnes	56m x 8m x 3m	1977–8	2 x 76mm guns, 2 x twin Exocet, 2 x TT
One or two 1970s 'La Combattante IIa' VOTSIS class FAC may also remain in service.						
Large Patrol Vessels (10)						
Patrol Vessel – PG	HSY-56A **MACHITIS**	4	575 tonnes	57m x 10m x 3m	2003–05	1 x 76mm gun
Patrol Vessel – PG	HSY-55 **KASOS**	2	575 tonnes	57m x 10m x 3m	1993–4	1 x 76mm gun
Patrol Vessel – PG	OSPREY 55 **ARMATOLOS**	2	550 tonnes	55m x 11m x 3m	1990	1 x 76mm gun
There is also one re-roled 'La Combattante IIa' FAC and one former US Navy ASHVILLE (PGM-84) class gunboat. These are supplemented by five coastal patrol vessels.						
Mine Countermeasures Vessels (3)						
Minehunter – MCMV	MHC-51 **EVNIKI**	2	925 tonnes	57m x 11m x 3m	2007	Close-in weapons only
Minehunter – MCMV	'Hunt' **EVROPI**	1	750 tonnes	60m x 10m x 3m	2000	Close-in weapons only
Major Amphibious Units (9)						
Tank Landing Ship – LST	'Jason' **CHIOS**	5	4,500 tonnes	116m x 15m x 3m	1994–2000	1 x 76mm gun (see text)
Hovercraft – LCUJ	Project 1232 **KEFALLINIA**	4[2]	550 tonnes	57m x 26m x 22m	2001–05	See text
There are also significant numbers of smaller landing craft ranging from c. 5 surviving Type 520 utility landing craft to between 40 and 50 smaller vehicle and personnel types.						

Notes:

1. Dates refer to induction of serving ships into the Hellenic Navy.
2. At least one of these vessels may be laid up.
3. The main fleet units are supported by a significant fleet of logistic support, auxiliary and specialist vessels. These include the c. 13,500-tonne *Etna* class replenishment oiler *Prometheus,* the c. 3,750-tonne logistic support ship *Aliakmon* and three former offshore support vessels re-roled as general-purpose support ships. Other assets include four hydrograhic survey vessels and a number of oil and water tenders, tugs and other yard craft.

Konstantinos Vlachos. The Chief of the HNGS also heads the Supreme Naval Council.

Three main Major Commands report to the Chief of the HNGS. These are:

- Fleet Headquarters.
- Navy Logistic Support Command.
- Naval Training Command.

In addition to these Main Commands, there are a number of independent naval agencies that also report directly to the HNGS. The most significant of these are the Centre for the Automation of Combat Systems (CACS), the Hellenic Maritime Communications Headquarters, the Hellenic Naval Academy, the Hellenic Navy Hydrographic Service and the NATO Maritime Interdiction Operational Training Centre

FLEET HEADQUARTERS

Headquartered in Salamis Naval Base, Fleet Headquarters is essentially responsible for the organisation, command, training, maintenance, safety and readiness of the HN's warships. A summary of the main warships currently in service is provided in Table 2.4B.1. The warships are allocated across a number of the Fleet Headquarters' subordinate commands, as set out below.

Submarine Command: The core of Submarine Command (COMHELSUB) comprises six remaining *Glavkos* class Type 209/1100 and *Poseidon* class Type 209/1200 boats, as well as four more modern Type 214 *Papanikolis* class submarines. They represent an important deterrent force, being capable of conducting a wide variety of missions in a national, allied and international context. They are entrusted with the surveillance of the EEZ and ports, the neutralisation of any intruder that might constitute a threat, intelligence-gathering operations, the reconnaissance of coasts and the insertion and extraction of Special Forces.

The two Type 209/1100 submarines – *Nereus* and *Triton* – were part of a batch of four boats delivered between 1971 and 1972. A major mid-life modernisation for the batch under the Neptune I programme included provision of Sub-Harpoon missiles, new flank array sonar, the Unisys fire-control system, a Sperry Mk 29 Mod 3 inertial navigation system and Argos electronic support measures (ESM). The work on *Triton* was completed in

The HN's Submarine Command, comprised of boats of German design, forms an important deterrent force. These pictures show the Type 209/1200 submarines *Poseidon* (S116) and *Okeanos* (S118). *Okeanos* was the only Type 209/1200 to complete the Neptune II upgrade, which included insertion of a hull plug to accommodate an AIP module. As such, she is essentially a distinct sub-class of her own. *(Guy Toremans/Hellenic Navy)*

The Type 214 AIP-equipped *Katsonis* was the last of four *Papanikolis* class submarines delivered to the HN, being commissioned in 2016 after considerable delay. This picture shows her surfacing in the course of the 'Noble Dina 2023' international exercise in the Eastern Mediterranean. *(Hellenic Navy)*

1993 and that on *Nereus* in 2000. The four later Type 209/1200 boats – *Poseidon*, *Amphitrite*, *Okeanos* and *Pontos* – that were delivered between 1979 and 1980 were scheduled to receive a more extensive upgrade under the follow-on Neptune II programme agreed in 2002.[2] In addition to an Atlas Elektronik ISUS 90 series combat management system (CMS), an optronic mast, CSU-90 sonar, Link 11 communications and Sub-Harpoon, this was to include insertion of a 6.5m hull-plug for a Siemens fuel-cell based air-independent propulsion (AIP) system. However, this programme was cancelled whilst work on *Okeanos*, the first to enter refit, was underway. As a result, she was the only Type 209/1200 to complete the upgrade when finally redelivered in October 2014. Given their age and the lack of recent modernisation, the status of many of the other HN Type 209s must now be considered doubtful.

The HN became the first Type 214 customer, announcing an order for three of the AIP-equipped submarines in October 1998. An option for a fourth was confirmed in 2002. The lead boat, *Papanikolis*, was launched at HDW in Kiel on 22 April 2004, arriving in Greek waters at the end of 2010 after being commissioned at Kiel the previous months. The three other members of the class – *Pipinos*, *Matrozos* and *Katsonis* – were assembled by Hellenic Shipyards in Skaramangas, commissioning between 2015 and 2016 after considerable delays resulting from a lengthy contractual dispute with thyssenkrupp Marine Systems (tkMS) and Greece's economic problems. They are undergoing incremental upgrades that include acquisition of new SeaHake Mod 4 heavyweight torpedoes and the installation of a Leonardo torpedo countermeasures system. They are amongst the most potent elements of today's Hellenic fleet.

COMHELSUB's inventory also includes three 1966-vintage Type 430A torpedo recovery vessels acquired from Germany between 1989 and 1991, and the Submarine Training School, where the command runs its own Submarine Officer Command Course.

Frigate Command: This operates the four *Hydra* (MEKO 200HN) class frigates *Hydra*, *Spetsai*, *Psara* and *Salamis*, commissioned between 1992 and 1998, and nine *Elli* class (*Kortenaer* class) frigates largely acquired second-hand from the Royal Netherlands Navy between 1993 and 2003.[3] These thirteen frigates are divided into two squadrons.

In April 2023, the Greek Parliament reportedly approved a budget in the region of €500m (c. US$535m) for a long-delayed mid-life upgrade of the four *Hydra* class frigates. The US State Department had previously approved the potential sale of equipment valued at as much as US$2.5bn that included integration of the Aegis based COMBATSS-21 CMS, TRS-4D multi-function radar, Mk 49 RAM missile launchers and various sonar upgrades amongst a host of other approvals. However, it would seem that this scheme will be much reduced in scope if the recently-reported budget figure is accurate. Once complete, the MLU should extend the *Hydra* class's lifespan out to the c. 2035 timeframe.

Turning to the *Elli* class, six – *Aegeon*, *Adrias*, *Elli*, *Limnos*, *Kountouriotis*, and *Navarinon* – received full MLUs that were completed from 2006 to 2010. The upgrade equipped the ships – inter alia – with a Thales TACTICOS combat management system; Thales Scout Mk 2 surface surveillance radar, a Mirador electro-optical (EO) sensor and an EDO CS-3701 ESM system. Their flight decks were reinforced to allow the operation of the Seahawk S-70B-6 helicopter. The three non-modernised units – *Kanaris*, *Themistoklis* and *Nikiforos Fokas* – have received only incremental improvement and are probably of questionable operational value.

The Frigate Command is also responsible for the fleet's 'at-sea' logistical support. The most important unit is the c. 13,500-tonne *Etna* class replenishment oiler *Prometheus*, delivered in 2003 and currently the largest ship in the fleet. She is supported by three former offshore support ships – *Atlas I*, *Herakles* and *Aias* – that were donated to the navy between 2019 and 2021 by a foundation controlled by Panagiotis Laskaridis, a leading Greek shipowner. These three ships are used to conduct a wide range of support roles, including the transport of cargo and fuel, emergency towing and firefighting, and pollution response. Two former West German Type 701 *Lüneburg* class logistic support vessels were also operated for many years but only one, *Aliakmon*, remained in service as of mid-2023.

Fast Attack Craft Command: Officially known as the 'Speed Boat Administration', the Fast Attack Craft (FAC) Command currently comprises c. 16 vessels and is homeported in the Amfiali Naval Station opposite the main part of Salamis Naval Base. These are split equally between two fast attack squadrons. The wide dispersal of Greek islands across the Aegean Sea makes these territories, their coastal zones and communications in between particularly vulnerable, therefore requiring the navy to patrol these waters on a 24/7 basis. As a consequence, a large part of the HN comprises vessels – fast attack craft, as well as the patrol ships of the Surveillance Vessels Command – that are optimised for this tasking. As well as playing a leading role in safeguarding Greece's waters, the command also participates in a wide range of national and multinational exercises and operations, including interdiction and peace support missions, such as NATO's 'Sea Guardian'.

The seven *Roussen* class fast attack craft, commissioned between 2005 and 2022, are at the core of the FAC Command.[4] Combining a powerful armament, high-performance sensors and modern command facilities, these vessels are suited to conduct a wide variety of missions in both high-intensity conventional combat and lower-intensity operations. Their tasks can vary from attacking surface combatants and hostile shore installations, either alone or within a task group, to minelaying operations. The HN envisages upgrades for the class in order to ensure commonality with the systems of forthcoming new frigates and corvettes, as well as the modernised *Hydra* class frigates.

The *Roussen* class are supplemented by the four 'La Combattante IIIa' *Laskos* and five 'La Combattante IIIb' *Kavaloudis* class FACs that entered the fleet between 1977 and 1981.[5] The two variants share common hulls but have variations in equipment. The *Laskos* class received a midlife upgrade that consisted of the installation of a Thales TACTICOS combat management system and DR3000 ESM system, a MIRADOR electro-optical sensor, SRBOC launchers, Harpoon Block 1B missiles and a Link 11 data link. A similar planned upgrade for the *Kavaloudis* class was never fully implemented because of Greece's economic woes.

The HN also retains three out of six members of the smaller 'La Combattante IIa' *Votsis* type that were originally built for Germany in the early 1970s and recommissioned between 1994 and 2000.

Aegeon, formerly the Royal Netherlands Navy's *Banckert,* is one of six Dutch-built *Kortenaer* class frigates in HN service that completed mid-life upgrades between 2006 and 2010. Another three members of the class in the navy's inventory have not been modernised. All are now somewhat long in the tooth. *(US Navy)*

The wide dispersal of Greek islands across the Aegean Sea has driven a continued emphasis on fast attack craft-based forces in the HN. The 'La Combattante IIIa' and 'IIIb' types – which share the same hull but have different equipment configurations – continue to dominate the FAC squadrons. This is the 'La Combattante IIIb' type *Kavaloudis*. Some sources suggest that she has been fitted with American Standard missiles since this photograph was taken. *(Guy Toremans)*

These are being withdrawn from the FAC Command as the remaining *Roussen* class are delivered, with at least one now serving with the Surveillance Vessels Command.

The HSY-56A *Machitis* class gunboat *Aittitos* pictured during exercises in the Aegean in February 2023. The HN's patrol vessels play a significant role complementing the fast attack craft in the surveillance and protection of Greece's islands. *(Hellenic Navy)*

Surveillance Vessels Command: This command's main tasks are defence of the plethora of islands across the Aegean, including the surveillance and control of local waters and shipping lanes. It assists the Hellenic Coast Guard and other security and safety-related agencies in activities that include counter-narcotics, the prevention of illegal immigration, SAR and medical evacuation missions. The command's inventory currently comprises around ten large patrol vessels (gunboats) and five coastal patrol vessels. Eight of the gunboats are from the related HSY-56A (four *Machitis* class), HSY-55 (two *Kasos* class) and 'Osprey 55' (two *Armatolos* class) series, which are based on a Danish design. These are supplemented by the former FAC *Votsis* and the veteran former US Navy *Ashville* (PGM-84) class gunboat *Tolmi* (previously PG-101 *Green Bay*). The coastal vessels encompass three 1960s-era *Andromeda* (re-roled *Nasty* class MTBs) and two 1970s *Antoniou* class vessels that are all in need of urgent replacement. The HN is reportedly receiving an initial batch of four former US Coast Guard 'Island' class cutters to replace some of the oldest patrol boats as an interim solution.

The mine countermeasures vessel *Evniki* – the former US Navy *Osprey* (MHC-51) class *Pelican* (MHC-53) – arrived in Greek waters in early 2008. She is now only one of three HN minehunters in commission following the constructive total loss of the 'Hunt' class *Kallisto* (the former Royal Navy *Berkeley*) to a collision in October 2020. *(Guy Toremans)*

Mine Warfare Command: The HN's Mine Warfare Command currently comprises only three units: the former British Royal Navy 'Hunt' class *Evropi* (ex-HMS *Bicester*) transferred in July 2000 and two US Navy *Osprey* class minehunters – *Evniki* (ex-MHC-53 *Pelican*) and *Kalypso* (ex-MHC-52 *Heron*) – that arrived in Greece in January 2008. The mine countermeasures fleet shrunk to three ships following the collision of *Kallisto* (ex-HMS *Berkeley*) on 27 October 2020 with a Portuguese-flagged container ship off Piraeus.

In October 2021 the Greek Directorate For Defense Investments and Armaments signed a letter of intent with the Netherlands Defence Materiel Organisation for the possible transfer of up to six of the Royal Netherlands Navy's (RNLN's) *Alkmaar* class ('Tripartite' type) minehunters that are scheduled to be phased out as the RNLN receives its new *Vlissingen* class MCM motherships.

Amphibious Forces Command: Vitally important for the security of Greece's numerous islands, Amphibious Forces Command's major units are focused on five *Chios* ('Jason') class tank landing ships (LSTs) and four Project 1232.2 'Zubr' (NATO 'Pomornik') air-cushion landing craft. The 'Jason' class were built in Greece commissioned between 1996 and 2000. They can embark up to four landing craft vehicle/personnel (LCVP) and have a military lift capacity that can include c. 300 fully equipped troops together with tanks and heavy vehicles. Their helicopter platform can support helicopters up to CH-47 Chinook size. A rather more unusual procurement was that of the four 'Zubr' hovercraft, which were built in Russia and Ukraine, being commissioned between 2001 and 2005. Capable of reaching speeds of 60 knots, they can embark around 140 tonnes of materiel including various combinations of troops, tanks and other equipment.

The command's inventory also includes around fifty smaller landing craft ranging in size from former c. 450-tonne West German Type 520 utility landing craft (LCUs) to small landing craft assault (LCA) and landing craft personnel (LCP) types.

Amongst the most unusual vessels in the HN are its giant Project 1232.2 'Zubr' class landing ships, which form part of the Amphibious Warfare Command. This photograph shows *Corfu*, which was delivered from Russia at the end of 2004. *(NATO)*

Naval Air Command: The HN Naval Aviation Command's operations are currently focused on the Kotroni Air Base north-east of Athens. It is comprised of two helicopter squadrons, one with eight Agusta Bell AB-212 and one with eleven S-70B/B-6 Seahawk/Aegean Hawk anti-submarine warfare rotorcraft. Two Alouette III SXA-139 helicopters may also still be used in the training role. The AB-212s will be replaced by a new fleet of seven Lockheed Martin Sikorsky MH-60R 'Romeo' Seahawk helicopters that are expected to enter operational service from the second half of 2023 onwards.

The *Hydra* (MEKO 200HN) class frigate *Psara* seen exercising with a Seahawk helicopter in March 2021. Hellenic Navy fleet modernisation plans will see new MH-60R Seahawk helicopters join the fleet whilst the *Hydra* class will receive a long-delayed mid-life modernisation. *(US Navy)*

The HN will also benefit from the reinstatement of a maritime patrol aircraft (MPA) capability with the modernisation and return to service of five P-3B Orions that were previously retired in 2009. Although one aircraft was delivered to an interim standard in 2019, completion of the fully upgraded aircraft has proved problematic and it is unlikely to be before 2026 that all will be fully operational. The P-3Bs will be allocated to the Hellenic Navy's Naval Aircraft Squadron based at the Elefsina Air Base.[6]

Other Commands: In addition to its warship and helicopter-based commands, Fleet Headquarters is also responsible for a number of other formations. Foremost amongst these is the Aegean Naval Command – officially the Aegean Naval Administration – that has responsibility, inter alia, for the various naval stations, radar and other surveillance facilities maintained across the Greek coast and islands. Since March 2022, the former Northern Greece and Ionian Commands have been incorporated into the Aegean Naval Command, becoming the North Hellenic Naval Station and Ionian Naval Station respectively.

Also subordinate to Fleet Headquarters are the

Naval Tactical Training School and the Underwater Demolition Command; the HN's Special Forces unit. Its inventory includes a range of fast interception and Special Operations craft. Recent arrivals have included four Mk V Special Operations Craft donated by the United States as part of the Excess Defense Articles program and *Agenor*, prototype of a new locally-designed and built equivalent.

NAVAL LOGISTICS AND NAVAL TRAINING COMMANDS

The Logistics Support Administration, headquartered in Athens, provides for all the fleet's logistical support and maintenance requirements to ensure that its ships remain ready to undertake their tasks. This department has under its authority the main naval bases in Salamis and in Souda Bay and a number of subsidiary support facilities, including logistical hubs in the Greek islands. It is also responsible for auxiliary units such as harbour craft and a range of administrative functions.

The Naval Training Directorate comprises a range of training and educational establishments with responsibilities ranging from the induction of conscripts and permanent ratings through the development of petty officers in specialist skills to the Naval War College. The command is also responsible for the Maritime Service, the HN's Naval Police Force.

FLEET REVITALISATION

The victory of Kyriakos Mitsotakis' New Democracy Party in the 2019 Greek elections brought to power an administration that was cognisant of the need to revitalise the Hellenic Armed Forces, including the HN. This has resulted in a significant rebound in defence expenditure alongside a September 2020 announcement of a major programme of capital investment in new and modernised equipment.

The most important naval investment is an agreement with France's Naval Group to acquire three new *Frégate de Défense et d'Intervention* (FDI) type frigates – alongside an option for a fourth – under an agreement reportedly valued in the region of €3bn (c. US$3.3bn). A memorandum of understanding relating to the deal was concluded in September 2021 and followed by a formal contract signed on 24 March 2022. The agreement includes a robust Hellenic Industrial Participation Plan that will see the involvement of numerous Greek subcontractors in FDI construction and develop the country's autonomy in the Greek ships' sustainment.

Displacing some 4,500 tonnes and with an overall length of c. 122m, the FDIs are multi-role frigates. They provide 'high end' capacity in anti-air, anti-ship and anti-submarine roles, whilst offering additional capabilities in roles such as Special Forces projection. The original French ships were also claimed to offer dedicated command facilities against asymmetric threats, as well as inbuilt cyber security. The design incorporates Naval Group's PSIM (Panoramic Sensors and Intelligence Module); a 150-tonne, 40m-high integrated mast structure that accommodates the ship's principal sensors and houses the combat management centre, data rooms and other facilities at its base. The main radar is Thales' Sea Fire 500, an active electronically-scanned array (AESA) that utilises four fixed panels. Armament includes Sylver A50 vertical launch cells for Aster surface-to-air missiles, Exocet MM-40 surface-to-surface missiles, a Super Rapid 76mm gun and twin ASW torpedo tubes. The main hangar and flight deck will allow operation of the HN's new MH-60R helicopters, whilst a dedicated hangar for UAV operations is also provided. A noteworthy design feature is the incorporation of an inverted, ram-type bow. Maximising waterline length, this is claimed to reduce hydrodynamic drag and improve stability at high speeds.

To date, the construction of the frigates is progressing at an impressive rate with work on two units currently underway at Naval Group's Lorient shipyard. These are to be built to a 'Standard 1' configuration aligned quite closely with their French counterparts. The keel-laying ceremony for the first, *Kimon*, was held on 21st October 2022.[7] She is scheduled to be launched before the end of 2023 prior to her anticipated delivery early in 2025. First steel cutting took place for her sister, *Nearchos*, on 13 July 2022. She should be handed over before the end of 2025 and be followed by the third vessel, *Phormion*, in the autumn of 2026. The last-mentioned will be built to a 'Standard 2' configuration that includes thirty-two A50 vertical launch cells and the RAM missile system. The earlier ships will be upgraded to this standard at a later date. If ordered, the optional ship will also be completed as a 'Standard 2' vessel.

The acquisition of the new frigates is to be supplemented by a HN corvette programme encompassing the procurement of up to four new corvettes (again three firm vessels plus one option). The value of the contract is expected to be around €1.6bn (c. US$1.8bn). The Greek government has short-listed Naval Group and Fincantieri to build the new

The seventh and final *Roussen* class fast attack craft, *Viahakos*, was commissioned at Amfiali Naval Station on 29 September 2022. With delivery of the class complete, the HN is now turning its attention to a much-needed renewal of its fleet of major surface combatants. *(Hellenic Navy)*

The lead HN FDI type frigate *Kimon* pictured under construction at Naval Group's Lorient facility. The acquisition of three of these frigates – plus an option for a fourth – is the focal point of Greece's current programme of fleet revitalisation. *(Naval Group)*

ships which, respectively, will be based on the companies' 2,800-tonne Gowind 2500 (Egyptian *El Fateh*) and 3,250-tonne FCX30 (Qatari *Al Zubarah*) designs. All but the first ship are to be built in Greece, with Naval Group looking to construct the follow-on vessels at Hellenic Shipyards and Fincantieri partnering with ONEX Elefsis Shipyards. Like the frigates, the corvettes are intended to be multi-role warships encompassing anti-air, anti-ship and anti-submarine missions. Once delivered, the new frigates and corvettes will gradually replace the *Elli* class frigates. Obviously, the introduction of so many new units will require some fine tuning to ensure their optimal use. However, a transition programme set up by the HNGS is based on a synchronised plan to balance the decommissioning of the legacy vessels with the arrival of their replacements.

In the longer term, Greece's membership of the European Patrol Corvette (EPC) Programme – part of the European Union's Permanent Structured Cooperation (PESCO) project to enhance defence collaboration between member states – offers the potential of further procurement, perhaps to strengthen the surveillance forces. Other requirements include a modern underway-replenishment capability and, given the size of the submarine flotilla, a dedicated submarine rescue ship.

Investment in new ships is being accompanied by further expenditure on upgraded weapons systems. The acquisition of new Atlas Elektronik SeaHake Mod 4 (DM2A4) torpedoes previously mentioned includes forty-four weapons, equipping the sole modernised Type 209/1200 *Okeanos* as well as four Type 214 submarines. In addition, Israeli Rafael Typhoon MLS-NLOS missile systems are to be acquired for use on patrol and Special Forces vessels. Broader maritime surveillance capabilities will be further enhanced by the pending acquisition of SeaGuardian MQ-9B unmanned aerial vehicles, for which the Greek parliament provided financial approval in 2022.

THE WAY AHEAD

It can be seen that recent years have marked the dawn of an ambitious HN procurement programme that offers the prospect of addressing the most critical elements of fleet capability gaps within the course of the coming decade. Given that the overall security situation across the Eastern Mediterranean remains subject to geopolitical instability, this investment is timely. A notable feature of the new procurement is the focus on acquiring larger-type vessels with high-end qualities. Whilst this partly reflects the pressing need to renew much of the obsolescent frigate force, this could also, perhaps, reflect less emphasis on the traditional flotillas of fast attack craft that have traditionally formed a major part of the fleet. In any event, the new investment augurs well for the maintenance of a flexible and reliable naval force, able to maintain a presence across the Eastern Mediterranean whilst being 'ready to fight' in time of need.

Notes

1. The Salamis base also encompasses facilities on the Greek mainland in the vicinity of Skaramangas.

2. The Neptune II programme contract covered three boats. It seems that the modernisation of the fourth, *Poseidon*, was a potential option.

3. Two of the *Elli* class were completed to Greek order in 1981 and 1982 and a further eight former Royal Netherlands Navy vessels acquired after the end of the Cold War. Of these, *Bouboulina* (previously *Willem van der Zaan*) was decommissioned in 2012 to be used for spare parts.

4. See the author's 'Roussen Class Fast Attack Craft: Thriving in Adversity', *Seaforth World Naval Review* 2016 (Barnsley: Seaforth Publishing, 2015), pp.141–53 for a detailed review of these vessels.

5. A sixth 'La Combattante IIIb', *Kostakos*, sank on 4 November 1996 after collision with a passenger ferry.

6. In addition to manned aircraft, the HN has also acquired five Spanish-designed Alpha 900 rotorcraft-type drones that will likely be deployed onboard the four *Hydra* class frigates.

7. The ships are being named after famous Greek admirals of the Classical era.

P779

3.1 SIGNIFICANT SHIPS

AUGUSTE BÉNÉBIG

First of France's New Patrouilleurs Outre-Mer

Author:
Bruno Huriet

Encompassing a total area of more than 11 million km², France has an immense Exclusive Economic Zone (EEZ); the second largest in the world. Well over 90 percent of this is away from Metropolitan France, being largely located in the Indian and Pacific Oceans.[1] Principal constituents of this EEZ include French Polynesia and New Caledonia in the Pacific, and Réunion and various scattered islands in the Indian Ocean, as well as Guadeloupe and Martinique in the Caribbean and French Guiana off South America's Atlantic coast. Policing the vast expanse of these disparate areas, spread across three oceans, requires substantial resources; a challenge long recognised by France's *Marine Nationale*. Construction of the new class of *patrouilleurs outre-mer* (POMs or overseas patrol vessels), of which *Auguste Bénébig* will be the first, forms an important part of the response to this need.

The constabulary missions required of these new vessels will be many and varied. Fighting illegal fishing that plunders marine resources, combatting drug and arms trafficking, preventing illegal immigration, providing assistance in the event of a maritime disaster and, of course, ensuring the security of the civilian population are amongst the most important tasks carried out by the navy in a country's EEZ. Overall, a dissuasive presence must be maintained. In the words of a previous French Chief of Naval Staff, most notably repeated by Édouard Philippe – French Prime Minister between 2017 and 2020 – 'What is not monitored is visited, what is visited is plundered, and what is plundered always ends up being contested.'

Left: *Auguste Bénébig*, the lead French *patrouilleur outre-mer* (POM), photographed on 1 April 2023 during the final leg of her voyage from France to her assigned base at Nouméa in New Caledonia. The POMs have been specifically designed to undertake lengthy constabulary patrol missions in the extensive waters of France's overseas EEZs. *(Thomas Trebern/Marine Nationale)*

The POMs are long-awaited replacements for the P400 class large patrol boats, which were completed during the late 1980s for overseas service. Lack of funding and indecision as to how best to meet the French Navy's requirements for new vessels meant that the class was largely retired before purpose-built replacements could be completed, giving rise to a gap in constabulary assets. This is the P400 *La Gracieuse* in 2008. *(Bernard Prézelin)*

CLASS ORIGINS

During the post-Cold War era, the policing of France's overseas waters has been primarily in the hands of three classes of warships, viz.

- Six c. 3,000-tonne *Floréal* class surveillance frigates (delivered from 1992 to 1994).
- Ten c. 500-tonne P400 class large patrol boats (1986–8).
- Five c. 1,350-tonne 'BATRAL' class light landing ships (1974–87).

Of these classes, all the 'BATRALs' have recently been decommissioned, being replaced by four new multi-role *D'Entrecasteaux* class *bâtiments de soutien et d'assistance outre-mer* (BSAOM). Quite similar to offshore support vessels, they can tow a vessel in difficulty, combat pollution, deploy a survey team and transfer – using a landing craft – a small vehicle or cargo ashore. The surveillance frigates remain

The three PAGs of the *La Confiance* class were commissioned between 2017 and 2020 for service off French Guiana and in the Caribbean. Designed and constructed by the same team that were subsequently responsible for the *patrouilleurs outre-mer*, they show a distinct family resemblance to the follow-on class but are considerably smaller. These pictures show *La Combattante* and *La Résolue. (Olivier Nicolas/Marine Nationale)*

active and their replacement is currently under consideration, possibly through the European Patrol Corvette (EPC) programme. This leaves the question of the patrol vessels, where a 'temporary breakdown in capability' – in the words of the French General Staff – has occurred. Here the P400 class has been progressively withdrawn without the arrival of modern replacements, leading to unsatisfactory 'ad hoc' solutions until the problem can be rectified.

The situation was summarised by a senior officer to the French Senate in October 2021: 'We benefit from an ambitious military programming law … however, the [patrol vessel replacement] programmes have been committed with a certain delay. In 2022 we will reach the low point in terms of overseas patrol boats, before the funding shows its effects from 2025. The Antilles-Guyana zone already has modern vessels. The other zones will have to wait until this time to have them. With ageing equipment that is certainly too little in number, it is a real challenge for us to be able to intervene and control all these areas which, without control, are plundered.'

Part of the delay arose from considerable uncertainty as to the most effective way that France's overall patrol vessel capacity should be modernised. Notably, in addition to the need to replace the P400s, the navy also had another class of patrol vessel that was reaching the end of its service life. These were the *patrouillers de haute mer* (PHMs), nine – now six – survivors of the once numerous c. 1,300-tonne A-69 corvette class that had been reclassified as patrol vessels. Based in Metropolitan France, these are used for a variety of missions ranging from escorting strategic submarines during 'near shore' transits to anti-piracy deployments off Africa.

The French Navy's initial thinking was to launch a programme to replace both patrol vessel types with a single class known as the BATSIMAR (*bâtiment de surveillance et d'intervention maritime*, or maritime surveillance and intervention vessel). This project was often discussed in the early years of the new Millennium but funding was never available to advance its launch. Finally, in 2017, then French Chief of Naval Staff Admiral Christophe Prazuck

decided to separate the two requirements, 'I initially intended to replace the metropolitan patrol boats and the overseas patrol boats with the same class of boats. I cannot do it, as I am told it would be too expensive. I therefore propose to deploy boats overseas that are two to three times cheaper so that I can get them faster. I am therefore ready to exchange the level of specification for a shortening of the timescale.'[2]

The most critical situation was that in French Guiana, whose waters were subject to pillaging by fishing fleets both from neighbouring countries and further away.[3] Moreover, the Guiana Space Centre at Kourou – from where the European Space Agency programme's rockets are launched – is located in the overseas department and its adjacent maritime zone must be 'cleared' during launches. As early as December 2014 – before the BATSIMAR programme was abandoned – it was decided to order two patrol boats specifically for the service in the area. In 2017, a third unit was ordered for deployment in the French West Indies.

This series of three ships are known as the *patrouilleurs Antilles Guyane* (PAGs) or the *La Confiance* class and were commissioned in 2017 and 2020. They were constructed by the Socarenam shipbuilding group to a design produced by the naval architects Mauric. To a large extent, these formed the basis for realising the subsequent overseas patrol vessel programme, which was ultimately entrusted to the same shipbuilders and architect. As such, images of the two designs show a clear family resemblance. However, the POMs are of significantly larger than both the P400 class and the PAGs, as illustrated by Table 3.1.1. This reflects

Table 3.1.1: FRENCH PATROL VESSEL COMPARISONS

TYPE	DISPLACEMENT	LENGTH	CORE CREW	COMMISSIONED
P400: *L'Audacieuse* class	477 tonnes	54.8m	24	1986–8
Patrouilleur Antilles Guyane: *La Confiance* class	750 tonnes	60.8m	24	2017–20
Patrouilleur Outre-Mer: *Félix Eboué* class	1,298 tonnes	79.0m	30	[2023–5]

both the evolution of patrol vessel requirements towards units with better range and endurance since the P400s entered service, as well as the different requirements of French Guiana and the Caribbean compared with the waters in which the POMs are destined to serve.

Following the decision to split the BATSIMAR programme, it was determined that tenders would be sought for a class of larger oversea patrol boats to be based in French Polynesia, New Caledonia and Réunion. A request for information (RFI) published in 2018 made clear that these vessels – designated *patrouilleurs outre-mer* – would be optimised for constabulary operations across large sea areas, with the following requirements being outlined:

- Design and construction of six vessels with either steel or aluminium hulls.
- A length of around 70m and a draft of no more than 3.8m.
- A maximum speed of at least 22 knots.
- Endurance of c. 30 days and a range of c. 5,500 nautical miles without refuelling.
- Suitability for operation from the intended overseas bases, including in conditions of high heat and humidity.
- Good manoeuvrability and sea-keeping characteristics.
- Operation by a crew of c. 35 with accommodation for up to 18 additional personnel.
- Capacity to accommodate and maintain an unmanned aerial vehicle (UAV) of up to 750kg in weight, as well as to carry two c. 8m rigid hulled-inflatable boats (RHIBs).
- Provision of handling equipment and the capacity to carry weapons and ammunition.
- Provision of tactical situational awareness equipment and integrated civilian and military communications.

Following a subsequent call for tenders, a €200m (c. US$215m) contract for the vessels' design and construction was awarded to Socarenam in December 2019. The award also included five years of operational maintenance – to be carried out by Brest-based CNN MCO – at an undisclosed cost.

Auguste Bénébig pictured on 17 January 2023 at the start of her long voyage to her assigned overseas station in New Caledonia. Her design was based on a specification that emphasised an ability to conduct constabulary operations across large sea areas, including good sea-keeping characteristics. The ship that resulted presents a slender silhouette with a panoramic 360° bridge sited virtually amidships. The main deck is enclosed for around three-quarters of the ship's length, opening out onto a working deck at the stern. Other points of note are the lightweight tubular mast structure carrying the main sensors, the large starboard opening for one of the two interception RHIBs and the platform aft of the bridge for aerial drone operations. *(Marine Nationale)*

CONSTRUCTION AND DELIVERY

Founded in 1961, Socarenam initially specialised in the construction of fishing vessels. Over time it has diversified its activities to encompass a wider range of ships. The latter have included c. 20–50m patrol boats for the French customs service, as well as 50m and 70m patrol vessels for, respectively, the Belgian Naval Component and the Polish Coast Guard. In addition to the previously mentioned *La Confiance* class, the company has also supplied the *Marine Nationale* with several series of tugs and support vessels. Headquartered at Boulogne sur Mer, Socarenam's principal construction sites are at Boulogne and at Saint Malo in Brittany. It has in the region of 250 employees.

Steel-cutting on the first POM – *Auguste Bénébig* – commenced at Saint Malo in October 2020.[4] She was floated out a year later prior to being towed to Boulogne for final outfitting. Initial sea trials commenced on 26 July 2022, with the ship subsequently sailing for the French naval base at Brest. Here, integration of military communications systems was followed by further trials, including live firing exercises. Subsequently, on 17 January 2023, *Auguste Bénébig* departed France to commence the long journey for her assigned base of Nouméa in New Caledonia. Passing via the Panama Canal, she arrived on 3 April 2023 after a 76-day voyage. She was subsequently officially delivered on 5 May 2023.

The original POM delivery programme was drawn up before the onset of the Covid pandemic, which has inevitably impacted the schedule. However, the target is to deliver all units of the class before the end of 2025. The second ship – *Teriieroo a Teriierooiterai* – was launched on 5 September 2022 and should be delivered before the end of 2023. The schedule will then accelerate, with two vessels to be handed over in 2024 and the final two in 2025.[5]

DESIGN DESCRIPTION

Technical details of *Auguste Bénébig* are summarised in Table 3.1.2. As previously mentioned, the POM design was drawn up by naval architects Mauric,

Auguste Bénébig pictured off Tahiti in French Polynesia on 14 March 2023 in the course of her voyage to New Caledonia. The patrol vessel *Arago*, a former hydrographic survey ship that has been pressed into service in the constabulary role pending completion of the POM programme, can be seen in the background. *(Thomas Trebern/Marine Nationale)*

who have previously collaborated with Socarenam on a number of other patrol boat projects.

Hull and General Arrangement: The POMs are 79.9m long, 12.0m in beam and have a draft of 3.5m. They have a displacement of 1,298 tonnes when fully loaded. As is now customary for the French Navy, the ships are being constructed under the surveillance of Bureau Veritas so as to fulfil the requirements of the classification society's specific naval rules.

Although, as previously mentioned, the POMs have a general resemblance to the previous PAGs, they are much larger vessels. As stated by the French defence procurement agency's (DGA's) programme manager, François Nicolas, the *Marine Nationale* required ships able to protect very large ocean areas; in Polynesia, New Caledonia and the Indian Ocean, EEZ patrol areas are far more significant than those in the Caribbean or Guiana.[6] As such, this mandated ships with greater endurance and longer-range surveillance systems (reflected in their endurance and capacity to operate a UAV), pushing up overall dimensions. The design achieves the RFI requirements for 30 days endurance and 5,500 nautical miles range.

Visually, the design presents a slender silhouette. The bridge is located in the middle of the ship and the main deck is enclosed for around three-quarters of its length, only opening up aft to facilitate crane and boat handling. The hull is fabricated out of steel up to the main-deck level but aluminium is used above. The connection between the two metals is made by means of a bi-metallic joint. The ship's bow incorporates a long and very tapered bulb bow form.

Moving from the ship's bottom upwards:

- The hold (20 level) contains various liquid bunkers and stores, as well as a sewage-treatment room. Like all recently-built French Navy ships, *Auguste Bénébig* complies with international standards for sewage discharge into the sea. The lower levels of the main machinery spaces also extend down into this level.
- The lower deck (10 level) houses the ratings' and petty officers' accommodation forward. This comprises four- and six-berth cabins with adjoining sanitary facilities. Further aft, from

Table 3.1.2.

AUGUSTE BÉNÉBIG PRINCIPAL PARTICULARS

Building Information:	
Fabrication Commenced:	8 October 2020 Launched: 15 October 2021 Delivered: 5 May 2023[1]
Builders:	Socarenam at their Saint Malo and Boulogne sur Mer shipyards
Dimensions:	
Displacement:	1,300 tonnes full load displacement.
Overall Hull Dimensions:	79.9m x 12.0m x 3.5m.
Equipment:	
Armament:	1 x Nexter 'Narwhal' 20B RWS. Light machine guns.
Aircraft:	Hangar and flight deck for 'Aliaca' SMDM UAV. Can operate a drone of up to 200kg in weight.
Principal Sensors:	Kelvin Hughes Mk11 SharpEye with Hensoldt MSSR 2000 IFF. 2 x navigation radar. 'Sea Eagle' EOSS surveillance system.
Combat System:	Hensoldt Nexeya 'Lyncea' CMS. Integrated communications suite with NATO Link compatibility.
Other:	2 x 6.7m RHIBs for boarding operations. 1 x 5m service RHIB. Two-tonne capacity crane and one/two 20ft/10ft containers.
Propulsion Systems:	
Machinery:	Hybrid diesel-electric/diesel. 2 x ENAG electric motors each rated at 550kW in PTI mode. 2 x ABC 16V DZC diesels each rated at 3.85MW in diesel mode. Can be combined for 'boost' power. Two shafts.
Speed:	Maximum speed is c. 24 knots in boost mode. Range is in excess of 5,500 nautical miles at 12 knots in PTI mode.
Other Details:	
Complement:	Core crew is 30, including four officers. Accommodation is provided for a total of 59 personnel, six in austere conditions.
Class & Base:	*Auguste Bénébig* (P779): Nouméa; *Teriieroo a Teriierooiterai* (P780): Papeete; *Auguste Techer* (P781): Port-des-Galets; *Jean Tranape* (P782): Nouméa; *Philippe Bernardino* (P783): Papeete; *Félix Éboué* (P784): Port-des-Galets.

Notes:

1. Refers to official delivery after arrival at Nouméa, New Caledonia. Sea trials commenced on 26 July 2022. See text for further details.

around the middle of the ship, are the main machinery compartments. These include the machinery control room and main switchboard, the main engine compartment and, then, the main auxiliary engine compartment. There are various spaces for stores further aft.

- The main deck (00 level) encompasses the ship's main catering facilities in its forward part. These include a galley, dry food stowage and cold stores, as well as a cafeteria and wardroom. A well-equipped sick bay is located on the ship's starboard side. Amidships, also to starboard, is a recess for a RHIB. To port is a room for divers and a modular compartment equipped with tables and folding bunks; it can be used to embark additional personnel (marines, soldiers, police etc.) or as a detention facility. The after-most compartments include hydraulic plant and a waste treatment and stowage room: no waste other than food waste can be disposed of into the sea. The deck then opens out into a weather deck that can house one 20ft or two 10ft containers with the support of a two-tonne crane. There is a ramp launching system for a second RHIB at the stern.
- Deck 01 contains officer and senior petty officer cabins, the communications room and a meeting room. Further aft, the UAV hangar leads to the aviation platform. Broad walkways run forward and aft to both port and starboard.
- Deck 02 is dominated by the bridge, which incorporates the command and control centre and aviation control facilities in its aft part. A passive stabilisation system and the ship's main 20mm 'Narwhal' remote weapons station can be found forward of the bridge.

Commanded by a lieutenant-commander, *Auguste Bénébig* has a core crew of 30 men and women. These comprise four officers, 20 senior petty officers and petty officers, and six ratings. There is additional accommodation for a total of 23 personnel – for example hydrographers or law-enforcement personnel – embarked dependent on mission. Accommodation is spacious and well-finished. In contrast to front-line combatants, portholes are incorporated from the lower deck up. The air-conditioning system is scaled for operation in tropical

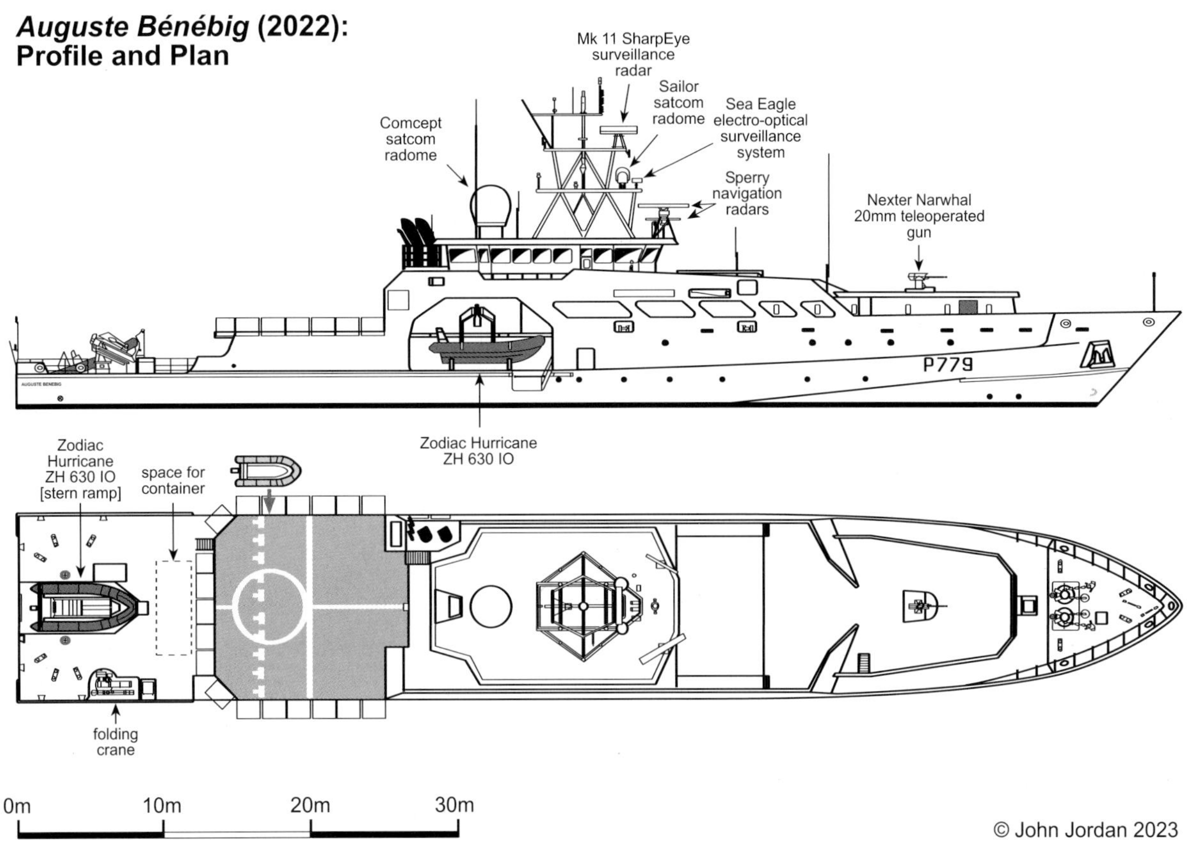

areas. When the six folding bunks in the modular compartment are taken into account, a maximum of 59 people can be housed onboard.

Engineering Details: *Auguste Bénébig* and her sisters are designed to patrol economically over long distances. This is reflected in the provision of a hybrid diesel-electric/diesel propulsion plant. For low-speed operation – up to a maximum 12 knots – the three 560kW generators installed in the auxiliary engine room can be used to supply electricity to two 550kW ENAG electric motors in power take in (PTI) mode. For higher-speed operation, power is supplied by the vessel's two main Anglo Belgian Corporation (ABC) 16VDZC diesels, which are each rated at 3.85MW. It is also possible to employ a 'boost' mode combining the power of both the electric motors and main diesels to achieve the ship's maximum speed of 24 knots. Other key elements of the propulsion train include two Reintjes gearboxes and twin shaft-lines equipped with fixed-pitch, five-bladed propellers. There are also two bow thrusters fitted to the forward part of the hull to facilitate manoeuvring at lower speeds.

In addition to the three generator sets in the hull – which meet ship 'hotel' needs as well as providing energy for PTI operation – there is also an emergency diesel generator installed at upper-deck level.

The small machinery control room is located ahead of the main engine compartment. This is equipped with a CMR Group-supplied control and monitoring system and, as noted previously, also contains the main electrical switchboard. In practice, however, the compartment will rarely be crewed whilst the ship is at sea, with control and monitoring normally performed from the bridge.

A passive stabilisation system, comprising two athwartship tanks of 10m^3, is installed in front of the bridge on 02 deck. This system was selected because it offered the best cost/efficiency ratio. Effective even at very slow speeds and even when the vessel is stationary, it also has the benefit of being a simple system. This is an important factor for ships that are destined to operate far away from maintenance specialists.

This stern view of *Auguste Bénébig* provides a good view of the aft working deck at 00 level, including the ramp used for speedy deployment of a RHIB. A hangar and aviation platform for UAVs is located at Deck 01 above. Note also the asymmetrical arrangement of the outlet for the ship's diesels, which – in conjunction with the electric motors – can produce a 'boost' speed of 24 knots. *(Marine Nationale)*

Aviation Equipment: It is in the area of aviation equipment that the POMs are arguably at their most innovative, being designed from the start to embark and operate an aerial drone system. The platform on 01 deck and the small hangar are designed to operate the SMDM (*Système Mini Drones Aériens Marine*), the French Navy's mini-UAV system. The SMDM was qualified at the end of July 2022 by the DGA after several test campaigns on offshore patrol

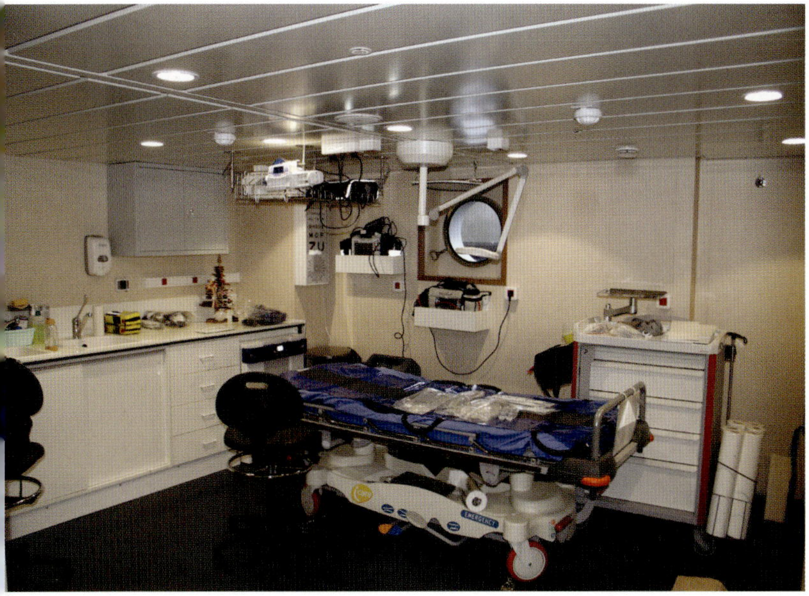

A picture of *Auguste Bénébig*'s well-equipped sick bay. This is located in the forward part of the ship at main-deck level. In contrast to front-line combatants, portholes are incorporated from the lower deck upwards. *(Bruno Huriet)*

In line with the mission requirements to undertake lengthy EEZ patrols, the POMs incorporate spacious and well-finished crew facilities. This is the cafeteria aboard *Auguste Bénébig. (Vincent Groizeleau)*

This photograph of *Auguste Bénébig*'s main engine room provides a good view of the two Anglo Belgian Corporation (ABC) 16VDZC diesels that are used for high-speed operation. A PTI arrangement utilising the ship's generators allows economical diesel-electric operation at lower speeds. *(Vincent Groizeleau)*

The POM's small machinery control room is located ahead of the main engine room and also houses the main switchboard. It is rarely crewed whilst the ship is at sea as monitoring is normally performed from the bridge. *(Vincent Groizeleau)*

The Airbus 'Aliaca' drone forms the basis of the French Navy's SMDM mini-UAV system. The POMs will be equipped with these, significantly enhancing their surveillance capabilities. *(NATO/Stéphane Dzioba)*

A view of the aft end of *Auguste Bénébig*'s superstructure, showing the small hangar that has been incorporated to support the maintenance of aerial drones. Operations are typically controlled from an 'aviation position' located in the bridge above. *(Bruno Huriet)*

vessels. Eleven systems have been ordered, each system comprising two 'Aliaca' UAVs and the associated launch, recovery and control equipment.

Designed by Survey Copter, an Airbus subsidiary, the 'Aliaca' has a wingspan of 3m and a length of 2.2m. Its mass is 16kg. Powered by an electric motor, it has a range of 27 nautical miles (50km) and can remain in flight for three hours. The UAV's cruising altitude is 150m but it can achieve a maximum altitude of 3,000m. The 'Aliaca' is equipped with a gyro-stabilised EO/IR camera capable of transmitting real-time video images to the ship; an AIS receiver allows it to read information sent out by ships in the area and also to detect those which have disconnected their AIS system to engage in illegal operations. After a short preparation time, just 10 minutes, it is catapulted into flight; recovery is performed automatically on board by means of a net. Both launch and recovery are performed on the class's aviation platform. The control system consists of two rugged laptops which are operated by two trained crew members. Operated from a dedicated position in the bridge, one computer controls the UAV's flight data and the other monitors its payload: information from the camera and the AIS.

The 'Aliaca' gives a patrol boat the capability of undertaking remote surveillance beyond the radar horizon. Silent and small, it can detect a vessel engaged in illegal operations, track it and secure images to be used as evidence, all without being detected by a suspect vessel.

The POM is designed with facilities dedicated to the use of the SMDM: a hangar for preparation and maintenance opening out onto the aviation platform, There is also a separate battery-charging room protected against fire. On the aft part of the bridge, the 'aviation position' provides a view of the platform and information on wind and platform conditions. It is worth noting that the platform cannot be used to accommodate a helicopter for structural reasons. However, it is designed for the use of larger rotary-wing UAVs, such as the Schiebel Camcopter S-100 that is already in service with the French Navy.

Command Systems and Sensors: *Auguste Bénébig* is equipped with sensors supplied by Hensoldt and other companies. These are integrated with a combat management system that is optimised for constabulary operations. The main radar system is a

Kelvin Hughes Mk11 SharpEye, which is produced by Hensoldt's British subsidiary. Co-located with a Hensoldt MSSR 2000 identification friend or foe (IFF) interrogator, it operates in the 'X' (NATO 'I/J' bands) and is primarily used to provide situational awareness. It is supplemented by two Sperry radars that are largely used for navigation. Another important sensor is a 'Sea Eagle' EOSS (electro-optical surveillance system), which is provided by another British company, Chess Dynamics. This stabilised system provides surveillance and target information data through a thermal imager and daylight TV camera.

The SharpEye radar and EOSS are installed on a lightweight tubular mast structure located atop the bridge. This also incorporates antennae for various radio communications systems, including the Sailor satellite array. The larger Comcept antenna is placed on the bridge roof behind the mast. The integrated communications system supports, inter alia, NATO Link connectivity, facilitating the exchange of tactical data with French and allied vessels and aircraft.

The POMs are also able to deploy a rather specific sensor, a multi-beam hydrographic sounder. A well is installed towards the forward part of the aft open deck and a rig allows the sounder to be lowered. A team of hydrographers from the *Service Hydrographique et Océanographique de la Marine* (SHOM), the French Navy hydrographic service, can embark and carry out hydrographic surveys. As the ships will sail in areas that were surveyed long ago with less efficient equipment, the prospect of obtaining more accurate soundings to update the charts is of particular value. The ship's meeting room is designed to be used as a mission control room when such surveys are conducted.

Coordination of sensors and other command and control functions is carried out from *Auguste Bénébig*'s bridge. In addition to the usual navigation equipment, this also consolidates the operations room and damage-control centre. It is a large room with a 360° panoramic view. During routine navigation, the bridge is manned by three persons: an officer of the watch, an assistant and a watchkeeper.

The forward part of the bridge is occupied by two banks of consoles. That located to starboard is used for navigation and incorporates an Electronic Chart Display Information System (ECDIS). The port position incorporates engine monitoring and control functions and is the location of the ship's

Auguste Bénébig's mast structure supports its main sensors. Here, the main Kelvin Hughes Mk11 SharpEye surveillance radar can be seen on a platform towards the top of the forward part of the structure, with Chess Dynamics' 'Sea Eagle' electro-optical surveillance system on the platform further below. Also visible are the two Sperry navigation radars and various communications arrays. *(Eugene Gillet/Bruno Huriet)*

These photographs of the forward part of *Auguste Bénébig*'s panoramic bridge show the two banks of consoles that occupy this area. The port position contains propulsion control and monitoring equipment and is occupied by the helmsman. The one to starboard is used primarily for navigation. The ship's chart table can be seen on the centreline further aft in the second view. *(Vincent Groizeleau)*

helmsman. Two control stations for the propulsion system are also provided outside the bridge to port and starboard.

A chart table is located aft of the forward console banks on the centreline. The ship's damage-control centre is positioned to port. It consolidates the various fire-detection and monitoring systems and can be used to operate the water mist type fixed fire-extinguishing equipment. It also displays images from the various cameras installed around the ship.

The starboard side incorporates a console that interfaces with the ship's communications equipment, although most of these systems – including the 'military' component – are controlled from the communications room on the deck below. The ship is equipped with two satellite communication systems: 'Comcept' from Airbus and Inmarsat's Sailor. While the latter is widely used in the civilian world, 'Comcept' was developed by Airbus to meet the

needs of the French Armed Forces. An 'all IP' (Internet Protocol) technology broadband satellite communications system whose initial operational capability was brought into service in the French Armed Forces in 2015, 'Comcept' provides an ultra-fast and secure network utilising the Franco-Italian Athena-Fidus satellite as well as some commercial satellite bands.

The aft part of the bridge is largely occupied by the combat information centre. This allows exploitation of information provided by the ship's various sensors and facilitates control of the drone and main gun. Two groups of consoles each provide space for two workstations that are equipped with the usual display screens to synthesise information and assist decision-making by the ship's command team. One of these stations is also used to control the 'Narwhal' weapons station.

The combat information centre is equipped with a Lyncea combat management system supplied by Nexeya, a French branch of Germany's Hensoldt. A multi-mission systems-management and decision support tool, it is optimised to support typical patrol-vessel missions such as fisheries control and wider EEZ protection. Situational awareness is provided through two monitors integrated into the mission-management console.

A photograph of one of the two Zodiac Hurricane ZH 630 IO RHIBs embarked in the POMs. This one is launched from the ship's starboard side by means of a wave-compensating davit system supplied by Vestdavit. *(Bruno Huriet)*

Armament: As *Auguste Bénébig* and her sisters are essentially dedicated to surveillance and other constabulary missions, conventional armament is limited. As previously discussed, the main weapon is a Nexter 'Narwhal' remote weapons station (RWS). The variant fitted in the POMs is a Narwhal 20B. Fully stabilised and remotely controlled from the bridge, it fires 20mm ammunition at a rate of around 700 rounds per minute. Largely developed as a response to asymmetric threats, it has been in service with the French Navy since 2013, initially aboard the FREMM multi-mission frigates. It has also been fitted to other major units but is also fully capable of being used in light naval platforms.[7] Sighting is performed by daylight/infrared cameras in conjunction with a laser rangefinder and motion tracking system.

The main gun is supplemented by positions for four additional machine guns that are located to provide all-round protection. One of these is located to each side of the ship forward of the bridge, one to starboard aft the bridge and one to the port side of the stern. These are equipped with two 12.7mm and two 7.62mm calibre weapons.

Given the likely mission profile, the POM's RHIBs also form an important part of their broader armament. Two Zodiac Hurricane ZH 630 IO 6.7m RHIBs are embarked for interception and inspection operations; equipped with an inboard engine they can reach 30 knots with five people aboard and up to 20 knots when carrying an inspection team of up to 14 people. A machine-gun mount is installed in the bow. One of the two RHIBs is launched from the starboard side by means of a davit supplied by Vestdavit: this uses an A frame single-point system fitted on the RHIBs and the winch includes a wave compensating system. There is also a step access flush with the water to facilitate access to the RHIB that divers can

Auguste Bénébig's aft working deck contains an inclined ramp used for launching and recovering the ship's second Zodiac Hurricane ZH 630 IO RHIB. Also evident to starboard is the two-tonne crane that is primarily used to handle mission-specific containers. *(Bruno Huriet)*

also use to get in and out of the water. The other RHIB utilises an inclined-ramp system equipped with a tilting door and winch at the stern. Additionally, a third boat – a 5m RHIB with an outboard motor that is used as a service craft – is stowed on the port side of the quarterdeck.

If mandated by mission requirements, the POMs could alternatively embark ETRACOs, larger RHIBs used by the Special Forces. These are 8m long, equipped with two outboard engines for a maximum speed of up to 45 knots and can carry eleven commandos.

Since the POM's missions are often likely to require the use of divers, a room is provided for dressing, showering, storing their equipment, inflating tanks and rinsing equipment. This compartment is linked with the multi-purpose room that has been described previously. This, for example, would facilitate the embarkation of Special Forces for a particular operation.

The overseas patrol ships are also fitted with dedicated tanks to store dispersants and recovered oil to assist with pollution-control missions. Provision is made to embark equipment such as skimmers, dispersant application systems and spill containment booms. These can be handled by the deck crane. *Auguste Bénébig* and her sisters also have a limited firefighting capability through fixed firefighting equipment installed on 02 deck. This can also be used as a non-lethal weapon.

Auguste Bénébig pictured in the Pacific on 1 April 2023. Her arrival in the region marks the start of a new era of policing France's large and disparate overseas EEZs. *(Thomas Trebern/Marine Nationale)*

CONCLUSION

Although long-awaited, the *patrouilleurs outre-mer* will make a significant contribution to ensuring the security of France's large and disparate overseas EEZs. It is clear that all will be required to maintain a high operational tempo as they arrive at their assigned bases over the next two years. Some days after first-of-class *Auguste Bénébig* reached Nouméa's naval base, the last P400 class patrol boat – *La Glorieuse* – in *Marine Nationale* service was finally decommissioned. A new era in French patrol vessel operations has arrived.

Notes

1. The extensive waters of what is known as Overseas France are essentially a legacy of France's previous empire. They belong to former colonies that decided to remain under French administration, often with a degree of local autonomy.

2. The order for the patrol vessels to be based in Metropolitan France has yet to be finalised. This element of the former BATSIMAR programme was initially to comprise ten vessels, which would be known as *patrouilleurs océaniques*. The vessels are being designed by Naval Group but will be built by the smaller shipyards CMN, Piriou and Socarenam. The French Military Programming Law 2024–30 announced in April 2023 re-designated these ships as *patrouilleurs hauturiers* and stated that seven would be completed within the law's timespan. It suggests the remaining three will be delivered by 2035 but other sources have speculated the programme will be truncated.

3. It is worth noting that the importance of combatting illegal fishing is such that, in 2015, the French Navy took delivery of a small, 24m unit specifically designed to pick up the nets that fishermen leave on the bottom when a control vessel approaches with the aim of recovering the nets later. Clearly, seizing these nets is a blow to this illicit activity. The ERF (*engin de récupération de filets* or net recovering unit) is probably the only vessel of this type in naval service in the world.

4. The *patrouilleurs outre-mer* will be named after Companions of the Liberation – people from the military and civilian communities who distinguished themselves in the work of liberating France and its empire – from Overseas France; largely people associated with the territories where the ships will be based. For example, Auguste Bénébig (1915–93) was a French soldier from Nouméa who distinguished himself during the Battle of Bir Hakeim in North Africa in 1942. Amongst other decorations, he was also a Knight of the Legion of Honour.

5. Strangely, the class is to be named with reference to *Félix Eboué*, the sixth and final ship scheduled for delivery, rather than *Auguste Bénébig*, the first vessel completed.

6. The DGA – *Direction Générale de l'Armement* – is France's defence procurement agency, a branch of the French Ministry of Defence. It is responsible for providing equipment to the French Armed Forces in compliance with their operational and technical needs. The DGA has over 10,000 employees and its facilities include a number of test sites for weapons and systems. In the naval sector, these include a large model test facility encompassing different basins; the largest being 500m long. There are also missile ranges on both the Mediterranean and Atlantic coasts.

The author acknowledges with gratitude the assistance of Mme Mano, DGA's Head of Communications, in arranging a visit to *Auguste Bénébig* and interview with the POM programme manager.

7. The Nexter 'Narwhal' has also been exported to Albania, Egypt, Gabon, Saudi Arabia and Senegal.

D63

3.3 **SIGNIFICANT SHIPS**

KOLKATA CLASS DESTROYERS

The Indian Navy's Project 15A and Project 15B Designs

Author:
Mrityunjoy Mazumdar

Some 13 years ago, *Seaforth World Naval Review 2011* assessed the Indian Navy's Project 15 *Delhi* class destroyers. Devised in the early 1980s, these three ships were commissioned between 1997 and 2001 after protracted building periods to become the fleet's most powerful surface combatants. Over subsequent years, India has put two variants of the original design, the Project 15A *Kolkata* and the P15B *Visakhapatnam* classes, into service. This chapter looks at these follow-on ships, reportedly the first in the Indian Navy to be equipped with network-centric warfare capabilities.

PROGRAMME OVERVIEW

The Project 15A *Kolkata* class destroyer was conceived as a successor to the Project 15 *Delhi* class, utilising the same hull and propulsion system as the previous ships but incorporating improvements in signature management (stealth) and more advanced combat systems. Development of the improved design was carried out by the Indian Navy's Directorate of Naval Design (DND) – reorganised in 2022 as the Warship Design Bureau – and benefitted from DND's previous work on the Project 17 *Shivalik* class stealth frigates.[1] Incorporating almost 2,500 modifications from the Project 15, the Project 15A can be regarded as effectively a new design in many respects.

Initial design work on the Project 15A was completed soon after the turn of the Millennium.[2] The most visually obvious revision from the Project 15 design was the incorporation of a much cleaner topside arrangement to reduce radar cross section. However, revisions from the *Delhi* class also included many internal changes, with a particular emphasis on improving ergonomics and habitability in working and living spaces. Inevitably, hull, machinery and electrical layouts had to be modified to cater for new equipment. Power-generation and cooling requirements were also much greater in the Project 15As than in their predecessors. Final government approval to proceed with the construction of three ships was obtained in June 2001, albeit the design's outfit of combat equipment had still to be finalised.

Early iterations of the Project 15A design incorporated weapons and sensors that had a distinct Russian orientation. For example, a model of the ship exhibited in 2005 – after construction of the lead ship had commenced – had an equipment outfit that included vertically-launched 3S90M 'Shtil-1' (SA-N-12) surface-to-air missiles, M2EM 'Fregat' radar and an AK-190 main gun. However, significant changes made from around this time onwards saw these systems being replaced by Israeli Barak 8 missiles and MF-STAR radar, as well as a Leonardo-designed 76mm Oto gun. The substitution of the Israeli equipment may well have been a reflection of the developing defence links between India and Israel during this period and the consequent availability of more effective equipment.

The DND's completion of work on the Project 15A design was followed by studies to see how the design could be further evolved. This process of incremental improvement saw further enhancement in areas such as stealth, survivability, seakeeping and manoeuvrability, habitability and internal layout. There was also an increase in the proportion of Indian-sourced equipment in the design, as well as the use of Indian-manufactured steel. Final approval to proceed with the construction of four of the resulting Project 15B destroyers was obtained in December 2010.

CONSTRUCTION TIMELINE AND COSTS

At the time approval for Project 15A production was obtained in 2001 it was anticipated that construction of the lead ship would begin by March 2003 to meet a planned 2008 delivery schedule. The two follow-on ships would be delivered at annual intervals; allowing project completion by March 2010. Estimated programme cost was INR 35.8bn (c. US$760m at 2001 exchange rates), a figure based on

Left: The lead Project 15A destroyer *Kolkata* is seen here in November 2020 whilst participating in the Malabar 2020 exercise in the North Arabian Sea. The Indian Navy's Project 15A and Project 15B classes are significantly upgraded derivatives of the original Project 15 *Delhi* class, most notably in their utilisation of the Israeli MF-STAR multi-function radar and Barak 8 missile system. *(US Navy)*

A busy scene at the then Mazagon Dock Ltd – now Mazagon Dock Shipbuilders Ltd (MDSL) – in April 2010. The Project 17 frigate *Sahyadri* is in the centre foreground with two Project 15A destroyers behind. The one forward of *Sahyadri*'s bows is *Kochi*, which is in the course of fitting out. The newly launched *Chennai* is to her left. The simultaneous construction of Project 17 frigates and Project 15A destroyers at MDSL before planned infrastructure upgrades had been completed strained shipyard capacity, exacerbating programme delays. *(Mrityunjoy Mazumdar)*

the cost of *Mumbai*, the final Project 15 destroyer. Given that the Project 15A design's weapon and sensor outfit had not been finalised at the time, it was understood that costs would need to be revisited when full details were known. Perhaps unsurprisingly, both timescales and costs were to exceed these initial estimates.[3]

Construction of the lead P15A, *Kolkata*, commenced in March 2003 on the basis of a letter of intent to Mazagon Dock Shipbuilders Ltd (MDSL) to construct all three ships. Formal keel-laying followed on 26 September that year. Delays in defining the weapons package meant that it was not until February 2006 that revised government financial approval for the programme could be obtained, finally leading to a formal construction contract with MDSL in June 2008. By this time total programme cost had increased to INR 116.6bn (c. US$2.7bn at 2008 exchange rates). The main reason was a seven-fold increase in the cost of major equipment and material to INR 52.3bn. Shipyard inflation also played a significant part.

Production also suffered significant delays. Again, much of this was associated with changes to weapons and sensors after construction had commenced but a myriad of other problems also played a part. Supply chain issues – which also bedevilled original Project 15 construction – were a major factor, most notably through ongoing dislocation of equipment supplies from Russia and Ukraine as the post-Soviet industrial base continued to adapt. For example, the ships' shaft-lines and propellers had to be re-ordered from

Chennai – the third and final Project 15A destroyer – pictured at the time of her launch on 1 April 2010. It would be another six and a half years before she was finally commissioned into the Indian Navy, the time between her keel-laying and commissioning amounting to no fewer than 127 months. An interesting detail visible in the photograph is the pontoon welded to the forward part of the ship's hull. This method was adopted to increase the hull's buoyancy in the shallow waters off the shipyard, thereby allowing a greater launch weight. *(Mrityunjoy Mazumdar)*

Russia when a Ukrainian contractor failed to deliver the equipment, resulting in *Kolkata* being launched without the equipment in place. Supplies of Russian D40S high-tensile steel were another area of delay, pushing back completion of the second and third ships. Subcontractor problems were not confined to former Soviet countries, as the insolvency of a German supplier or air conditioning and ventilation equipment also caused delay. Another issue related to capacity constraints at MDSL, which was involved in simultaneous construction of the Project 17 frigate and Project 15A destroyer designs.[4]

In the end, *Kolkata* was delivered in July 2014 and commissioned the following month. Commissioning had occurred some 135 months after the commencement of production and construction taken 129.5 months from keel laying to delivery, more than double the 60 months initially envisaged. Her acceptance was followed by that of *Kochi* in September 2015 and *Chennai* in August 2016. A detailed analysis of construction timescales is provided in Table 3.2.1.

The contract to construct the follow-on Project 15B class was signed with MDSL in January 2011 at a cost of INR 296.4bn (c. US$6.4bn at 2011 exchange rates). At this stage it was envisaged that the lead ship, *Visakhapatnam*, would be delivered in July 2018 with the remaining three following at biennial intervals through to 2024. *Visakhapatnam* was laid down on 12 October 2013 and finally delivered on 28 October 2021 prior to commissioning on 21 November that same year. *Mormugao*, the second P15B, was delivered in November 2022 whilst the third vessel, *Imphal,* commenced sea trials in April 2023. The programme will be concluded with the delivery of the final vessel, *Surat*, which is likely to commission in 2026. Whilst construction has taken considerably longer than initially envisaged, overall progress has showed a marked improvement over the Project 15As, as evidenced by the table. This seems to be a creditable achievement given the impact of the Covid-19 pandemic. Whilst some reports suggest that total costs have increased to over INR 350bn, programme inflation has been considerably less than that experienced with the preceding class.

The improvement in MDSL's performance with

Kolkata was delivered to the Indian Navy on 10 July 2014 after a lengthy trials process, subsequently commissioning on 16 August that year. This picture dates from October 2013 when the destroyer was undertaking sea trials. *(MDSL)*

Table 3.2.1: PROJECT 15A KOLKATA AND PROJECT 15B VISAKHAPATNAM CONSTRUCTION DETAILS

SHIP	CONTRACTED	START OF PRODUCTION	KEEL LAID	LAUNCHED	DELIVERED	COMMISSIONED	BUILD TIME[1]
Project 15A							
Kolkata (D63)	June 2008[2]	12 March 2003	26 September 2003	30 March 2006	10 July 2014	16 August 2014	129.5 months
Kochi (D64)	June 2008[2]	Not Known	25 October 2005	18 September 2009	Not Known	30 September 2015	Not known
Chennai (D65)	June 2008[2]	Not known	21 February 2006	1 April 2010	21 August 2016	21 November 2016	126 .0 months
Project 15B							
Visakhapatnam (D66)	January 2011	23 January 2013	12 October 2013	20 April 2015	28 October 2021	21 November 2021	96.5 months
Mormugao (D67)	January 2011	29 July 2014	04 June 2015	17 September 2016	24 November 2022	18 December 2022	89.5 months
Imphal (D68)	January 2011	26 July 2016	19 May 2017	20 April 2019	[2023]	[2023]	[To be determined]
Surat (D69)	January 2011	18 July 2018	7 November 2019	17 May 2022	[2026]	[2026]	[To be determined]

Notes:

1. Construction time from keel laying to delivery to the nearest half month.
2. Construction proceeded on the basis of a letter of intent issued in 2001.

Two pictures of the third Project 15B *Visakhapatnam* class destroyer *Imphal* taken off Mumbai on 24 April 2023 at the start of her preliminary sea trials. Constructed using modular building methods like the rest of the Project 15B series, some of her blocks were fabricated at the Shoft Shipyard. As part of the process towards a 'Self-Reliant India', she is constructed from Indian-manufactured DMR 249A high tensile steel. *(Indian Navy)*

respect to Project 15B deliveries can be put down to a number of factors. Lessons learned from building the previous class have been put to good use building their successors, whilst continuity in terms of much of the combat systems and other equipment installed has clearly helped. The introduction of 3D and virtual reality modelling – a first for MDSL – has brought further gains. For example, it has helped with assessing the impact of proposed changes during the build period and allowed cabling and pipework interfaces to be checked before physical outfitting commences.

Another influence has been modernisation of MDSL's facilities to allow greater use of modular building methods. The P15As, like the P15s before them, were built using 'traditional' methods incorporating small blocks that were outfitted as the ships were assembled. However, the P15Bs have been built from larger 'mega blocks' that incorporate a greater level of pre-assembly. For the last two P15Bs, some blocks were sub-contracted to Shoft Shipyard in Bharuch, Gujarat in a further effort to speed completion. However, levels of pre-outfitting are believed to remain low compared to similar warship programmes elsewhere. Delays have also continued to impact equipment deliveries, particularly from former Soviet countries. These have reportedly included elements of the propulsion and the shaft-lines.

Construction of the P15A and P15B series has also seen the progressive indigenisation of production under a process that has been championed as a move towards a self-reliant India – *Aatmanirbhar Bharat* – by the administration of current Indian premier Narendra Modi. Whilst claims relating to the actual amount of indigenisation are not always consistent, it seems that the value of Indian-sourced labour, materials and equipment has increased from less than 50 percent in the original Project 15 *Delhi* class to around 75 percent in the Project 15B *Visakhapatnam* design. One major advance has been in the area of steelwork. Here the problems with the supply of Russian D40S steel for the Project 15As mentioned above resulted in the development of a local alternative, DMR 249A, by India's Defence Metallurgical Research Laboratory (DMRL) that was then used in the Project 15Bs. In other areas, 'indigenous' equipment either relates to the licensed production of overseas systems or the completion of systems from sub-assemblies sourced from overseas. In some important areas, particularly with respect to propulsion, almost total reliance on overseas suppliers remains.

DESIGN DESCRIPTION: OVERVIEW

According to shipbuilders MDSL, the role of the Project 15A and Project 15B destroyers is to co-ordinate a task force in the exercise of sea control whilst operating in a multi-threat environment. As multi-role destroyers, they are capable of undertaking strikes against sea and land-based targets whilst providing area air defence and engaging in anti-submarine warfare. In addition to commanding naval formations, they also have a significant part to play as a leading component of carrier groups formed by the Indian Navy's two aircraft carriers.

Whilst the Project 15A and Project 15B classes carry a strong family resemblance to the preceding Project 15 design, there are two significant visual differences. One is the attention to radar cross section across the superstructure, giving a less cluttered appearance. The other is the presence of the distinctive housing for the MF-STAR multifunction radar system atop the forward mast.

The principal technical characteristics of the Project 15A destroyer design are provided in Table 3.2.2. Overall length is c. 164m and maximum beam some 17.4m at the hull's 'knuckle'. Draught at the designed standard displacement of 6,800 tonnes is 5.3m, increasing to 6.5m at full load displacement of c. 7,400 tonnes.[5]

This November 2020 overhead view of *Kolkata* provides a good overview of the Project 15A destroyer design, including the overall emphasis on stealth and the dominant MF-STAR radar atop the foremast. Extensive deckhouses for missile launchers are located forward of the bridge superstructure whilst helicopter landing and maintenance facilities dominate the stern. *(US Navy)*

This picture of *Kolkata* in company with the British Type 45 destroyer *Defender* taken at India's 2016 International Fleet Review makes an interesting comparison with respect to the emphasis on stealth inherent in the two designs, which are broadly contemporaneous. *(US Navy)*

Hull Structure and Layout: The Indian Navy describes the Project 15A as having a full beam superstructure with a flared hull and canted sides. In profile, the sheer line (knuckle line) runs forward from the helicopter platform at 1 Deck (main deck) level for about two-thirds of the ship's length, gradually sloping upwards to 01 Deck level in the area of the forecastle. As was the case with the Project 15 class, the hull is fitted with bilge keels and two pairs of stabilisers to assist stability.[6]

There are a total of four principal deck levels – Deck 01 to Deck 04 – above the main deck. The main 76mm gun on the forecastle is located forward of extensive deckhouse spaces for vertical-launch missile cells and rocket launchers that stretch up to 02 Deck level. These, in turn, are located ahead of the main bridge superstructure block. This contains a flag bridge on 02 Deck and the main bridge on 03 Deck above, with 04 Deck forming the structure's roof. This also acts as a platform for the foremast and its MF-STAR radar. Immediately aft is the forward funnel and, then, two twin torpedo tubes. This is followed by a further raised structure that houses the 'cornered' arrangement of AK630M guns at 02 Deck level and acts as the base for the mainmast with its LW-08 surveillance radar. A windowed emergency control position is located in the mast structure. Moving aft, one comes to the second funnel and, then, the hangar. Its roof is also located at 02 Deck level and incorporates various weapons systems and sensors. The helicopter deck is at the stern.

Decks from the main, Deck 1, level downwards are numbered sequentially. For example, the quarter-deck located immediately beneath the helicopter deck is at Deck 2 level. Although full details have not been published, it is believed that approximately fifteen transverse bulkheads ensure the hull's water-tight integrity, whilst the ship is also split into a number of firefighting and gas-tight citadel zones for damage control purposes. The turbines in the forward and aft engine rooms are mounted asymmetrically, with the two spaces separated by an auxiliary machine room housing a diesel alternator and other equipment. Overall, the Project 15A design is

Table 3.2.2.

KOLKATA PRINCIPAL PARTICULARS

Building Information:				
Keel Laid:	26 September 2003	Launched: 30 March 2006	Commissioned:	16 August 2014[1]
Builders:	Mazagon Dock Shipbuilders Ltd, Mumbai, India.			
Dimensions:				
Displacement:	7,400 tonnes full load displacement.[2]			
Hull Dimensions:	164.0m (overall) x 17.4m x 6.5m at full load. Length between perpendiculars is 151.5m.			
Weapons Systems:				
Missiles:	4 x 8-cell vertical launchers for Barak 8 surface-to-air missiles. 2 x 8-cell launchers for BrahMos PJ-10 surface-to-surface missiles.			
Guns:	1 x 76mm Oto gun. 4 x AK-630M guns as part of CIWS. Light weapons.			
Torpedoes/ASW:	2 x twin DTA-53 533mm torpedo mountings. 2 x 12-tube RBU-6000 A/S rocket launchers.			
Aircraft:	Up to 2 x AgustaWestland Sea King Mk 42B helicopters or equivalent. MH-60R to replace Sea King in due course.			
Countermeasures:	Ellora Mk 1 electronic warfare suite. 4 x Kavach Mod II decoy launchers. Nayan communications intelligence system. Fitted for Mareech torpedo defence system.			
Principal Sensors:	1 x ELM-2248 MF-STAR multi-function radar. 1 x RAWL-02 (Thales Nederland LW-08) 2D long-range search. 1 x Garpun Bal 3TS-25E target designation radar for SSMs. Surface search/navigation radars. HUMSA NG hull-mounted sonar. Fitted for Atlas Elektronik Advanced Towed Array Sonar (ATAS).			
Combat System:	CMS-15A combat management system. Link II datalink. CEC (JTF mode of Barak 8).			
Propulsion Systems:				
Machinery:	COGAG. Zorya Mashproekt M36E.1 plant with two pairs of DT-59 reversible gas turbines. Plant provides in excess of 48MW (64,000shp) through two shafts.			
Speed and Range:	Designed maximum speed is in excess of 30 knots. Range is at least 3,300 nautical miles at 18 knots.			
Other Details:				
Complement:	A typical crew comprises c. 330–390 personnel, including c. 30–40 officers.			
Class:	Three Project 17A ships have been commissioned: *Kolkata* (D63), *Kochi* (D64) and *Chennai* (D65).			

Notes:

1. Delivery was on 10 July 2014
2. This is the official figure. Actual full load displacement could be as much as c. 8,100 tonnes.

reported to have over 500 separate compartments, lobbies and passageways.

As already mentioned, stealth has been a major design consideration. The hull sides and superstructure are inclined and shaped to reduce overall radar cross section (RCS) and the level of deck clutter has been significantly reduced compared with the original Project 15 design. To give one example, the two telescopic accommodation ladders – one aft on the port side and one forward on the starboard side – are mounted in recessed housings with covers. There is also evidence of the use of radar-absorbent materials and coatings to help reduce radar reflections. Notably, panels with black radar absorbent material have been installed in areas behind some of the surface-surveillance and fire-control radars. There are indications that infra-red suppression systems (IRSSs) are fitted to gas turbine and diesel engine exhausts.

Propulsion and Platform Management Systems: The Project 15As utilise a combined gas and gas (COGAG) propulsion system incorporating with two Ukrainian Zorya Mashproekt M36E.1 gas-turbine power plants. Each unit consists of two DT-59 gas turbines paired with a RG54 reduction gearbox. The M36E.1 is an improved version of the M36E power plant used in the Project 15 *Delhi* class, benefitting from a power plant control system that incorporates greater levels of automation. Total power output is in excess of 64,000shp (48MW). The propulsion units are reversible, with each gearbox driving a five-bladed, fixed propeller.[7] As previously mentioned, the plants are fitted in

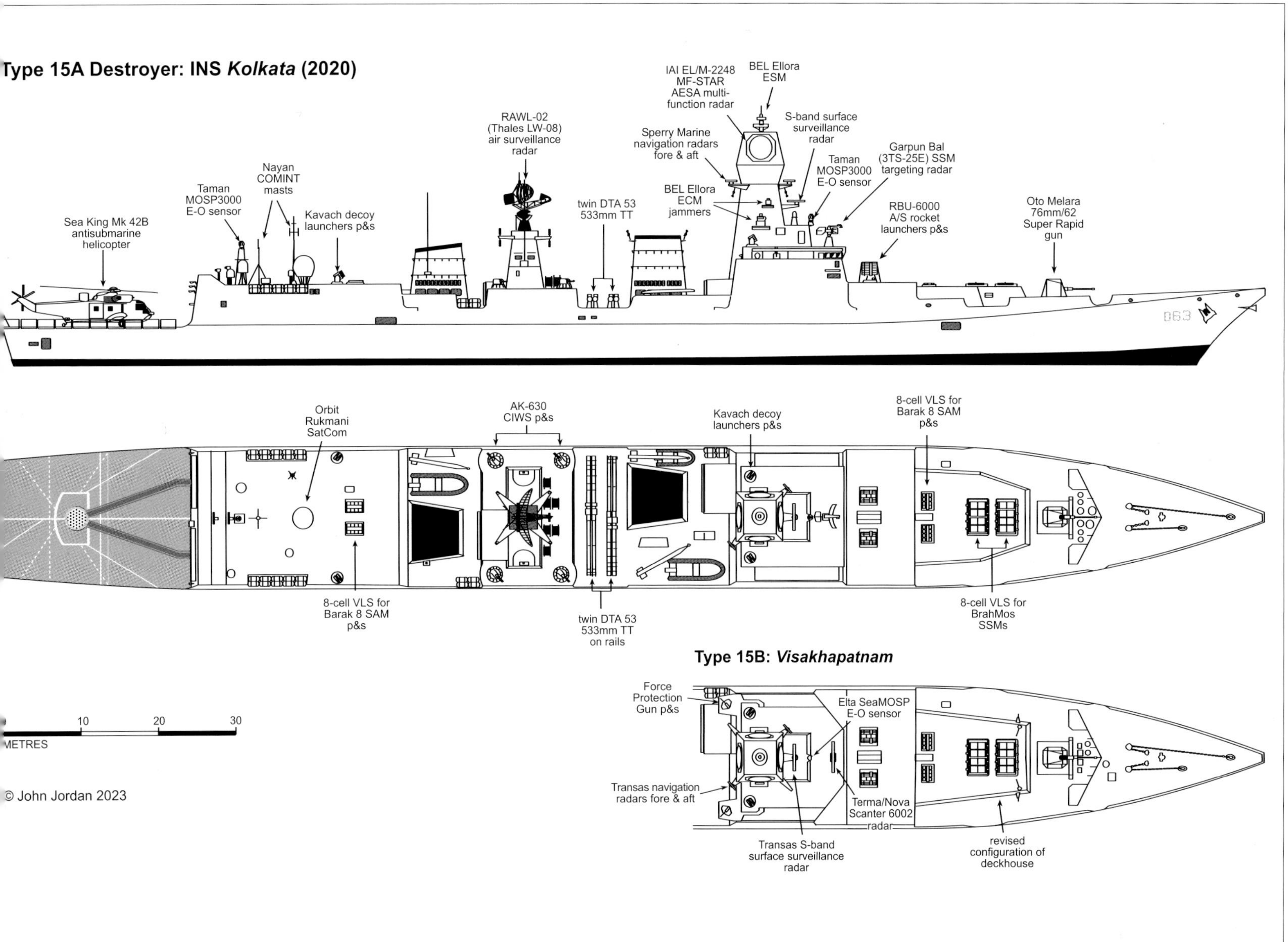

Chennai – top – pictured conducting exercises with the Japanese *Murasame* class destroyer *Ikazuchi* (DD-107) in 2020. An interesting feature evident in both designs is the asymmetrical positioning of the two funnels, reflecting the layout of their propulsion plant. *(Indian Navy)*

forward and aft engine rooms, resulting in asymmetrical shaft lengths. Maximum speed is quoted as being in excess of 30 knots, whilst range is reportedly at least 3,300 nautical miles at 18 knots. There are twin rudders.

Power-generation requirements are met by a combination of four GTG-1250 2E gas turbine generators and one Wärtsilä diesel alternator providing a total of around 4.5MW of electrical power for shipboard requirements. A small emergency diesel generator is also fitted. Power distribution is carried out through a main switchboard and various subsidiary power panels, transformers and automatic change over switches. An Automatic Power Management System (APMS) controls overall electrical power distribution whilst a separate Auxiliary Control System (ACS) provides many of the remote control and monitoring functions for ship equipment associated with a modern integrated platform management system (IPMS).[8] As well as its control and monitoring role, the ACS is a key tool in ensuring the co-ordination of, for example, damage control and the response to any nuclear, biological or chemical (NBC) attack. Control system data is transferred by means of a so-called Asynchronous Transfer Mode-based Integrated Ship Data Network (AISDN), a modular, multi-services broadband network that is also used to integrate weapons, sensors and communication systems into the combat management system.

The Project 15As are equipped with a comprehensive heating, ventilation and air-conditioning (HVAC) system, which encompasses equipment cooling and air filtration requirements. Around twenty-five air treatment units, sixty heat exchangers, ninety ventilation fans and ten air filtration units are installed in each member of the Project 15A class. According to MSDL, there are also over 35km of piping in each ship.

COMMAND AND CONTROL

The Project 15A's weapons and sensors are controlled and co-ordinated through a Project 15A Combat Management System (CMS-15A), about which published details remain sparse. CMS-15A is believed to have been developed from the Russian Meridian Research & Production Enterprise's 'Trebovaniye' ('Request' in English) series of fully distributed combat management systems. These have formed the basis for combat management systems found in other Indian Navy surface combatants, including the original Project 15 destroyers. This technology has been progressively enhanced with indigenous input from Bharat Electronics Limited (BEL) under the oversight of the Indian Navy's Weapons and Electronics Systems Engineering Establishment (WESEE). A major element of CMS-15A development will have been the interface with the Israeli-designed MF-STAR radar and Barak 8 missiles that form the class's principal anti-air defence. Integration has also involved a number of indigenously developed modules, such as BEL's IAC-Mod C anti-submarine fire-control system. Data transfer is means by means of the AISDN broadband network that has been previously described.

Radar and Other Sensors: The class's primary radar is the Israeli Elta ELM-2248 MF-STAR. This is a modern multi-function, active electronically scanned array (AESA) operating in the S-band (NATO E/F-bands). It is able to perform long-range surveillance and tracking, provide mid-course guidance for the ship's Barak 8 surface-to-air missiles, and undertake gunnery-control functions. Its four fixed arrays can be installed in various configurations and sizes, with those fitted atop the Project 15A design's foremast measuring 3m by 3m and reportedly weighing circa two tonnes each. The radar provides all round coverage in azimuth and from -20° to +85° in elevation. Elta state that the maximum instrumented range is in excess of 450km (c. 250 nautical miles).

MF-STAR's surveillance capabilities are supplemented by the venerable RAWL-02, a locally developed variant of the Thales LW-08. It is a solid-state 2D air-search radar operating in the L-band (NATO C/D-bands) and has a claimed range of over 250km. The radar is arguably superfluous given the MF-STAR's superior surveillance performance but was probably specified due to Indian Navy concerns about over-reliance on a single multi-function array and a consequent desire to provide a level of redundancy. Other radars include a Russian Garpun Bal 3TS-25E, which provides targeting data for the class's BrahMos surface-to-surface missiles. The Project 15As were also initially fitted with Consilium

This photograph of *Kolkata* provides a good view of the four-faced MF-STAR multi-function radar that is the primary sensor on both the Project 15A and Project 15B classes. The Russian Garpun Bal 3TS-25E radar that can be used to provide targeting data for the ship's BrahMos missiles is located at the base of the foremast atop the bridge. Other equipment visible includes the array for the ESM element of the Ellora Mk 1 electronic warfare measures system on top of the mast, as well as the sided pairs of jammers on platforms to its sides. Further aft, the mainmast provides a platform for the ship's RAWL-02 2D surveillance radar. *(US Navy)*

Selesmar navigation radars, although these had been replaced by Sperry Marine sets by 2021.

In addition to the various radar arrays, the Project 15As are equipped with two optronic directors; one at the base of the forward mast and one on a stub-mast towards the aft of the hangar roof. These are likely Israel Aerospace Industries (IAI) Taman MOSP-3000 multi-sensor units and can be used for both surveillance and fire-control functions as a supplement to the primary MF-STAR array.

Anti-submarine warfare (ASW) detection is currently focused on an indigenous, hull-mounted HUMSA NG sonar. This was developed by the Defence Research and Development Organisation (DRDO) as its third generation of hull-mounted sonar systems and is manufactured by BEL. Primarily an active sonar, it is also capable of simultaneous passive operation. It incorporates multiple waveforms and both omni and directional transmission. It is optimised for operations in the salinity levels typical of the Indian Ocean. Maximum range is c. 15km (eight nautical miles) and up to eight targets can be tracked simultaneously.

The Project 15As are also designed to operate a towed array. However, as of mid-2023, it is unclear whether the Atlas Elektronik Advanced Towed Array Sonar (ATAS) system that the Indian Navy has acquired in limited numbers has been fitted to any of the ships.

Electronic Warfare and Countermeasures: The BEL-developed Ellora Mk 1 electronic warfare system provides the Project 15As' electronic countermeasures (ECM) and electronic support measures (ESM) capability. There are two pairs of jammers on either side of the forward mast and a distinctive ESM array at its top. The ships are also equipped with arrays for the Nayan communications intelligence system atop the hangar roof.

Physical countermeasures are launched from the Kavach Mod. II decoy launching system. This comprises two pairs of short-range and two pairs of medium-long range decoy launchers to counter incoming missiles at a variety of ranges. The short-range launchers are located atop the bridge structure on either side of the foremast and the long-range launchers are on top of the hangar.

This close-up view of *Chennai*'s hangar roof dates from January 2023. Two eight-cell launchers for Barak 8 missiles can be seen either side of the centreline towards its forward end, with sided Kavach decoy launchers located slightly further aft. The large satellite dome for the Indian Navy's Rukmani Integrated Communication Network System is supplemented by smaller domes for commercial satellite communications and the arrays of the Navan communications intelligence system. The stub mast towards the hangar's aft end supports an optronic director. Two new remote weapons stations – not installed when the ship was first commissioned – are positioned at the aft hangar roof corners. *(Marine Nationale)*

Communications and Data Links: The Project 15As are fitted with an integrated Composite Communications System Mk III suite manufactured by BEL. It has the usual comprehensive range of ship-to-ship, ship-to-shore and ship-to-air communications, including satellite terminal access to both the Indian Navy's bespoke Rukmani Integrated Communication Network System (ICNS) and commercial satellite services. The suite incorporates the main Indian Navy tactical data link system, which is known as Link II. This was introduced around the turn of the Millennium and has been progressively upgraded with faster data transfer speeds. The Project 15As are believed to utilise the Link II Mod 3 variant.

In addition to its standard data links, a notable feature of the Project 15A design is its capacity to operate its Barak 8 missiles in what is known as Joint Taskforce Coordination (JTC) mode. This utilises a network of data links to allow any destroyer equipped with Barak 8 to control a missile irrespective of whether or not it was the original launch platform. This capacity, which is similar to the US Navy's Cooperative Engagement Capability, is discussed further in the accompanying text box.

ARMAMENT

As a multi-role design, the Project 15A destroyers are equipped with a wide range of weapons systems. This equipment is summarised further below:

Surface-to-Air Missiles: A total of thirty-two Barak 8 surface-to-air missiles are carried in four eight-cell vertical launchers. Two of these are located in the missile silo complex forward of the bridge superstructure and two in the forward part of the hangar structure.

The Barak 8 was co-developed with Israel's IAI and partly funded by India's DRDO. Assembly in India is by Bharat Dynamics Limited and includes some indigenous content. It is designed to counter a wide variety of airborne threats, including aircraft, anti-ship missiles and UAVs. Somewhat confusingly

Two views of test firing of the Indo-Russian BrahMos surface-to-surface missile from, respectively, the Project 15A class destroyer *Chennai* and its Project 15B counterpart *Mormugao*. The images give a good impression of the missile's size: it is some 8.4m in length and weighs around three tonnes. In this regard, it makes an interesting contrast with the 3.4m, 400kg Naval Strike Missile discussed elsewhere in this edition. *(Indian Navy)*

described in Indian Navy literature as both a medium-range (MRSAM) and long-range surface-to-air missile (LRSAM), the variant used aboard the Project 15As appears to correspond to the long range member of what is now known as IAI's Barak MX family. This has a stated range of 70km (c. 38 nautical miles), although it appears that over 90km has been achieved in tests. IAI are also developing an extended range 150km variant that includes an additional booster section and is claimed to have an anti-ballistic missile defence (ABMD) capability.[9]

The Barak 8 missile – interceptor in IAI parlance – has a length of approximately 4.5m and a diameter that expands from 0.225m at the body to 0.54m at the booster. Wingspan is 0.94m. Weight, including a 60kg proximity-fuze warhead, is just 275kg. Missile guidance is provided by data uplinks from the MF-STAR radar, with an active seeker being used for terminal guidance. Maximum speed is in excess of Mach 2, with thrust vectoring used to allow high gravity manoeuvring during interception. As installed in the Project 15As, Barak 8 is capable of engaging multiple targets during saturation attacks. First test firings of the missile were concluded from *Kolkata* in December 2015.

Surface-to-Surface Missiles: The Project 15As are fitted with two eight-cell UVLM (universal vertical launcher modules) for the supersonic BrahMos cruise missile. The Indo-Russian BrahMos, also known as the PJ-10, is essentially derived from the NPO Mashinostroyenia-developed Yakhont/P-800 Oniks missile. It was developed and then placed into production with the help of Indian Ministry of Defence funding. A New Delhi-headquartered joint venture, BrahMos Aerospace, was established in 1998 to manage the programme, with the first test-firing taking place in 2001. It is believed to have entered operational service with the Indian Navy later in the decade after the conclusion of a series of

PROJECT 15A AND 15B COOPERATIVE ENGAGEMENT CAPABILITY

On 15 May 2019, the Project 15A destroyers *Kochi* and *Chennai* successfully demonstrated the Cooperative Engagement Capability inherent in their Barak 8 surface-to-air missile system during a series of test firings in the Arabian Sea. In the demonstration, missiles launched by both ships were controlled by just one ship to intercept a number of aerial targets at extended ranges. The capacity – previously publicly demonstrated only by US Navy and Royal Australian Navy Aegis-equipped warships – gives the Indian Navy an operational edge possessed by few fleets.

The Cooperative Engagement Capability inherent in the Project 15A and Project 15B cases is based on the Barak 8 missile system's Joint Taskforce Coordination (JTC) operating mode. This utilises the network-centric capabilities of Barak 8 and the associated MF-STAR radar to share information between platforms and provide relevant updates to a missile via a network of data links. A missile's flight path can be continuously updated by any ship equipped with the appropriate technology until the interceptor enters its terminal engagement phase and the active radar seeker assumes control.

The ability to maintain a shared picture of the 'battlefield' that has sufficient depth and clarity to allow a ship to take control of missiles installed on multiple platforms has obvious advantages. For example, it provides an enhanced capacity to respond to saturation attacks and can help overcome complications resulting from the use of stealth and/or jamming. The main current limitation faced by the Indian Navy appears to be the limited number of ships – the Project 15A and Project 15B and the aircraft carrier *Vikrant* – equipped with the relevant technology. However, the seven new Project 17A *Nilgiri* class frigates will also be fitted with the Barak 8/MF-STAR combination, significantly increasing the Indian Navy's Cooperative Engagement Capability potential.

The Project 15B *Visakhapatnam* class destroyers are visually similar to the Project 15A *Kolkata* class, incorporating only minor differences. The most obvious changes are revisions to the shapes of the bridge face and forward deck houses to enhance stealth and provide better firing arcs for the ASW rocket launchers. This photograph of *Visakhapatnam* was taken whilst she was undergoing sea trials in the summer of 2021. *(Indian Navy)*

trials and has remained under constant improvement. The majority of components were originally sourced from Russian suppliers but the level of indigenisation has steadily increased, currently standing at c. 80 percent. It is produced in land, sea and air launched variants and can be used as an anti-shipping or land-attack missile. It is claimed to be the fastest cruise missile in the world.

The current ship-launched variant of the missile is 8.4m long, weighs about 3,000kg, and carries a 200–300kg warhead. It uses a solid-propellant rocket for initial acceleration and a ramjet to maintain cruise speed. BrahMos flies at a speed in excess of Mach 2 and has a range of more than 500km.

Guns: The main gun is a licence-built Leonardo Oto 76mm mounting in a stealthy turret. The guns are built by Bharat Heavy Electricals Limited (BHEL) at its Haridwar plant. Consideration had previously been given to fitting the class with larger-calibre 127mm guns from either Leonardo or BAE Systems but these plans were never progressed. However, it is likely that the 76mm mounting will be equipped with advanced munition types in due course. Four Russian-designed AK-630M guns are also fitted as close-in weapons systems (CIWS).

A number of crew-served heavy and light machine guns were installed in Project 15A *Kolkata* class ships as force protection weapons after completion. These mountings typically include two Russian-origin 12.7m heavy machine guns in the forward bridge superstructure and two more atop the hangar deck. However, the *Kolkata* class are now being re-equipped with locally assembled Elbit remotely-operated heavy machine guns in line with similar guns found aboard the Project 15Bs. For example, in January 2023, *Chennai* was seen with two of these Elbit remote weapons stations in place of the former crew-served weapons on the hangar.

Anti-Submarine Weapons: Two sets of Larsen and Toubro built DTA 53 twin heavyweight launchers of Russian design (known locally as Indian Torpedo Tube Launchers) are fitted amidships. One pair fires to starboard and the other to port. They fire SET 65E and similar heavyweight torpedoes of Russian origin. Production versions of the indigenous Varunastra heavyweight torpedo are also starting to enter service and these are likely to be used in due course.

Two RBU 6000 Smerch 2 ASW rocket launchers are located forward of the bridge. These are also license built – with some modifications – by Larsen & Toubro and are believed to be equipped with 23kg, RGB-60 rounds. Extended range rounds, with a maximum range of 8,900m instead of 5,000m, were test fired from *Chennai* in April 2023.

Defence against enemy torpedoes is intended to be provided by the locally-developed Mareech anti-torpedo decoy system. However, it is unclear whether this system has yet been actually installed.

Aviation Facilities: The Project 15As are fitted with

a large flight deck equipped with a Larsen and Toubro-supplied helicopter handling system and two hangars each able to accommodate a medium-sized helicopter. Principal embarked types are Westland Sea King Mk 42B ASW and HAL Chetak utility helicopters, although these will likely be supplanted by the new Sikorsky MH-60R and HAL Dhruv MK III types in due course.[10]

PROJECT 15B DESIGN VARIATIONS

Whilst there have been assertions that the Project 15B *Visakhapatnam* design represents a significant advance over the preceding Project 15A class, these claims appear to be overblown. The Project 15Bs were ordered whilst their predecessors were still under construction and largely share the same configuration and equipment fit as their predecessors. Although consideration was, for example, originally given to equipping them with a different propulsion train built around the GE LM2500 gas turbine, this plan was cancelled when similar engines destined for Project 17 frigates were delayed due to American export restrictions. As such, changes have largely been incremental in nature.

Visually, the most obvious external differences between the Project 15A and Project 15B designs have been a number of small revisions to the forward superstructure to achieve further enhancements to stealth and provide better firing arcs for the ASW rocket launchers. The hangar structure is also slightly different, incorporating a revised arrangement for life-raft stowage and dispensing with the Project 15A's distinctive 'hump' by the hangar doors. Key external equipment changes include the substitution of a Terma Scanter 6002 radar for the previous Russian Garpun Bal set. Primarily used for surface surveillance, it operates in the X-band (NATO I/J-bands) and can also be used to monitor the near airspace around the ship and perform helicopter-control functions. The navigation radar suite has been further refined through the specification of Transas S and X-band sets. Remote weapons stations – two on platforms on the aft bridge structure and two on the hangar roof – have replaced the manually-operated machine guns initially fitted to the Project 15As. A further visual difference is the use of a rail-less helicopter handling system manufactured by GRSE in conjunction with McTaggart Scott.

There have also been a number of internal changes. These reportedly include installation of a more sophisticated Total Atmosphere Control System (TACS) that provides better NBC protection than that accorded to the Project 15As. The previous ACS has been replaced with a new system that provides more comprehensive integrated platform-management capabilities. Other enhancements have arisen through ongoing improvements made to previous iterations of equipment. For example, the M36E.2 variant of the main power plant encompasses further upgrades to its control equipment and a new fuel delivery system whilst the HUMSA NG (Mod) sonar incorporates the new Near-field Acoustic Characterisation System (NACS). NACS

The second Project 15B destroyer, *Mormugao*, is seen here in September 2022, shortly before her official delivery. Whilst external changes from the Project 15A design are modest, the opportunity was taken to incorporate a number of internal upgrades in the new class. *(Indian Navy)*

monitors self-noise, measures the magnitude and phase characteristics of the sonar's transmission and reception electronics, and makes calibration adjustments at sea for improved sonar performance. The Link II Mod III SDR-TAC data link is also improved, including a further increase in transmission rates. Another change has been specification of the new Shakti electronic warfare suite. *Visakhapatnam* was the first Indian Navy warship to use this new system.

The delivery of the Project 15Bs is taking place alongside mid-life upgrades to the original Project 15 *Delhi* class. These are further detailed in the text box.

CONCLUSION

Members of the Project 15A and Project 15B series have been extremely active in the period since

PROJECT 15 DELHI CLASS MID-LIFE UPGRADE

The three Project 15 *Delhi* class destroyers are in the course of a mid-life upgrade programme. *Delhi* was the first to enter the programme at the naval dockyard in Mumbai and has now returned to operational service. *Mumbai* will also complete her upgrade in her namesake port. *Mysore*'s modernisation has been allocated to the naval dockyard in Visakhapatnam, where work is reportedly drawing to a conclusion.

The mid-life upgrade is essentially focused on replacing legacy equipment, much of Russian origin, with updated technology. Some of this will be newer variants of Russian-produced systems but, in line with the tenets of *Aatmanirbhar Bharat*, there is also a heavy focus on indigenisation.

Changes made to *Delhi* include substitution of the Russian-origin AK-100 main gun and its T-91E (MR 145) fire-control system with a BHEL built 76.2mm Super Rapid gun mount and a BEL manufactured Lynx U2 (Upgrade 2) fire-control director. Two inclined quad launchers for BrahMos have been installed in place of the original four sets of quad launchers for Kh-35 Uran surface-to-surface missiles. The Garpun Bal radar target designation radar previously used with these missiles has been replaced by a Terma Scanter array. The Fregat MAE target-acquisition radar has also been landed in favour of the newer Fregat M2EM variant. Although consideration was given to replacing the original single-arm 3S90 launchers of the Kashmir surface-to-air system with vertical launch cells, these have been retained. However, the system itself has been refurbished and upgraded.

There have also been less obvious internal changes. These include replacement of the original Russian Trebovaniye E based combat management system with the latest indigenous development and revisions to the shipboard communications to incorporate updated BEL technology. The original gas turbine power control system has been replaced with more automated technology similar to that already fitted in the P15Bs. A HUMSA-NG sonar array has been substituted for the legacy APSOH hull-mounted sonar, whilst BEL's IAC-Mod C anti-submarine fire-control system has also been installed to provide ASW fire-control solutions. Atlas Elektronik towed array sonar sets are also slated for installation on these ships, replacing the previous HUMVAAD system. The Ellora Mk 1 electronic warfare suite has been upgraded and existing decoy launchers replaced by the Kavach system.

It remains to be seen to what extent all three *Delhi* class hulls will end up receiving the same standard of upgrades upon the completion of their mid-life refits. However, it is believed that at least one unit could receive a licence-built Spanish Indra Lanza 3D radar, one of 23 units the Indian Navy ordered for production by TATA Advanced Systems Ltd (TASL) in 2020.

The original Project 15 *Delhi* class destroyers are being upgraded to a standard that brings them closer to their Project 15A and Project 15B half-sisters. This has included replacement of 'legacy' equipment with new or upgraded systems, many indigenously manufactured. These photographs show *Mysore* as originally built and the forecastle of the newly-modernised *Delhi*. Notable enhancements include replacement of the original Russian AK-100 main gun with a licence-built Oto 76mm mounting and substitution of inclined BrahMos missile launchers for the previous Kh-30 Uran surface-to-surface missiles. *(Mrityunjoy Mazumdar/Arjun Sarup)*

delivery. They have participated in numerous Indian Navy deployments across the Indian Ocean and beyond whilst making their presence felt in many international exercises. A few examples of these include Exercise 'Konkan 2018' involving *Kolkata* and the British Type 45 destroyer *Dragon*, *Kochi*'s participation in the inaugural Exercise 'Al-Mohed Al-Hindi 2021' with the Royal Saudi Navy, and *Chennai*'s involvement in Exercise 'Varuna 2023' with France's *Marine Nationale*. A notable illustration of defence diplomacy was *Kolkata*'s visit to Qingdao in China to attend the international fleet review held to mark the People Liberation Army Navy's 70th anniversary in April 2019. An important aspect of these deployments has been to demonstrate to friend and foe alike the Indian Navy's growing capacity to design, build and operate modern, 'high end' warships.

In spite of their undoubted qualities, some concerns have been raised. One relates to the design's relatively low missile load-out at a time when there is an international trend towards increasing missile capacity. This might be a reflection of the inevitable compromises that had to be made in fitting a much more sophisticated level of equipment into an existing hull. A more valid criticism might relate to the lengthy construction times that have typified delivery of the ships which, whilst improving, are still considerably behind international best practice.

The Project 15A and Project 15B classes have been extremely active since delivery, demonstrating the Indian Navy's growing capacity to design, build and operate modern, 'high end' warships to friend and foe alike. This is *Chennai* on 10 January 2023 during Exercise 'Varuna 2023' with the French Navy. *(Terence Walet/Marine Nationale)*

The Project 15A *Kolkata* and Project 15B *Visakhapatnam* class destroyers are undoubtedly powerful warships that reflect the Indian Navy's desire to project maritime power across the Indian Ocean region. Alongside the upgraded Project 15 *Delhi* class, they will form the centrepiece of the fleet's destroyer force for the foreseeable future.

Notes

1. The Project 17 frigate design was described by the author in 'Shivalik Class Stealth Frigates', *Seaforth World Naval Review 2013* (Barnsley: Seaforth Publishing, 2012), pp.148–65.

2. The conceptual and basic design work for the Project 15A and Project 15B designs was completed by the DND's Surface Ship Group. Detailed design work was subsequently carried out by the appointed building yard, Mazagon Dock Shipbuilders Ltd.

3. This section relies heavily on two reports, a *Performance Audit of the Indigenous Construction of Indian Naval Warships* (New Delhi: Comptroller and Auditor General of India, 2011), available at cag.gov.in/en/audit-report/details/2444, and a Public Accounts Committee report on *Indigenous Construction of Indian Naval Warships* (New Delhi: Lok Sabha Secretariat, 2015), available at eparlib.nic.in/

4. Another constraint impacting construction of the Project 15 series has been limited water depth at MDSL, limiting the weight at which ships could be launched. For the second and third P15As, this was mitigated by the use of pontoon assistance, by which pontoons were welded to the forward and aft portions of the hull to enhance buoyancy. This increased potential launch displacement from around 3,000 tonnes to over 4,000 tonnes. However, this method has not been followed for the P15Bs, possibly because the different build approach makes it easier to fit superstructure blocks after launch. In the case of the final vessel, *Surat*, many of the hull blocks were manufactured and joined together at Shoft Shipyard before being towed to MDSL for the ship's final integration.

5. A number of sources suggest that these official figures are likely to be underestimates, with a full load displacement of c. 8,100 tonnes possible.

6. The Project 15 series' hull form is described in detail in the author's 'Delhi Class Destroyers', *Seaforth World Naval Review 2011* (Barnsley: Seaforth Publishing, 2010), pp.102–19. The Project 15 series adopt generally fine hull lines, with a length to beam ratio in excess of 9:1. Model tests on the hull form were carried out at SSPA Maritime Center Sweden and validated at the Krylov Institute in St Petersburg, Russia.

7. It has been reported that the Indian Navy and shipbuilders MDSL have initiated a study at the Stichting Maritiem Research Instituut in the Netherlands to improve the cavitational properties of these propellers. This may result in use of an enhanced propeller design.

8. The separation of the design's power-management system from the broader platform management system is also a feature of the broadly contemporary Project 17 *Shivalik* class and appears to have been driven by decisions by India's Directorates of Marine Engineering and Electrical Engineering to follow separate developmental paths.

9. A detailed review of the Barak 8's development entitled 'BARAK-8: Advanced Air & Missile Defence System' was by *SP's Naval Forces* – spsnavalforces.com/default.asp – in their 3/2022 edition and available by searching their archive.

10. Trial landings of the MH-60R helicopter were carried out aboard *Kolkata* in May 2023.

3.3 SIGNIFICANT SHIPS

S-80 CLASS SUBMARINES

Demonstrating the Benefits of Perseverance

Author:
Conrad Waters

On Thursday, 30 March 2023, the lead Spanish S-80 class submarine *Isaac Peral* (S-81) completed its first static dive in the waters of Cartagena Bay off the La Algameca naval station. The successful test marked another step towards the delivery of Spain's first truly indigenous submarine, which shipbuilder Navantia plans to hand over to the *Armada Española* before the end of 2023.[1] Ordered nearly two decades ago in March 2004, the four-strong S-80 programme has needed to overcome many challenges in the intervening years. Nevertheless, the imminent commencement of deliveries places Spain amongst the ranks of the mere handful of countries that can design and build a modern submarine.

PROGRAMME ORIGINS

The S-80 class submarine programme traces its origins as far back as preliminary studies initiated by the Spanish Navy towards the end of the 1980s. The aim was to identify a replacement for its quartet of 1970s-era S-60 *Delfín* class boats. These had been licence-built to the French *Daphné* class design. The reduction in defence expenditure that followed the end of the Cold War meant that initial progress with the project was slow. Accordingly, it was not until late 1997 that preliminary staff objectives were drafted. This ultimately paved the way for the formal approval of staff requirements in October the following year. Subsequently, in November 1999, the then Empresa Nacional Bazán was awarded a two-year project definition contract to develop a

Left: The lead S-80 submarine *Isaac Peral* (S-81) pictured after being floated out at Cartagena in May 2021. *Isaac Peral* is the first modern submarine to be designed and constructed in Spain. *(Navantia)*

A S-70 *Galerna* (*Agosta*) class submarine undergoing maintenance at Cartagena in April 2023. Prior to the S-80 class, Navantia had built a number of submarines under licence to the designs of what is now France's Naval Group. *(Conrad Waters)*

The Malaysian submarine *Tun Abdul Razak* is one of a number of 'Scorpène' type units built as a result of a joint venture between France and Spain. This collaboration exerted an influence on early design studies for the S-80 class until revised Spanish Navy requirements resulted in development going down a different track. *(Navantia)*

A computer-generated image of the S-80 design that was initially ordered from the then IZAR in March 2004. This original 71m design was later lengthened by approximately 10m to address buoyancy issues. *(Navantia)*

new submarine design in accordance with this approval.[2]

At the time the S-80 project definition contract was awarded, Bazán and France's DCN (now Naval Group) had achieved a mutually beneficial record of co-operation in submarine construction. As well as the S-60 series, Spain had also built the successor S-70 (*Agosta*) class under licence to French design. More recently, the two companies had started to achieve export success for their jointly-developed 'Scorpène' submarine, which had been unveiled at the October 1990 naval exhibition at Le Bourget. First sold to Chile in 1997, it was subsequently adopted by several other navies.[3]

Given this backdrop of Franco-Spanish collaboration, construction of a 'Scorpène' variant was one clear option to meet the Spanish Navy's needs. The experience gained from the programme – and previous collaboration – certainly exerted an important influence on the initial S-80 design effort. At the same time, the Spanish Navy's requirements mandated a somewhat bigger boat with equipment provided by a more diverse supplier base than the joint venture's French-dominated supply chain. The resultant draft design, designated P650, was a single-deck submarine with a slightly larger-diameter pressure hull than that found in the 'Scorpène'.[4] It incorporated an option for the addition of air-independent propulsion (AIP).

The conclusion of this initial project definition phase coincided with a shift in the Spanish Navy's operational requirements for their new submarines. This reflected the post-Cold War environment that emphasised global naval power projection, particularly in the littoral. As such, the capacity to undertake missions such as intelligence and reconnaissance, land attack, and the deployment of Special Forces from coastal waters began to assume at least equal importance to more traditional 'blue water' assignments focused on anti-surface and anti-submarine warfare. The shift in emphasis was reflected in the issue of a revised set of staff requirements in July 2002. Accordingly, a further project definition contract was signed with what was now IZAR in November that year. The Spanish strategic defence review of 2003 essentially confirmed the change in the submarine flotilla's priorities.

The new staff requirements inevitably had a significant impact on the original S-80 design, which effectively had to be entirely re-engineered to meet the new mission focus.[5] In particular, the submarines were to incorporate reformer-based AIP technology from build and be equipped with the capacity to launch land attack cruise missiles. The additional demand for space that these changes mandated resulted in the adoption of a two-deck hull of increased diameter. The land attack mission likely also influenced selection of the international partner chosen to assist with development of key elements of the combat management system, as few navies were equipped with this capacity at the time. The American defence conglomerate Lockheed Martin was eventually contracted to perform this role. The redesign process also cemented the S-80 programme's status as an indigenous project, independent of previous Franco-Spanish collaboration.

PROJECT IMPLEMENTATION

Government approval for the S-80 programme was received in September 2003. This was followed by the award of a design and build contract to IZAR in March 2004. At this stage it was envisaged that construction would begin early in 2005, with delivery of the lead submarine taking place in October 2011. The following boats were to be completed at annual intervals, bringing the programme to completion by the end of 2014. However, this timetable soon began to slip. An early delay was caused by uncertainty over the preferred partner for developing the class's combat management system; a decision only resolved in favour of Lockheed Martin in July 2005. Following fabrication of its initial rings, a keel-laying ceremony for the first submarine subsequently took place at Cartagena on 13 December 2007. Later, the Spanish economic crisis at the turn of the decade resulted in a further re-profiling of deliveries. By 2011, scheduled completion of the first submarine had been pushed back to the middle of the decade.

Unfortunately, this was not the end of the programme's difficulties. As the constituent sections of the lead boat began to be joined together in 2012, it began to emerge that the submarine's weight had grown by up to 100 tonnes. This increase impacted reserve buoyancy to such an extent that it was later reported that it could potentially reduce a submerged submarine's ability to surface in certain circumstances, necessitating extensive redesign at a comparatively late stage in construction. The nature of the problem was publicly announced by the now Navantia in May 2013. At this time a further project delay of between 12 and 24 months was anticipated;

A general view of Navantia's Cartagena's shipyard, where a keel-laying ceremony for the first S-80 class submarine took place on 13 December 2007. The main construction hall can be seen in the background, with the floating dock used to launch the submarines positioned in front of its doors. *Isaac Peral* is at the trials berth under the cranes in the left foreground, with a decommissioned S-70 class boat berthed immediately ahead. *(Conrad Waters)*

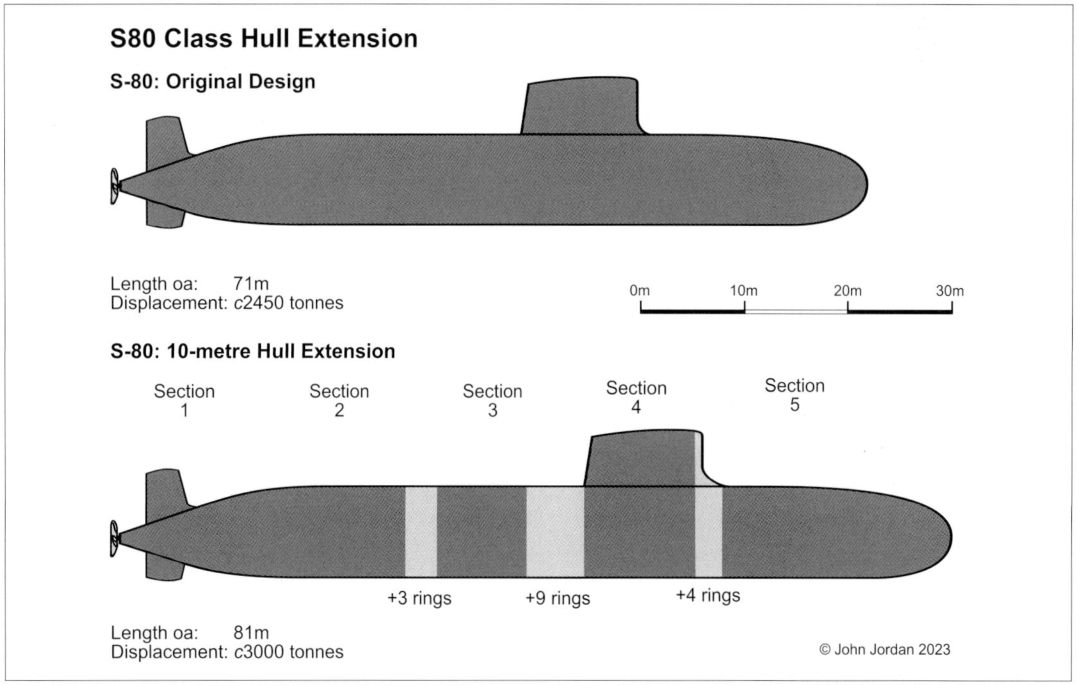

an estimate that was to prove overly optimistic. The following month it was confirmed that General Dynamics Electric Boat (GDEB) had been appointed to advise Navantia on the optimal way forward to address the issue under a three-year Foreign Military Sales contract. In addition to assessing various redesign options, GDEB also recommended project management enhancements to strengthen the systems engineering philosophy that underpinned the programme's realisation. The technical solution eventually chosen was to extend the design's hull by c. 10m through the insertion of additional hull rings in three separate locations, as illustrated in the diagram. Although overall displacement increased from just under 2,500 tonnes to nearly 3,000 tonnes as a result of these changes, the space within these extensions provided the additional buoyancy necessary to resolve the problem that had been identified.[6]

It was not until mid-2016 that the Spanish Ministry of Defence approved the critical design review of the lengthened S-80, clearing a major hurdle on the journey to the resumption of production. The necessary contract revisions were subsequently inked at the end of 2018. A further major step forward was achieved on 18 December 2019 when an event was held to mark the closure of the first boat's pressure hull with the joining of the final two constituent sections. Although the onset of the Covid pandemic in 2020 provided an additional challenge, a formal ceremony to name the lead submarine *Isaac Peral* took place at Cartagena on 22 April 2021. The importance of the programme was reflected in the attendance of King Felipe VI and other members of the Spanish royal family at the celebrations. Leonor de Borbón, Princess of Asturias and heir to the Spanish throne, acted as the boat's sponsor. The submarine was floated out of Navantia's floating dock on 7 May that year prior to completing harbour acceptance tests. Initial sea trials

These images of S-81 under assembly in Cartagena's ship hall in early 2012 give a good indication of how far construction had advanced before the emergence of buoyancy issues led to the project's suspension for redesign. The top image shows Sections 4 (left foreground) to Section 1 (far background) in January of that year. The bottom was taken the following month when the boat's electric motor – manufactured by Gamesa Electric – was installed in No. 1 Section. It was not until 2018 that a contract to complete the submarines to the revised lengthened configuration was agreed. *(Navantia)*

commenced just over a year later on 27 May 2022 with a short maiden voyage into Cartagena Bay.

THE CONSTRUCTION AND ASSEMBLY PROCESS

Construction of the S-80 class is focused on Navantia's shipyard at Cartagena in the Region of Murcia in south-east Spain. The facility has a lengthy track record in submarine production, including the licensed-build of all the previous S-60 and S-70 class boats as well as participation in the 'Scorpène' joint venture. After fabrication of a boat's constituent components, main assembly and integration activities are carried out at the yard's main ship hall. This is able to support the construction of two boats simultaneously. Each submarine is outfitted in five sections numbered from aft to forward. Section 1 comprises the electric motor and aft control surfaces, Section 2 the diesel generators, Section 3 the AIP module, Section 4 the main command and control area and Section 5 the accommodation and weapons-handling spaces. Sections are typically outfitted and joined in numerical sequence. However, there is sufficient flexibility to alter this arrangement to accommodate variations in the speed with which each section has been outfitted. Once the sections have been joined and final outfitting completed, the submarine is rolled out of the assembly hall into the facility's floating dock to be floated out into the waters of Cartagena harbour.

Although assembly is located at Cartagena, construction of the S-80 class also encompasses companies located across Spain. For example, Navantia's own in-house systems development subsidiary, Navantia Sistemas (formerly FABA), has played an important role in supplying both combat management and platform management technology for the new boats, whist Spanish defence and technology conglomerate Indra has provided radar, electronic warfare and communications equipment. Other important indigenous suppliers include system equipment manufacturer Sainsel, underwater signal processing expert SAES and Gamesa Electric, the last-mentioned being responsible for manufacturing the submarines' electric motors. The contract for designing and installing the accommodation spaces was awarded to Coruña-based marine outfitting specialists Gabadi. In addition to reportedly accounting for around seven percent of industrial employment in the Murcia region, the programme

Two pictures showing different stages of *Isaac Peral's* float out from Cartagena in May 2021. The process was completed on 7 May. Although assembly of all boats in the S-80 class is focused on Cartagena, their construction has supported employment in companies across Spain. *(Navantia)*

has brought employment to hundreds of Spanish enterprises. This is very much in line with the government's objective of stimulating economic activity by developing an indigenous industrial base for submarine construction.

Another benefit of establishing S-80 acquisition as a fully-indigenous programme has been the greater freedom of action gained to select international equipment suppliers compared with previous licence-builds. This is most notably evidenced in Lockheed Martin's appointment to assist with combat management system development, as well as to source key elements of the sonar suite.[7] Other significant international equipment selections have included the contract with L3 Harris KEO's Italian Calzoni subsidiary to supply periscopes and other hoistable masts. The class's weapons-handling and discharge equipment – including its torpedo tubes – have been provided by Britain's Babcock International with the assistance of a Spanish supply chain. This reflects the use of equipment contracts to boost Spain's capacity to indigenise the future production of key components. For example, forward and aft pressure hull domes for the first two submarines were entirely constructed by BAE Systems in Barrow-in-Furness. However, final assembly of those for the second pair has taken place in Cartagena as Navantia gained the technology and experience necessary to fabricate these crucial components.

Table 3.3.1.

ISAAC PERAL (S-81) PRINCIPAL PARTICULARS

Building Information:	
Laid Down:	13 December 2007 Floated Out: 7 May 2021[1] Commissioned: To be confirmed
Builders:	Navantia at its Cartagena Shipyard, Murcia, Spain.
Dimensions:	
Displacement:	2,695 tonnes surface displacement, 2,965 tonnes dived displacement.
Overall Hull Dimensions:	81.0m x 11.6m x 6.3m. Hull diameter is 7.3m
Weapons Systems:	
Armament:	6 x bow 533mm torpedo tubes. Space for up to 19 torpedoes (inc. one emergency position) or equivalent. Weapons outfit includes:
	Atlas Elektronik DM2 A4 Sea Hake heavyweight torpedo. Active/passive homing and fibre optical guidance to 50km (27nm) at speeds of up to 50 knots.
	SAES MINEA multi-influence naval mine.
	Equipped to launch anti-surface and land attack missiles.
Countermeasures:	Indra Pegaso ESM. 4 x 5-tube Babcock International decoy launchers.
Principal Sensors:	Lockheed Martin integrated sonar suite plus SAES Solarsub digital towed-array sonar.
	L3 Harris KEO Model 2010 AP attack periscope and Model 2010 OS optronic mast.
	Indra Aries-S low probability of intercept surveillance radar.
Combat System:	S-80 CMS jointly developed by Navantia Sistemas and Lockheed Martin utilising SCOMBA and SUBICS technology.
	Integrated communications including NATO Links 11 and 22.
Propulsion Systems:	
Machinery:	Diesel-electric with auxiliary AIP propulsion;
	3 x MTU 16V 396 SE 84L diesel generators each rated at 1.2MW
	1 x Gamesa Electric synchronous permanent magnet electric motor rated at 3.5MW
	1 x BEST (Bio-Ethanol Stealth Technology) AIP plant rated at 350 kW.
Speed and Range:	Over 10 knots surfaced, over 19 knots submerged. Up to 3 weeks underwater endurance on AIP.
Diving Depth:	Classified but in excess of 350m.
Other Details:	
Complement:	Normal crew is 32. Accommodation is provided for 46 personnel.
Class:	Four – S-81 *Isaac Peral*, S-82 *Narciso Monturiol*, S-83 *Cosme García* and S-84 *Mateo García de los Reyes*.

Note:
1. A formal naming/sponsorship ceremony was held on 22 April 2021.

DESIGN DESCRIPTION

Key technical details of the S-80 class submarine are set out in Table 3.3.1. The design has a submerged displacement approaching 3,000 tonnes, an overall length of c. 81m and a pressure hull diameter of 7.3m. This places it towards the larger end of contemporary 'Western' diesel-electric submarines. Australia's veteran *Collins* and Japan's more recent *Soryu* and *Tagei* classes are, perhaps, its closest comparators. This essentially reflects the decision to acquire submarines capable of global expeditionary deployment compared with the more defensive mission characteristics of previous, smaller Spanish Navy designs.

Overview: The S-80 design incorporates a single-hull 'teardrop' form that can trace its recent lineage to the US Navy's research submarine *Albacore* (AGSS-569). It is primarily intended to minimise acoustic signature. In addition to computer simulations, the hull design was subject to tow-tank testing at SSPA Maritime Center in Sweden and MARIN in the Netherlands to validate its hydro-dynamic characteristics. Attention to stealth is apparent throughout the design. For example, the navigating position on the fin (US Navy sail) can be closed off to avoid underwater turbulence when the submarine is submerged. In contrast to recent US and Royal Navy submarines, there is no use of anechoic tiles. However, these could be retrofitted if ever required.

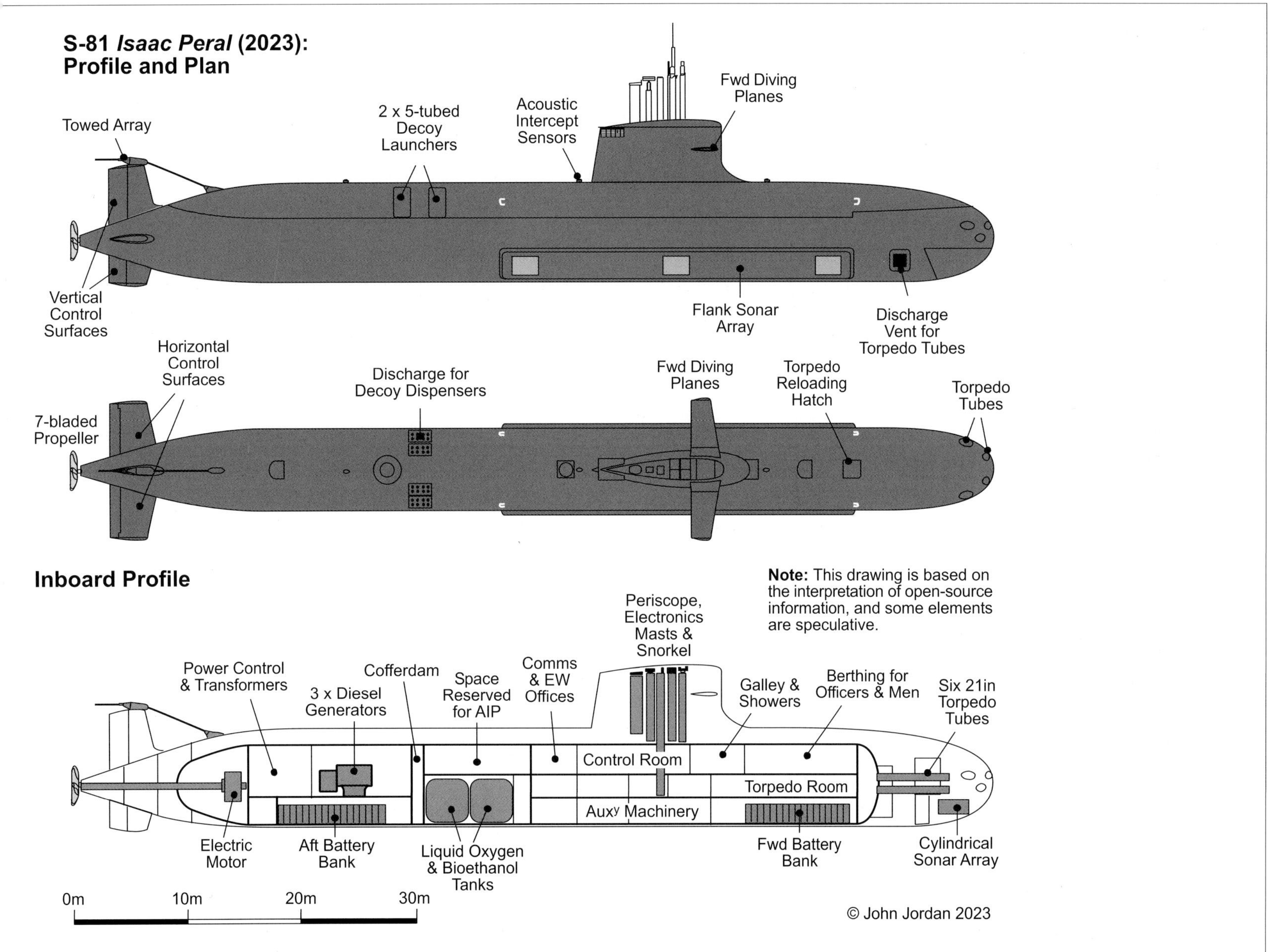

Isaac Peral is pictured in Navantia's floating dock in May 2021 after completion of the assembly process. The photograph gives a good impression of the class's 'teardrop', *Albacore*-type hull form as well as its relatively large diameter, facilitating the adoption of what is essentially a two-deck design. *(Navantia)*

This Navantia-produced cutaway of the S-80 design gives a particularly good impression of the after part of the boat, comprising Section 1 (motor), Section 2 (diesel generators) and Section 3 (AIP plant) assemblies. Points of interest include the framing of the AIP section's fuel tanks and the large battery compartment under the generators and associated control/ conversion equipment. Also apparent are the cruciform arrangement of the rudder and aft hydroplanes, as well as the solution adopted to deploy the towed-array sonar. *(Navantia)*

The pressure-hull structure is manufactured from high strength HLES 80 steel.

Internally, the S-80 class's relatively large diameter facilitates adoption of what is largely a two-deck design. Commencing at the pressure hull's forward end, the upper deck of No. 5 section is occupied by the galley, sanitary facilities and crew accommodation. This is arranged so that that the commanding officer's cabin – the only single-berth unit – is closest to the command centre. A total crew of thirty-two is required to operate the boat on a three-watch system. There is also provision for up to eight Special Forces personnel. However, up to forty-six people can be accommodated if the need arises. The lower deck in this area is largely taken up with torpedo stowage, with the forward battery compartment located in the hold below.

Moving aft from the accommodation on the upper deck, No. 4 section is dominated by the combat information centre/control room. This is located immediately below the fin (US Navy sail). There is a total of seven combat management system

The Gamesa Electric-supplied synchronous permanent magnet motor pictured in S-81's hull. Of lightweight, shock-resistant design, the motor has a power output in the order of 3.5MW. *(Navantia)*

Isaac Peral pictured off Cartagena in the course of preliminary surface sea trials in May 2022. The class's surface speed is quoted as being in excess of 10 knots, whilst more than 19 knots can be achieved underwater. Actual figures are likely to be higher. *(Navantia)*

consoles to the starboard side of the command and control facility, whilst platform management consoles and a position for the helmsman are located to port. This leaves the centreline of the space free for the commanding officer and the traditional, hull-penetrating attack periscope. Immediately aft of the command centre are separate compartments for communications and electronic warfare, an arrangement probably facilitated by the lengthening of the hull in this area. The lower deck areas in No. 2 section are largely occupied by electrical equipment.

The boat's No. 3 section is occupied by the AIP plant. Liquid oxygen and bioethanol tanks are positioned on the lower deck and a reformer plant and polymer membrane (PEM) fuel cells on the deck above. Although the relevant tanks have been fitted to the first two members of the class from build, installation of the upper-level AIP plant will only commence with the third S-80 submarine due to developmental delays. Immediately aft of the AIP module is an airlock that can be used to facilitate the deployment of Special Forces or to assist crew escape in the event of an accident. There is a platform for a deep-submergence rescue vehicle (DSRV) above the airlock's escape hatch.

The aftermost No. 2 and No. 1 sections are largely occupied by the main propulsion machinery. The three diesel generators are mounted in parallel in No. 2 section and encompass much of the hull depth at this point. There are spaces for power control and conversion equipment further aft whilst the aft battery compartment is located in the hold. The major part of No. 1 section is taken up with the electrical motor.

A notable design decision was to maintain a conventional cruciform rudder configuration rather than the 'X' type arrangement that is becoming increasingly popular in recent submarine designs. The 'X' configuration – in which no distinction is made between a boat's rudder and aft hydroplanes – is regarded as improving manoeuvrability and facilitating safe operation in shallow water. However, Navantia's design team determined that the traditional cruciform arrangement remained easier to control in manual reversionary mode, enhancing overall survivability. Moreover, the S-80 design will still be highly responsive. It is reportedly able to dive from periscope depth to 100m in just 50 seconds and perform a 'crash stop' in 80 seconds (the equivalent of about five boat-lengths).[8]

Propulsion and Platform Management: The S-80 class is powered by three licence-built MTU 16V 396 SE 84L diesel generators delivering a combined output of 3.6 MW. These are linked to alternator rectifier equipment to enable the AC to DC power conversion required for battery charging. In similar fashion to much other equipment, the generators are elastically mounted as part of the overall focus on reducing acoustic stealth. The provision of three

A unique feature of the S-80 class design is its BEST (Bio-Ethanol Stealth Technology) auxiliary AIP plant, which will be installed from build in the third boat. This uses the now well-established PEM fuel cell technology under which the reaction of hydrogen and oxygen is used to produce electricity but incorporates a bioethanol processor to create hydrogen onboard. This picture shows the equipment under test in factory conditions. *(Navantia)*

This picture of the S-80 class's combat management system consoles – taken in the tactical simulator at Cartagena Naval Base – replicates the layout of the starboard side of the actual boats' command and control centre. The seven Sainsel dual-screen CONAM SUB multi-function common consoles can be used to present a wider range of sensor data and to perform weapons targeting and control functions. *(Navantia)*

separate generators speeds battery recharging whilst snorkelling, thereby reducing vulnerability. Each of the two battery compartments are equipped with 180 separate lead acid cells supplied by Exide's Spanish Tudor subsidiary. The S-80's design was completed before recent developments in Lithium-ion (Li-ion) technology have seen them emerge as an attractive alternative for energy storage in modern submarines. However, Navantia has undertaken to assess their potential retrofit at a later date.

Propulsion is by means of a synchronous permanent magnet motor linked by a single shaft to a skew-bladed fixed-pitch propeller incorporating seven blades. Ordered from Cantarey Reinosa – now part of Siemens Energy's Gamesa Electric – the motor is of lightweight, shock-resistant design. It has an output of 3.5MW. Submerged speed is quoted as being in excess of 19 knots and over 10 knots can be achieved on the surface. It seems likely that both these figures will be comfortably exceeded in practice.[9]

The planned 300 kW BEST (Bio-Ethanol Stealth Technology) auxiliary AIP plant is intended to allow a significant extension in underwater endurance without the need for snorkelling, albeit at a significantly reduced speed. The Spanish Navy's original requirement was reportedly to allow underwater operation for 15 days at a speed of four knots. However, this figure could be increased to around three weeks by reducing a boat's 'hotel' load. Utilising PEM fuel cells manufactured by Collins Aerospace, the AIP plant's basic operating principle is essentially similar to that found, for example, in thyssenkrupp Marine Systems' Type 212A and Type 214 submarines. It relies on the conversion of chemical energy produced by the reaction of hydrogen and oxygen into electricity. However, Navantia's solution differs by producing hydrogen as and when required by means of a bioethanol processor rather than by devising specific arrangements to store relatively large quantities of hydrogen aboard. Navantia argues that this approach is inherently safer, as only small quantities of the potentially dangerous gas are required at any one time. Moreover, the use of industrial alcohol in the reformer process simplifies logistics, as supplies are readily available at most major ports and no special facilities are required for refuelling. Development of the BEST system has proved challenging, as evidenced by the fact that it will only be ready in time for installation in the third S-80.[10] Nevertheless, its potential benefits represent a major step forward in AIP operation.

The S-80 class's platform management system is based on the principal of multiple redundancy; thereby reflecting the Spanish Navy's emphasis on overall survivability. Primary control and monitoring of non-combat-related equipment is performed by an integrated platform management system (IPMS) developed by Navantia Sistemas. This is the first submarine-based IPMS developed by the company. The system is operated from two Sainsel-supplied consoles in the command and control room. The IPMS is supplemented by a fully independent, non-integrated platform management system that provides direct connections to important equipment in case of need. Certain critical systems can also be directly operated in fall-back mode.

Navigation functions are performed from the helmsman's position in the command and control centre. This is used to operate a steering and diving control system provided by GE's Italian Avio Aero business. The system encompasses Avio Aero's GAUDI (Guidance Automation Unit Distributed Intelligence) autopilot. It maintains automatic control of the submarine's course, depth and trim in a wide range of operating conditions.

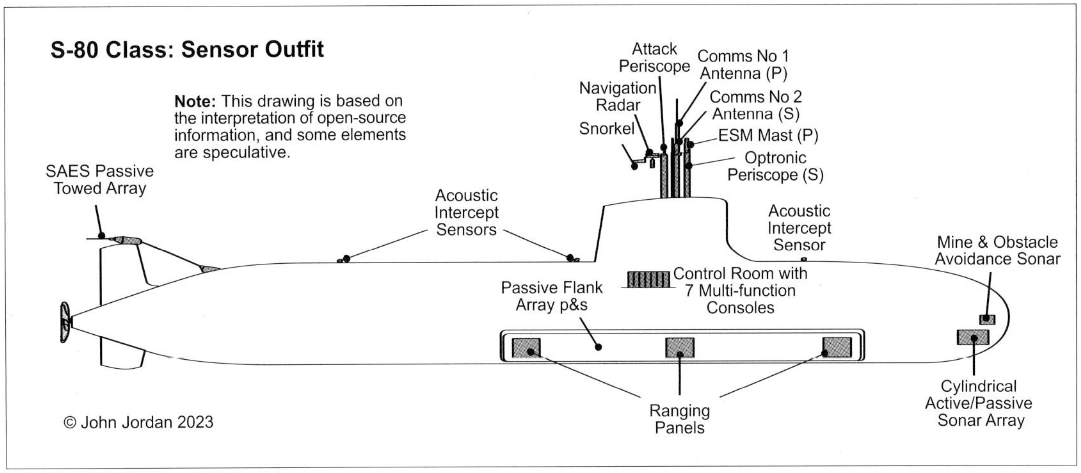

Combat Management System and Sensors: The heart of the S-80 class's warfighting capabilities is provided by its combat management system. Its underlying architecture and hardware share many similarities with the Navantia Sistemas SCOMBA (*Sistema de Combate de los Buques de la Armada*) that is widely used in the Spanish Navy's surface vessels. However, in certain key areas it is overlaid by technology provided by design partner Lockheed Martin that is based on its scalable International Diesel-Electric Submarine Integrated Combat System (SUBICS). This is, in turn, derived from the American company's experience supplying combat systems to US Navy submarines.

The combat management system (CMS) is controlled from seven Sainsel dual-screen CONAM SUB multi-function common consoles situated in the command centre and which are broadly similar to those used by the IPMS. They are used to present sensor data and perform weapons targeting and control functions. There is also a large tactical display screen that is essentially used to support overall situational awareness. Information for these displays is processed and distributed by two Ares S-80 servers. These are connected to relevant sensors and weapons via the usual network of data cables and various weapon processor and weapon interface units. The CMS is also integrated with an own noise management system to help manage acoustic signature. In line with current practice, the CMS makes full use of commercial off the shelf (COTS) equipment and utilises an open systems architecture to facilitate future upgrades.

The CMS forms an integral part of what is commonly referred to as the S-80's integrated combat system core (ICSC). This also encompasses the design's sonar array suite, which is largely supplied by Lockheed Martin. Its main elements include:

- A cylindrical array sonar located in the submarine's chin.
- Flank array sonar panels attached to the port and starboard sides of the hull.
- Ranging panels on the flank arrays.
- A mine and obstacle-avoidance sonar in the vicinity of the torpedo tubes.
- Acoustic intercept arrays atop the submarine's hull.

These arrays are supplemented by an indigenous Solarsub S-80 digital towed-array sonar (DTAS) manufactured by SAES. This has been developed on the basis of experience gained from the previous production of towed arrays for the S-70 class. Comprising a long towed passive antenna, it is deployed by means of a reel-able handling system that passes it through a rigid tube extending from the hull to the upper rudder mounting.

In addition to the sonar system, the S-80 design is also equipped with a comprehensive range of above-water sensors. These are largely deployed by means of hoistable masts located atop the fin that have been

This May 2023 photograph of *Isaac Peral* at Cartagena provides a good view of the tube used to deploy her SAES Solarsub S-80 digital towed-array sonar. Other points of interest are the two five-tube decoy launchers that can be seen on the hull aft of her fin (sail) and the raised snorkel. *(Conrad Waters)*

This view of *Isaac Peral* in the Cartagena assembly hall provides a good view of her six 533mm torpedo tubes. The gap between the two lower torpedo tubes is probably occupied by the mine and obstacle avoidance sonar. The class's Babcock International-supplied weapon handling and discharge equipment can handle a wide range of torpedoes, mines and missiles. *(Navantia)*

An overhead view of *Isaac Peral* in Navantia's floating dock. Her torpedo tubes and weapons stowage area are all located forward of the fin. Two pairs of five-cell decoy launchers are mounted on each side of the hull roughly a third of the way between the fin and the stern. *(Navantia)*

supplied by L3 Harris KEO's Calzoni. In total, the suite of seven masts supports:

- A low probability of intercept Aries-S surveillance radar supplied by Indra.
- An ESM antenna for Indra's Pegaso system.
- Two communications antennae that, inter alia, provide NATO Link 11 and Link 22 connectivity for the integrated communications suite.
- Two periscopes.
- A snorkel.

A noteworthy feature of this outfit is the Spanish Navy's selection of a configuration that combines a conventional, hull-penetrating attack periscope (a L3 Harris KEO Model 2010 AP) with a non-penetrating optronic surveillance mast (Model 2010 OS). Both are fitted with a thermal imaging camera supplied by Indra alongside TV equipment. The optronic mast also has a colour camera and laser rangefinder.

Weapons Systems: The S-80 class's principal armament comprises six 533mm (21in) torpedo tubes. These are arranged in a four (upper) plus two (lower) configuration, the latter being divided by the position for the mine and obstacle avoidance sonar. The tubes utilise a positive air discharge system provided by two rotary air-turbine pumps.

Weapons stowage is provided in the pressure hull just aft of the tubes. A total of twelve torpedoes can be carried in the two double-tier weapons racks (i.e. three weapons at each level in each rack). A further six torpedoes could be carried in the tubes themselves. In addition, there is provision for a nineteenth weapon to be stowed on the centreline between the two racks in an emergency. The principal weapon carried will be Atlas Elektronik's widely-used DM2A4 (SeaHake mod 4) heavy weight electric torpedo. Adopting a modular approach that allows configuration with two, three or four battery sets, DM2A4 uses fibre-optic guidance to engage targets up to reported ranges of over 25 nautical miles. An alternative loadout could include SAES' MINEA multi-influence naval mine. One reported feature of the class's weapon-handling and discharge equipment is the ability to eject mines automatically in sequence using all six tubes.

The weapon-handling system has the capacity to handle a wider range of weapons than those currently in the Spanish Navy's inventory. This includes anti-surface and land attack missiles.

A picture of *Isaac Peral* making her first static test dive in the waters of Cartagena Bay on 30 March 2023. The picture provides a good view of her non-hull penetrating L3 Harris KEO Model 2010 optronic surveillance mast. As of mid-2023, a full programme of trials was expected to conclude with the submarine's acceptance by the end of the year. *(Navantia)*

Somewhat ironically, given the significant influence the land attack mission had on the original design process, budgetary constraints have meant that the Tomahawk cruise missiles originally envisaged for the class have not yet been acquired, although this remains a possibility. Given, however, the current US Navy trend to use vertical launch systems for submarine-deployed cruise missiles, a decision will be required soon if the S-80 class are ever perform their intended land attack mission.

In addition to their weapons, the S-80s are equipped with acoustic countermeasures launchers that can deploy decoys to counter incoming torpedoes and disrupt enemy sonar. Like the torpedo handling and discharge system, these have been supplied by Babcock International. Two pairs of five launchers are mounted on each side of the hull aft of the fin in the vicinity of No. 3 section.

INTO SERVICE

With *Isaac Peral*'s diving trials now underway, the S-80 programme is in the final stages of achieving the long-awaited delivery of its first submarine. A full programme of phased tests is planned for much of the remainder of 2023 which, all being well, will culminate with delivery of the lead boat by the end of the year. Navantia states that the submarine's Spanish Navy crew have been very satisfied with the submarine to date. For example, the performance of the sonar suite is considered a significant step forwards by personnel with experience of the equipment found in the previous S-70 design.

At the time of writing, the second and third

Ensuring the safety of submarine operation is a high priority for both the Spanish Navy and Navantia. The acquisition of the new BAM-IS submarine rescue vessel *Poseidon* is one of a number of investments made to support this focus. *(Navantia)*

Isaac Peral pictured sailing in the waters of Cartagena Bay on 27 May 2022. The submarine continues to progress through a series of trials that should result in her delivery before the end of 2023. Her imminent arrival reflects great credit on both Navantia and the Spanish Navy. *(Navantia)*

members of the class – respectively *Narciso Monturiol* (S-82) and *Cosme García* (S-83) – are in the course of integration in Navantia's Cartagena assembly hall. It is anticipated that S-82's pressure hull will be closed in the course of 2023, with delivery scheduled during 2024. Delivery of S-83 is anticipated in 2026, with additional time required to complete installation of the full AIP plant for the first time in the class. The current programme will reach its conclusion with completion of the fourth boat – *Mateo García de los Reyes* (S-84) – in 2028.

The delivery of the class is being supported by an extensive training programme that has included the installation of two simulators in the Submarine School at Cartagena Naval Base. One is a tactical simulator designed to train sailors to operate the combat management system. The other is a platform simulator that is intended to facilitate tuition relating to platform management and steering systems. Both simulators replicate the relevant areas of the actual submarines. In addition, the platform simulator is designed to pitch and roll in line with the boat's manoeuvring characteristics.[11]

The S-80 programme's status as a truly indigenous project has been reflected in the creation of a national submarine technical certification programme. This is focused principally (1) on ensuring watertight integrity and (2) facilitating safe recovery if flooding does occur. Managed by the Submarine Technical Certification Office, its work encompasses certifying the overall S-80 design and each individual member of the class. The process includes both initial entry into service and subsequent overhaul. Technical assistance from the US Navy's Submarine Safety (SUBSAFE) programme was sought in drawing up the certification process. The importance attached to ensuring submarine safety is also demonstrated by the November 2021 order for the BAM-IS submarine rescue vessel *Poseidon*, which will be completed at Navantia's Puerto Real shipyard in the Bay of Cádiz.

Once in service, each member of the S-80 class is designed to have a service life of 36 years. It is intended that a submarine will be able to operate for six years between major overhauls, at which stage each boat will be withdrawn from service for one and a half years. With four major overhauls scheduled in each submarine's lifetime, it will be well into the 2060s before the last is retired.

CONCLUSION

It is apparent that successful realisation of the S-80 submarine programme has posed major challenges to both Navantia and the Spanish Navy. Notably, the significant delays associated with the boats' redesign have had a major impact on the navy's underwater flotilla. This has been forced to resort to costly life-extensions to two of the legacy S-70 class to maintain a residual operational capability until the new vessels arrive. Moreover, overall project costs have increased from an initial €1.75bn (c. US$1.9bn) to approximately €3.9bn (c. US$4.2bn), further stretching an already limited defence budget.

To an extent, these challenges are not surprising. The design and construction of a modern submarine is widely acknowledged as being one of the most complex endeavours known to mankind, sometimes being compared to the demands associated with space travel. Many other countries have encountered significant problems renewing their submarine flotillas with new units as a result of the loss of technical expertise in the aftermath of the Cold War. The challenges faced by Navantia – which effectively had to develop many essential skills from scratch – have been all the greater.

Despite all these challenges, Navantia and the Spanish government have persevered with the S-80 programme, now reaching the point where its successful delivery is imminent. In addition to providing a vital capability for the Spanish Navy, this success will bring major benefits to both the country's maritime sector and its larger economy. Just one example of the fruits of this perseverance is S-80 sub-contractor Indra's recent export success in selling electronic equipment to the new South Korean KSS-III and joint German/Norwegian Type 212CD submarine programmes.

A major outstanding question is what the future holds for Spanish submarine construction. The renewal of East-West tensions has certainly reinforced the importance of submarine operations in European navies. This could hold out the prospect of the future expansion of Spain's underwater flotilla towards its late Cold War structure of eight boats should funding become available. Alternatively, the S-80's relatively unusual status as a large conventional submarine suitable for lengthy deployment could make it attractive for other navies needing this capability. The requirements of the proposed Indian Project 75I and of the Canadian Patrol Submarine Project (CPSP) seemingly align closely with these characteristics.

In any event, the imminent delivery of *Isaac Peral* reflects great credit on Navantia and the Spanish Navy. The new submarine is a fitting legacy to the achievement of her namesake, designer of the first *Peral*, over a hundred years ago.

Notes

1. Spain has a long and distinguished history of submarine construction. Most notably, the indigenously designed and innovative submersible *Peral* – product of the S-81's namesake Isaac Peral – was delivered in 1889. However, subsequent deliveries to the Spanish Navy were dominated by licensed construction of overseas designs, occasionally supplemented by the transfer of boats from overseas. More recently, the export-focused 'Scorpène' type was developed as a joint project with what is now Naval Group of France.

2. The former Empresa Nacional Bazán was subsequently merged into IZAR in 2000 as part of a consolidation of Spanish state-owned naval and mercantile shipbuilding interests. A further corporate reorganisation in 2005 saw the creation of Navantia, which is largely focused on naval construction and support activities.

3. The 'Scorpène' design originated from French plans to replace their *Daphné* class submarines with new diesel-electric boats that were intended to draw heavily on technology previously developed for their nuclear-powered submarines. The agreement to proceed with the project as an export-focused joint venture with Spain was finalised in 2001. The alliance was eventually terminated in 2010 due to French dissatisfaction with the development of the S-80, which they regarded as a competitor. In addition to the inaugural sale to Chile, two 'Scorpènes' have been built for Malaysia. There has been licensed construction of six Indian and four Brazilian variants; the latter to a lengthened design. Construction of the Chilean and Malaysian submarines was shared between Naval Group and Navantia. This arrangement saw the forward sections of the boats being completed in Cherbourg and the aft sections in Cartagena. Each shipyard then undertook the final assembly of one of each of the two pairs of boats. The basic 'Scorpène' design has a submerged displacement of c. 1,750 tonnes, a length of c. 67m and a diameter of 6.2m. It is equipped with six 533mm (21in) torpedo tubes and can carry a total of eighteen torpedoes or equivalent weapons.

4. A variant of the P650 design was reportedly favoured for an ultimately abortive plan to construct diesel-electric submarines for Taiwan's Republic of China Navy in the United States.

5. The re-designed submarine was referenced as the S-80A for a period. Later, when the design was lengthened to address buoyancy issues, it became known as the S-80 Plus. At the time of writing, the S-80 designation is back in favour.

6. The emergence of the class's buoyancy issue broadly coincided with separate difficulties with development of the intended AIP plant. This ultimately resulted in a decision to fit the first two S-80s 'for but not with' AIP pending retrofit at a later date.

7. Although Lockheed Martin is the principal contractor for key elements of the class's sonar suite, secondary sources suggest some arrays have been subcontracted to other manufacturers.

8. These figures were reported by Richard Scott in 'Spain's S-80A submarine comes up to the surface', *Jane's Navy International* – December 2007 (Coulsdon: IHS Jane's, 2007) and refer to the S-80 design prior to lengthening. The impact of the subsequent design changes is not known.

9. The previous, less efficient S-70 class is generally stated to have a maximum underwater speed in excess of 20 knots and over 12 knots on the surface.

10. Abengoa, a subcontractor for BEST, experienced significant difficulties producing an effective bioethanol processing plant within the space and weight margins provided in the S-80 class. This resulted in the development of a competitor solution by Técnicas Reunidas. In the event, it was decided to proceed with Abengoa's proposal in 2020.

11. A more detailed description of the simulators is contained in Ginés Soriano Forte's dual language *Perfiles ids: S-80 El Submarino Española Puesto A Flote* (Madrid: Ancares Artes Gráficas, 2021), pp.66–9.

12. The author acknowledges with thanks the considerable assistance of Germán Romero Valiente, Submarine Business Managing Director; Jaime Diáz Diáz, Engineering Manager, Cartagena Shipyard; Esther Benito Lope, Navantia Communications Directorate; José Andrés Elgarresta, Head of Communications and Institutional Relations, Cartagena Shipyard; and the many other engineering and production staff at Navantia's Cartagena shipyard in the preparation of this article.

4.1 TECHNOLOGICAL REVIEW

Author:
David Hobbs

WORLD NAVAL AVIATION

A Review of Recent Developments

The past 12 months have seen a significant increase in the use of unmanned combat air vehicles (UCAVs) – commonly referred to as drones – by several navies. Stimulated by Ukraine's often innovative measures against Russian invasion forces, these have included commercially available, 'off-the-shelf' quadcopters and their derivatives, which can be brought into service more quickly than the more advanced air vehicles being developed by, for example, the US Navy. The Royal Navy (RN) sees drones as adding mass and expanded capabilities to its carrier air wings but the US Navy still has reservations about the extent to which UCAVs should replace manned aircraft over the next decade. Other navies see 'drone carriers' as a means of taking aircraft to sea for roles that range from simple over-the-horizon surveillance to strike missions. Appropriately, this review includes a detailed description of the US Navy's MQ-25A Stingray aerial tanker, which is intended to join carrier air wings from 2026.

Queen Elizabeth arrives in New York on 25 September 2022 ahead of hosting the Atlantic Future Forum, a gathering of senior politicians, policymakers, military leaders and academia aimed at strengthening the Euro-Atlantic alliance. She had been re-assigned to act as the venue for the forum at short notice following her sister's mechanical failure. *(Crown Copyright 2022)*

UNITED KINGDOM: ROYAL NAVY

Carrier Aviation: The 2021 deployment of the *Queen Elizabeth* task force to the Pacific and the more recent NATO deployment of *Prince of Wales* into the Arctic are examples of the aircraft carriers' role as instruments of the United Kingdom's maritime strategy. The movements of these ships generate headlines but these have not always been positive. In August 2022 *Prince of Wales* sailed from Portsmouth for a Western Atlantic deployment that was to include developmental testing of F-35B shipborne rolling vertical landing techniques and unmanned aircraft, as well as the embarkation of USMC MV-22 Ospreys. Within hours of sailing, she had to anchor off the Isle of Wight for divers to examine a problem with the starboard propeller shaft. Examination revealed a failed shaft coupling which required her to be dry-docked at Rosyth for repairs. The various trials she was to have carried out were re-scheduled for the autumn of 2023 and *Queen Elizabeth* was re-programmed to replace her as the floating venue for the September 2022 Atlantic Future Forum in New York. She was welcomed by the British Ambassador to the United States, Dame Karen Pierce, who described her presence as 'a fantastic demonstration of soft power and the close working relationship between the United Kingdom and United States of America'.

Once *Prince of Wales* was docked in Rosyth, the port shaft was also examined and found to have issues similar to those which had led to the failure of components on the starboard shaft. These had caused damage to the propeller and rudder as well as the shaft itself. Media reports describe the failure as possibly being due to shaft misalignment during construction. An examination of *Queen Elizabeth's* shafts has revealed no similar problems. *Prince of Wales'* ship's company remained on board throughout the repair period to assist with the work and carry on with synthetic training exercises; work is due to be complete in mid-2023 after which she will resume her original programme beginning with an upgrade period in Portsmouth intended to bring her up to the same operational standard as her sister before sailing for the delayed West Atlantic deployment in the autumn.

The RN's ability to support carrier task forces continues to expand in a number of ways. A contract for the construction of three new fleet auxiliaries – the fleet solid support ships – was awarded in January 2023.[1] They will provide the ammunition, spare parts and solid logistics needed to maintain the carriers and their aircraft in global operations. While their primary carrier-support role caught the headlines, these ships are to be significant helicopter-operating platforms in their own right, capable of embarking every helicopter type in current British service up to and including the large Chinooks. In addition to hangar space for two Merlins (with accommodation for aircrew and maintenance personnel) there is to be space for drones or other unmanned systems and their operators. As the latter evolve, they could be either pilotless target aircraft or operational systems, capable of data-linked sorties

Left: The carrier *Prince of Wales* departs Portsmouth Harbour on 27 August 2023 at the start of what was described as a 'landmark mission to shape the future of stealth fighter jet and drone operations off the coast of North America'. Unfortunately, the emergence of a defect with the ship's starboard shaft-line meant that the deployment had to be cancelled within hours of sailing. As of mid-2023, she remained under repair at Rosyth. *(Crown Copyright 2022)*

within a widely dispersed task force. Ashore, the *Queen Elizabeth* class carrier forward logistics centre in Portsmouth contains the spare parts, tools and documentation the ships need during maintenance periods. It opened in June 2022 as the first net-zero carbon structure in the RN and one of the most advanced facilities of its kind anywhere.

Britain's joint F-35B Lightning II force continues to grow slowly towards maturity. Tranche 1 deliveries continue, with thirty of the forty-eight aircraft delivered by December 2022 and the last due in 2025.[2] The next programme milestone is the commissioning of 809 Naval Air Squadron (NAS), due in the second half of 2023. It is expected to mature to operational capability in March 2025. At this point the carrier strike force will have two carriers and two operational F-35B squadrons, the force level defined in the UK Defence Equipment Plan 2022 as full operational capability (FOC). A Tranche 2 buy of a further twenty-six F-35Bs has also been authorised. This will bring total British F-35B acquisitions up to seventy-four aircraft, allowing a third front-line squadron to be commissioned by 2033. It also extends the planned F-35B out-of-service date (OSD) to 2069, the same date as the *Queen Elizabeth* class carriers.

A graphic of a F-35B Lightning II launching a Meteor BVRAAM from its internal weapons bay. The Meteor air-to-air missile and the SPEAR 3 air-to-surface missile systems are both scheduled to enter service with the F-35B in 2028 as part of the aircraft's Block 4 software upgrade. *(MBDA)*

One of the underlying factors slowing the growth of the F-35B force has been insufficient numbers of RN and Royal Air Force (RAF) maintenance personnel. Steps have been taken to remedy this including increases in the numbers allocated to the force, with benefits expected to appear from 2023. During 2022 the training unit at Marham, 207 Squadron RAF, trained eight F-35B pilots, of whom four had previously flown other types of fighter, two were straight from pilot training, one was from the Royal Australian Air Force (RAAF), and one from the US Air Force. Four British F-35 pilots are serving with allied F-35 units including one in Australia and three in the United States. Pilot training was planned to increase during 2023.

A significant F-35B capability upgrade is planned for 2028 when the Meteor air-to-air missile and the SPEAR 3 air-to-surface missile systems are due to enter service. Both are designed and manufactured by MBDA and their introduction forms part of the aircraft's Block 4 software upgrade. Meteor is an active radar-guided beyond visual range air-to-air missile (BVRAAM). It is powered by a solid fuel ramjet motor that gives a maximum speed in excess of Mach 4 and an effective range of over 55 nautical miles. It allows the aircraft to engage multiple targets simultaneously, even in a high-ECM environment. Initial guidance is inertial but a two-way datalink allows mid-course updates or re-targeting by either the launch aircraft or a third party. Mid-course updates can also initiate missile acceleration and final target interception is by terminal active radar homing. Both impact and proximity fuses initiate the blast/fragmentation warhead. Meteor is already in service in a number of European aircraft, including the French Navy's Rafale. Italian Navy F-35Bs are also to get Meteor as part of the Block 4 software package. Meanwhile, SPEAR 3 (Select Precision Effects At Range Capability 3) is a subsonic stand-off attack weapon with a range in excess of 80 nautical miles evolved from the earlier Brimstone missile. The F-35B's two internal weapon bays can carry various combinations of the two missiles.

The loss of F-35B ZM 152 from *Queen Elizabeth* off Egypt on 17 November 2021 was mentioned in last year's review and an interim report has now outlined its probable cause.[3] 'Red Gear', the generic name for engine intake blanks and protective covers, was fitted for the passage of the Suez Canal a day earlier but work had been carried out on the aircraft overnight to prepare it for flight. During this, some Red Gear was removed by engineers but no entry was required in the aircraft technical log about its fitment or removal. A local accounting procedure was in place but had not been used for the mass fitting and removal during the Suez transit. On 17 November the aircraft taxied onto the runway for launch at 11.37, the pilot conducted engine run-up checks and confirmed all indications were normal before selecting take-off power, 97 per cent engine thrust request (ETR) and released the brakes. Initial acceleration felt normal but then decreased and the pilot noted that ETR was only 74 percent. He selected 100 percent but engine power remained low. The pilot attempted to abort the take-off but was unable to stop the aircraft and he ejected, the parachute deployed and he landed on the flight deck with only minor injuries. The aircraft passed down the port side of the ship before it sank but, as it did so, the left-hand intake blank was seen to float clear of the wreckage and was recovered and impounded. The report studied an analysis of the flight data recorder conducted by Lockheed Martin and completed an independent airworthiness review before stating its opinion that a single engine intake blank remained inside the intake at the time of launch, causing a restriction in airflow sufficient to prevent the engine from producing the power required for take-off. This was most likely due to a combination of human, organisational and procedural factors.

Project Crowsnest, the delivery of airborne surveillance and control (ASaC) capability for use as alternative role equipment in the Merlin HM 2 fleet, has made some progress during the past year. Written answers to Parliamentary Questions about the system in December 2022 stated that negotiations with industry about re-baselining the contract for the outstanding aspects of Crowsnest were due to conclude by mid-2023. Details of the quantity and performance of equipment were classified but requirements in terms of the number of trained people, ASaC role equipment deliveries, modified aircraft, training equipment and support had already been met. In many cases the minimum numbers required had been exceeded. A software update needed to deliver initial operational capability (IOC), as well as final flight testing, safety and airworthiness clearance was also forecast to be complete by mid-2023. Although these statements give hope that Crowsnest will achieve IOC sometime in 2024, this will be five years after the original target deadline and cannot be described as good. Some analysts have speculated that early development was hampered by incompatibilities between Merlin HM 2 software and the Crowsnest role equipment, which revealed the capability was far more than a straightforward 'plug-in and play' role change. The ASaC mission has clearly been hampered by being seen as one of three missions taking equal priorities within a single squadron, when experience has shown that it needs to be the dedicated specialisation of one. It is difficult to understand why the RN does not revert to having a dedicated ASaC unit, as it did so successfully with the Sea King ASaC 7 fleet for decades.

The RN continues to explore Project Vixen – a potential carrier-compatible, medium-sized, fixed-wing unmanned aircraft – with industry. The objective remains the delivery of a persistent, wide-area surveillance and airborne early warning (AEW) capability from about 2030 onwards, a timeframe that is getting tighter as time passes. The RN sees Vixen as a key enabler, using autonomous operation to add mass to carrier air groups. The system selected needs not only to focus on the air vehicle but also on its payload and, most importantly, the digital connectivity required to control and employ the system under operational conditions. It has to align with future RN digital architecture, including the naval strike network, and to integrate with the manned aircraft that will operate alongside it from the carrier deck. Many commentators believe that the *Queen Elizabeth* class will need to be adapted to permit catapult assisted take-off but arrested recovery (CATOBAR) alongside short take-off and landing (STOL) operations to take full advantage of UAV technology. Accordingly, a project known as 'Ark Royal' is being pursued to evaluate potential options, albeit for implementation in the longer term. In the meantime – in May 2023 – the British Ministry of Defence announced that trials of the General Atomics' Mojave STOL UAV would be carried out during *Prince of Wales*' West Atlantic deployment.

Unmanned Aircraft: Project Vixen is just one strand in a number of Fleet Air Arm (FAA) initiatives to exploit the benefits of developing UAV technologies. In July 2022, the RN announced Project Proteus, a £60m (c. US$75m) contract with Leonardo to design and develop an unmanned helicopter for use as a technology demonstrator. Initial tests will focus on its ability to lay sonobuoy patterns for interpretation use by other platforms. Rear Admiral James Parkin, the RN Director Develop, told the press in 2022 that Proteus would be cost-effective to run and production examples would, potentially, reduce the amount of flying time required from manned helicopters. With an air vehicle in the three-tonne (6,500lb) class – roughly the same weight as a US Navy MQ-8C Fire Scout – Proteus is expected to fly in 2025 after which it will aid decision-making about future investment in naval unmanned air systems. If successful, Proteus would provide a platform capable of delivering improved surveillance and intelligence-gathering as well as carrying a significant payload in harsh environmental conditions. Beyond anti-submarine warfare, other potential uses for unmanned helicopters include casualty evacuation and ship-to-ship resupply.

In late 2022 the Type 23 frigate *Lancaster* served as a command hub for a variety of autonomous unmanned systems in NATO Exercise REPMUS 22 off Portugal, trialling an autonomous asset-ready combat system which successfully distributed unmanned system data to the task group. It was the first exercise under NATO command to use autonomous underwater vehicles but *Lancaster* also had an RQ-20 hand-launched UAV from 700X NAS embarked, which was used for over-the-horizon intelligence-gathering. In another 'first', 700X NAS has taken its UAV expertise a step further by designing and building its own remotely-piloted UAV at RNAS Culdrose in December 2022. The 44lb (19.9kg) quadcopter was named Walrus after the amphibian flying boats flown by 700 NAS from battleships and cruisers during the Second World War. It was built to high aviation standards and will be used as a testbed for sensors and other sensitive payloads. Independent of outside input, the squadron sees it as a yardstick against which systems from industry can be evaluated and Walrus is, therefore, an important tool.

Subsequently, in February 2023, the RN announced that it had procured a single Schiebel S-100 unmanned helicopter for operational use in the Persian Gulf and its approaches. Thales will act as the systems integrator for the programme, which

A Schiebel S-100 Camcopter of the Royal Australian Navy's 822X Naval Air Squadron embarked onboard the frigate *Ballarat*. The MH-60R Seahawk helicopter in the background gives an idea of the diminutive rotary UAV's size. In February 2023, the British Royal Navy announced that it had procured a single Schiebel S-100 – to be known as the Peregrine – for operational deployment in the Persian Gulf. *(Australian Department of Defence)*

The Royal Navy has ordered seven Banshee Jet80+ drones as it expands its operations with remotely-piloted air systems. A new flight has been formed at 700X Naval Air Squadron based at RNAS Culdrose to operate these jet-powered aircraft, with trial operation scheduled to commence in the summer of 2023. *(Crown Copyright 2023)*

Admiral Parkin described as an excellent capability for introduction to the front line. The air vehicle will form part of a long-endurance system with the ability to find, fix and track surface contacts using a range of Thales sensors that include I-Master radar. This can be operated in either synthetic aperture or maritime moving target modes fused with the CarteNav AIMS mission system, which cues the air vehicle's electro-optical/infrared sensor onto a radar contact to identify it. Both high-definition imagery and the radar picture can be downloaded to the host ship's combat management system and data-linked to other units. The S-100 can be operated from a frigate or fleet auxiliary flight deck alongside the embarked manned helicopter flight and can be launched rapidly by day or night, even in adverse weather conditions. It is to be known as the Peregrine in RN service.[4] The S-100 Camcopter is already in service with a number of operators including the Royal Australian Navy, where it equips 822X NAS. Peregrine is to be deployed directly into the operational theatre in 2024, initially for two years but with the option to extend. It is powered by a 55hp Austro Engine AE 50R Wankel engine, giving a maximum level speed of 120 knots. Maximum take-off weight is only 441lb (200kg) and it can remain airborne for six hours. Some operators have fitted weapons to the S-100 but the RN has not announced any intention to do so.

A year ago the RN announced that the QinetiQ Banshee Jet 80+ had been selected to meet the Project Vampire requirement for a fixed-wing, remotely-piloted air system (RPAS). Several aircraft have now been delivered to Royal Naval Air Station (RNAS) Culdrose to form a new flight within 700X NAS. Banshees have a wingspan of 8ft (2.4m) and their two 88lb thrust turbojet engines give speeds in excess of 400 knots for up to 40 minutes. They are accelerated into flight from a 60ft (18.3m) pneumatic launcher which was trialled aboard *Prince of Wales* in 2021. However, 700X's first launches are to be from Culdrose's satellite airfield at Predannack.

Manned Rotary Aircraft: Progress has also been made with the manned Wildcat HMA 2 and its weapon systems. In late 2022 a specially-instrumented Wildcat carried out successful ship helicopter operating limitation (SHOL) trials on the Royal Fleet Auxiliary, *Argus*, over a period of 19 days in both the Atlantic and Mediterranean. In 87 hours of flight it carried out 894 deck landings by day and

In late 2022 a specially-instrumented Wildcat HM 2 helicopter carried out ship helicopter operating limitation trials on the Royal Fleet Auxiliary *Argus*. The trials included tests with various weapons configurations; this photo shows a full load out of twenty of the new Martlet lightweight missiles. In late 2022, Martlet missiles were fired from a Wildcat as part of a 'Sinkex' involving the decommissioned US Navy frigate *Boone* (FFG-28). *(Crown Copyright 2022)*

night and tested seven different weapon configurations, including asymmetric stub wing attachments. Weapons included both variants of the future air-to-surface guided-weapon (FASGW) programme air-to-surface missiles and Stingray torpedoes. FASGW includes both the supersonic Martlet missile – intended to take out smaller threats such as fast attack boats – and the larger Sea Venom, which has greater range and is fitted with a larger warhead. Martlet was already operational as of 2023 but Sea Venom's IOC has been delayed due to integration problems. The asymmetric wing fit is intended to leave one side of the helicopter clear for the fitting of a 0.5in heavy machine gun, considered a more suitable weapon for anti-piracy missions. It also allows a winch to be used for rescue or personnel transfer, allowing operational flexibility within a task force.

In late 2022 a Wildcat HM 2 from the frigate *Westminster* took part in Exercise 'Atlantic Thunder', a rare 'Sinkex' in the North Atlantic. During this, the specially-prepared former US Navy frigate *Boone* (FFG-28) was attacked by a range of live weapons. *Westminster* and a US Navy P-8A Poseidon first launched Harpoon anti-ship missiles which struck the target simultaneously. Subsequently, the Wildcat launched Martlet missiles against it before using its laser targeting pod to illuminate the target for an RAF Typhoon, which then dropped Paveway IV precision-guided bombs successfully. This was the first time an RAF Typhoon had dropped live weapons on a warship target, as well as the first time that a RN helicopter had guided a Paveway IV onto its target. *Boone* finally sank after being hit by a Standard SM-6 missile from the destroyer *Arleigh Burke* (DDG-51) after several JDAM joint direct attack munitions had also been dropped on the ship by US Air Force F-15E Eagles.

The Royal Marines' new Future Commando Force structure – which will include the forward-deployed Littoral Response Groups (LRGs) – has conducted a series of exercises stretching from Northern Norway to the Indo-Pacific over the past year. For example, Exercise 'Ssangyong 23' in Korea saw Bravo Company of 40 Commando operating alongside US and Korean Marines with seventy aircraft and numerous amphibious assets. They operated as part of a surveillance team which directed air strikes onto their targets using new technologies that included compact solar panels to charge their tactical systems. Meanwhile Commando Helicopter Force (CHF) Merlin HC 4 helicopters now use cover sheets that can be deployed quickly over the aircraft's nose, cockpit, cabin, engines and rotors to prevent them freezing in temperatures as low as minus 60 degrees Celsius. They can be removed quickly to allow them to get airborne without having to wait for systems to warm up, a potential game-changer in extreme conditions. The covers can be equally effective in hot or humid conditions in temperatures up to 80 degrees Celsius, as well as protecting the aircraft against salt and extreme humidity. In November 2022 two Merlin HC 4 helicopters were refuelled on the ground from an RAF C-130J Hercules, demonstrating that replenishment can be carried out at remote locations from the Arctic to Middle East deserts when necessary. The technique is known as the air-landed aircraft refuelling system (ALARS) and is expected to be commonplace by 2025.

UNITED STATES: US NAVY AND US MARINE CORPS

Aircraft Carriers: The US Navy continues to try to expedite timely delivery of new aircraft carriers as the current force remains under operational strain. Newport News Shipbuilding has described how the future aircraft carrier *Enterprise* (CVN-80) is being assembled by workers using individual laptops that instruct them about what is required in every shift. *Enterprise* was designed using the same 3D virtual technology now being used in its 300 assembly modules. She is the first ship in a two-carrier buy agreed in 2019 which is believed to have saved US$4bn; the second is *Doris Miller* (CVN-81). The US Navy has already calculated that a follow-on two-carrier buy for CVN-82 and CVN-83 would be equally cost-effective but Congress has not yet agreed. Captain Brian Metcalf USN, project manager for the class, has briefed the US Naval Institute's *USNI News* that the navy and Huntingdon Ingalls Industries (HII), who own

Huntington Ingalls Industries' Newport News Shipbuilding division re-delivered the aircraft carrier *George Washington* (CVN-73) to the US Navy in late May 2023 after a protracted refuelling and complex overhaul. Delays with the refit exacerbated the strain on an aircraft carrier force that is already struggling to meet the demands placed on it. *(Huntington Ingalls Industries)*

The carrier *George H. W. Bush* (CVN-77) pictured alongside at Suda Bay, Crete in October 2022. The carrier spent eight months in the Mediterranean during 2022-3 as the US Navy maintained a high operational tempo in the European region as part of the response to Russia's invasion of Ukraine. *(US Navy)*

Newport News Shipbuilding, are putting up a joint case to Congress for a decision that must be taken no later than FY 2025.[5]

The existing carrier force is stretched to its limits because national tasking exceeds the number of available hulls. Newport News Shipbuilding finally redelivered *George Washington* (CVN-73) to the navy in May 2023 after completion of a protracted refuelling and complex overhaul (RCOH) that had been delayed by workforce shortages caused by the COVID-19 pandemic and an expanded work package. The yard states that 'steady progress' is being made with *John C. Stennis* (CVN-74), which commenced her own RCOH in May 2021. East coast-based carriers, in particular, have endured back-to-back, extended deployments in order to meet forward-deployed combat commanders' demands. Most recently, the US Secretary of Defence, Lloyd Austin, extended the Mediterranean deployment of *George H. W. Bush* (CVN-77) to eight months as the navy maintained a high tempo of operations in Europe as part of the response to the Russian attack on Ukraine. The carrier finally returned to its base at Norfolk Virginia on 23 April 2023 after spending 230 days in the Mediterranean Sea.

CVN-77's replacement in Europe was the lead *Ford* class carrier, *Gerald R. Ford* (CVN-78). She briefly deployed from Norfolk for Canada and the United Kingdom with about 80 percent of her air wing aboard in October 2022 as a short 'stress test' to prepare for operational deployment proper in 2023. Returning at the end of November that year, it was reported that many of the problems associated with her new technologies over the past five years have now been resolved. Notably, reliability of her electro-magnetic launch system (EMALS) has improved significantly with more than 10,000 launches now completed and her advanced weapons elevators (AWEs) are now fully operational. Able to operate 150 percent faster than the cable and pulley technology lifts in the *Nimitz* (CVN-68) class, they are a key factor in increasing the new ship's sortie generation rate. Subsequently, in March 2023, *Ford* departed from Norfolk for a composite training unit exercise (COMPTUEX), the last hurdle before being certified ready for national tasking throughout the world at the direction of the President via the Secretary of Defence. This was the first period at sea with her full air wing – comprising four F/A-18E/F Super Hornet squadrons, one EA-18G Growler squadron, an E-2D AEW squadron and two helicopter squadrons – embarked. With certification completed, *Ford* then embarked on her inaugural full-length operational deployment on 3 May 2023.

The second *Ford* class carrier, *John F. Kennedy* (CVN-79), is now due to be delivered in 2025, a year later than originally planned. However, she is still expected to make her first operational deployment on the predicted date because work formerly planned for a post-delivery package will now be completed during build. She will be the first of class capable of operating the F-35C Lightning II and is expected to operate in the Indo-Pacific.[6]

Last year's *World Naval Review* mentioned a 'pre-decisional' discussion within the US Navy about retaining *Nimitz* in service for a year beyond her projected out of service date in 2025. That decision has now been taken and the navy's budget for FY 2024 requests her retention for an extra 13 months until May 2026. This will essentially allow one more deployment to be squeezed out of her operational life before she is retired. Despite this, the ship's eventual disposal is such a complicated process that work on planning it began in 2023 using the experience gained with the former *Enterprise* (CVN-65) as a yardstick. Under present plans *Dwight D. Eisenhower* (CVN-69) is to be withdrawn from service in 2027 but this could also be extended.

Table 4.1.1: US NAVY PLANNED AIRCRAFT PROCUREMENT: FY2023–FY2028

TYPE	MISSION	FY2023 Authorised[1]	FY2024 Requested	FY2025 Planned	FY2026 Planned	FY2027 Planned	FY2028 Planned	FYDP[2] Planned
Fixed Wing (Carrier Based)								
F-35B Lightning II JSF	Strike Fighter (STOVL)	15 (15)	16	16	16	17	20	**85**
F-35C Lightning II JSF	Strike Fighter (CV)	19 (13)	19	19	19	18	15	**90**
FA-18E/F Super Hornet	Strike Fighter (CV)	8 (0)	0	0	0	0	0	**0**
E-2D Advanced Hawkeye	Surveillance/Control	7 (5)	0	0	0	0	0	**0**
Fixed Wing (Land Based)								
KC-130J Hercules	Tanker	5 (5)	2	0	0	0	0	**2**
E-XX (TACAMO)[3]	Communications	0 (0)	0	0	0	3	6	**9**
T-45 Replacement[4]	Training	0 (0)	0	7	12	12	12	**43**
T-44 Replacement[5]	Training	10 (10)	26	27	0	0	0	**53**
Rotary Wing								
CH-53K King Stallion	Heavy-Lift	12 (10)	15	21	21	21	21	**99**
C/MV-22/B Osprey	Transport	5(0)	0	0	0	0	0	**0**
TH-73A[6]	Training	26 (26)	0	0	0	0	0	**0**
Unmanned Aerial Vehicles								
MQ-25 Stingray	Refuelling	1 (4)	3	4	4	4	7	**22**
MQ-4C Triton	Maritime Patrol	3 (3)	2	0	0	0	0	**2**
MQ-9A Reaper	Surveillance/Strike	5 (5)	5	0	0	0	0	**5**
Totals FY2024:		**116 (96)**	**88**	**94**	**72**	**75**	**81**	**410**
[Totals FY 2023]:		**[96]**	**[89]**	**[91]**	**[72]**	**[72]**	**[N/a]**	**[420]**

Notes:

1. FY2023 authorised numbers reflect numbers actually funded in the Consolidated Appropriations Act signed into law on 29 December 2022; figures in brackets reflect aircraft numbers set out in the Biden Administration's Presidential Budget Request of 28 March 2022. As is frequently the case, the US Congress added material numbers of aircraft over the original request.
2. Total five-year FYDP (Future Years Defense Program) numbers for FY2024–28 as at time of the FY2024 Presidential Budget Request
3. E-XX TACAMO (Take Charge And Move Out) is a planned replacement for the E-6B Mercury aircraft that form part of the United States' system of survivable communications links that are used to maintain communications between decision-makers and the triad of strategic weapon delivery systems. It will be based on a C-130J Hercules variant.
4. Refers to replacement of the T-45 Goshawk training aircraft. Unlike the current aircraft, the replacement will reportedly only be required to perform touch-and-go landings on the US Navy's aircraft carriers.
5. Refers to replacement of the T-44 Pegasus (Beechcraft King Air series) twin-engined turboprop trainer.
6. Refers to the Leonardo AW119 variant selected to replace the TH-57 Sea Ranger (Bell 206 series) training helicopter.

Naval Aircraft: In the absence of further Congressional action, the Department of the Navy's FY2024 Presidential Budget Request will see final termination of F/A-18E/F Super Hornet procurement.[7] Instead fixed-wing fighter production will be focused exclusively on varying proportions of F-35B/F-35C Lightning II aircraft at a steady total rate of thirty-five units per year. Overall aircraft acquisition over the five years of the Future Years Defense Program is largely in line with previous plans, with the MQ-25 Stingray UAV and US Marine Corps' CH-53K King Stallion heavy lift helicopter accounting for the lion's share of other future front-line type production. Full details are set out in Table 4.1.1.

The Next Generation Air Dominance Program (NGAD) – pronounced En-JAD by the US Navy – remains central to its longer-term plans to modernise its carrier air wings, replacing the Super Hornet in the 2030s. Details are classified but the navy describes it as a family of manned and unmanned systems centred on the F/A-XX which is expected to be a manned fighter. With a greater radius of action than the F/A-18E/F, the new fighter is to have both active and passive sensor technologies as well as new, longer-ranged weapons. The latest generation F-35C gives carrier air wings an effective strike radius of about 700 nautical miles. However, F/A-XX must have a radius greater than 1,000 nautical miles to keep the carrier out of range of Chinese ballistic anti-ship missiles such as the DF-21 and DF-26. The deployment of MQ-25A Stingray unmanned aerial-refuelling UAVs from 2026 will begin to increase strike radii of action ahead of F/A-XX but the US Navy is considering a wider range of unmanned combat air vehicles.

Rear Admiral Andrew Loiselle, the US Navy's Air Warfare Director (OPNAV N98), briefed *USNI News* in July 2022 that these are expected to fall into three categories.[8] The first would be able to penetrate a hostile, high-threat environment and stay there. The second would be capable of penetrating the same high-threat environment to perform a given mission before exiting with a high probability of returning to the carrier. The third would be smaller, less expensive and considered 'attritable'. It might be capable of performing a number of NGAD missions ranging from acting as a 'wingman' for the F/A-XX with extra air-to-air missiles, through electronic attack to forming a node within a distributed architecture command and control network. Despite the continuing stated interest in UAV technology, however, it is now ten years since the first arrested landing by an unmanned aircraft on an aircraft carrier; a Northrop Grumman X-47B – call-sign Salty Dog 502 – which landed on *George H. W. Bush* in July 2013. Progress since then cannot be described as rapid.

Meanwhile, the US Congressional Budget Office (CBO) continues to express concern over Super Hornet availability. Worryingly, a February 2023 report states that F/A-18E/Fs have suffered more adversely from time in service than earlier F/A-18C/D Hornets.[9] Specifically, comparisons between Hornets and Super Hornets of the same age showed significantly lower availability rates for the latter type. Moreover, the report found that numbers of hours flown, alone, could not explain the difference, as Super Hornets have flown fewer averaged hours per month. The CBO feels, however, that increased maintenance funding might stabilise the situation.

In addition to investigating future aircraft types, the US Navy is introducing new airborne weaponry. Notably, it announced in November 2022 that its high-altitude, anti-submarine warfare weapon capa-

A F/A-18F Super Hornet from the 'Mighty Strikers' of Strike Fighter Squadron 94 (VFA-94) prepares to launch from the aircraft carrier *Nimitz* (CVN-68) in May 2023. Boeing intends to wind down production of the Super Hornet at its St. Louis plant by the end of 2025 as it transitions to new programmes. Meanwhile, the US Congressional Budget Office continues to express concern over Super Hornet availability. *(US Navy)*

bility (HAAWC), had achieved IOC. It consists of a modular air launch accessory kit that is attached to a Mark 54 torpedo to transform it into a precision-guided glide weapon able to be released from a P-8A Poseidon at its search altitude. A contract for HAAWC to be put into full rate production was awarded to Boeing in August 2022 and the system will also likely be acquired by other nations that use the P-8A. HAAWC is to be rolled out to operational squadrons through 2024 with the potential to remain in production until 2030 under the initial contract. US Navy Poseidon maritime patrol aircraft (MPA) have now amassed more than 450,000 mishap-free operational flight hours.

The loss of a F-35C operating from *Carl Vinson* (CVN-70) in January 2022 was the subject of an inquiry report published in February 2023.[10] It explained that a pilot from Strike Fighter Squadron 147 (VFA-147), the 'Argonauts', had attempted an expedited recovery by breaking overhead the carrier to carry out a hard 360-degree turn. This is a common manoeuvre known in the US Navy as a 'Sierra Hotel Break' but one that he had not attempted before. In the break the pilot uses G-forces to slow the aircraft, lowering the landing gear as speed drops below its limiting speed. In this instance, the pilot failed to appreciate the reduced time available to carry out pre-landing checks in the hard turn. Specifically he failed to engage the fighter's two landing-assist systems – the approach power compensation mode (APC) and delta flight path (DFP) – which automate some of the pilot's vital actions when landing on a carrier. When activated, DFP automatically adjusts the throttle to maintain the correct speed on final approach while APC maintains the aircraft's angle of attack. By the time the pilot realised his error, the aircraft was very slow and descending rapidly. The landing signal officer warned that speed was low and ordered afterburner as he waved the aircraft off. The pilot selected maximum afterburner but it was too late; two seconds later the F-35C hit the ramp at the rear of the flight deck, shearing off the main landing gear. Part of the jet caught an arrester wire which caused it to spin as it slid down the deck on its belly at 85 knots, gouging it and causing damage. Flying debris injured six sailors and badly damaged an EA-18G before the F-35C went over the side into the sea. The pilot safely ejected. Data recovered after its recovery a month later showed that after its turn onto finals the F-35C's engine had been at flight idle and remained there until afterburner was selected. Other aircraft airborne at the time were diverted to *Abraham Lincoln* (CVN-72), which was nearby, to refuel but were later recovered to *Vinson* after repairs to the deck.

US Marine Corps Aviation: The US Marine Corps (USMC) continues to emphasise the achievements of the F-35Bs of Marine Fighter Attack Squadron 211 (VMFA-211), the 'Wake Island Avengers', during their time deployed aboard *Queen Elizabeth* during 2021. As an example, a USMC aircraft first flew from the British carrier, then landed on the amphibious assault ship *America* (LHA-6) to be refuelled and rearmed to pursue follow-on objectives before returning to *Queen Elizabeth*. Described as the first time in modern history that the United States had cross-decked aircraft for a mission utilising a foreign aircraft carrier, this achievement demonstrated exactly the sort of flexibility and interoperability that the Corps wants.[11] The USMC spent much of 2022 evaluating the 'Lightning Carrier' concept aboard *America*'s sister *Tripoli* (LHA-7). It has plans to use amphibious ships as maintenance bases for aircraft operating from expeditionary advanced bases on Pacific islands, embarking alternative fighter or helicopter focused air wings for use as light carriers or assault ships as the situation demands. Vice Admiral Karl Thomas USN, Commander US 7th Fleet, elaborated on this flexibility at an event in October 2022, briefing that the LHAs are flexible ships that could have F-35Bs on deck one day and MV-22s the next.[12] However, there is no getting away from the fact that they lack the airborne early warning and electronic attack aircraft embarked in the nuclear-powered carriers.

In addition to the F-35B, the USMC also increasingly operates the F-35C, the tail-hook variant of the Lightning II, alongside their US Navy counterparts on the navy's large carriers. The second front-line USMC F-35C squadron, VMFA-311 – the 'Tomcats' – was stood up at MCAS Miramar in April 2023.

Away from the F-35, the USMC's most important aircraft procurement programme is that for the Sikorsky CH-53K King Stallion heavy-lift helicopter. This was approved for full-rate production in December 2022, with Table 4.1.1 suggesting procurement will ramp up to fifteen in FY2024 and then twenty-one in each year from 2025. Full operational capability is expected to be achieved in 2029. Total production of 200 is ultimately planned.

In January 2023 it was revealed that the USMC

The US Navy amphibious assault ships *Tripoli* (LHA-7) and *America* (LHA-6) pictured operating in company in September 2022. Both vessels have been active in advancing new operating concepts for the US Marine Corps' F-35B Lightning II strike fighters, which are an increasing feature of its fixed-wing aviation operations. *(US Navy)*

The US Marine Corps is to take delivery of two Kratos XQ-58 Valkyrie UAVs as part of its ongoing efforts to experiment with a wide range of unmanned aircraft. This picture shows a Valkyrie taking off from the US Army Yuma Proving Ground in December 2020; its ability to be launched from a standard shipping container could fit well with evolving Distributed Maritime Operations concepts. *(US Air Force)*

A concept image of the proposed Liberty Lifter X-Plane, a proposed long-range flying boat relying on wing-in-ground-effect technology to transport heavy loads to distributed bases across the vast expanse of the Pacific. Two consortia led by General Atomics and Aurora Flight Sciences have been awarded contracts by the Defense Advanced Research Projects Agency to develop designs; this image appears to be based on the General Atomics' concept. *(DARPA)*

had ordered two Kratos-produced XQ-58 Valkyrie stealthy UAVs. The type is already being used by the US Air Force to evaluate its 'loyal wingman' programme but the USMC's airframes could be adapted for experimentation across a range of future mission requirements, including intelligence, surveillance and reconnaissance, as well as electronic warfare. The XQ-58A can operate without a runway and carry a variety of payloads out to a range of roughly 3,000 nautical miles at a cruising speed of c. 475 knots. The USMC has already tested remote landing areas to support F-35B operations and the same approach could be adopted for the XQ-58A. The UAV is just one of a number of unmanned aircraft that the Marines are currently using for experimentation, ranging from the MQ-9 Reaper to the TRUAS (tactical resupply unmanned air system) quadcopter.

The focus of much of this experimentation has been driven by the demands of supplying small units operating from island to island across the Pacific as part of the developing Distributed Maritime Operations (DMO) concept. In February 2023, the Defense Advanced Research Projects Agency (DARPA) signed two contracts to develop designs for a long-range flying boat that might provide an innovative way of meeting this requirement. Known as the Liberty Lifter X-Plane programme, the project aims to produce an amphibian similar in size and capacity to the C-17 Globemaster III transport aircraft. It will use wing-in-ground-effect technology to fly at less than 100ft over the sea with up to 90 tonnes of cargo over ranges in excess of 6,500 nautical miles. One contract was awarded to General Atomics working with the Maritime Applied Physics Corporation and the other to Aurora Flight Sciences working with Gibbs & Cox and ReconCraft. Their approaches are significantly different. General Atomics has selected a twin-hulled, mid-wing design to optimise on-water stability with distributed propulsion using twelve turboshaft engines. Aurora Flight Sciences design resembles a conventional flying boat with a single hull, high wing and eight turboprops for propulsion. Liberty Lifter has the obvious advantage that it needs no fixed base at the point of delivery when resupplying distributed marine forces, although there must be some means of refuelling it. The Soviet Union experimented with ground effect air vehicles – known as ekranoplans – for use as transports and missile carriers but they did not survive long in service.

AUSTRALIA: ROYAL AUSTRALIAN NAVY

The Royal Australian Navy (RAN) is in the course of implementing the surprise December 2021 decision to replace the Australian Defence Force's MRH-90 Taipan helicopters a decade earlier than planned. The MHR-90s were withdrawn from naval service in April 2022, having failed to provide the intended number of flight hours and being proved difficult to operate at sea. Typically, 808 NAS was required to deploy two or three operational flights but had only been able to generate one. The Taipans were placed into maintained storage at the Airbus facility in Brisbane in order to retain value in case a third party wanted to buy them. However, 808 NAS was not stood down when the Taipans were grounded as it is to transition to the Lockheed Martin MH-60R Seahawk helicopter, commonly referred to as the 'Romeo'. An additional twelve have been procured under Project Sea 9100 Phase 1 to ensure a continued embarked logistic support helicopter capability. All are expected to be delivered between mid-2025 and mid-2026, joining twenty-three MH-60Rs already in service.[13] The RAN was the first overseas customer for the 'Romeo' and it currently equips a training squadron, 725 NAS, and a front-line squadron, 816 NAS. To date they have flown more than 30,000 flight hours.

The Royal Australian Navy is consolidating its front-line helicopter operations on the Sikorsky MH-60R Seahawk after dissatisfaction with the MRH-90 Taipan led to a decision to retire the type. Here a MH-60R is seen operating from the frigate *Arunta* in September 2022. *(Australian Department of Defence)*

Commander Christopher Smith RAN, 808 NAS's commanding officer, briefed *Seaforth World Naval Review* in November 2022 that he expected the squadron to form its first 'Romeo' flight in mid-2023 and then continuously grow its number of embarked aircraft. Its mission will encompass regular deployments to the two Australian amphibious assault ships, broadening the type's operational use in RAN service. The switch from the Taipan will also mean that the RAN's Fleet Air Arm will benefit from operating a single type at sea rather than two, whilst potentially increasing interoperability with the US Navy.

An illustration of RAN/US Navy cooperation with respect to the MH-60R was provided in late 2022 when a US Navy 'Romeo' commenced a periodic maintenance inspection (PMI) in Australia as part of an evaluation of alternative maintenance capabilities in the Indo-Pacific. The work will take 10 months and involve a thorough strip-down and rebuild at the Sikorsky Australia facility at Naval Air Station Nowra. New components sourced from Australian industry will be used where appropriate. The PMI is not a guarantee of future work but is seen as a natural extension of the interchangeability between the US Navy and RAN. Commodore Darren Rae, Director General of RAN Naval Aviation and Aircrew Training briefed reporters that the work was strategically significant as it would deepen logistical interchangeability between Australia and the United States. He added that if a US Navy pilot was to jump into an RAN 'Romeo' they would feel completely at home and able to operate it as if it were a US Navy aircraft and the same would apply with an RAN pilot in a US Navy aircraft. The PMI contract demonstrates that depot level maintenance has achieved the same level of interoperability using Australian industry to maintain a US Navy 'Romeo' within combined maintenance practices.[14]

In another example of growing defence ties between Australia and the United States, the first MQ-4C Triton autonomous, high-altitude, long-endurance UAV for the Royal Australian Air Force (RAAF) was rolled out at Northrop Grumman's Palmdale, California, factory in March 2023. It is intended to complement the P-8A Poseidon as part of a family of systems. Australian personnel are already in the United States working with the US Navy and industry to acquire experience. Tritons will be controlled from RAAF Edinburgh but they will be flown from RAAF Tindal by 9 Squadron, which has been re-activated for the task. A single MQ-4C mission is capable of staying airborne for over 24 hours and searching over a million square miles, an area larger than Western Australia. The first aircraft is due in Australia in mid-2024 and IOC is planned for late 2025 or early 2026. Critically, the Australian Defence Force will share data collected by its Tritons with that collected by US Navy aircraft. Three MQ-4Cs have been ordered to date but the RAAF hopes eventually to have seven.

CHINA: PEOPLE'S LIBERATION ARMY NAVY

The use of drones in the war between Ukraine and Russia has been widely reported and many armed forces are studying the practical application of this relatively cheap, commercially-available technology to naval warfare. Press reports in early 2023 claimed that China was testing a catamaran drone carrier that can launch and recover small swarms of aerial drones designed to carry out electronic attacks on ships. Although it is believed to be an experimental platform, the rapid advances being made in digital drone technology mean that this is a significant development. Indeed, one Asian analyst has made the point that Taiwan might be better able to mount its own asymmetric defence if it built a small fleet of networked, unmanned drone carriers, observing that it has the shipbuilding and semiconductor industries to do so. Rapid technological advances already indicate that this view might not be as fanciful as it seems.

Aside from experimental new concepts, the two completed Chinese aircraft carriers have deployed into the Western Pacific on several occasions during the past year. Typical of these, the *Shandong* strike group passed through waters to the south-east of Taiwan in April 2023 and through the Taiwan Strait itself the following month. The deployment came as China's first carrier, *Liaoning*, underwent a period of scheduled maintenance and the third carrier, *Fujian*, continued to be fitted out. Launched at Shanghai in June 2022, she has an overall length in excess of 300m and is expected to have a full load displacement of more than 80,000 tonnes. Unlike her two predecessors she has no ski-jump but, instead, will be equipped with Chinese-designed electromagnetic catapults and arrester gear that will allow the more effective operation of fighters and fixed-wing AEW aircraft. The People's Liberation Army Navy (PLAN) reportedly intends to commence the ship's trials programme by late 2023 prior to delivery in the course of 2024. *Fujian*'s embarked strike fighters will likely initially be modified J-15B versions of the Shenyang J-15 Flying Shark, fitted with a nose-tow catapult launch system similar to those used in US Navy carrier aircraft. Another J-15 variant, designated the J-15D, is also being evaluated. This is a two-seat aircraft with wingtip electronic support measures/intelligence gathering pods as well as several conformal antennae, which analysts believe to be intended for the embarked electronic attack role. The use of J-15 variants aboard *Fujian* is, however, likely to be a temporary expedient as the PLAN is believed to be developing a carrier-capable variant of the fifth-generation J-31 long-range stealth fighter for service aboard the new ship.

A PLAN press release in February 2023 revealed that it has begun to recruit both male and female graduates from non-military colleges to be naval aviators. Candidates have to pass through several phases of physical, psychological and political testing before flight assessment. Volunteers are being sought 'who love national defence, are committed to the sea and the air…so that they can dedicate their youth to building a world class navy and contribute to the great rejuvenation of the Chinese nation'. Those selected undergo two months of basic training before entering the Naval Aviation University at Yantai, Shandong Province for up to four years of flight and aviation theory training before graduating for appointment to an operational unit.

Meanwhile, the PLAN is also making considerable progress bringing 'large deck' amphibious assault ships similar to those operated by the US Navy into service. The first of these, the Type 075 class *Hainan,* is now believed to be fully operational and two sisters – *Guangxi* and *Anhui* – have also been delivered. The class is believed to displace around 40,000 tonnes at full load and can embark up to 30 helicopters; the dock aft can operate air-cushion landing craft and the design is believed to be capable of embarking up to 1,600 marines.

The lead PLAN Type 075 class amphibious assault ship *Hainan* pictured during a maritime training exercise in March 2023. Three Type 075 vessels have now been commissioned into Chinese naval service. *(China Military Online)*

FRANCE: MARINE NATIONALE

The French nuclear-powered carrier *Charles de Gaulle* left Toulon with its strike group in November 2022 for Operation 'Antares', a deployment to the Mediterranean Sea and Indian Ocean. In January 2023, the group and a French Navy Atlantique MPA took part in exercises with the Indian Navy off the western coast of India, including Mig-29K, P-8I Poseidon and Dornier 228 MPA and surface warships. On completion of the exercise *Charles de Gaulle* launched three of her Rafale fighters to link up with a French Air Force A330 multi-role tanker/transport aircraft and fly 2,000 nautical miles to Singapore, where they landed at Paya Lebar air base. Once there they carried out exercises with the Republic of Singapore Air Force before returning to the carrier, again with the A330 in support.

The latest appearance of the projected 75,000-tonne, nuclear-powered *Porte-Avions de Nouvelle Génération* (PANG) was revealed at the Euronaval 2022 Exhibition, having altered significantly since the first artist's impressions were released in 2020. The original cone-shaped structure on top of the island has been replaced by an array of satellite communication domes underneath which the observation deck – with its panoramic view – has a more angular appearance. Lower down, conventional bridge and flying control positions have been maintained. However, the flight-deck layout has also been changed to allow for the possible incorporation of a third electromagnetic catapult. Under current plans, the project's development and production phase will be launched in the mid-2020s, with the as-yet unnamed vessel to replace *Charles de Gaulle* in 2038.

INDIA: INDIAN NAVY

The indigenously-built aircraft carrier *Vikrant* was commissioned into the Indian Navy on 2 September 2022 during a ceremony that also revealed a new Indian naval ensign. She had previously been handed over by builders Cochin Shipyard on 28 July of that year. The commissioning event was described by Prime Minister Narendra Modi as a landmark achievement, with 76 percent of the new carrier's components made in India. However, the ambitious project has encountered significant problems, not least being delivered many years late at a much greater cost than first envisaged. She is recognised as a major national asset, however, capable of operating Mig-29K fighters and Kamov-31, SH-60R and Dhruv helicopters.

The Indian Navy regards the Mig-29K as a dated design with its origins in the Cold War and hopes to replace it with either the F/A-18E/F Super Hornet or the Rafale M. A decision is expected before the end of 2023. In July 2022 Boeing revealed that it had successfully completed a series of operational demonstration flights with a pair of US Navy F/A-18Es from the Indian naval air station at Hansa in Goa. During these the fighters completed multiple ski-jump launches from the dummy deck on the airfield together with roll-in and fly-in arrested landings at a variety of weights in air-to-air and strike configurations. The US Navy had already carried out F/A-18E/F ski-jump launches at NAS Patuxent River, Maryland during 2020 to prove that the type was capable of the short take off but arrested recovery (STOBAR) operation required by the Indian Navy. Boeing is offering the Block III Super Hornet with shoulder-mounted conformal fuel tanks in both single-seat 'E' and two-seat 'F' variants. They could operate from the former Soviet *Vikramaditya* and the new *Vikrant*. A limiting factor appears to be the ships' Russian-designed arrester gear, an old design that would limit maximum landing weights. India has already procured two US Navy types, the P-8I Poseidon MPA and the MH-60R Seahawk multi-role helicopter, so the addition of the Super Hornet would

The design of the French *Porte-Avions de Nouvelle Génération* (PANG) continues to evolve as development work progresses prior to an expected production contract in 2025. These two images show, firstly, the configuration as of mid-2022 and, then, by the time of the Euronaval exhibition in the autumn. The original cone-shaped structure on top of the island has been replaced by an array of radomes and provision has been made for installation of a third catapult. *(Naval Group)*

Boeing's F/A-18 Super Hornet successfully completed operational demonstration tests at Indian Naval Station Hansa in Goa in the course of 2022. This photograph shows the US aircraft lined up with a ski-jump similar to those installed in Indian aircraft carriers. *(Indian Navy)*

New Zealand received the first of four Poseidon P-8A maritime patrol aircraft ordered from Boeing at a ceremony held on 7 December 2022. The aircraft subsequently arrived at RNZAF Base Ohakea on 12 December that year. *(Boeing)*

be a logical step; that said, the Indian Air Force has already selected the land-based Rafale derivative so the decision might be finely balanced. Meanwhile, in February 2023, a naval prototype of the Indian-built Tejas light fighter was the first fast jet to land and take off from *Vikrant*, an event described by Admiral Harl Kumar, Chief of the Naval Staff, as a momentous step forward towards Prime Minister Modi's vision of Indian self-reliance known as *Aatmanirbhar Bharat*.[15]

Until 2022 the Indian Navy wanted to follow *Vikrant* with a larger Indian-built carrier equipped with catapults and arrester wires. However, in December 2022 Admiral Kumar announced at a press conference ahead of India's Navy Day that these plans had been put on hold, with construction of a sister-ship to *Vikrant* now a potential option. A new design would require considerable foreign involvement, running counter to the policy of Indian self-reliance which the navy is under pressure to achieve by 2047, the centenary of independence. The option of building a repeat carrier with greater indigenous content would clearly be preferable to politicians, whilst ensuring that the Cochin shipyard's recent carrier construction expertise could be retained and exploited.

JAPAN: JMSDF

The first phase of work to modify the Japan Maritime Self Defence Force (JMSDF) 'helicopter-carrying destroyer' *Kaga* (DDH-184) for F-35B Lightning II operations was well underway at Kure in 2023. It includes the application of a heat-resistant coating to the flight deck and the fitting of a reshaped bow section that will be square rather than trapezoidal. The hull will also be rebalanced and structurally reinforced to take the weight of the fighters, which are considerably heavier than the SH-60J helicopters she was originally designed to operate. Her sister-ship *Izumo* (DDH-183) had already undergone an initial phase of modification but the reshaped bow will not be fitted until a second phase of work, which will also include internal alterations. Modification of both ships is expected to be completed by 2027. Japan has ordered forty-two F-35Bs, which are to be operated by the Japan Air Self-Defence Force. The first six are expected to be delivered in 2024 and another two in 2025.

NEW ZEALAND: ROYAL NEW ZEALAND AIR FORCE

The first of the Royal New Zealand Air Force's four new P-8A Poseidon aircraft arrived at RNZAF Base Ohakea on 12 December 2022 and was followed by a second aircraft in March. However, the air force's remaining P-3K2 Orion aircraft were retired prematurely in January 2023, as there were insufficient available aircrew to maintain them in operation whilst transitioning to the new type. The Poseidon force is expected to achieve IOC for search and rescue missions at the end of June 2023 and for humanitarian and disaster relief operations in July. IOC for anti-submarine and surface search operations is expected to follow in due course.

NORWAY: ROYAL NORWEGIAN AIR FORCE

In mid-2022 the Norwegian Ministry of Defence announced that it had decided to axe its fleet of NH-90 helicopters – which are operated by the Royal Norwegian Air Force's 334 and 227 Squadrons for deployment aboard the navy's frigates and for coast guard duties – and effectively ask for its money back. The acquisition had been heavily criticised from its early stages and the final statement about its failure spoke of late delivery and unreliability. Norway has followed Australia in discarding the type, which has allegedly proved to be expensive both to fly and maintain in addition to other failings. However, Airbus – which manufactures the NH-90 – has called the Norwegian decision 'legally groundless' and contested it. In March 2023, it was announced that Norway would purchase six MH-60R Seahawks from Lockheed Martin to fill the gap at a cost of NOK.12bn (c. US$1.1bn). Deliveries are scheduled for between 2025 and 2027.

SOUTH KOREA: REPUBLIC OF KOREA NAVY

The CVX project to build a 'Lightning Carrier' in the Republic of Korea received a setback in September 2022 when funding for its development was withdrawn by President Yoon Suk Yeol's new administration in favour of capabilities more directly aimed at deterring North Korean aggression. However, the navy retains ambitions to field an aircraft carrier and is even reportedly considering a larger design suitable for operating a navalised variant of the indigenous KF-21 fighter.

A Kizilelma drone seen on the deck of the newly commissioned Turkish amphibious assault ship *Anadolu*. The jet-powered UAV might eventually form an alternative for the F-35B fighters that were previously planned to be deployed aboard the ship. *(Devrim Yaylali)*

TURKEY: TURKISH NAVY

The Turkish Navy commissioned its first amphibious assault ship, *Anadolu*, on 10 April 2023. She is based on Spain's *Juan Carlos I* design but incorporates a number of modifications. Following its removal from the F-35B programme in 2019, Turkey has being developing alternative options for the ship's air group and has increasingly favoured operating her as a drone carrier. A navalised, TB3 variant of the widely-used Baykar Bayraktar TB2 UAV is being developed to operate from the ship but the company's jet-powered Kizilelma (meaning 'Red Apple') drone may be a preferred option in the medium term. Kizilelma has a single-engine, low-observable, low radar cross-section, canard delta airframe with a maximum take-off weight of 13,200lb (c. six tonnes). Prototypes first flew in 2022 and IOC for a carrier variant is expected to be achieved by 2025. It is supersonic, has a lightweight active electronically scanned array (AESA) radar and can carry payloads of up to 1,500lb (680kg) which give it a significant capability in the strike role. However, many analysts believe that the software, artificial intelligence and processing power it would need for an air-to-air capability are beyond Turkey's reach at present. It is said to be capable of taking off from *Anadolu* without a catapult but recovery would need to be into some form of arresting system.

THE BOEING MQ-25A STINGRAY

Origins: The MQ-25A Stingray under development for the US Navy is a single-engine, unmanned combat air vehicle (UCAV), capable of operation from an aircraft carrier and intended initially for use in the air-to-air refuelling role. Its origins can be traced back to research into a naval unmanned combat air vehicle – N-UCAV – by the navy and DARPA that commenced around the turn of the millennium.[16] By 2006, ongoing research and development had given rise to the Unmanned Combat Air System Demonstration (UCAS-D) programme, which was intended to demonstrate the technical feasibility of operating unmanned air combat systems from an aircraft carrier. Northrop Grumman's X-47B was subsequently selected for this technology demonstration programme, ultimately carrying out the world's first carrier landing by an unmanned aircraft on 10 July 2013. The X-47B was a relatively small aircraft that was not taken any further by the US Navy but it provided valuable information about command and control software, the interface between unmanned aircraft and the ship and the integration of unmanned aircraft into the deck-operating cycle.

Whilst X-47B trials were underway, the navy continued to refine its requirements for an operational carrier UCAV capacity. This resulted in the launch of the Unmanned Carrier-Launched Airborne Surveillance and Strike (UCLASS) programme in 2011. This was initially to have been an autonomous, stealthy platform capable of penetrating sophisticated enemy air defences, releasing precision-guided munitions and returning to its carrier over a considerable radius of action. However, by late 2012, this requirement had shifted to a more limited focus on the intelligence-gathering, surveillance and reconnaissance (ISR) mission. This was not the end of the debate and considerable procrastination followed as the navy struggled to finalise what the new UCAV's mission focus should be. Finally, in February 2016, the US Navy decided to prioritise production of an UCAV about the size of a Super Hornet to act as a specialised air-to-air refuelling aircraft, freeing F/A-18E/Fs from this task and thereby allow them to concentrate on their primary missions.[17] The project was renamed the Carrier-Borne Aerial Refuelling System (CBARS), although it was accepted that a UCAV large enough to meet the requirement would also have a latent, non-penetrating, ISR capability that could be developed in due course. The manned strike fighter community had continuing doubts about the introduction of UCAVs to the carrier air wing and the US Navy believed that CBARS would help ease the way to the planned unmanned element of its Next Generation Air Dominance Program.

Four design development contracts for what was officially designated the MQ-25A Stingray were awarded during 2016. Of the contracted companies, Boeing had already built a suitably-sized drone intended for UCLASS. It had not been designed for the refuelling mission but Boeing had considered it to be an important capability and factored it into the design. Other firms that offered proposals were General Atomics with its Sea Avenger concept (based on an enlarged Predator C/Avenger airframe) and Lockheed Martin with its Sea Ghost (based on the RQ-170 Sentinel). Northrop Grumman, which had designed and built the X-47B, announced in 2017 that it would not enter a design since it did not regard the request as being sufficiently advanced. The existence of the Boeing prototype, known as 'Tail Number 1' or simply T-1, gave the firm an edge and it was awarded a US$805m contract to develop its design and build an initial tranche of four developmental Stingrays in August 2018. A further three system demonstration aircraft were ordered in 2020. The US Navy programme of record calls for an eventual total of seventy-two MQ-25As to be acquired, with twenty-two planned for procurement between FY2023 and FY2028. Boeing is to construct a new 300,000ft^2 facility at MidAmerica St. Louis Airport, Illinois to build the new UCAVs.

A Northrop Grumman X-47B UCAV technology demonstrator makes an arrested landing on *George H. W. Bush* (CVN-77) on 10 July 2013 in what was claimed to be the world's first carrier landing by an autonomous unmanned aircraft. The success of the X-47B trials helped pave the way for the procurement of the MQ-25A Stingray. *(US Navy)*

Description: The MQ-25A has a stealthy wing-body-tail design with a flush engine inlet on top of the fuselage to shield the turbine blades from radar interrogation and a slit exhaust. Whilst these features are the legacy of its UCLASS origins, they give the design considerable development potential for the ISR and strike roles once the US Navy has integrated the type into carrier air wings. It is powered by a single 10,000lb thrust Rolls-Royce AE 3007N turbofan, a variant of the engine used in the MQ-4C Triton. It has a length of 51ft (15.5m) and a wingspan of 75ft (22.8m) with the wings spread, 31ft (9.4m) when folded. Empty weight is 14,000lb (6.4 tonnes) and maximum take-off weight is 44,500lb (20.4 tonnes). In comparative terms it is about the size of an E-2D Advanced Hawkeye but somewhat lighter. It has a nose-tow attachment for catapult launch and a tail hook aft for arrested recovery. Height is 9ft 8in (2.9m) with the wings spread and 15ft 7in (4.7m) with the wings folded.

The US Navy requires the MQ-25A to be capable of delivering 16,000lb (7.25 tonnes) of fuel to other aircraft from a position 500 nautical miles from the parent carrier. Role equipment is a single Cobham

The MQ-25 T-1 became the first unmanned aircraft to transfer fuel to another aircraft in flight when it refuelled a navy Super Hornet on 4 June 2021. It has also conducted successful refuelling trials with a F-35C Lightning II and E-2D Hawkeye (pictured). *(Boeing)*

aerial refuelling store carried on an underwing hardpoint, which uses the hose and drogue method standard in the US Navy. A second hardpoint under the other wing can be fitted with a drop tank. Once it has streamed the drogue, the Stingray maintains a steady flight path and it is the receiving pilot's responsibility to join, plug into the drogue and withdraw. The T-1 prototype made its first flight in September 2019 and flew with the aerial refuelling store in 2020. It subsequently became the first unmanned aircraft to transfer fuel to another aircraft in flight when it refuelled a navy Super Hornet on 4 June 2021. It successfully completed similar inaugural transfers with an E-2D Advanced Hawkeye and F-35C Lightning II in, respectively, August and September that year. In December 2021 it completed a deck-handling evaluation aboard the carrier *George H. W. Bush* at sea.

The prototype Boeing MQ-25 T-1 UCAV seen aboard *George H. W. Bush* (CVN-77) during handling trials in December 2021. Boeing's continued development of the T-1 prototype gave it a clear edge in its eventually successful bid for the MQ-25A contract. *(US Navy)*

Current Programme Status: Despite the early optimism that the existence of T-1 would allow rapid progress, there have been delays with the programme. In April 2023 Rear Admiral Stephen Tedford USN, the programme executive officer, briefed the Navy League Sea, Air and Space Symposium that IOC would be delayed by a year from 2025 to 2026. Apparently this is because of challenges encountered as the production line developed. A subsequent Boeing briefing to *USNI News* said that the company had suffered quality issues with delivered items, especially with coatings applied to metal components.[18] These, together with the lingering impact of COVID-19 throughout the supply chain, have led to delays. However, things are improving and the US Navy still hopes to get Stingrays to sea in 2026. Under current plans, the first carrier to be fitted with control stations and data links to operate an MQ-25A flight is *Theodore Roosevelt* (CVN-71) at some point in 2026. She will be followed by *Bush* as soon as possible thereafter.

Admiral Tedford briefed *USNI News* that the Navy has created what he called a slim list of requirements for the MQ-25A. The first step is 'Stingray to the Fleet': to get Stingrays to sea in a permissive environment to take over the tanking role. The second phase is 'Stingray to the Fight': opening up more capabilities in a non-permissive environment once the Navy has perfected deck control, launch and recovery with low probability of intercept/low probability of detection (LPI/LPD) waveforms. Another developmental factor is the optimum control of the aircraft whilst it is airborne. Although the MQ-25A is autonomous rather than remotely-piloted it still has to be given mission commands from the carrier's combat information centre as well as being operationally adaptive to multiple environments and able to work with a variety of operating systems. This will require early expansion of management tools to include other airborne platforms including those of allies. However, the enhancement of open architecture software management to do this is a big 'ask' and Tedford said that US Navy needs industry's help 'to figure out how best to do it quickly'.

The US Navy formed a new squadron, Unmanned Carrier Launched Multi-Role Squadron 10 (VUQ-10), in October 2021 to provide service input to the MQ-25A development programme, train operators and maintenance personnel and, eventually, to become the fleet replacement squadron for the type. It is based at Naval Air Station Point Mugu within Naval Base Ventura County, California. Specialised aviation warrant officers are being trained as operators to embark with the operational flights which will eventually be provided by two further squadrons to be designated VUQ-11 and VUQ-12.

Analysis: With its wings folded the Stingray has the same deck spotting factor as the Super Hornet, which helps give flexibility to its movement on deck and in the hangar. Manned aircraft are initially manoeuvred by aircraft handlers using tractors. However, after engine start their pilots take over under the control of 'yellow-shirt' handlers using hand signals. Obviously the MQ-25A cannot do this and so this is the one occasion where it is remotely-operated; a deck controller uses a wearable control unit to taxi the drone in response to yellow-shirts' conventional signals just as if he or she were a pilot in the aircraft. Apart from the need for a human deck crew no other special procedures are needed and, once it is in the air, the MQ-25A operates as an autonomous platform, not a remotely-piloted one. The operator loads a digital pre-briefed mission plan before the flight and then clicks a mouse to have the drone execute it. The control station operator in the carrier is responsible for communicating with other parties involved in the flight such as the carrier air traffic control centre (CATC), or shore-based ATC if the drone needs to enter commercial airspace. The operator can execute mission changes if necessary and the drone's software has provision for emergency situation management. For instance if communications are lost, the drone will switch to backup systems. If it still has power it will always make its own way back to the carrier and attempt to re-join the landing pattern.

Apart from its potential to change the way US Navy carrier air wings operate, the Stingray has significant design implications for Boeing in that it has introduced a new era of digital design, simulation and engineering practice. The computational power, big data and fidelity of the latest computers have allowed significant increases in the quantity and speed of design and development work that can be done digitally to include factors such as aerodynamics and structural load factors. They also affect the so-called 'soft' production engineering processes such as ergonomics. Like the shipyard workers at Newport News, the mechanics on the Stingray's new production line start by downloading their task onto a laptop which will show them where their task is, how to address it and what the finished work should

Although the MQ-25A is autonomous in flight, it has to be manoeuvred by a deck controller whilst on the flight deck or in the hangar. Here, the MQ-25 T-1 prototype is seen positioned on the deck of *George H. W. Bush* (CVN-77). A drop tank is positioned under its port wing. *(US Navy)*

look like. As can be imagined, this has made a significant difference to the way cabling and pipework are installed. This 'digital thread' now has the ability and power to track every physical aircraft with a virtual history from the earliest staff requirement through its construction, delivery, maintenance, supply chain management and modernisation to its eventual disposal. As computer power evolves still further, a 3D model of the aircraft will evolve to give a virtual single 'source-of-truth' analysis of structure, fuel-flow, hydraulics and electrics and other systems to be used to initiate and monitor design evolution.

It is clear that internal arguments over the place of UCAVs in the carrier wing that led to the switch from UCLASS to CBARS have 'watered down' the original concept of a penetrating stealth strike platform into an aerial tanker. At the same time, the US Navy clearly accepts that Stingray has the potential for future growth into other missions, such as carrier-based ISR. At the very least the drone's low-observable shape and autonomous operation mean that it may challenge enemies who try to take out tankers or use them as a means of locating the carrier's position. Boeing believes that there is export potential for the Stingray, although at present the French Navy is the only carrier operator likely to be interested in it.[19]

In conclusion, Stingray must be seen as one of the most significant emerging naval aircraft projects from a number of angles. The fact that it is intended to be the first unmanned fixed-wing fast jet to form part of a carrier air wing, one of the United States' principal tools of diplomacy and power-projection, is reason enough to follow its progress. However, its ability to expand the radius of action of the current manned strike fighters is also highly significant. This will enable the carrier strike group to operate further from the outer limit of the anti-access/area-denial (A2/AD) 'bubble' created by Chinese ballistic anti-ship missiles and give existing strike fighters greater lethality while F/A-XX is evolved. Its successful operation is seen as the key to overcoming the suspicion of the aviator-dominated air wing against autonomous UCAVs, paving the way towards increasing the number of unmanned systems at sea. Even a partially unmanned air wing will have enormous benefits in terms of reduced fuel burn, cost and manpower that will be of great benefit to the naval budget. UCAVs do not need to carry out refresher flying, nor do they need to disembark when the carrier is in port since they only fly when necessary. From Boeing's perspective the successful delivery of the MQ-25A would prove the maturity and de-risking of its computer model-based systems engineering and model-based analysis when applied to military aircraft. It might not be too much to say that the company's future as a provider of military aircraft depends on it.

Notes

1. The contract was awarded to Team Resolute, which is headed by Spanish shipbuilder Navantia but involves assembly by Harland & Wolff, Belfast to a British BMT design. Team Resolute had previously been selected as preferred bidder in November 2022.

2. This information was provided by then Minister of State for Defence Procurement, Alex Chalk, in a letter to the Chair of the British House of Commons' Defence Committee on 9 January 2023 and is available in the correspondence section of the Committee's website: committees.parliament.uk/committee/24/defence-committee/

3. *Service Inquiry investigating the accident involving F-35B ZM152 on HMS Queen Elizabeth on 17 November 2021 - Interim Report* available by searching: gov.uk

4. The name was inspired by the former HMS *Peregrine*, the RN air station at Ford, West Sussex and the Fleet Air Arm's test and development centre for carrier-borne jet aircraft after 1945.

5. See Sam LaGrone, 'HII Argues for Aircraft Carrier Block Buy as New Enterprise Takes Shape' posted to the *USNI News* website – news.usni.org – on 28 August 2022.

6. For further detail, see Mallory Shelbourne, 'Ford Aircraft Carrier John F. Kennedy to Deliver a Year Later' posted to news.usni.org on 23 March 2023.

7. In the past, Congressional action has seen F/A-18E/F production extended on a number of occasions but further US Navy orders seem unlikely, with Boeing planning to shutter the assembly line in 2025 unless foreign orders materialise. FY2023 also marked the planned end of US Navy procurement of, inter alia, the E-2D Advanced Hawkeye and CMV-22/MV-22B Osprey tiltrotor.

8. See another Sam LaGrone article, 'Several UAVs Under Development for Next-Generation Carrier Air Wing' posted to news.usni.org on 13 July 2022.

9. *Availability and Use of the F/A-18E/F Super Hornet Fighter Aircraft* (Washington DC: Congressional Budget Office, 2023). The report is available at: cbo.gov/publication/58937

10. The Flight Safety Foundation's *Aviation Safety Network* site provides links to a range of sources relating to the incident, including a redacted copy of the US Navy's investigation report, at: aviation-safety.net/wikibase/274659

11. The cross-deck mission was first reported on the USMC's official website – marines.mil – on 24 August 2021.

12. See further Stavros Atlamazoglou, 'The US's experimental "lightning carriers" are "much more capable" than China's current carriers, US admiral says' posted to the *Business Insider* website – businessinsider.com – on 6 December 2022.

13. An additional MH-60R was lost in October 2021 but, despite expectations to the contrary, does not appear to be included in the current contract.

14. Commodore Rae was quoted by Ben Felton in 'US Navy Seahawk to undergo maintenance in Australia' posted to *Australian Defence Magazine* website – australiandefence.com.au – on 1 December 2022.

15. Although the navalised variant of the Tejas has undergone trials aboard both *Vikramaditya* and *Vikrant,* it is unlikely to ever see operational service with the Indian Navy. Instead, the navy's preference for a twin-engined aircraft is ultimately likely to be met by the proposed HAL Twin Engine Deck Based Fighter (TEDBF).

16. The subsequent journey from N-UCAV to UCLASS went through several phases. A Congressional Research Service report by Jeremiah Gertler, *History of the Navy UCLASS Program Requirements: In Brief* (Washington DC: Congressional Research Service, 2015) provides further detail on a complicated story.

17. It had been estimated that Super Hornets were spending up to 30 percent of their flight time on tanking missions.

18. Sam LaGrone, 'MQ-25A Stingray IOC Pushed to 2026 Following Manufacturing Delays' posted to news.usni.org on 4 April 2023.

19. The previously-mentioned Royal Navy 'Ark Royal' project might change this assessment. This would undoubtedly be a game-changer for the F-35B's limited radius of action and make a significant difference to the ships' strike radius.

4.3 TECHNOLOGICAL REVIEW

NAVAL PROPULSION

Some Considerations

Author:
Norman Friedman

For the most part, warship propulsion follows a pattern set in the 1970s in which gas turbines and large diesels replaced steam as the usual prime mover. Both seem to have won out as ways of reducing engine-room personnel – a vital point for navies – and of improving safety. Steam plants gain efficiency by operating at higher temperatures and pressures. However, post-1945 experience, at least in the US Navy, showed that really high pressure could be quite dangerous. After some bad experiences, the US Secretary of the Navy decided to lay up high-temperature/high-pressure ships. The US Navy did not retain them after the end of the Cold War. This decision was somewhat controversial, as it appeared that such plants could operate very successfully when safety rules were followed rigorously. None of the plants involved survive.

The Russians used pressure-fired steam plants in many of their larger warships, including their aircraft carriers. Three of these carriers have survived: the Russian *Admiral Kuznetsov*, her Chinese sister *Liaoning* (the former *Riga*/*Varyag*) and the Indian Navy's *Vikramaditya* (formerly *Baku*/*Admiral Gorshkov*). Of these, *Kuznetsov* is being refitted after suffering failures in the Mediterranean; this work may never be completed. *Vikramaditya* is operational, but only after burning out her boilers during her initial post-modernisation trials. The Chinese are not reported to have had problems with *Liaoning*. The Chinese have also built a sister-ship, presumably with the same type of power plant. The Russians also retain two large cruisers with unique combined nuclear and steam (CONAS) power plants. They chose this combination – nuclear plus steam boost for higher speed – because the submarine-type reactors they were producing were not powerful enough. It is not clear how successful the combination has been.[1]

American *Charles F. Adams* (DDG-2) class destroyers laid up at Philadelphia Naval Shipyard in the early 1990s. The last steam turbine-powered destroyers to be completed for the US Navy, their high-temperature/high-pressure plants presented operational challenges and were a major factor in their retirement. *(Conrad Waters)*

STEAM PLANTS TODAY

Steam plants survive in major navies only in the form of nuclear power plants. These are currently used in carriers and submarines; no nuclear surface combatants have survived. The driving forces behind recent reactor designs have been the need to reduce refuelling – which is when most of the maintenance money for a nuclear ship is spent – and to reduce crewing. At least in the US Navy, the lifetime of nuclear cores has been extended to the point where new submarines have 'one-shot' reactors which need not be refuelled during a boat's lifetime. The French, on the other hand, chose to use less highly-enriched fuel ('caramel'), probably because that best matched the capabilities of their indigenous nuclear sector. As a consequence, their reactors need more frequent refuelling, as has been evident with the carrier *Charles de Gaulle*.

In submarines, a major issue is how to silence a powerful power plant which has to run continuously. Both the US Navy and the Royal Navy adopted a British idea that involved rigidly mounting machinery on a raft which could be

The Russian aircraft carrier *Admiral Kuznetsov* emits large clouds of smoke as she passes through the English Channel on the way to the Mediterranean in October 2016. Her high-pressure steam plant has proved unreliable in practice and a refit intended to resolve these problems has been problematic. *(Crown Copyright 2016)*

sound-mounted to deaden the sound involved. In the late 1970s the Russians apparently made the same choice. When the US Navy adopted rafting, Admiral Hyman Rickover, the father of submarine nuclear power plants, was outraged at what he considered an inelegant solution to the noise problem. He much preferred inherently quiet turbo-electric power, in which the submarine turbine

The French *Rubis* class nuclear-powered attack submarine *Émeraude* pictured whilst operating in the Pacific in December 2020. Nuclear-powered submarines are amongst the few remaining steam-powered ships serving in major navies today, with the precise technology used differing from fleet to fleet. The *Rubis* class use less highly-enriched fuel than their American and British counterparts, mandating periodic refuelling. *(US Navy)*

would drive a generator rather than gears driving a propeller. That turned out to be impossibly inefficient at the time. Admiral Rickover was influential enough to force the US Navy to try turbo-electric power in the submarine *Glenard P. Lipscomb* (SSN-685), which was generally considered an expensive failure. Reportedly the *Lipscomb* experience initially caused the US Navy to reject electric drive when it was again proposed in the 1990s.

However, when they built nuclear-powered attack submarines during the 1980s, the French adopted turbo-electric propulsion.[2] The new American and British strategic submarines are also to be driven electrically as part of a larger programme to keep them quiet and, hence, difficult to detect through their expected service lives. Reportedly the same type of propulsion is planned for the US Navy's next class of attack submarines.

GAS TURBINE AND DIESEL PROPULSION

Gas turbines took over from their steam equivalents because they offer high power in a compact package. However, they are inefficient, particularly when running at a fraction of full power.[3] They are also inherently quiet, though they require loud reduction gearing. By contrast, diesels are efficient over a wide range of powers, but they are much more massive and they are inherently loud (though not as loud as petrol engines). The typical solution to the inefficiency of large gas turbines was – and has remained – to combine them with other power plants, for example in a combined diesel and gas (CODAG) or combined diesel or gas (CODOG) arrangement.

The Rolls-Royce MT-30 gas turbine, which typically produces up to 40MW of power, first entered service on the lead *Freedom* (LCS-1) class Littoral Combat Ship. Gas turbines took over from their steam equivalents because they offer high power in a compact package. *(Rolls-Royce)*

The alternatives are to combine large gas turbines with smaller ones used for lower-speed cruising. This is combined gas and gas (COGAG) or combined gas or gas (COGOG) propulsion, depending on whether the smaller ones are or are not combined with the main high-powered ones for full power. The main recent development in gas-turbine power plants is the willingness to rely on a single gas turbine geared to multiple shafts (split operation).

For some years there have been attempts to improve the fuel economy of big gas turbines by capturing energy lost in their exhausts. For example, in the 1970s and early 1980s the US Navy experimented with RACER, a regenerative gas turbine which used the waste heat in a boiler. RACER was much disliked because of its complexity and because it was difficult to maintain; its piping leaked constantly. It was abandoned after its main Congressional advocate, Tony Battista, retired. However, the idea of regeneration still reappears from time to time.

Diesel-powered ships generally employ at least one diesel per shaft, sometimes with a clutch which makes it possible to cut some of the diesels out for more economical cruising. Perhaps surprisingly, big diesels dominate the market for small fast attack craft. The main exceptions to this have been hydrofoils, which need really high power in the smallest possible package. The American Littoral Combat Ships (LCS) are the principal current examples of very fast ships which would be impossible to achieve their design aim without gas turbines.

The tendency in high-powered ships has been towards larger higher-powered gas turbines, but not towards any basically new kind of gas turbine. No real alternative seems to have appeared. However, some years ago there was interest in fuel cells. They are inherently more efficient than gas turbines. Moreover, they apparently produce no observable exhaust plume and, hence, offer stealthy operation. Nor do they necessarily produce much noise, apart from the sound of the pumps feeding them their oxidant and fuel. Their exhaust product is water. Thus far fuel cells have apparently not been scaled up to the point of becoming effective competitors to gas turbines or diesels.[4]

ELECTRIC PROPULSION

Probably the most important current trend in warship propulsion is the shift towards electric ships. In the British *Queen Elizabeth* class aircraft carriers,

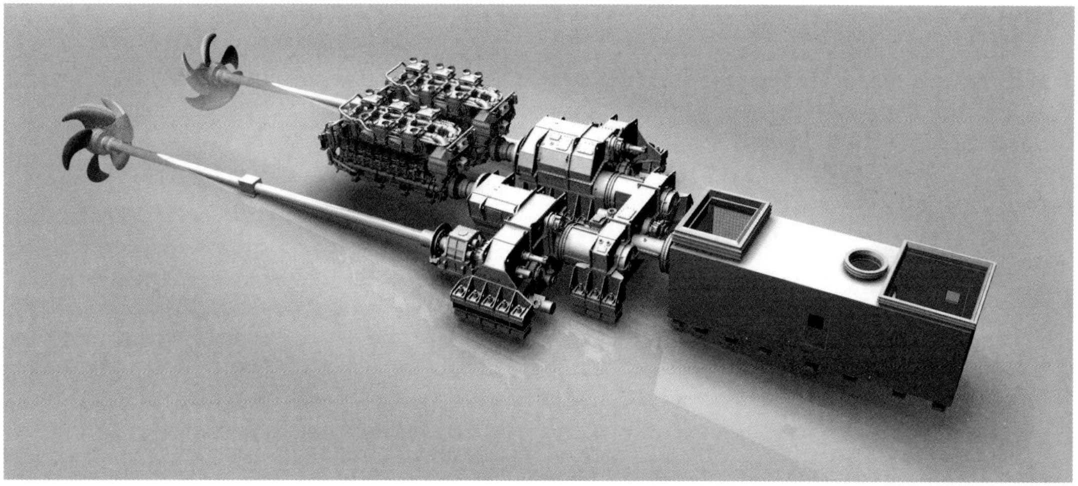

An example of a typical combined diesel and gas (CODAG) propulsion arrangement, with two MTU diesels and a single gas turbine linked to two propulsion shafts via gearing. The inefficiency inherent in running gas turbines at less than full power has typically been resolved by combining them with other power plants, or with smaller gas turbines used for lower-speed cruising. *(Rolls-Royce)*

The most important recent shift in naval propulsion has been the increased use of electric solutions, either in the form of full integrated electric propulsion (IEP) or as part of a hybrid solution in combination with other technology. This photograph shows an MT-30 gas turbine being installed in the British *Queen Elizabeth* class aircraft carrier *Prince of Wales*, which utilises IEP. The fact that there is no direct mechanical link between the turbine and the shaft lines means that power can be generated anywhere in the ship. *(Aircraft Carrier Alliance)*

for example, gas turbines in the bases of the two island structures drive alternators, whose output in turn drives motors near the two propellers.[5] Electric drive offers an important degree of flexibility, since the generated power can be used anywhere in the ship, for any desired purpose. That was not the case with earlier prime movers. Given electric drive, if the two carriers were ever to be fitted with catapults, they would presumably be electric units driven indirectly by the main generators. Similarly, if the ships were fitted with arresting gear, they would have something like the latest US Navy type, with energy absorbed by arresting gear being turned into usable electricity. Fitting with steam catapults and conventional arrester gear would require much more complex reconstruction.

Going electric – always with some prime mover driving generators – has several advantages. These were identified at least as early as 1989 by a US Navy panel on future surface warships. The most obvious, visible in the *Queen Elizabeth* class, is that turbo-generators can be located anywhere in a ship. Placing them well above the waterline limits vulnerability to underwater hits, including standoff hits causing shock. Turbo-generators can also be separated fore and aft, again limiting damage from any one hit. Moreover, the buses linking the generators and motors can be duplicated, so that hits cutting any one bus do not disable it.

Many cruise liners already employ electric propulsion; their generators typically driving propellers in azimuth thruster pods which can be turned as desired to manoeuvre the ship.[6] Advantages include freeing valuable space inside the hull and providing excellent manoeuvrability for use in small harbours where tugs may not be available. In theory, a warship might be fitted with azimuth thrusters fore and aft. Thus equipped, the vessel could keep going even with her bow or stern blown off. On the other hand, a really significant underwater shock might detach the pods altogether, or at least so damage them that they jammed.

Whilst podded propulsion might not be the way forward, drastically shortening propeller shafts – which electric drive makes possible – could be used to limit the effects of shock. Shock is potentially dangerous because it might distort long propeller shafts and cause them to open up a ship's hull to rapid flooding. It was this sort of damage that doomed the battleship *Prince of Wales* in 1941. Moreover, a single turbo-generator can drive more than one propeller shaft, making for much greater fuel economy at low speed. Another important argument for electric drive is that long, vulnerable propeller shafts take up valuable ship space. This was a pertinent point at the end of the 1980s, when large refits of the US Navy *Spruance* (DD-963) incorporating vertical launch systems were planned. It turned out that – although there was sufficient hull depth forward of the bridge for such an installation – the propeller shafts occupied too much hull depth for this to be replicated aft without significant redesign, as in the Aegis cruisers.

Electric drive is sometimes associated with anti-submarine warfare (ASW). This is because it is considered inherently quiet compared to gearing. When the British Royal Navy designed its Type 23 'Duke' class frigates, it was particularly interested in achieving very quiet operation at low speed, when the ships would be towing their passive sonar arrays. The navy hit on a solution involving sound-mounted diesel generators driving their propellers (through low-powered motors) only at low speed. The diesels were inherently noisy, but the British had long experience with effective sound-mounting. Later, when extreme silencing was no longer a cardinal virtue in the post-Cold War era, the British also observed that as prime movers the diesels offered considerable fuel economy, despite losses inherent in the separate generators and motors.

Against its advantages, electric drive has always been associated with additional weight. This is due both to the complication of adding both generators and motors, and to the sheer weight of a high-powered electric motor. The US Navy adopted turbo-electric drive during the First World War and built a number of capital ships employing it, including the carriers *Lexington* (CV-2) and *Saratoga* (CV-3). In these ships, adopting turbo-electric drive made it possible to subdivide a ship much more minutely, with turbines concentrated on the centre-line, surrounded by individual boiler rooms. After the inter-war naval treaties limited ship weight, the US Navy considered and rejected reviving turbo-electric drive because of the weight penalty it imposed. During the Second World War, *Saratoga* was disabled when the shock of an underwater hit, which was not in danger of sinking her, caused circuit-breakers to jump. The US Navy did adopt electric drive for destroyer escorts during the conflict, but only because of a lack of the gear-cutting capacity which would have been needed

Electric drive is sometimes associated with ASW operations, often as part of a hybrid propulsion system in which the electric element is used as a low-speed but silent mode. The British Royal Navy Type 23 'Duke' class frigates are a good example of this approach; the photograph shows *Portland* in June 2022. *(Derek Fox)*

otherwise. Some diesel-engine ships also had electric propulsion, presumably for the same reason.[7]

FUTURE TRENDS

The US Navy eventually became particularly interested in electric drive because of its hopes to put electric weapons, such as lasers and rail guns, into service. An electric prime mover was needed to provide the peak power involved, just as a substantial increase in electric power was required to energise the electric catapults of *Ford* class (CVN-78) class carriers.[8] The hope of building electric lasers powerful enough to destroy incoming missiles has not yet been met. However, existing lasers are powerful enough to destroy drones. The war in Ukraine has demonstrated that, because they are so cheap, drones can saturate an air defence system and cause it to expend its finite missile magazine, opening the way for attacks by more massive, and far more destructive, weapons. A laser defence against drones and similar decoys would still leave conventional surface-to-air missile magazines full enough to deal with the heavy-missile threat. The US Navy is already mounting lasers on some *Burke* (DDG-51) class destroyers, both to deal with drones and to beat off attacks by swarm boats.

A key technical issue has been the need to find a way to switch smoothly from propulsion to firing weapons and back again, in a very short time. A ship needed, in effect, software-controlled switchboards capable of shifting smoothly. Generally the electric weapons use pulses of electric power, drawing not directly on the ship's power plant, but rather on a storage device, such as a bank of capacitors (in the case of the catapults of the *Ford* class, a bank of flywheels). The storage device is comparable to the magazine of a ship with more conventional weapons. As such, its destruction would be the equivalent of a magazine hit.

Electric drive has another important aspect. It can be viewed as a bridge to future propulsion systems. That is, it divorces the propeller driving a ship from

A F/A-18F Super Hornet attached to the 'Blacklions' of Strike Fighter Squadron 213 (VFA-213) prepares to launch from the aircraft carrier *Gerald R. Ford* (CVN-78) in March 2023. Whilst the *Ford* class retain conventional steam turbines for their main propulsion, they were designed from the outset with significant turbo-generating capacity for their 'all-electric' auxiliary systems, such as their Electromagnetic Aircraft Launch System (EMALS). *(US Navy)*

The US Navy is particularly interested in electric drive because of its hopes to put electric weapons – such as lasers and rail guns – into service as an electric prime mover would help to provide the peak power involved. The US Navy is already mounting lasers on some *Burke* (DDG-51) class destroyers; this is a graphic of the Lockheed Martin HELIOS system that was first installed aboard *Preble* (DDG-88) in 2022. *(Lockheed Martin)*

the source of power. In a conventional ship, the propeller shaft is connected to a steam or gas turbine or to a diesel. Re-engining is inherently difficult and, if even possible, expensive. In an electric ship, there is only a limited connection between the propeller and whatever provides electric power.

EXAMPLES OF PROPULSION TRENDS IN CURRENT WARSHIPS

The *Zumwalt* (DDG-1000) class destroyers were the first fast US Navy turbo-electric surface ships to be laid down since 1921. They utilise an integrated electric propulsion arrangement. Drawings of *Zumwalt*'s internal arrangement suggest that little or no attempt was made to shorten her propeller shafts. Given her peripheral missile launcher arrangement, there was little need to conserve centreline space. However, reportedly the ship did benefit from having multiple electric power buses to limit the effect of any damage. She has often been described as a test-bed for future electric weapons, such as high-powered lasers. It has also been claimed that means have been found to reduce motor (and generator) weight drastically. Placing really heavy weights far aft in a large ship can cause girder-strength and trim problems. It is sometimes suggested that the solution is high-temperature superconductivity; meaning high relative to the near absolute zero typically needed to induce superconductivity in the past. Presumably shock can also be mitigated.

Typically a fully-electric ship integrates propulsion and auxiliary power, since she has a single set of main generators. In theory, such a ship can be designed so that both motors can run using power by one of several main engines. For example,

The *Zumwalt* (DDG-1000) class – which use integrated electric propulsion – are the first fast US Navy major surface combatants to incorporate turbo-electric drive since the 1920s. Their propulsion plants combine two large Rolls-Royce MT-30 gas turbines with a pair of the company's smaller RR4500 models. These provide energy for both propulsion motors and 'hotel' services. This is *Michael Monsoor* (DDG-1001) in June 2022. *(US Navy)*

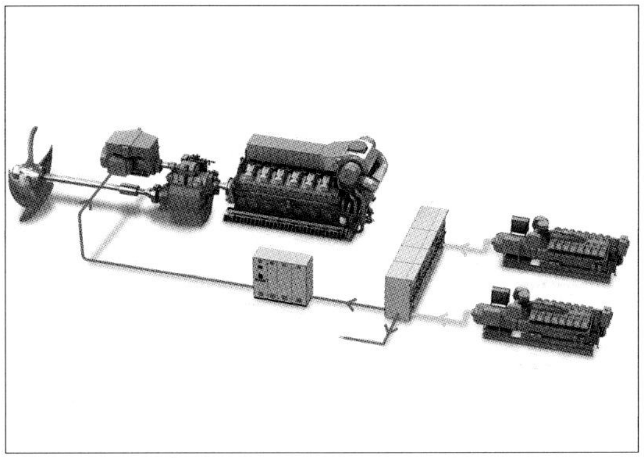

The Italian FREMM variants – this is *Virginio Fasan* pictured with *George H. W. Bush* (CVN-77) during operations in the Mediterranean in early 2023 – provide a good example of the hybrid combined diesel-electric and gas (CODLAG) propulsion plants found in many current frigates; their French 'half-sisters' use an alternative combined diesel-electric or gas (CODLOG) arrangement that is also increasingly popular. The schematic shows another hybrid arrangement, combining diesel-electric and diesel (CODLAD) propulsion, which is, for example, often found in auxiliary warships. *(Italian Navy/Rolls-Royce)*

Zumwalt has two main Rolls-Royce MT30 gas turbines. The inherent simplicity of the fully-integrated system can drastically reduce a ship's engine-room complement. On the other hand, like all turbines, a gas-turbine generator is inefficient when operating at a small fraction of full power. This inefficiency makes it attractive to adopt a hybrid power plant in which a gas turbine provides full-speed power but diesels, which are efficient over a broad power range, are used for lower speeds. In *Zumwalt* and her sisters, the solution adopted was to include two smaller Rolls-Royce RR4500 gas turbines in the integrated electric power system.

Several frigate designs have hybrid power plants that include electric elements. The previously mentioned Royal Navy Type 23, which used two Rolls-Royce Spey turbines to supplement its diesel-electric propulsion system to achieve sprint speed, was a trendsetter in this field. A more recent example is provided by the Franco-Italian multi-mission FREMM type frigates, including the US Navy's derivative *Constellation* (FFG-62) class design. These are driven by a combined gas-turbine and diesel-electric propulsion arrangement. At high speeds a single high-powered gas turbine drives the ships through gearing linked to two propeller shafts. For lower-speed operation – for example, in silent ASW mode – four diesel-driven generators supply electric power to motors on the propeller shafts. The French FREMM variant power plant utilises a combined diesel electric or gas (CODLOG) arrangement whereas the Italian FREMMs have a combined diesel and gas (CODLAG) configuration, in which the electric motors can be used in combination with the gas turbine at high speeds. However, the overall concept of operation is broadly similar in both cases. The South Korean *Daegu* (FFX Batch II) and German F125 *Baden-Württemberg* classes have, respectively, similar CODLOG and CODLAG type hybrid propulsion systems.

Another example is provided by the British Type 26 design. This has a CODLOG configuration with a single powerful gas turbine driving two shafts through gearing for sprint operation and four diesels driving generators for lower and silent speeds. This arrangement offers a combination of quieting – the diesel-electric element does not require gearing – and the flexible use of available diesel power, which can be split as needed between propulsion and, say, weapons and sensors. The diesels are mounted in acoustic enclosures, which is practical because they are not connected directly to the shafts.

Another recent development is the use of waterjets to transmit really high power to the sea, as in the US Navy's *Freedom* (LCS-1) class Littoral Combat Ship variant. This has two high-power Rolls-Royce MT-30 gas turbines coupled with a pair of lower-rated Pielstick diesels in a combined diesel and gas turbine (CODAG) configuration. The rather powerful machinery was adopted to drive the class's relatively inefficient 'semi-planing' – meaning a flat broad-beamed hull – at the desired 45 knots. Effective propulsion would have been impossible using conventional propellers, which would have cavitated badly and, thus, lost their efficiency. Waterjets, however, do not cavitate. They pump high-speed water into the sea. The US Navy had previously used waterjet propulsion in its *Pegasus* (PHM-1) class hydrofoils, but to transmit much less power. Waterjets were also used by the Italians in their *Sparviero* class hydrofoils and in similar ships built in Japan. Again, these ships generated far less power than the *Freedom* variant LCS.

The alternative to the displacement-hull *Freedom* class is the trimaran *Independence* (LCS-2) class, with a significantly more efficient hull, driven by less powerful LM 2500 gas turbines and diesels. Neither LCS class seems to have made its designed speed. The *Freedom* class in, particular, has been widely criticised for its very limited range; a consequence of the significant power required to reach the desired speed.

The *Freedom* (LCS-1) variant Littoral Combat Ships *Billings* (LCS-15) and *Wichita* (LCS-13) utilise waterjets and a high-powered combined diesel and gas (CODAG) propulsion arrangement to drive a relatively inefficient hull form in an attempt to achieve the class's high design speed of 45 knots. *(US Navy)*

Notes

1. Pressure firing, which was also tried by the US Navy, employs a gas turbine to pressurise air going into a ship's boiler, boosting its output. The gas turbine is driven by boiler exhaust.

2. The French did not use turbo-electric drive for the main propulsion system of their earlier and much larger *Le Redoutable* class strategic submarines, which adopted the traditional arrangement of steam turbines with reduction gearing. This difference with the subsequent attack submarines was probably due to the sheer weight required for a sufficiently powerful electric propulsion motor to propel these large vessels at an acceptable speed.

3. Probably the fundamental problem of gas-turbine economy is that the turbine is designed to spin at a speed optimum for maximum power. At that speed it has considerable inertia: it does not want to spin at any other speed. Moreover, at that speed it is operating at maximum efficiency. Throttling-down therefore costs efficiency.

4. A partial exception is the use of fuel-cell technology in submarine air-independent propulsion (AIP) systems. However, here the cells are being used for auxiliary propulsion, the main power plant remaining diesel electric.

5. The *Queen Elizabeth* class's integrated electric propulsion (IEP) system also utilises four diesel generators.

6. These are commonly known as Azipods, a trademarked azimuth thruster pod design developed in Finland in the 1980s. Azipods were seriously considered for use in the *Queen Elizabeth* class and are, for example, a feature of the Navantia-designed *Juan Carlos I* series of amphibious assault ships.

7. Minesweepers, however, had electric drive because they needed extra electric power to sweep magnetic mines.

8. Whilst the *Ford* class retain conventional steam turbines for their main propulsion, they were designed from the outset with significant turbo-generating capacity – four main turbine generators (MTGs) – for what have been described as 'all-electric' auxiliary systems. An important argument in favour of electric power was that hydraulics – and direct steam power, as in catapults – involve miles of piping, which can and does leak in service and hence requires continuous surveillance and repair. The continually rising cost of personnel can make any substantial reduction in such efforts worthwhile, as long as it works. It is not clear whether the problems the *Ford* has encountered with her electric power systems are just teething troubles or something worse. In the case of *Ford,* of course electric power also offers the possibility of improved self-defence using future high-powered lasers.

More broadly, the use of electric power in ship systems has another important advantage in that – compared to hydraulics – it is relatively easy to control electronically. For example, in the past few decades many ships have been fitted with computer-controlled damage control systems. Compartments are fitted with flooding and fire sensors, which are wired to a central computer. The computer creates a picture of the situation in the ship, analogous to the tactical picture created on the basis of external sensor data. Given the damage picture, the computer can recommend action that the damage control officer can try to implement by controlling, for example, watertight door activators and pumps. It is difficult to imagine the computer controlling the situation by activating hydraulic valves.

4.3 TECHNOLOGICAL REVIEW

NAVAL STRIKE MISSILE

Striker from the North

Author:
Richard Scott

The last decade has seen Norway's Kongsberg Defence & Aerospace capture a number of major orders for its Naval Strike Missile (NSM), both from navies across NATO and further afield. Conceived at the very end of the Cold War to provide the Royal Norwegian Navy (RNoN) with a compact, survivable and cost-effective anti-surface guided weapon able to engage and defeat surface ships in both open-ocean and littoral environments, NSM is some three decades later establishing itself as the de facto replacement for the Harpoon anti-ship missile employed by numerous Western navies since the 1980s. Indeed, some observers have latterly applied the moniker 'NATO Strike Missile' to reflect its take-up across the alliance.

As is so often the case, success did not come overnight. Development and testing of NSM encountered major cost overruns and a series of technical challenges that at one stage put the programme's future in doubt. Furthermore, NSM came into an anti-ship missile market already crowded with competing solutions from manufacturers in France, Israel, Sweden and the United States. That NSM has succeeded in this market is testament to a number of factors: a demanding but far-sighted RNoN staff requirement that shaped an anti-ship cruise missile design unlike anything that had gone before; the willingness of the Norwegian state to keep faith in a small but proficient sovereign guided weapons enterprise; and a global marketing strategy led by Kongsberg that has carefully cultivated market opportunities for NSM worldwide.

PENGUIN HERITAGE

In 1947, just two years after the end of the Second World War, the Norwegian Defence Research

A Norwegian Naval Strike Missile (NSM) pictured immediately after launch. Conceived at the end of the Cold War to provide the Royal Norwegian Navy with a compact, survivable and cost-effective anti-surface guided weapon, the missile has gone on to achieve international sales success. *(Kongsberg)*

Establishment (NDRE) was given seed funding to nurture an indigenous capability in missile design and technology. Over the next decade, a small team of scientists and engineers were engaged on a series of studies and development projects: early work was focused on unguided, free-flight rocket weapons but, over time, the focus switched to the development of guided missiles. By the late 1950s, NDRE was starting to investigate ship-launched anti-surface guided-weapon concepts. Its first efforts – code-named Albatross and Mikkel – explored relatively large missiles. However, these projects foundered because the navy lacked the resources and personnel to operate the large surface combatants that would be needed to carry these weapons.

Instead, the focus switched to a smaller missile better suited to an evolving future fleet concept subsequently enshrined as *Flåteplan* 1960 (Fleet Plan 1960). This new naval blueprint would reshape the RNoN into a sizeable force primarily comprising small but nimble fast attack boats designed for sea denial in coastal waters.

Attendant to this shift, NDRE conceived of a lighter weight anti-ship missile that could be carried by motor torpedo boats. Equally important, the new weapon would be required to operate effectively within a complex littoral replete with myriad islands, islets and fjords. What was needed was a weapon system that could navigate precisely through archipelagic waters and terrain waters – indeed, that could exploit the topography to achieve tactical advantage – and then select and home onto its intended target. This drove the adoption of a guidance system combining midcourse inertial navigation and infrared (IR) terminal homing.

This research and concept development work gave birth to the Penguin anti-ship missile and, consequentially, the creation of Norway's sovereign guided-weapons industry. Although NDRE had designed and developed all major subsystems for Penguin, it was not set up for volume manufacture. Consequently, Kongsberg Våpenfabrikk (now Kongsberg Defence & Aerospace) was brought into the programme as prime industrial partner. The original Mk 1 ship-launched version of Penguin entered service with the RNoN in 1972. A first export order was received from Turkey the same year. Penguin was subsequently evolved through several distinct design iterations, spawning the helicopter-launched Mk 2 Mod 7 variant – sold to Australia, Brazil, Greece, Spain, Turkey and the United States – and the fast-jet Mk 3 version, developed to equip Royal Norwegian Air Force (RNoAF) F-16 fighters.

The Penguin anti-ship missile was effectively the NSM's predecessor, playing a major part in the creation of Norway's sovereign guided weapons industry. This photograph shows a Mk 2 Mod 7 variant – designated the AGM 119 in American service – being launched from a US Navy SH-60B helicopter in July 1998. *(US National Archives 6510480)*

NAVAL STRIKE MISSILE GENESIS

Towards the end of the 1980s the RNoN began to consider its need for a new anti-ship missile to meet the needs of the 2010–40 timeframe. Top-line requirements emerged for a survivable and highly discriminative precision stand-off guided weapon that would be able to defeat ship (primary) and land (secondary) targets in complex maritime and littoral environments. Unlike Penguin, which had been designed to counter relatively small and lightly armed vessels up to corvette/light frigate size, this follow-on missile would be required to achieve a mission kill against much larger and better defended targets at range. The RNoN would eventually distil its requirement – codified as P6026 – into four broad categories:

- First, the new missile needed to be suitable for launch from a range of platforms, including a projected new frigate class, a type of new fast patrol boat (FPB), coastal batteries, and helicopters.[1]
- Second, the navy wanted to assure a high level of mission success, also referred to as probability of kill. This necessitated high system availability; the ability to penetrate shipborne defences (both hard-kill weapons and soft-kill countermeasures); a robust and reliable means by which to acquire the selected target against a complex background; and the delivery of a lethal effect sufficient to either destroy the target, or achieve a 'mission kill'.
- Third, the new missile would be required to engage targets in diverse and complex mission scenarios, in both littoral and open-sea conditions, while bound by restrictive Rules of Engagement. This demanded a high level of flexibility in mission planning with regard to geography, no-fly areas/no-attack areas and the avoidance of enemy air defences.
- Fourth, but by no means last, the Norwegian customer was focused on affordability. This meant a low unit cost, a reduced inventory requirement – on the basis of a much higher probability of kill per missile – and reduced life-

cycle costs. The last-mentioned factor could be achieved, for example, by extended test and maintenance intervals and an upgrade path to enable technology insertions/capability upgrades over a planned 30-year service life.

At the outset, the RNoN and the Norwegian Ministry of Defence (MOD) explored a range of options for a 'military off-the-shelf' solution that would avoid the non-recurring engineering costs associated with a brand new development programme. However, as market survey studies progressed it became clear that none of the anti-ship weapons then available or in development could meet the requirements set for low signature, target discrimination/recognition and defence penetration. The analyses concluded that most of these missiles were based on technology from the late 1970s or early 1980s that would fast become obsolete, even with planned upgrades. Size was another factor. Early design work on the new FPB envisaged the installation of missiles in the forward part of the vessel, which would necessarily constrain both dimensions and mass. No existing anti-ship weapon would fit this envelope.

As a result, the decision was taken to start a brand new national development programme under the name *Nytt sjømålsmissil*, translated as 'new naval target missile'.[2] In 1991, Kongsberg – at that stage known as Norsk Forsvarsteknologi – began early definition work, under contract to the MOD to consider how best to engineer a new anti-ship guided weapon solution to meet the stressing requirements previously identified by NDRE and the RNoN.

A picture of the lead Norwegian *Fridtjof Nansen* class frigate taken in June 2014 with canisters for four NSMs visible aft of her distinctive mast. The NSM was developed with a view to equipping, inter alia, new frigate and corvette designs that were ultimately to be delivered as, respectively, the *Nansen* and *Skjold* classes. *(Kongsberg)*

NDRE had by this stage already begun to explore a next-generation infrared sensor providing sufficient resolution to 'image' the target. Kongsberg meanwhile would look to leverage experience from Penguin while at the same time venturing into some high-technology areas previously outside Norway's guided weapons enterprise. At this early stage, there was an emphasis on re-using existing Penguin systems where possible or practical.

With defence penetration a key requirement, Kongsberg had to make a fundamental choice between speed and stealth at an early stage. It quickly settled on the latter approach, judging that a supersonic missile would be ill-suited to the target recognition requirements and complex littoral warfare scenarios envisaged by the RNoN. Instead of relying on speed to puncture the defensive screen, the design philosophy and operational concept underpinning NSM placed emphasis on the penetration of defences though a combination of:

- Low signature: both radar cross section (RCS) and thermal signature.
- Advanced engagement planning and precision navigation: exploiting local topography to mask the approach to target.
- A very low sea-skimming flight profile.
- The use of a high-resolution passive imaging infrared (IIR) seeker for terminal homing
- High terminal agility.

A NSM pictured during the final phase of its approach to the target during testing carried out at Point Mugu, California between 2006 and 2007. Key design requirements to maximise the chances of penetrating enemy defences included low radar and thermal signatures, a sea-skimming flight profile, the use of a passive seeker, and high terminal agility. *(Kongsberg)*

This image of the NSM Coastal Defence System provides a clear view of the Naval Strike Missile's overall design. One particular characteristic is the missile's carefully, contoured low-observable airframe. To reduce RCS, Kongsberg adopted a distinctive chined airframe manufactured from lightweight composite material. Attention was also paid to shroud the inlet feeding the turbojet engine in order to suppress radar returns. *(Kongsberg)*

A NSM – designated RGM-184 in US Navy service – pictured being launched from the Littoral Combat Ship *Gabrielle Giffords* (LCS-10) in March 2021. Launch and fly-out/acceleration to cruise is enabled by a solid rocket boost motor produced by the defence group Nammo. *(US Navy)*

In June 1996 Kongsberg was awarded a preliminary development contract by Naval Materiel Command while negotiations continued on a full development award. These concluded in December that year, with Kongsberg receiving a fixed-price contract initially valued at NOK.1.2bn (c. US$110m at mid-2023 exchange rates). At that time, it was planned that development would conclude by the end of 2002, leaving sufficient time for follow-on production contracts to deliver series weapons matched to the entry into service of the new frigates and strike craft.[3]

NAVAL STRIKE MISSILE DESIGN

The development phase saw Kongsberg, working closely with NDRE, shape and mature a stealthy, turbojet-powered, precision guided weapon incorporating a number of advanced technologies and novel design features. The company has subsequently gone on to characterise NSM as the world's first 'fifth-generation' anti-ship missile, reflecting its core attributes of survivability, precision, intelligence and lethality.

Platform constraints imposed at the outset of the programme conditioned a missile length of 3.5m (3.9m with booster) and an all-up mass of 415kg (again with booster). This was only a modest increase on Penguin, and significantly less than competing over-the-horizon anti-ship weapons. One very evident characteristic of NSM is its carefully contoured low-observable airframe. To reduce RCS, Kongsberg adopted a distinctive chined airframe body manufactured from lightweight composite materials; significant attention was also paid to shroud the inlet feeding the turbojet engine in order to suppress radar returns.

French company Microturbo – now subsumed within Safran – was selected to supply its TRI-40 compact turbojet power plant. A single-shaft engine equipped with a four-stage axial compressor, the JP-10 fuelled TRI-40 can sustain high subsonic speeds up to Mach 0.95 and achieve ranges in excess of 200km. Launch and fly-out/acceleration to cruise is enabled by a solid rocket boost motor produced by Norwegian-headquartered defence group Nammo.

Aerodynamically, NSM features two mid-body

A test launch of an NSM. One launched, NSM uses a multi-sensor precision navigation system that is designed to guide the missile to a predefined error-circle that defines the start of the terminal phase. The navigational accuracy afforded to the missile allows it to execute complex flight profiles over land and sea in order to take advantage of prevailing geography. *(Kongsberg)*

wings – which extend after launch – and cruciform control surfaces aft. The missile manoeuvres in the same way as an aircraft – executing a bank to turn – so as to confer excellent agility. This is particularly important in the terminal phase. Here the missile combines sustained, pseudo-random high-g manoeuvres in three dimensions with a high subsonic end-game speed, exploiting a greater than 1:1 thrust-to-weight ratio to continuously change acceleration without losing speed.

Perhaps the single most important innovation embodied in NSM is its advanced dual-band wide-field-of-view IIR seeker. Conceived and prototyped by NDRE, this seeker – fitted inside a roll-stabilised nose section – is designed to be able to detect, classify and select targets in confined and congested waters, being pivotal to achieving the levels of stealth and target discrimination required. NSM is unique in its class by virtue of using IIR homing. Competing long-range anti-ship guided weapons all use active radar seekers for terminal homing, with their manufacturers claiming that a radio frequency (RF) seeker is necessary to deliver all-weather performance in the maritime environment. Kongsberg takes a contrary view, arguing that its modelling and analysis indicates that there are very few conditions in which fog or precipitation would prevent the IIR seeker acquiring the target. Furthermore, the company argues, radar seekers will have significant 'electronic fog' – natural or man-made – to contend with. A seeker operating in the infrared portion of the electromagnetic spectrum also has the key advantage that it is passive, and so cannot be detected by shipborne sensors. In contrast, an active RF seeker must radiate and so is inherently vulnerable to detection/identification by shipboard electronic support measures.

Importantly, the resolution afforded by the IIR seeker and its associated image processing enables a high level of functionality with regard to target acquisition, selection and countermeasures immunity, supporting the implementation of automatic target-recognition algorithms for ship classification and aim-point selection. So as well as being able to discriminate target vessels from nearby land masses or other ships, NSM can actually identify a vessel by ship class by comparing the seeker image with a 'target library' resident in the missile's main computer. Also, the target aim point can be selected during the mission planning process to meet the command aim for a surgical kill or controlled/proportionate damage.

Another important technology enabler for NSM is a multi-sensor precision navigation system that is used to guide the missile to a predefined error-circle that defines the start of the terminal phase. It consists of a tactical grade inertial measurement unit (IMU) aided by a military L1/L2 Selective Availability Anti-spoofing Module GPS receiver, and a laser altimeter to provide terrain correlation for overland flights and height estimation over water. It is important to note that the system is GPS-aided rather than GPS-dependent: that is to say that GPS information is only used to augment the primary inertial system.

The fibre-optic IMU is the core sensor in the navigation system. Inertial navigation system algorithms integrate IMU measurements, which are combined with measurements from the GPS receiver and a laser altimeter in a Kalman filter.[4] Correction algorithms calculate position, velocity and attitude based on the IMU measurements and the error estimates. The IMU also provides aiding data to the GPS during flight, aiding initial acquisition and ensuring rapid reacquisition after satellite outages due to manoeuvres or jamming. The low-power laser altimeter, housed in the stabilised nose section to ensure it always points downward, provides the capability for terrain matching over land – comparing its measurements to digital maps stored on a hard disk on board – and sea-skimming and 'super' sea-skimming flight profiles over sea. The navigational accuracy afforded to the missile allows it to execute complex flight profiles over land and sea incorporating multiple waypoints in order to take advantage of prevailing geography. By approaching the target at a very low altitude, NSM is able to stay below the radar horizon – and thus undetected – until the very last seconds of flight.

NSM's lethal payload – carried in what is effectively a 'bomb bay' within the missile – is a 120kg MBDA TDW semi-armour-piercing blast/fragmentation insensitive munition-qualified warhead. This combines a titanium alloy warhead casing, with a steel grid for fragmentation effect, and high explosive fill. Warhead initiation is by a void-sensing programmable intelligent multi-purpose fuze (PIMPF) designed to optimise effect against hard targets; PIMPF enables selectable penetration (using bulkhead counting) to maximise warhead effect internally.

Onboard mission preparation/engagement planning, using a dedicated operator console, is another key part of the NSM weapon system. Mission plans can be generated automatically – based on tactical situational/scene data and pre-set doctrine – or manually using a highly intuitive graphical user interface. Various selectable parameters can be programmed including time of flight; minimum probability of target counter-detection; target approach heading; maximised search area; delineation of attack and no-attack/no-fly zones; and precise time on target. Complex and coordinated salvo attacks, involving simultaneous arrival of multiple missiles from different axes, can be generated to saturate target defences. A reversionary 'point

The NSM underwent a lengthy period of trials and evaluation that began in 2000 and ultimately progressed to operational firings after the first missiles were delivered in 2012. These photographs of the results of trials of the NSM against the decommissioned frigate *Trondheim* in June 2013 give an indication of the potency of the MBDA TDW 120kg warhead used by the missile. Key features of the NSM demonstrated in this test included the missile's ability to impact a precise aim-point (the forward superstructure housing the combat information centre); the functionality of the programmable fuze; and the destruction wrought by the warhead. *(Peder Torp Mathisen/Norwegian Armed Forces)*

and shoot' mode is also available as a subset of manual planning functionality. In this case, the missile flies a straight path out along a given bearing with no target data.

Finally, the launch infrastructure associated with NSM needed to be both compact and lightweight to enable installation on smaller ships down to fast strike craft/corvette size. To achieve this, Kongsberg developed a lightweight launch missile module (LMM) serving as a common canister for storage, transportation and launch. The modular philosophy was intended to allow for different 'pack sizes' to suit specific installation constraints; in practice, LMMs are typically stacked into ramped four-pack (two x two) launcher groups.

TRIALS AND TRIBULATIONS

The first NSM ballistic test firing was undertaken at the Andøya range in northern Norway in October 2000, followed by a second ballistic trial in May 2001. Testing then moved to the Centre d'Essais de la Mediterranee (CEM) test range on the Ile du Levant in southern France for controlled flight trials. It was at this stage that the test campaign began to encounter challenges, with controlled flight tests undertaken at the CEM range in 2002 and 2003 revealing a series of technical issues. With doubts growing in the minds of the Norwegian customer, a comprehensive programme review was undertaken by Kongsberg in conjunction with NDRE. This audit concluded that the programme's technical footing remained fundamentally sound, but that the development phase would need to be re-baselined and extended. Having accepted a fixed-price development contract, Kongsberg was subsequently obliged to dig into its own pocket and accept a NOK.150m (c. US$14m) charge against its earnings.

The turning point came in June 2004 with NSM test firing U-6. Launched from the Ile du Levant, the fully-instrumented missile covered almost 150km at prescribed altitudes and velocities, banking to execute turns of various radii before making a controlled entry into the sea. The test was judged flawless, and provided a huge volume of data on the performance of the missile in flight. U-6 provided a conclusive demonstration that the NSM concept worked, and removed significant risk from the programme. With confidence restored, the MOD awarded Kongsberg a NOK.200m (c. US$18m) transition contract in December 2004 to prepare for NSM production start-up and deliver associated shipboard systems while the development flight test programme continued.

Following a further test success at CEM in June 2005, the flight test programme migrated to the US Naval Air Weapons Center Weapons Division's Point Mugu range in California, where four successful firings were carried out against both moving and static sea targets between late July 2006 and early January 2007. These included an attack from open water towards a target with background land clutter, and an attack against an anchored target 'in harbour'. These operational firings, the culmination of a ten-year development programme amounting to approximately two million man-hours of effort, gave full confidence that NSM was ready to enter series production. Following a final design review, the conclusion of contract negotiations and approval by the Storting (Norway's parliament), Kongsberg was awarded a full-scale production contract worth NOK.2.74bn (c. US$250m) in June 2007. This marked the biggest single order in Kongsberg Defence & Aerospace's history, securing direct employment for between 200 and 250 company employees and providing work to about 120 subcontractors across Norway.

INTO SERVICE

A first batch of NSM Block 1 missiles was formally signed over to the RNoN in a ceremony aboard the frigate *Roald Amundsen* at Haakonsvern Naval Base, Bergen on 30 May 2012. Phased deliveries over the next two years saw the service's five *Fridtjof Nansen* class frigates and six *Skjold* class surface effect ship corvettes all outfitted with the NSM. Each frigate received eight missiles, with two four-pack launcher assemblies fitted athwartships. The smaller *Skjolds* also received two four-pack launchers, in their case recessed into the stern of the hull. The launcher group elevates 25° to fire and then retracts back into the vessel's hull.

A first operational firing from a Norwegian vessel was conducted from the corvette *Glimt* at Andøya Test Centre in northern Norway in October 2012. The telemetered missile – the first production-standard warshot to be fired – followed a sea-skimming flight profile, executing a number of waypoints during a flight extending more than 100km. In the terminal phase, the missile acquired its target – the decommissioned corvette *Aeger* anchored in the Anfjorden – and impacted as planned.

However, it was the RNoN's second operational firing – executed on the Andøya range on 4 June 2013 – that provided the most visible proof of NSM's performance and potency. The first firing of an NSM equipped with a live warhead, this event saw a missile launched from the corvette *Steil* strike the decommissioned frigate *Trondheim.* Three key features of the NSM design were demonstrated in this end-to-end test: the ability of the missile to impact a precise aim-point on the target (in this case

Images of an NSM strike against a land target; the *Skjold* class corvette *Storm* demonstrated this capability against a simulated command and control facility during a joint Norwegian/Polish exercise in mid-2016. Note that the two four-pack NSM launchers are recessed into the stern of the *Skjold* class's hull. The launcher group elevates 25° to fire and then retracts into the vessel's hull. *(Kongsberg)*

COASTAL DEFENDER

An early requirement that helped shaped the final design of NSM was Norway's plan for a new mobile coastal defence system – the Medium Weight Missile Battery (MWMB) – which would replace existing fixed coastal fortifications. This project was important because it emphasised the need for a missile that could achieve an extended range beyond the fjords – something over 100km – while being of a suitable size and weight to engender a high degree of mobility. In the event, budget pressures and the end of the Cold War saw the MWMB programme cancelled. However, Kongsberg remained confident that there was a role for NSM in coastal defence. To address this market, the company designed a highly mobile NSM Coastal Defence System combining a command and control node – or fire distribution centre – with a number of truck-mounted NSM launcher firing units, and a suitable surface surveillance/tracking radar.

The wisdom of this development was borne out in 2008 when Poland's Ministry of National Defence awarded Kongsberg a contract for the procurement of an NSM system for the Polish Navy's coastal defence squadron. A follow-on order was placed in late 2014 covering equipment and missiles for a second coastal defence squadron. In January 2023, Romania became the second European NATO customer for the NSM Coastal Defence System when Raytheon was awarded a US$208m contract under the US Foreign Military Sales (FMS) process. Subsequently, FMS approval covering an NSM Coastal Defense System and related equipment for Latvia was announced in April 2023.

However, it is the US military where the biggest market has emerged for NSM as a so-called 'cross-domain fires' effector. Going back to 2015, the US Army Research, Development and Engineering Command Aviation & Missile Center (AMRDEC) began to investigate options that could be pursued to provide a near-term multi-domain fires capability. This concept recognised that, by employing land-based anti-ship missiles, the Army could potentially target enemy ships and restrict movement in the maritime domain. In 2016 the Mobile Land Based Anti-Ship Fires FCT project was established. NSM was one of the options identified to meet this requirement.

In July 2018, as part of the RIMPAC 2018 exercise, the US Army fired a single NSM missile from a Palletized Load System truck on Hawaii's Kauai Island as part of a 'cross domain fires/cross domain integration' demonstration. The missile successfully struck the hulk of the retired tank landing ship *Racine* (LST-1191) at a range of just over 100km.

The US Marine Corps has now sought to evolve the cross-domain fires concept further as part of its Force Design 2030 modernisation plan, enshrining the so-called Navy/Marine Corps Expeditionary Ship Interdiction System (NMESIS) as part of new Marine Littoral Regiments based in the Pacific. Designed to provide a ground-based anti-ship capability to strike at maritime and land targets while remaining highly survivable within an adversary's weapons engagement zone, NMESIS combines NSM with the Oshkosh Defense Remote Operated Ground Unmanned Expeditionary (ROGUE) fires system – an uncrewed vehicle based on a Joint Lightweight Tactical Vehicle chassis – and a fire-control system. Each remotely-operated ROGUE Fires vehicle is able to carry two encanistered NSM missiles. Raytheon and the US Marine Corps completed a first NMESIS firing in November 2020 off the California coast. A second live firing trial was performed in August 2021 during Large Scale Exercise 21 in Hawaii.

Another concept, given the name StrikeMaster, has been proposed by Kongsberg to fulfil the Australian Army's requirement for deployable, land-based anti-ship missiles. StrikeMaster would use the Bushmaster utility vehicle to transport and fire NSM, with two missiles equipping each vehicle.

Air-launched Option

Keen to repeat the earlier success of Penguin, Kongsberg also continues to market an air-launched version of NSM known as NSM-AL. The missile would utilise a standard MIL-STD 1760 electrical interface and be drop-launched from a standard BRU-14 bomb rack.

The main marketing effort for NSM-AL is focused on integration with the MH-60R/MH-60S helicopter family. Kongsberg has completed fit checks with both types: as of mid-2023, the first full integration was awaiting a customer. NSM-AL is also suitable for launch from maritime patrol aircraft. Another opportunity relates to uncrewed air systems (UAS): according to Kongsberg, NSM is sufficiently small and lightweight to be carried by a medium altitude/long endurance UAS such as the MQ-9.

The US Marine Corps has been trialling the NMESIS concept. This combines NSM with the Oshkosh Defense Remote Operated Ground Unmanned Expeditionary (ROGUE) fires system – an uncrewed vehicle based on a Joint Lightweight Tactical Vehicle chassis – and a fire-control system to provide a highly mobile anti-ship system capable of rapid deployment to islands across the Pacific.

the forward superstructure housing the combat information centre); the functionality of the programmable PIMPF fuze; and the destructive blast and fragmentation effects wrought by the warhead.

The RNoN went on to prove NSM in a coastal suppression role during a joint Norwegian/Polish exercise conducted on the Andøya range in May/June 2016. In this case, a single missile launched from the corvette *Storm* was targeted on a GPS coordinate and successfully destroyed a simulated coastal command and control facility.

NSM ENTERS THE INTERNATIONAL STAGE

It was recognised from the outset that the investment in the development of NSM could not be justified on the basis of national offtake alone. As with Penguin, the success of the programme would hinge on securing orders from allies and partners looking to modernise their own capabilities. So began a marketing campaign that sought to convince potential customers of the merits of a 'fifth generation' anti-ship missile in the face of fierce competition from incumbents such as Boeing, MBDA and Saab. As well as addressing the market for ship-launched weapons, the company also identified opportunities for NSM as part of a coastal defence system (see text box) as well as a helicopter-launched variant.

Malaysia was an early target, with the Royal Malaysian Navy having articulated a requirement for a new anti-ship missile as part of its Littoral Combat Ship programme. In April 2015, Kongsberg received a €20m (c. US$20m) award from Boustead Naval Shipyard – the programme's prime contractor – to prepare the new vessels to receive NSM. The scope of this award covered fixed installations such as launchers, cables, electronics and integration to the combat management system. A follow-on contract to supply NSM rounds was announced in April 2018.[5]

However, Kongsberg had its eyes on a much bigger prize. Having sold Penguin to the US Navy in the early 1990s, the company saw an opportunity to position NSM as a replacement for the ageing Harpoon Block 1C missile. While there was initially no programme of record for such a weapon, Kongsberg – with the backing of the Norwegian government – began an information campaign in an effort to shape requirements and carve out a market. It saw the US Navy's Littoral Combat Ships (LCS) – derided by many for their lack of offensive punch – as a prime target. Accordingly, it completed a set of engineering studies to examine the integration of NSM missiles into the space/weight envelopes associated with LCS mission modules. The 'gear-shift' in its campaign came in 2014 as the navy's surface warfare community, stung by criticism of the LCS programme, established a task force to look hard at the offensive potential of its small surface combatant force. This work complemented wider deliberations on future force architecture and warfighting requirements from which ultimately emerged the operational concept of 'Distributed Lethality'.

To provide the US Navy and other allies with a first-hand demonstration of the potential of NSM, the RNoN frigate *Fridtjof Nansen* participated in the 'Sinkex' phase of the RIMPAC 2014 exercise in the Pacific. A single missile was fired from the ship, impacting the hulk of the decommissioned amphibious ship *Ogden* (LPD-5). Shortly afterwards, the Naval Sea Systems Command (NAVSEA) issued a pre-solicitation notice for the procurement of two NSM missiles plus technical support for a

Persistent efforts by Kongsberg to seek the NSM's acquisition by the US Navy were assisted by the service's adoption of the 'Distributed Lethality' concept, finally resulting in an initial contract for a first shipset of misisles and equipment in May 2018. The first US Navy ship equipped with NSM was the Littoral Combat Ship *Gabrielle Giffords* (LCS-10), seen here undertaking a test firing in October 2019. In addition to equipping the *Independence* (LCS-2) Littoral Combat Ship variant, NSM will also be installed in the new *Constellation* (FFG-62) class frigates. *(US Navy)*

demonstration under the Foreign Comparative Test (FCT) programme. The FCT was designed to act as a demonstration of LCS's potential to execute an increased offensive anti-surface warfare role. While there was at that time no stated requirement for such a capability, NAVSEA acknowledged that it would 'additionally provide insights into the weapon's stated capabilities of increased range, survivability, and lethality'. The FCT test firing was performed from *Coronado* (LCS-4) on 23 September 2014. A single missile was fired from a launch canister installed on the ship's flight deck, flying a pre-planned 'straight-line' trajectory to a mobile sea target approximately 100 nautical miles away. For the purposes of the demonstration, the NSM mission planning system was self-contained and not integrated with the ship's combat system.

During 2015, the US Navy's surface warfare leadership promulgated the idea of 'Distributed Lethality'. This new operational concept set out a vision of a surface fleet re-equipped, re-configured and re-purposed to assume a more overtly 'offensive' posture. Attendant to this was the identification of a requirement for a c. 120-nautical mile range surface-to-surface missile that could be retrofitted to the LCS, and equip a follow-on frigate class from build. Following detailed requirements analysis, NAVSEA subsequently released a request for information (RFI) for a new Over The Horizon-Weapon System (OTH-WS) in mid-2015. The RFI specifically referenced the navy's preference for a non-developmental solution that could be delivered in a short timeframe. In anticipation of a formal requirement emerging, Kongsberg and Raytheon had formalised a teaming arrangement to address US and international opportunities for NSM in April 2015. In July that same year, the companies disclosed plans to qualify a second NSM production line at Raytheon's plant in Tucson, Arizona and move construction of launchers to the company's factory in Louisville, Kentucky.

NAVSEA released a Request for Proposals for the OTH-WS in February 2017. While the navy had sought to promote full competition, in the event only Raytheon/Kongsberg submitted a bid. Following detailed evaluation, NAVSEA awarded Raytheon an initial contract for a first shipset of 'encanistered' missiles (tactical, telemetered and inert operational), launchers, a single fire-control suite, mission-support equipment, training, and engineering services on 31 May 2018. Several contract options for additional missiles and ship equipment have been exercised since.

The NSM weapon system solution delivered under OTH-WS is essentially the same as the existing RNoN baseline. Designated RGM-184 by the US Navy, the system is being rolled out onto the *Independence* (LCS-2) variant of the LCS, and will later also equip the new *Constellation* (FFG-62) class frigates. Each LCS installation comprises a fire-control system, launcher equipment, and eight encanistered NSM missiles; the *Constellation* class frigates will each receive sixteen encanistered missiles.

The original OTH-WS programme schedule called for initial delivery 24 months after contract. However, the first installation – on *Gabrielle Giffords* (LCS-10) – was accelerated, with integration completed just 15 months after contract. The NSM rounds themselves were obtained from RNoN stocks to expedite rapid delivery, with LCS-10 competing a first NSM firing on 1 October 2019 off Guam as part of Exercise 'Pacific Griffin'. Missile deliveries from the Raytheon production line subsequently commenced in May 2021.

GROWTH POTENTIAL

NSM is a weapon system still at a relatively early stage of its lifecycle. Kongsberg's product philosophy, informed by the RNoN's original requirement, recognised that NSM would need to evolve through-life to meet changing mission needs and threat priorities. Pre-planned product improvement options identified during the development phase included the possible addition of a two-way data link for mid-course target updates and target confirmation; automatic target recognition enhancement to enable land target recognition; provision for additional terminal sensors such as a passive RF seeker; alternative warheads/payloads; and a mid-body stretch to increase fuel capacity and, hence, range. NSM also stands to benefit from the Norwegian government's investment in the development of the Joint Strike Missile (JSM). Building on the technology matured in the NSM programme, JSM will provide Norwegian F-35A fighters with a survivable precision strike weapon able to prosecute maritime and land targets from stand-off ranges. The latest NSM Block 1A production standard offers first evidence of this philosophy in action. As well as resolving some component obsolescence in the missile baseline, and introducing an upgraded mission computer (common to that in JSM), this latest iteration introduces a capability for seeker-assisted land attack, and software improvements in the propulsion management system to tease out additional range.

In February 2018 the governments of Norway and Germany reached a joint agreement on procurement of NSM, including development of an improved version to meet the long-term anti-surface warfare needs of the German Navy and the RNoN. Concluded as an extension to a strategic Norwegian/German partnership on future submarines announced that same month, the agreement called for a single common missile to meet the operational needs of the two navies, while at the same time promoting cooperation in the fields of maintenance, training and logistics.

Germany's new F126 multirole frigate will be the first German Navy ship to be equipped with NSM. Over the longer term, the missile is intended to become the standard offensive anti-surface weapon system for all German frigates. The Norwegian government has aligned a planned Mid-Life Update (MLU) of the RNoN's stocks with Germany's new production requirements under a bilateral project arrangement. In October 2021 the Norwegian Ministry of Defence announced the award of two separate contracts to Kongsberg covering the MLU and recertification of existing missiles, and a buy of new-build NSM Block 1A missiles common to those being acquired by Germany. In parallel to this initial acquisition, Norway and Germany are looking to jointly evaluate concepts to meet their respective navies strike needs after 2035. Kongsberg was in June 2018 awarded a NOK.220m (c. US$20m) contract by the Norwegian MOD for a 12-month study to explore different concept options.

Kongsberg is continuing to capture more international sales to existing Harpoon users. Canada confirmed its selection of NSM in 2020, and during 2022 Australia, the Netherlands and Spain also announced their intention to procure the system. Another success has come from the UK. Following abandonment of an earlier competitive effort to acquire an interim surface-to-surface guided weapon, the UK MOD announced in November 2022 that it had concluded a government-to-government agreement with Norway to acquire NSM to meet its Maritime Offensive Surface Strike requirement. A total of eleven ship sets are being procured for retrofit to Type 23 frigates and Type 45 destroyers: missile stocks to equip an initial three

An early graphic of Kongsberg's Joint Strike Missile (JSM). Building on the technology matured in the NSM programme, JSM will provide Norwegian F-35A fighters with a survivable precision strike weapon able to prosecute maritime and land targets from stand-off ranges. *(Kongsberg)*

ships are being provided from Norway's inventory. The RN plans to have an initial capability at sea by the time Harpoon is retired at the end of 2023. The Type 23 frigate *Somerset* is the first RN ship to receive NSM.

Notes

1. The new frigate programme ultimately delivered five *Fridtjof Nansen* class frigates built by Navantia. The new FPB programme resulted in the acquisition of the six *Skjold* class corvettes from Umoe Mandal.

2. The anglicised name 'Naval Strike Missile' was adopted by Kongsberg in the early 2000s.

3. An important, if now historical, footnote to the NSM development programme was the involvement of an overseas industrial partner to develop the propulsion subsystem, whilst also adding impetus to Kongsberg's overseas marketing efforts. Following a competition, Aerospatiale Missiles (later to be subsumed within MBDA) – manufacturer of the Exocet missile – was identified as partner of choice in August 1997. At that time, there appeared to be a good fit between the anti-ship missile portfolios of the two companies. Penguin and Exocet were expected to continue selling through to 2005; thereafter, NSM would occupy the 'intermediate' market for a compact, stealthy and manoeuvrable weapon compatible with smaller surface and air platforms, while Aerospatiale planned to target 'high end' requirements with its somewhat larger supersonic Anti-Navire Futur (ANF). In the event, market dynamics were ultimately to break this relationship. Development of ANF was cancelled in early 2000, spurring MBDA to evolve its MM40 Exocet to a new turbojet-powered Block 3 standard and thereby spawn a rival competing head-on with NSM. While MBDA fulfilled its obligations to the NSM development programme, the two companies later dissolved their marketing arrangement and are now competitors on the export stage.

4. Kalman filtering is an algorithm that uses a series of measurements observed over time to produce estimates of unknown variables that tend to be more accurate than those based on a single measurement.

5. Owing to severe delays impacting the Littoral Combat Ship programme, the RMN is now reportedly considering installation of NSM on at least two existing *Kedah* class patrol vessels.

Contributors

Richard Beedall: Richard is an IT Consultant with an interest in the Royal Navy and naval affairs in general. He served in the Royal Naval Reserve as a rating and officer for 14 years, often in the Arabian Gulf working with the US Navy and local naval forces. In 1999 he founded *Navy Matters*, one of the earliest websites on the Royal Navy. He has contributed to *Seaforth World Naval Review* since the initial 2010 edition and has written on naval developments for publications such as *AMI International*, *Naval Forces*, *Maritime Defence Monitor* and *Warships IFR*. He lives in Ireland with his wife and daughters.

Norman Friedman: Norman Friedman is one of the world's best-known naval historians and the author of over forty books. He has written widely on issues of military interest and with respect to warship development. Amongst recent works, *Winning a Future War: War Gaming and Victory in the Pacific War* – a description of how war gaming at the US Naval War College helped the US Navy prepare for the Pacific War produced for the Naval History & Heritage Command – stands out as a notable contribution to naval history. His latest book, *British Coastal Forces*, forms part of a wider series on British warship types. In June 2022, he received the Anderson Medal for lifetime achievement from the Society for Nautical Research and, in August that year, the Dudley W. Knox medal for lifetime achievement in naval history from the (US) Naval Historical Foundation. The holder of a PhD in theoretical physics from Columbia, Dr. Friedman is a regular commentator on television and lectures widely on defence issues. He resides with his wife in New York.

Alexandre Galante: A journalist specialising in military affairs, Alexandre Galante is editor-in-chief of the Brazilian trilogy of websites: *Naval Power* (naval.com.br), *Air Power* (aereo.jor.br), and *Land Forces* (forte.jor.br). He previously served in the Brazilian Navy at the end of the Cold War, including aboard the frigate *Niterói* (F40). Upon leaving naval service, he wrote for various defence magazines, also working for the newspaper *O Globo* for 12 years. From 2011 and 2015, he edited and published the print magazine *Forças de Defesa (Defence Forces).*

David Hobbs: David Hobbs is a naval historian with an international reputation. He has written over twenty books, the latest of which, *The Fleet Air Arm and The War in Europe 1939–1945*, was published by Seaforth in 2022. He has also written for several journals and magazines and in 2005 won the award for the Aerospace Journalist of the Year, Best Defence Submission, in Paris. He also won the essay prize awarded by the Navy League of Australia in 2008. He has lectured on naval subjects worldwide and has been broadcast in several countries. He served in the Royal Navy for 33 years and retired with the rank of Commander. He is qualified as both a fixed and rotary wing pilot and his log book contains 2,300 hours with over 800 carrier deck landings, 150 of which were at night. For eight years he was the Curator of the Fleet Air Arm Museum at Yeovilton. His next book, *Aircraft of the Royal Navy since 1908*, describes over 450 types of fixed wing, rotary wing and lighter-than-air aircraft and is due to be published in 2024. He lives in Northumberland with his wife Jandy, a former WRNS officer.

Bruno Huriet: Bruno Huriet is a French merchant navy officer, holding a dual bridge & engine certificate. After a few years on bulk carriers he worked ashore as ship superintendent on a major naval export contract. Subsequently – over a period extending for more than 20 years – he has been employed by companies in insulation and interior outfitting for both civilian and naval projects. Having worked on several naval projects in different countries, he is particularly interested in comparing the varying design solutions adopted by different navies. He is a long-standing contributor to *Seaforth World Naval Review.*

Mrityunjoy Mazumdar: Mr Mazumdar, who studied applied physics & mechanical engineering, has been a regular contributor to *Seaforth World Naval Review* since its inception. His interests are the sea services of South and Southeast Asian countries, as well as the lesser-known naval and air forces around the world. His words, pictures, and research have appeared in many naval and military aircraft publications including *Jane's Navy International*, IQPC's *Defence Industry Bulletin*, *Shephard Media*, *Ships of the World*, *Warship Technology* and *Air Forces Monthly* as well as the standard naval reference books. Having grown up in India and Nigeria, Mr Mazumdar lives in the 'wine country' north of San Francisco with his wife.

Felipe Salles: Felipe Salles is the owner and anchor of the Portuguese language *BaseMilitar* video magazine (basemilitar.com.br), one of Brazil's most trusted sources of defence information and available on YouTube at: youtube.com/basemilitarvideomagazine. He also acts as an analyst and consultant for overseas defence companies looking to enter the Brazilian and South American markets. Having a lifelong interest in military matters, he migrated to defence journalism after an extensive sales and marketing career in high-technology products both within and beyond Brazil. He holds a Master's degree in maritime studies from the Brazilian Navy's civilian-focused post graduate programme.

Richard Scott: Richard Scott is a UK-based analyst and commentator who has specialised in coverage of naval operations and technology for over 25 years, with particular interests in the fields of naval aviation, guided weapons and electronic warfare. He has held a number of editorial positions with Jane's, including the editorship of *Jane's Navy International* magazine, and is currently group Consultant Editor – Naval. Mr Scott is also a regular contributor to other periodicals, including the *AOC Journal of Electromagnetic Dominance* and *Warship World.*

Guy Toremans: Guy Toremans is a Belgian-based, maritime freelance correspondent and a member of the Association of Belgian & Foreign Journalists, an association accredited by NATO and the UN. His reports, ship profiles and interviews are published in the English language naval magazines *Jane's Navy International*, *Naval Forces* and *Warships IFR*, as well as in the French *Marines & Forces Navales* and the Japanese *J-Ships*. Since 1990, he has regularly embarked on NATO, Asian, South African and Pacific-based warships, including aircraft carriers, destroyers, frigates, mine-countermeasures vessels and support ships.

Conrad Waters (editor): See front flap.